Anderson's Business Law and the Legal Environment

Created for Drexel University, BLAW 201

Author: David P. Twomey, Marianne Moody Jennings, Stephanie M. Greene

 CENGAGE
Learning·

Australia • Brazil • Japan • Korea • Mexico • Singapore • Spain • United Kingdom • United States

Anderson's Business Law and the Legal
Environment: Created for Drexel University,
BLAW 201

Anderson's Business Law and the Legal Environment, Comprehensive
Volume
David P. Twomey, Marianne Moody Jennings, Stephanie M. Greene

©2017 Cengage Learning. All rights reserved.

For product information and technology assistance, contact us at
Cengage Learning Customer & Sales Support, 1-800-354-9706

For permission to use material from this text or product,
submit all requests online at **cengage.com/permissions**
Further permissions questions can be emailed to
permissionrequest@cengage.com

This book contains select works from existing Cengage Learning resources and
was produced by Cengage Learning Custom Solutions for collegiate use. As such,
those adopting and/or contributing to this work are responsible for editorial
content accuracy, continuity and completeness.

Compilation © 2016 Cengage Learning

ISBN:978-1-337-44249-7

Cengage Learning

Cengage Learning is a leading provider of customized learning solutions with
office locations around the globe, including Singapore, the United Kingdom,
Australia, Mexico, Brazil, and Japan. Locate your local office at:
www.international.cengage.com/region.

Cengage Learning products are represented in Canada by Nelson Education, Ltd.

For your lifelong learning solutions, visit **www.cengage.com/custom.**

Visit our corporate website at **www.cengage.com.**

Printed at CLDPC, USA, 03-19

Brief Contents

The Nature and Sources of Law

Learning Outcomes ‹‹‹

After studying this chapter, you should be able to

LO.1 Discuss the nature of law and legal rights

LO.2 List the sources of law

LO.3 Describe the classifications of law

1-1 Nature of Law and Legal Rights

Why have law? If you have ever been stuck in a traffic jam or jostled in a crowd leaving a stadium, you have observed the need for order to keep those involved moving in an efficient and safe manner. The issues with bloggers' use of others' materials and continuing downloading of music and films without compensation to copyright holders illustrate the need for rules and order in this era of new technology. When our interactions are not orderly, whether at our concerts or through our e-mail, all of us and our rights are affected. The order or pattern of rules that society uses to govern the conduct of individuals and their relationships is called **law.** Law keeps society running smoothly and efficiently.

Law consists of the body of principles that govern conduct and that can be enforced in courts or by administrative agencies. The law could also be described as a collection or bundle of rights.

law–the order or pattern of rules that society establishes to govern the conduct of individuals and the relationships among them.

1-1a Legal Rights

A **right** is a legal capacity to require another person to perform or refrain from performing an act. Our rights flow from the U.S. Constitution, state constitutions, federal and state statutes, and ordinances at the local levels, including cities, counties, and boroughs. Within these sources of rights are also duties. A **duty** is an obligation of law imposed on a person to perform or refrain from performing a certain act.

Duties and rights coexist. No right exists in one person without a corresponding duty resting on some other person or persons. For example, if the terms of a lease provide that the premises will remain in a condition of good repair so that the tenant can live there comfortably, the landlord has a corresponding duty to provide a dwelling that has hot and cold running water.

right–legal capacity to require another person to perform or refrain from an action.

duty–an obligation of law imposed on a person to perform or refrain from performing a certain act.

1-1b Individual Rights

The U.S. Constitution gives individuals certain rights. Those rights include the right to freedom of speech, the right to due process or the right to have a hearing before any freedom is taken away, and the right to vote. There are also duties that accompany individual rights, such as the duty to speak in a way that does not cause harm to others. For example, individuals are free to express their opinions about the government or its officials, but they would not be permitted to yell "Fire!" in a crowded theater and cause unnecessary harm to others. The rights given in the U.S. Constitution are rights that cannot be taken away or violated by any statutes, ordinances, or court decisions. These rights provide a framework for the structure of government and other laws.

1-1c The Right of Privacy

One very important individual legal right is the right of privacy, which has two components. The first is the right to be secure against unreasonable searches and seizures by the government. The Fourth Amendment of the U.S. Constitution guarantees this portion of the **right of privacy.** A police officer, for example, may not search your home unless the officer has a reasonable suspicion (which is generally established through a warrant) that your home contains evidence of a crime, such as illegal drugs. If your home or business is searched unlawfully, any items obtained during that unlawful search could be excluded as evidence in a criminal trial because of the Fourth Amendment's exclusionary rule. **For Example,** in *Riley v. California*, 134 S. Ct. 2473 (2014), David Riley was stopped by a police officer for driving with expired registration tags. The officer discovered that Mr. Riley's license had been suspended, so his car was impounded and searched. Officers

right of privacy–the right to be free from unreasonable intrusion by others.

also found Mr. Riley's smart phone and, in going through the phone, found pictures and information related to a gang shooting, and Mr. Riley was then charged with that earlier shooting. However, the court held that evidence from the smart phone could not be used at trial because there was no warrant and Mr. Riley had a right of privacy in the data on that phone.[1]

A second aspect of the right of privacy protects individuals against intrusions by others. Your private life is not subject to public scrutiny when you are a private citizen. This right is provided in many state constitutions and exists through interpretation at the federal level through the landmark case of *Roe v. Wade*,[2] in which the U.S. Supreme Court established a right of privacy that gives women the right to choose whether to have an abortion.

These two components of the right to privacy have many interpretations. These interpretations are often found in statutes that afford privacy rights with respect to certain types of conduct. **For Example,** a federal statute provides a right of privacy to bank customers that prevents their banks from giving out information about their accounts except to law enforcement agencies conducting investigations. Some laws protect the rights of students. **For Example,** the Family Educational Rights and Privacy Act of 1974 (FERPA, also known as the *Buckley Amendment*) prevents colleges and universities from disclosing students' grades to third parties without the students' permission. From your credit information to your Social Security number, you have great privacy protections.

1-1d Privacy and Technology

Technology creates new situations that may require the application of new rules of law. Technology has changed the way we interact with each other, and new rules of law have developed to protect our rights. Today, business is conducted by computers, wire transfers of funds, e-mail, electronic data interchange (EDI) order placements, and the Internet. We still expect that our communication is private. However, technology also affords others the ability to eavesdrop on conversations and intercept electronic messages. The law has stepped in to reestablish that the right of privacy still exists even in these technologically nonprivate circumstances. Some laws now make it a crime and a breach of privacy to engage in such interceptions of communications.[3]

CASE SUMMARY

If You Shout It Out the Window or on Facebook, Is It Private?

FACTS: Gina L. Fawcett (plaintiff) and her then-minor son, John, sued Sea High School and the parents of Nicholas Altieri (defendants) to recover damages for John's eye injury that he sustained in an altercation with Nicholas during a tennis match with St. Joseph High School. The defendants made a discovery request for access to John's social media accounts, including Facebook, MySpace, Friendster, Flickr,

and others. Ms. Fawcett moved for a protective order to prevent discovery of the information on these sites because John's sites were not publicly available.

DECISION: The court held that a variety of factors must be considered before granting broad access to social media accounts, including privacy settings by the holder of the

---

[1] Police officers do not need a warrant in order to use the content of an incoming text message on a suspect's phone that is received while they are questioning the suspect because the sender does not have a right of privacy in the suspect's smart phone's content. *State v. Varle,* 337 P.3d 904 (Or. App. 2014).

[2] 410 U.S. 113 (1973).

[3] *Luangkhot v. State,* 722 S.E.2d 193 (Ga. App. 2012).

If You Shout It Out the Window or on Facebook, Is It Private? continued

account, relevancy of the information to the litigation, and protections afforded by the various social media sites. The court's decision provides the guidelines for determining whether the litigants in cases will be able to have discovery access to each other's social media sites. The parties will have to do depositions and then renew the request once more factual information is available for the analysis of the request for access. [*Fawcett v. Altieri*, 960 N.Y.S.2d 592 (2013)]

ETHICS & THE LAW

Maybe a Little Too "LinkedIn"

LinkedIn, the popular professional connection service, has a tool called "Reference Search." A premium service, employers and recruiters are using the tool to cull their connections to see who knows job applicants in order to get background on them. Employers are checking with references that the applicants did not list, references that may not have all good things to say about them. The service provides employers with the list of LinkedIn contacts that they have who worked at the same companies as the applicants and at the same time.*

Applicants are worried that employers are basing employment decisions on the information that they receive, information that may not be true or verified or verifiable. The applicants do not always know that the employer is checking with other sources or which ones and do not have the opportunity to respond to negative information.

Discuss the ethical issues in the use of this LinkedIn service by employers.

*Natasha Singer, "Funny, They Don't Look Like My References," *New York Times Magazine*, November 10, 2014, p. BU4.

E-COMMERCE & CYBERLAW

A University's Access to Your Computer

Scott Kennedy, a computer system administrator for Qualcomm Corporation in San Diego, California, discovered that somebody had obtained unauthorized access (or "hacked into," in popular parlance) the company's computer network. Kennedy contacted the Federal Bureau of Investigation (FBI). Working together, Kennedy and the FBI were able to trace the intrusion to a computer on the University of Wisconsin at Madison network. They contacted Jeffrey Savoy, the University of Wisconsin computer network investigator, who found evidence that someone using a computer on the university network was in fact hacking into the Qualcomm system and that the user had gained unauthorized access to the university's system as well. Savoy traced the source of intrusion to a computer located in university housing, the room of Jerome Heckenkamp, a computer science graduate student at the university. Savoy knew that Heckenkamp had been terminated from his job at the university computer help desk two years earlier for similar unauthorized activity.

While Heckenkamp was online and logged into the university's system, Savoy, along with detectives, went to Heckenkamp's room. The door was ajar, and nobody was in the room. Savoy entered the room and disconnected the network cord that attached the computer to the network. In order to be sure that the computer he had disconnected from the network was the computer that had gained unauthorized access to the university server, Savoy wanted to run some commands on the computer. Detectives located Heckenkamp, explained the situation, and asked for Heckenkamp's password, which Heckenkamp voluntarily provided. Savoy then ran tests on the computer and copied the hard drive without a warrant. When Heckenkamp was charged with several federal computer crimes, he challenged the university's access to his account and Savoy's steps that night, including the copy of the hard drive, as a breach of his privacy.

Was Heckenkamp correct? Was his privacy breached?

[*U.S. v. Heckenkamp*, 482 F.3d 1142 (9th Cir. 2007)]

1-2 Sources of Law

Several layers of law are enacted at different levels of government to provide the framework for business and personal rights and duties. At the base of this framework of laws is constitutional law.

1-2a Constitutional Law

constitution–a body of principles that establishes the structure of a government and the relationship of the government to the people who are governed.

Constitutional law is the branch of law that is based on the constitution for a particular level of government. A **constitution** is a body of principles that establishes the structure of a government and the relationship of that government to the people who are governed. A constitution is generally a combination of the written document and the practices and customs that develop with the passage of time and the emergence of new problems. In each state, two constitutions are in force: the state constitution and the federal Constitution.

1-2b Statutory Law

statutory law–legislative acts declaring, commanding, or prohibiting something.

Statutory law includes legislative acts. Both Congress and the state legislatures enact statutory law. Examples of congressional legislative enactments include the Securities Act of 1933 (Chapter 45), the Sherman Antitrust Act (Chapter 5), the bankruptcy laws (Chapter 34), and consumer credit protection provisions (Chapter 32). At the state level, statutes govern the creation of corporations, probate of wills, and the transfer of title to property. In addition to the state legislatures and the U.S. Congress, all cities, counties, and other governmental subdivisions have some power to adopt ordinances within their sphere of operation. Examples of the types of laws found at this level of government include traffic laws, zoning laws, and pet and bicycle licensing laws.

1-2c Administrative Law

administrative regulations–rules made by state and federal administrative agencies.

Administrative regulations are rules promulgated by state and federal administrative agencies, such as the Securities and Exchange Commission (SEC) and the Environmental Protection Agency (EPA). For example, the restrictions on carbon emissions by businesses have all been promulgated by the EPA. These regulations generally have the force of statutes.

1-2d Private Law

private law–the rules and regulations parties agree to as part of their contractual relationships.

Even individuals and businesses create their own laws, or **private law.** Private law consists of the rules and regulations parties agree to as part of their contractual relationships. **For Example,** landlords develop rules for tenants on everything from parking to laundry room use. Employers develop rules for employees on everything from proper computer use to posting pictures and information on bulletin boards located within the company walls. Homeowner associations have rules on everything from your landscaping to the color of your house paint.

1-2e Case Law, Statutory Interpretation, and Precedent

case law–law that includes principles that are expressed for the first time in court decisions.

Law also includes principles that are expressed for the first time in court decisions. This form of law is called **case law.** Case law plays three very important roles. The first is one of clarifying the meaning of statutes, or providing statutory interpretation. **For Example,** in *King v. Burwell,* the U.S. Supreme Court interpreted the phrase, "an Exchange established by the State" in the Affordable Care Act to determine whether tax credits were available to insurance exchanges operated by the federal government and not the states. The court held that "State," meant either the federal government or any of the states so that all exchanges qualified for the tax credits.[4] The second role that courts play is in creating precedent. When a court decides a new question or problem, its decision becomes a **precedent,** which stands as the law in future cases that involve that particular problem.

precedent–a decision of a court that stands as the law for a particular problem in the future.

Using precedent and following decisions is also known as the doctrine of ***stare decisis.*** However, the rule of *stare decisis* is not cast in stone. Judges have some flexibility. When a court finds an earlier decision to be incorrect, it overrules that decision. For example, in *National Federation of Independent Business v. Sebelius*, 132 S.Ct. 2566 (2012) the U.S. Supreme Court held that the Affordable Care Act (Obama Care) was constitutional. However, in 2014, the Court held, based on new issues raised, that a portion of the act violated the First Amendment because it mandated health care coverage of certain types of birth controls that were in violation of the religious beliefs of the owners of a corporation. *Burwell v. Hobby Lobby Stores, Inc.*, 134 S. Ct. 2751 (2014).

stare decisis–"let the decision stand"; the principle that the decision of a court should serve as a guide or precedent and control the decision of a similar case in the future.

The third role courts play is in developing a body of law that is not statutory but addresses long-standing issues. Court decisions do not always deal with new problems or make new rules. In many cases, courts apply rules as they have been for many years, even centuries. These time-honored rules of the community are called the **common law. For Example,** most of law that we still follow today in determining real property rights developed in England, beginning in 1066. Statutes sometimes repeal or redeclare the common law rules. Many statutes depend on the common law for definitions of the terms in the statutes.

common law–the body of unwritten principles originally based upon the usages and customs of the community that were recognized and enforced by the courts.

1-2f Other Forms of Law: Treaties and Executive Orders

Law also includes treaties made by the United States and proclamations and executive orders of the president of the United States or of other public officials. President Obama's executive order altering immigration policy is the subject of a constitutional challenge to the scope of executive orders.

1-2g Uniform State Laws

To facilitate the national nature of business and transactions, the National Conference of Commissioners on Uniform State Laws (NCCUSL), composed of representatives from every state, has drafted statutes on various subjects for adoption by the states. The best example of such laws is the Uniform Commercial Code (UCC).[5] (See Chapters 22–30, Chapter 33.) The UCC regulates the sale and lease of goods; commercial paper, such as checks; fund transfers; secured transactions in personal property; banking; and letters of credit. Having the same principles of law on contracts for the sale of goods and other commercial transactions in most of the 50 states makes doing business easier and less expensive. Other examples of uniform laws across the states include the Model Business Corporation Act (Chapter 43), the Uniform Partnership Act (Chapter 41), and the Uniform Residential Landlord Tenant Act (Chapter 50). The Uniform Computer Information Transactions Act (UCITA) as well as the Uniform Electronic Transactions Act

---

[4] *King v. Burwell*, 135 S.Ct. 2480 (2015).

[5] The UCC has been adopted in every state, except that Louisiana has not adopted Article 2, Sales. Guam, the Virgin Islands, and the District of Columbia have also adopted the UCC. The United Nations Convention on Contracts for the International Sale of Goods (CISG) has been adopted as the means for achieving uniformity in sale-of-goods contracts on an international level. Provisions of CISG were strongly influenced by Article 2 of the UCC.

(UETA) are two uniform laws that have taken contract law from the traditional paper era to the paperless computer age.

1-3 Classifications of Law

1-3a Substantive Law vs. Procedural Law

substantive law—the law that defines rights and liabilities.

procedural law—the law that must be followed in enforcing rights and liabilities.

Substantive law creates, defines, and regulates rights and liabilities. The law that determines when a contract is formed is substantive law. **Procedural law** specifies the steps that must be followed in enforcing those rights and liabilities. For example, once that contract is formed, you have rights to enforce that contract, and the steps you take through the court system to recover your damages for a breach of contract are procedural laws. The laws that prohibit computer theft are substantive laws. The prosecution of someone for computer theft follows procedural law.

1-3b Criminal Law vs. Civil Law

criminal laws—the laws that define wrongs against society.

civil laws—the laws that define the rights of one person against another.

Criminal laws define wrongs against society. **Civil laws** define the rights of one person against another. Criminal law violations carry fines and imprisonment as penalties. Civil laws carry damage remedies for the wronged individual.

For Example, if you run a red light, you have committed a crime and you will be punished with a fine and points on your license. If you run a red light and strike a pedestrian, you will also have committed a civil wrong of injury to another through your

SPORTS & ENTERTAINMENT LAW

When Players Break the Law and Owners Are Offensive

During 2014, professional sports had three events that resulted in a public engaged in the business decisions of the teams and their leagues. Baltimore Ravens player Ray Rice was accused of striking his fiancé (who would shortly become his wife) in an elevator. Local authorities declined to prosecute because his wife refused to cooperate with the investigation or the prosecution. Nonetheless, Roger Goodell, the NFL commissioner, suspended Mr. Rice from play indefinitely. Public opinion swung both ways, and Mr. Rice eventually won his appeal on the suspension and was reinstated. However, he lost his endorsement contracts with various companies, including Nike.

In the NBA, Donald Sterling was forced by the league to sell the LA Clippers franchise after an audio tape emerged of him making racist comments to his girlfriend. Steve Ballmer, the former CEO of Microsoft, bought the team for $2 billion. The team owners in the NBA made the decision by a vote to require Sterling to sell the team, a provision permitted under the bylaws of the corporation.

Back in the NFL, Adrian Peterson of the Minnesota Vikings was arrested for child abuse. Mr. Peterson entered a no-contest plea to the charges, which were based on his using a branch to hit his four-year-old son. The court's determination of guilt was postponed for two years as Mr. Peterson serves 80 hours of community service and pays a $4,000 fine. Under its bylaws, the NFL imposed a temporary suspension, and Mr. Peterson and the NFL are locked in a court and arbitration dispute over the suspension.

The three cases have these topics in common:

Private conduct affected business ownership and employment.

There were private bylaws involved that permitted league action against team owners and players.

There were also civil and criminal laws involved that required prosecution in two of the cases.

The law at various levels, including the authority of the leagues to do what they did, was at the center of these very public controversies.

carelessness. Civil laws provide that in addition to taking care of your wrong to society, you must take care of your wrong to the pedestrian and pay damages for the cost of her injuries (see Chapter 8 for more information about recovery of damages for accidents such as this).

1-3c Law vs. Equity

equity—the body of principles that originally developed because of the inadequacy of the rules then applied by the common law courts of England.

Equity is a body of law that provides justice when the law does not offer an adequate remedy or the application of the law would be terribly unfair. Equity courts developed in England as a means of getting to the heart of a dispute and seeing that justice was done. **For Example,** Christian Louboutin shoes have a distinctive red bottom that is their trademark. Yves Saint Laurent began producing its shoes with a red bottom. Common and statutory law provide for Louboutin to collect damages—the amount the company lost in sales through the copycat efforts of Yves Saint Laurent. However, if the Yves Saint Laurent shoes continue in production, Louboutin is never adequately compensated. Equity provides for an injunction, a court order to stop Yves Saint Laurent from making the red-soled shoes.[6]

At one time, the United States had separate law courts and equity courts, but today these courts have been combined so that one court applies principles of both law and equity. A party may ask for both legal and equitable remedies in a single court.[7] **For Example,** suppose a homeowner contracts to sell his home to a buyer. If the homeowner then refuses to go through with the contract, the buyer has the legal remedy of recovering damages. The rules of equity go further and could require the owner to convey title to the house, an equitable remedy known as *specific performance*. Equitable remedies may also be available in certain contract breaches (see Chapters 2, 11, and 19).

Make the Connection

Summary

Law provides rights and imposes duties. One such right is the right of privacy, which affords protection against unreasonable searches of our property and intrusion into or disclosure of our private affairs.

Law consists of the pattern of rules established by society to govern conduct and relationships. These rules can be expressed as constitutional provisions, statutes, administrative regulations, and case decisions. Law can be classified as substantive or procedural, and it can be described in terms of civil or criminal law. Law provides remedies in equity in addition to damages.

The sources of law include constitutions, federal and state statutes, administrative regulations, ordinances, and uniform laws generally codified by the states in their statutes. The courts are also a source of law through their adherence to case precedent under the doctrine of *stare decisis* and through their development of time-honored principles called the common law.

[6] *Christian Louboutin S.A. v. Yves Saint Laurent America, Inc.,* 778 F. Supp. 2d 445 (S.D.N.Y. 2011). The court eventually held that other companies could not copy the distinctive red sole. They could have colored soles but not the Louboutin trademark red sole.
[7] For example, when Jennifer Lopez and Marc Anthony were married, they filed suit against the manufacturer of a British company that produces baby carriages for using their images on its Web site and in ads without permission; they asked for $5 million in damages as well as an injunction to stop use of their photos and likenesses in the company's ads. *Lopez v. Silver Cross,* 2009 WL 481386 (C.D. Cal.). The case was settled prior to the dissolution of the Lopez and Anthony marriage. Silver Cross no longer uses the images of Lopez and Anthony in its ads.

Learning Outcomes

After studying this chapter, you should be able to clearly explain:

1-1 Nature of Law and Legal Rights

LO.1 Discuss the nature of law and legal rights

See Ethics & the Law for a discussion on the use of LinkedIn for finding more honest references about potential employees, page 6.

See E-Commerce & Cyberlaw for a discussion of a university student's privacy rights in using the university's server, page 6.

1-2 Sources of Law

LO.2 List the sources of law

See the *For Example* discussion of landlords developing rules for tenants on everything from parking to laundry room use, page 7.

See the list and explanation of uniform laws, page 8. See the Sports & Entertainment Law discussion of leagues taking action against players for their private conduct, page 9.

1-3 Classifications of Law

LO.3 Describe the classifications of law

See the discussion of law, equity, procedural, substantive, criminal, and civil, pages 9–10.

See the Christian Louboutin example on its red-bottomed shoe being copied and footnote 8 with the discussion of the Jennifer Lopez/Marc Anthony suit. Explain uniform state laws, page 10.

Key Terms

administrative regulations	duty	right
case law	equity	right of privacy
civil law	law	*stare decisis*
common law	precedent	statutory law
constitution	private law	substantive law
criminal law	procedural law	

Questions and Case Problems

1. The Family Educational Rights and Privacy Act (FERPA) protects students' rights to keep their academic records private. What duties are imposed and upon whom because of this protection of rights? Discuss the relationship between rights and duties.

2. List the sources of law.

3. What is the difference between common law and statutory law?

4. Classify the following laws as substantive or procedural:

    a. A law that requires public schools to hold a hearing before a student is expelled.

    b. A law that establishes a maximum interest rate for credit transactions of 24 percent.

    c. A law that provides employee leave for the birth or adoption of a child for up to 12 weeks.

    d. A law that requires the county assessor to send four notices of taxes due and owing before a lien can be filed (attached) to the property.

5. What do uniform laws accomplish? Why do states adopt them? Give an example of a uniform law.

6. Cindy Nathan is a student at West University. While she was at her 9:00 A.M. anthropology class, campus security entered her dorm room and searched all areas, including her closet and drawers. When Cindy returned to her room and discovered what had happened, she complained to the dorm's senior resident. The senior resident said that this was the university's property and that Cindy had no right of privacy. Do you agree with the senior resident's statement? Is there a right of privacy in a dorm room?

7. Professor Lucas Phelps sent the following e-mail to Professor Marlin Jones: "I recently read the opinion piece you wrote for the *Sacramento Bee* on affirmative action. Your opinion is incorrect, your reasoning and analysis are poor, and I am embarrassed that you are a member of the faculty here at Cal State Yolinda." Professor Jones forwarded the note from Professor Phelps to the provost of the university and asked that

Professor Phelps be disciplined for using the university e-mail system for harassment purposes. Professor Phelps objected when the provost contacted him: "He had no right to forward that e-mail to you. That was private correspondence. And you have no right of access to my e-mail. I have privacy rights." Do you agree with Professor Phelps? Was there a breach of privacy?

8. Under what circumstances would a court disregard precedent?

9. What is the difference between a statute and an administrative regulation?

10. The Eminem ad for Chrysler that ran during the Super Bowl in February 2011 was rated as one of the best ads for the game. In May 2011, Audi ran an ad at a German auto show that had the "feel" of the Eminem Chrysler "Lose Yourself" ad. Subsequently, the German auto show ad made its way onto the Internet.

    The German ad caught the attention of Eminem and 8 Mile, Eminem's publishing company. They notified Audi that the ad constituted an unauthorized use of their intellectual property. Explain what rights Eminem and 8 Mile have and how the courts can help.

11. Give examples of areas covered by federal laws. Give examples of areas covered by city ordinances. What are the limitations on these two sources of laws? What could the laws at these two levels not do?

12. What is the principle of *stare decisis*?

13. Explain how Twitter, Facebook, and LinkedIn have resulted in the development of new laws and precedent.

14. During the 2001 baseball season, San Francisco Giants player Barry Bonds hit 73 home runs, a new record that broke the one set by Mark McGwire in 2000 (72 home runs). When Mr. Bonds hit his record-breaking home run, the ball went into the so-called cheap seats. Alex Popov was sitting in those seats and had brought along his baseball glove for purposes of catching any hits that might come into the stands.

    Everyone sitting in the area agreed that Mr. Popov's glove touched Bonds's home-run ball. Videotape also shows Mr. Popov's glove on the ball. However, the ball dropped and, following a melee among the cheap-seat fans, Patrick Hayashi ended up with Bonds's home-run ball.

    Mr. Popov filed suit for the ball, claiming it as his property. Such baseballs can be very valuable. The baseball from Mr. McGwire's record-breaking home run in 2000 sold for $3 million. List those areas of law that will apply as the case is tried and the owner of the baseball is determined.

15. Janice Dempsey has just started her own tax preparation firm. She has leased office space in a building, and she is incorporating her business as a Subchapter S corporation under the Internal Revenue Code. She has purchased desks, chairs, computers, and copiers from Staples through a line of credit they have established for her. Janice is a CPA in the state of Arizona and her license fees and continuing education hours are due within 90 days. Janice will begin with only a clerical person as an employee to serve as receptionist and bookkeeper. List all of the areas of the law that affect Janice in her new business.

The Court System and Dispute Resolution

Learning Outcomes ‹‹‹

After studying this chapter, you should be able to

LO.1 Explain the federal and state court systems

LO.2 Describe court procedures

LO.3 List the forms of alternative dispute resolution and distinguish among them

2-1 The Court System

court—a tribunal established by government to hear and decide matters properly brought to it.

Despite carefully negotiated and well-written contracts and high safety standards in the workplace or in product design and production, businesses can end up in a lawsuit. **For Example,** you could hire the brightest and most expensive lawyer in town to prepare a contract with another party and believe the final agreement is "bulletproof." However, even a bulletproof contract does not guarantee performance by the other party, and you may have to file a suit to collect your damages.

jurisdiction—the power of a court to hear and determine a given class of cases; the power to act over a particular defendant.

Business disputes can be resolved in court or through alternative dispute resolution. This chapter covers the structure of the court system and the litigation process as well as the forms of alternative dispute resolution.

A **court** is a tribunal established by government to hear evidence, decide cases brought before it, and provide remedies when a wrong has been committed. As discussed in Chapter 1, sometimes courts prevent wrongs by issuing the equitable remedy of an injunction. **For Example,** in March 2012, a federal court issued an injunction against Cardinal Health because it was shipping too much oxycodone to its pharmacies in Florida, and the FDA had discovered that the prescriptions were fraudulent. The FDA needed to stop the flow of the drug while it pulled the prescriptions.[1]

subject matter jurisdiction—judicial authority to hear a particular type of case.

original jurisdiction—the authority to hear a controversy when it is first brought to court.

2-1a The Types of Courts

general jurisdiction—the power to hear and decide most controversies involving legal rights and duties.

Each type of court has the authority to decide certain types or classes of cases. The authority of courts to hear cases is called **jurisdiction.** One form of jurisdiction, **subject matter jurisdiction,** covers the type of cases the court has the authority to hear. Courts that have the authority to hear the original proceedings in a case (the trial court) are called courts of **original jurisdiction. For Example,** in a court of original jurisdiction witnesses testify, documents are admitted into evidence, and the jury, in the case of a jury trial, hears all the evidence and then makes a decision.

limited (special) jurisdiction—the authority to hear only particular kinds of cases.

Other types of subject matter jurisdiction give courts the authority over particular legal topic areas. A court with **general jurisdiction** has broad authority to hear general civil and criminal cases. When a general jurisdiction trial court hears criminal cases, it serves as the trial court for those charged with crimes. General trial courts also have the authority to hear civil disputes, such as breach of contract cases and personal injury lawsuits.

appellate jurisdiction—the power of a court to hear and decide a given class of cases on appeal from another court or administrative agency.

A court with **limited or special jurisdiction** has the authority to hear only particular kinds of cases. **For Example,** many states have courts that can hear only disputes in which the damages are $10,000 or less. Other examples of limited or special jurisdiction courts are juvenile courts, probate courts, and domestic relations courts. States vary in the names they give these courts, but these courts of special or limited jurisdiction have very narrow authority for the types of cases they hear. In the federal court system, limited or special jurisdiction courts include bankruptcy courts and the U.S. Tax Court.

appeal—taking a case to a reviewing court to determine whether the judgment of the lower court or administrative agency was correct. (Parties—appellant, appellee)

A court with **appellate jurisdiction** reviews the work of a lower court. **For Example,** a trial court may issue a judgment that a defendant in a breach of contract suit should pay $500,000 in damages. That defendant could appeal the decision to an appellate court and seek review of the decision itself or even the amount of the damages.[2] An **appeal** is a

---

[1] *Holiday CVS, LLC. v. Holder*, 839 F. Supp. 2d 145 (D.D.C. 2012).

[2] A case that is sent back for a redetermination of damages is remanded for what is known as *remititur*. For example, an appeal of Oracle's $1.3 billion verdict against SAP was sent back for another determination of damages, with the judge indicating $272 million was in the right range. *Oracle USA, Inc. v. SAP AG*, 2012 WL 29095 (N.D. Cal.).

reversible error–an error or defect in court proceedings of so serious a nature that on appeal the appellate court will set aside the proceedings of the lower court.

review of the trial and decision of the lower court. An appellate court does not hear witnesses or take testimony. An appellate court, usually a panel of three judges, simply reviews the transcript and evidence from the lower court and determines whether there has been **reversible error.** A reversible error is a mistake in applying the law or a mistake in admitting evidence that affected the outcome of the case. An appellate court can **affirm** or **reverse** a lower court decision or **remand** that decision for another trial or additional hearings.

CASE SUMMARY

Horseback Riding Videos and Judging Hairy Chest Contests—Good Evidence?

FACTS: Mary Kay Stanford (Stanford) was driving a truck for V.F. in late evening of February 7, 2006, when she began to feel nauseous. She pulled into a truck scale house to rest for the evening. She parked the truck, and as she attempted to climb into the sleeper compartment, she tripped over a cooler. Stanford fell into the sleeper compartment and hit her head on the bed rail; the fall knocked her unconscious. Stanford's husband, William Stanford, who was riding with her, attempted to revive her. After she regained consciousness, William offered to take her to the emergency room. Stanford declined and decided to stay in the sleeper compartment and rest until morning. Stanford contacted V.F. dispatch and made the notifications to the company about her injury. The company arranged for the two to return home.

On February 8, 2006, Mary Kay went to Dr. Allie Prater whose notes reflect that Stanford's chief complaints were blackouts, syncope, and slurred speech. Stanford told Dr. Prater that her symptoms had begun one week prior to her visit. Dr. Prater's notes do not mention Stanford's fall in the truck or that she was knocked unconscious. Dr. Prater diagnosed Stanford with benign essential hypertension and ordered blood tests, an ultrasound, and a brain MRI.

Dr. Prater referred Mary Kay to Dr. Glenn Crosby, a neurosurgeon. Before seeing Dr. Crosby, Stanford went to Dr. Johnny Mitias, an orthopedic surgeon, on March 15, 2006. There was no mention of her fall in Dr. Mitias's notes. In fact, he noted that "[t]here was no injury that started this." Dr. Mitias diagnosed Stanford with right sciatica and ordered physical therapy.

Dr. Crosby recommended and performed spinal surgeries on August 8, 2006. After surgery, Stanford began complaining of pain in her left buttock and down her left leg. Dr. Crosby ordered a lumbar MRI, which revealed a large rupture of the lumbar spine at L4. On November 28, 2006, Dr. Crosby performed a diskectomy at the L4 level.

Dr. Crosby's notes indicate that Stanford "had a fall this past year" that may have aggravated her back. However, Dr. Crosby's notes do not mention that Stanford suffered a fall at work until her follow-up visit with Dr. Crosby on May 30, 2008. Dr. Crosby testified that prior to that visit, Stanford had not disclosed any history of an accident at work. However, he testified that the problems with her neck and back were probably related to her work injury.

A hearing was held before an administrative judge (AJ), who denied Stanford's claim for workers' compensation benefits. There was evidence submitted at the hearing that Stanford had taken a cruise despite her medical issues. In addition, there was video of her riding horses during the time of her treatment. There were also videos of Stanford at parties and bars. In one video she appeared to be having a great time as a judge in a "hairy chest contest." Stanford appealed the AJ's decision to the Commission, which affirmed the AJ's decision. Stanford appealed the Commission's decision to the Circuit Court of Union County, and the circuit court affirmed the Commission's decision denying benefits. Stanford then appealed.

DECISION: The court affirmed the denial of workers' compensation benefits because the evidence indicated clearly that Stanford did not tell the doctors about her work injury. The testimony about the cruise and the videos of horseback riding were damaging to Stanford's case, but they did not indicate bias particularly because the AJ had allowed evidence from Stanford's husband, friends, and relatives about her condition. Because evidence is damaging to one party does not mean that it should not be admitted. [*Stanford v. V.F. Jeanswear, LP*, 84 So. 3d 825 (Miss. App. 2012)]

affirm–action taken by an appellate court that approves the decision of the court below.

reverse–the term used when the appellate court sets aside the verdict or judgment of a lower court.

remand–term used when an appellate court sends a case back to trial court for additional hearings or a new trial.

federal district court–a general trial court of the federal system.

2-1b The Federal Court System

The federal court system consists of three levels of courts. Figure 2-1 illustrates federal court structure.

Federal District Courts

The **federal district courts** are the general trial courts of the federal system. They are courts of original jurisdiction that hear both civil and criminal matters. Criminal cases in federal district courts are those in which the defendant is charged with a violation of federal law (the U.S. Code). In addition to the criminal cases, the types of civil cases that can be brought in federal district courts include (1) civil suits in which the United States is a party, (2) cases between citizens of different states that involve damages of $75,000 or more, and (3) cases that arise under the U.S. Constitution or federal laws and treaties.

Federal district courts are organized within each of the states. There are 94 federal districts (each state has at least one federal district and there are 89 federal districts in the United States with the remaining courts found in Puerto Rico, Guam, etc.). Judges and courtrooms are assigned according to the caseload in that geographic area of the state.[3] Some states, such as New York and California, have several federal districts because

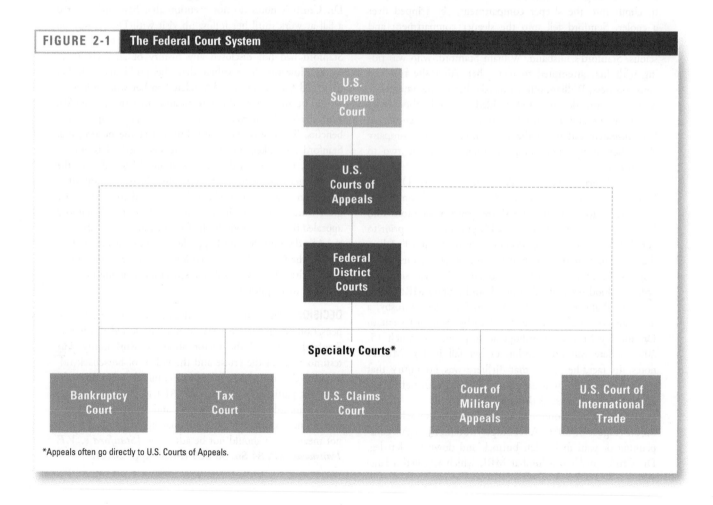

FIGURE 2-1   The Federal Court System

*Appeals often go directly to U.S. Courts of Appeals.

---

[3] For complete information about the courts and the number of judgeships, go to 28 U.S.C. §§81-144 and 28 U.S.C. §133.

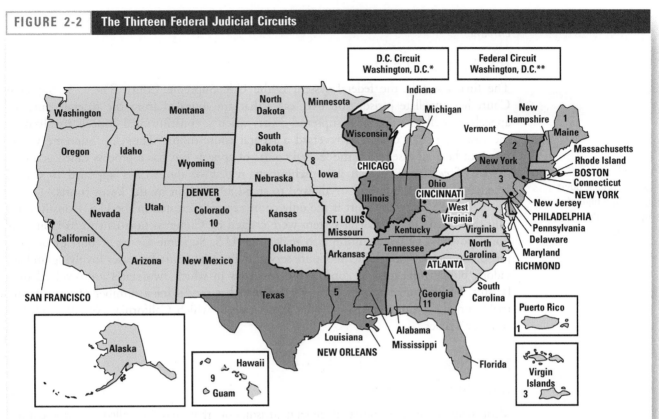

FIGURE 2-2 | **The Thirteen Federal Judicial Circuits**

*A sizable portion of the caseload of the D.C. Circuit comes from the federal administrative agencies and offices located in Washington, D.C., such as the Securities and Exchange Commission, the National Labor Relations Board, the Federal Trade Commission, the Secretary of the Treasury, and the Labor Department, as well as appeals from the U.S. District Court of the District of Columbia.

**Rather than being defined by geography like the regional courts of appeals, the Federal Circuit is defined by subject matter, having jurisdiction over such matters as patent infringement cases, appeals from the Court of Federal Claims and the Court of International Trade, and appeals from administrative rulings regarding subject matter such as unfair import practices and tariff schedule disputes.

of the population base and the resulting caseload. Figure 2-2 shows the geographic structure of the federal court system, including the appellate circuits.

The federal system has additional trial courts with limited jurisdiction, differing from the general jurisdiction of the federal district courts. These courts include, for example, the federal bankruptcy courts, Indian tribal courts, Tax Court, Court of Federal Claims, Court of Veterans Appeals, and the Court of International Trade.

U.S. Courts of Appeals

The final decision in a federal district court can be appealed to a court with appellate jurisdiction. In the federal court system, the federal districts are grouped together geographically into 12 judicial circuits, including one for the District of Columbia. Additionally, a thirteenth federal circuit, called the *Federal Circuit*, hears certain types of appeals from all of the circuits, including specialty cases such as patent appeals. Each circuit has an appellate court called the U.S. Court of Appeals, and the judges for these courts review the decisions of the federal district courts. Generally, a panel of three judges reviews the cases. However, some decisions, called ***en banc*** decisions, are made by the circuit's full panel of judges. **For Example,** in 2003, the Ninth Circuit heard an appeal on a father's right to challenge the requirement that his daughter recite the Pledge of Allegiance in the public school she attended. The contentious case had so many issues that the Ninth

en banc—the term used when the full panel of judges on the appellate court hears a case.

Circuit issued three opinions and the third opinion was issued after the case was heard *en banc.*[4]

U.S. Supreme Court

The final court in the federal system is the U.S. Supreme Court. The U.S. Supreme Court has appellate jurisdiction over cases that are appealed from the federal courts of appeals as well as from state supreme courts when a constitutional issue is involved in the case or a state court has reversed a federal court ruling. The U.S. Supreme Court does not hear all cases from the federal courts of appeals but has a process called granting a **writ of** *certiorari,* which is a preliminary review of those cases appealed to decide whether a case will be heard or allowed to stand as ruled on by the lower courts.[5]

The U.S. Supreme Court is the only court expressly created in the U.S. Constitution. All other courts in the federal system were created by Congress pursuant to its Constitutional power. The Constitution also makes the U.S. Supreme Court a court of original jurisdiction. The U.S. Supreme Court serves as the trial court for cases involving ambassadors, public ministers, or consuls and for cases in which two states are involved in a lawsuit. **For Example,** the U.S. Supreme Court has served for a number of years as the trial court for a Colorado River water rights case in which California, Nevada, and Arizona are parties.

writ of *certiorari*–the U.S. Supreme Court granting a right of review by the court of a lower court decision.

2-1c State Court Systems

General Trial Courts

Most states have trial courts of general jurisdiction that may be called superior courts, circuit courts, district courts, or county courts. These courts of general and original jurisdiction usually hear both criminal and civil cases. Cases that do not meet the jurisdictional requirements for the federal district courts would be tried in these courts. Figure 2-3 illustrates a sample state court system.

Specialty Courts

Most states also have courts with limited jurisdiction, sometimes referred to as *specialty courts*. **For Example,** most states have juvenile courts, or courts with limited jurisdiction over criminal matters that involve defendants who are under the age of 18. Other specialty courts or lesser courts in state systems are probate and family law courts.

City, Municipal, and Justice Courts

Cities and counties may also have lesser courts with limited jurisdiction, which may be referred to as *municipal courts* or *justice courts*. These courts generally handle civil matters in which the claim made in the suit is an amount below a certain level, such as $5,000 or

---

[4] *Newdow v. U.S. Congress*, 292 F.3d 597 (9th Cir. 2002) *(Newdow I)*; *Newdow v. U.S. Congress*, 313 F.3d 500, 502 (9th Cir. 2002) *(Newdow II)*; and *Newdow v. U.S. Congress*, 328 F.3d 466, 468 (9th Cir. 2003) *(Newdow III)*. The U.S. Supreme Court eventually heard the case. *Elkgrove Unified School District v. Newdow*, 542 U.S. 1 (2004). Another *en banc* hearing occurred at the Ninth Circuit over the issues in the California gubernatorial recall election. The three-judge panel held that the voting methods in California violated the rights of voters and therefore placed a stay on the election. However, the Ninth Circuit then heard the case *en banc* and reversed the decision of the original three-judge panel.

[5] For example, the Supreme Court refused to grant *certiorari* in a Fifth Circuit case on law school admissions at the University of Texas. However, it granted *certiorari* in a later case involving law school admissions at the University of Michigan. *Gratz v. Bollinger*, 539 U.S. 244 (2003). A case challenging undergraduate admissions at the University of Texas (*Fisher v. University of Texas*) was heard by the U.S. Supreme Court (133 S. Ct. 2411 (2013)) and remanded, but the appellate court refused to remand the case for trial on a strict scrutiny basis. That decision of the federal court of appeals is on appeal again with *certiorari* granted. *Fisher v. University of Texas at Austin*, 2015 WL 629286.

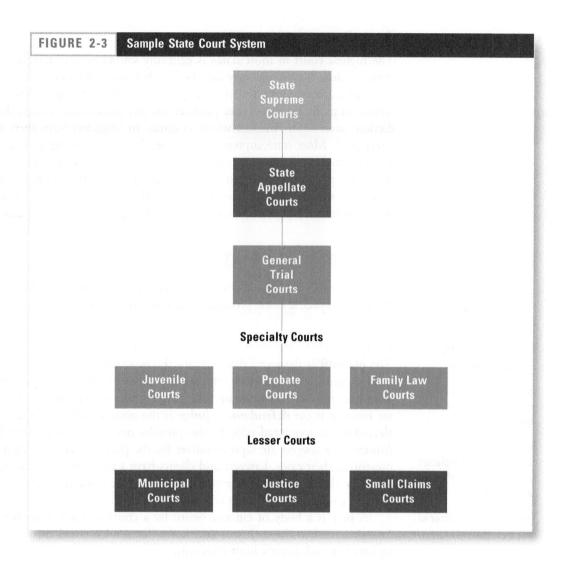

FIGURE 2-3 | Sample State Court System

$10,000. These courts may also handle misdemeanor types of offenses, such as traffic violations or violations of noise ordinances, and the trials for them.

Small Claims Courts

small claims courts—
courts that resolve
disputes between parties
when those disputes do
not exceed a minimal
level; no lawyers are
permitted; the parties
represent themselves.

Most states also have **small claims courts** at the county or city level. These are courts of limited jurisdiction where parties with small amounts in dispute may come to have a third party, such as a justice of the peace or city judge, review their disputes and determine how they should be resolved. A true small claims court is one in which the parties are not permitted to be represented by counsel. Rather, the parties present their cases to the judge in an informal manner without the strict procedural rules that apply in courts of general jurisdiction. Small claims courts provide a faster and inexpensive means for resolving a dispute that does not involve a large amount of claimed damages.

State Appellate Courts

Most states also have intermediate-level courts similar to the federal courts of appeals. They are courts with appellate jurisdiction that review the decisions of lower courts in that state. Decisions of the general trial courts in a state would be appealed to these courts.

State Supreme Courts

The highest court in most states is generally known as the *state supreme court*, but a few states, such as New York, may call their highest court the *court of appeals*; Maine and Massachusetts, for example, call their highest court the *supreme judicial court*. State supreme courts primarily have appellate jurisdiction, but some states' courts do have original jurisdiction, such as in Arizona, where counties in litigation have their trial at the supreme court level. Most state supreme courts also have a screening process for cases. They are required to hear some cases, such as criminal cases in which the defendant has received the death penalty. A decision of a state supreme court is final except in those circumstances in which a federal law or treaty or the U.S. Constitution is involved. Cases with these federal subject matter issues can then be appealed to the U.S. Supreme Court.

2-2 Court Procedure

Once a party decides to use the court system for resolution of a dispute, that party enters a world with specific rules, procedures, and terms that must be used to have a case proceed.

2-2a Participants in the Court System

plaintiff–party who initiates a lawsuit.

prosecutor–party who originates a criminal proceeding.

defendant–party charged with a violation of civil or criminal law in a proceeding.

judge–primary officer of the court.

attorney-client privilege–right of individual to have discussions with his/her attorney kept private and confidential.

jury–a body of citizens sworn by a court to determine by verdict the issues of fact submitted to them.

The **plaintiff** is the party that initiates the proceedings in a court of original jurisdiction. In a criminal case in which charges are brought, the party initiating the proceedings would be called the **prosecutor.** The party against whom the civil or criminal proceedings are brought is the **defendant.** A **judge** is the primary officer of the court and is either an elected or an appointed official who presides over the matters brought before the court. Attorneys or lawyers are representatives for the plaintiff and the defendant for purposes of presenting their cases. Lawyers and clients have a privilege of confidentiality known as the **attorney-client privilege.** Lawyers cannot disclose what their clients tell them unless the client is committing, or plans to commit, a crime.

A **jury** is a body of citizens sworn by a court to reach a verdict on the basis of the case presented to them. Jurors are chosen for service based on lists compiled from voter registration and driver's license records.

2-2b Which Law Applies—Conflicts of Law

When a lawsuit is brought, there is not just the question of where a case will be tried but also of what law will be applied in determining the rights of the parties. The principle that determines when a court applies the law of its own state—the law of the forum—or some foreign law is called *conflict of laws*. Because there are 50 state court systems and a federal court system, as well as a high degree of interstate activity, conflicts of law questions arise frequently.

Some general rules apply. For example, the law of the state in which the court is located governs the case on procedural issues and rules of evidence. In contract litigation, the court applies the law of the state in which the contract was made for determining issues of formation. Performance disputes and damages for nonperformance are generally governed by the law of the state where the contract is to be performed. International contracts follow similar rules. **For Example,** a California court will apply Swiss law to a contract made in Switzerland that is to be performed in that country.

However, it is becoming more common for the parties to specify their choice of law in their contract.[6] In the absence of a law-selecting provision in the contract, there is a

---

[6] For example, when tourists from other countries engage in activities there, they sign a combination waiver and contract that provides in the event of an injury that they agree to be governed by the laws of that country in terms of recovery and not those of the United States. *E & H Cruises, Ltd. v. Baker*, 88 So. 3d 291 (Fla. App. 2012).

growing acceptance of the rule that a contract should be governed by the law of the state that has the most significant contacts with the transaction.

For Example, assume the buyer's place of business and the seller's plant are located in Nebraska, and the buyer is purchasing goods from the seller to resell to Nebraska customers. Many courts will hold that this is a contract governed by the law of Nebraska. In determining which state has the most significant contacts, the court considers the place of contracting, negotiating, and performing; the location of the subject matter of the contract; and the domicile (residence), states of incorporation, and principal place of business of the parties.

2-2c Initial Steps in a Lawsuit

The following steps in a lawsuit generally apply in cases brought in courts of original jurisdiction. Not every step applies in every case, but understanding litigation steps and terms is important for businesspeople.

Commencement of a Lawsuit

A lawsuit begins with the filing of a **complaint.** The complaint generally contains a description of the wrongful conduct and a request for damages, such as a monetary amount. **For Example,** a plaintiff in a contract suit would describe the contract, when it was entered into, and when the defendant stopped performance on the contract. A copy of the contract would be attached to the complaint.

Service of Process

Once the plaintiff has filed the complaint with the proper court, the plaintiff has the responsibility of notifying the defendant that the lawsuit has been filed. The defendant must be served with **process.** Process, often called a *writ*, *notice*, or *summons*, is delivered to the defendant and includes a copy of the complaint and notification that the defendant must appear and respond to the allegations in the complaint.

The Defendant's Response and the Pleadings

After the defendant is served with process in the case, the defendant is required to respond to or **answer** the complaint within the time provided under the court's rules. In answering the plaintiff's complaint, the defendant has several options. For example, the defendant could make a **motion to dismiss,** which is a request to the court to dismiss the lawsuit on the grounds that, even if everything the plaintiff said in the complaint were true, there is still no right of recovery. A motion to dismiss is also called a **demurrer.**

A defendant could also respond and deny the allegations. **For Example,** in a contract lawsuit, the defendant-seller could say he did not breach the contract but stopped shipment of the goods because the plaintiff-buyer did not pay for the goods in advance as the contract required. A defendant could also **counterclaim** in the answer, which is asking the court for damages as a result of the underlying dispute. The defendant-seller in the contract lawsuit might ask for damages in the counterclaim for the plaintiff-buyer's failure to pay as the contract required.

All documents filed in this initial phase of the case are referred to as the **pleadings.** The pleadings are a statement of the case and the basis for recovery if all the facts alleged can be proved.

Discovery

The Federal Rules of Civil Procedure and similar rules in all states permit one party to obtain from the adverse party information about all witnesses, documents, and any other items relevant to the case. **Discovery** requires each side to name its potential witnesses

complaint–the initial pleading filed by the plaintiff in many actions, which in many states may be served as original process to acquire jurisdiction over the defendant.

process–paperwork served personally on a defendant in a civil case.

answer–what a defendant must file to admit or deny facts asserted by the plaintiff.

motion to dismiss–a pleading that may be filed to attack the adverse party's pleading as not stating a cause of action or a defense.

demurrer–a pleading to dismiss the adverse party's pleading for not stating a cause of action or a defense.

counterclaim–a claim that the defendant in an action may make against the plaintiff.

pleadings–the papers filed by the parties in an action in order to set forth the facts and frame the issues to be tried, although, under some systems, the pleadings merely give notice or a general indication of the nature of the issues.

discovery–procedures for ascertaining facts prior to the time of trial in order to eliminate the element of surprise in litigation.

and to provide each side the chance to question those witnesses in advance of the trial. Each party also has the opportunity to examine, inspect, and photograph books, records, buildings, and machines. Even examining the physical or mental condition of a party is part of discovery when it has relevance in the case. The scope of discovery is extremely broad because the rules permit any questions that are likely to lead to admissible evidence.

Deposition. A **deposition** is the testimony of a witness taken under oath outside the courtroom; it is transcribed by a court reporter. Each party is permitted to question the witness. If a party or a witness gives testimony at the trial that is inconsistent with her deposition testimony, the prior inconsistent testimony can be used to **impeach** the witness's credibility at trial.

Depositions can be taken either for discovery purposes or to preserve the testimony of a witness who will not be available during the trial. Some states now permit depositions to be videotaped. A videotape is a more effective way of presenting deposition testimony than reading that testimony at trial from a reporter's transcript because jurors can see the witness and the witness's demeanor and hear the words as they were spoken, complete with inflection.

Other Forms of Discovery. Other forms of discovery include medical exams, particularly in cases in which the plaintiff is claiming damages for physical injuries. Written **interrogatories** (questions) and written **requests for production of documents** are discovery requests that can be very time consuming to the answering party and often lead to pretrial legal disputes between the parties and their attorneys as a result of the legal expenses involved.

Motion for Summary Judgment

If a case has no material facts in dispute, either party can file a **motion for summary judgment.** Using affidavits or deposition testimony obtained in discovery, the court can find that there are no factual issues and decide the case as a matter of law. **For Example,** suppose that the parties can agree that they entered into a life insurance contract but dispute whether the policy applies when there is a suicide. The facts are not in dispute; the law on payment of insurance proceeds in the event of a suicide is the issue. Such a case is one that is appropriate for summary judgment.

Designation of Expert Witnesses

In some cases, such as those involving product safety, the parties may want to designate an expert witness. An **expert witness** is a witness who has some special expertise, such as an economist who gives expert opinion on the value of future lost income or a scientist who testifies about the safety of a prescription drug. There are rules for naming expert witnesses as well as for admitting into evidence any studies or documents of the expert.[7] The purpose of these rules is to avoid the problem of what has been called *junk science*, or the admission of experts' testimony and research that has not been properly conducted or reviewed by peers.

2-2d The Trial

Selecting a Jury

Jurors drawn for service are questioned by the judge and lawyers to determine whether they are biased or have any preformed judgments about the parties in the case. Jury selection is called *voir dire* **examination. For Example,** in the trial of Martha Stewart, the multimedia home and garden diva, it took a great deal of time for the lawyers to question

---

deposition–the testimony of a witness taken out of court before a person authorized to administer oaths.

impeach–using prior inconsistent evidence to challenge the credibility of a witness.

interrogatories–written questions used as a discovery tool that must be answered under oath.

request for production of documents–discovery tool for uncovering paper evidence in a case.

motion for summary judgment–request that the court decide a case on basis of law only because there are no material issues disputed by the parties.

expert witness–one who has acquired special knowledge in a particular field as through practical experience or study, or both, whose opinion is admissible as an aid to the trier of fact.

voir dire examination–the preliminary examination of a juror or a witness to ascertain fitness to act as such.

---

[7] *Daubert v. Merrell Dow Pharmaceuticals, Inc.*, 509 U.S. 579 (1993).

E-COMMERCE & CYBERLAW

Google's Impact on Trials

The courts continue to struggle with the effects of the Internet on the jury selection process as well as with the jurors themselves in accessing social media sites while serving on a jury. There have been 134 cases in the past three years that involved issues with Google and jurors. In *McGaha v. Com.*, 414 S.W.3d 1 (Ky. 2013), the court held that a juror's failure to disclose being a friend of the defendant's wife on Facebook is not a presumed reason for disqualification of that juror on the basis of bias or lack of impartiality. In *People v. Levack*, 2014 WL 2118088 (Mich. App.), the jurors used Google Maps to determine whether there was a shortcut to the victim's home, as claimed in the testimony. The jurors did not consider the Google information in their deliberations and the court found that a new trial was not necessary.

The key points of these cases are that prospective jurors should disclose online connections with any of the parties in a case and that jurors should not consider any information that was not provided through the trial process. The courts follow these basic principles when evaluating whether a mistrial is necessary when the Internet has affected jurors or prospective jurors. In fact, judges often include an instruction similar to this one in turning the case over to a jury:

> *Do not visit or view any place discussed in this case, and do not use any internet maps or Google Earth or any other program or device to search for or view any place discussed in the testimony.**

**State v. Feliciano*, 2014 WL 1577768 (N.J. Sup.).

---

opening statements— statements by opposing attorneys that tell the jury what their cases will prove.

admissibility— the quality of the evidence in a case that allows it to be presented to the jury.

direct examination— examination of a witness by his or her attorney.

cross-examination— the examination made of a witness by the attorney for the adverse party.

redirect examination— questioning after cross-examination, in which the attorney for the witness testifying may ask the same witness other questions to overcome effects of the cross-examination.

recross-examination— an examination by the other side's attorney that follows the redirect examination.

the potential jurors about their prior knowledge concerning the case, which had received nationwide attention and much media coverage. Lawyers have the opportunity to remove jurors who know parties in the case or who indicate they have already formed opinions about guilt or innocence. The attorneys question the potential jurors to determine if a juror should be *challenged for cause* (e.g., when the prospective juror states he is employed by the plaintiff's company). Challenges for cause are unlimited, but each side can also exercise six to eight peremptory challenges.[8] A peremptory challenge is a challenge that is used to strike (remove) a juror for any reason except on racial grounds.[9]

Opening Statements

After the jury is chosen, the attorneys for each of the parties make their **opening statements** to the jury. An opening statement, as one lawyer has explained, makes a puzzle frame for the case so jurors can follow the witnesses and place the pieces of the case—the various forms of evidence—within the frame.

The Presentation of Evidence

Following the opening statements, the plaintiff presents his case with witnesses and other evidence. A judge rules on the **admissibility** of evidence. Evidence can consist of documents, testimony, expert testimony, medical information from exams, and even physical evidence.

In the case of testimony, the attorney for the plaintiff conducts **direct examination** of his witnesses during his case, and the defense attorney conducts **cross-examination** of the plaintiff's witnesses. The plaintiff's attorney can then ask questions again of his witnesses in what is called **redirect examination.** Finally, the defense attorney may question the plaintiff's witnesses again in **recross-examination.** The defendant presents her case after the plaintiff's case concludes. During the defendant's case, the lawyer for the

---

[8] The number of peremptory challenges varies from state to state and may also vary within a particular state depending on the type of case. For example, in Arizona, peremptory challenges are unlimited in capital cases.
[9] *Felkner v. Jackson*, 562 U.S. 594 (2011).

THINKING THINGS THROUGH

Why Do We Require Sworn Testimony?

There is a difference between what people say in conversation (and even what company executives say in speeches and reports) and what they are willing to say under oath. Speaking under oath often means that different information and recollections emerge. The oath is symbolic and carries the penalty of criminal prosecution for perjury if the testimony given is false.

The *Wall Street Journal* has reported that the testimony of executives in the Microsoft antitrust trial and their statements regarding their business relationships outside the courtroom are quite different. For example, the following quotations indicate some discrepancies. Eric Benhamou, the chief executive officer (CEO) of Palm, Inc., said:

We believe that the handheld opportunity remains wide open …. Unlike the PC industry, there is no monopoly of silicon, there is no monopoly of software.

However, at the Microsoft trial, another officer of Palm, Michael Mace, offered the following testimony:

We believe that there is a very substantial risk that Microsoft could manipulate its products and its

standards in order to exclude Palm from the marketplace in the future.

Likewise, Microsoft has taken different positions inside and outside the courtroom. For example, an attorney for Microsoft stated that Microsoft had "zero deployments of its interactive TV middleware products connected to cable systems in the United States." However, Microsoft's marketing materials provide as follows:

Microsoft's multiple deployments around the world now including Charter-show Microsoft TV is ready to deploy now and set the standard for what TV can be.*

Explain why the executives had differing statements. For more information on the Microsoft antitrust cases, go to **http://www.usdoj.gov** or **http://www.microsoft.com**.

*Rebecca Buckman and Nicholas Kulish, "Microsoft Trial Prompts an Outbreak of Doublespeak," *Wall Street Journal*, April 15, 2002, B1, B3.

---

defendant conducts direct examination of the defendant's witnesses, and the plaintiff's lawyer can then cross-examine the defendant's witnesses.

Motion for a Directed Verdict

directed verdict—a direction by the trial judge to the jury to return a verdict in favor of a specified party to the action.

A motion for a **directed verdict** asks the court to grant a verdict because even if all the evidence that has been presented by each side were true, there is either no basis for recovery or no defense to recovery.

For Example, suppose that a plaintiff company presented evidence that an employee who quit working for the company posted on his Facebook page, "I just wasn't happy there." The company might not feel good about the former employee's post, but there is no false statement and no breach of privacy. The evidence is true, but there is no legal right of recovery. The defendant employee would be entitled to a directed verdict. A directed verdict means that the party has not presented enough evidence to show that there is some right of recovery under the law.

summation—the attorney address that follows all the evidence presented in court and sums up a case and recommends a particular verdict be returned by the jury.

Closing Arguments or Summation

After the witnesses for both parties have been examined and all the evidence has been presented, each attorney makes a closing argument. These statements are also called **summations;** they summarize the case and urge the jury to reach a particular verdict.

mistrial—a court's declaration that terminates a trial and postpones it to a later date; commonly entered when evidence has been of a highly prejudicial character or when a juror has been guilty of misconduct.

Motion for Mistrial

During the course of a trial, when necessary to avoid great injustice, the trial court may declare a **mistrial.** A mistrial requires a do-over, a new jury. A mistrial can be declared for jury or attorney misconduct. **For Example,** if a juror were caught fraternizing with one of the lawyers in the case, objectivity would be compromised and the court would most likely declare a mistrial. See also E-Commerce & Cyberlaw (Google's Impact on Trials) for more information on juror misconduct and case dismissals.

Jury Instructions and Verdict

instruction–summary of the law given to jurors by the judge before deliberation begins.

After the summation by the attorneys, the court gives the jurors **instructions** on the appropriate law to apply to the facts presented. The jury then deliberates and renders its verdict. After the jury verdict, the court enters a judgment. If the jury is deadlocked and unable to reach a verdict, known as a hung jury or a mistrial, the case is reset for a new trial at some future date.

Motion for New Trial; Motion for Judgment *n.o.v.*

judgment n.o.v.–or non obstante veredicto (notwithstanding the verdict), a judgment entered after verdict upon the motion of the losing party on the ground that the verdict is so wrong that a judgment should be entered the opposite of the verdict.

A court may grant a **judgment** *non obstante veredicto* or a **judgment** *n.o.v.* (notwithstanding the verdict) if the verdict is clearly wrong as a matter of law. The court can set aside the verdict and enter a judgment in favor of the other party. Perhaps one of the most famous judgments n.o.v. occurred in Boston in 1997 when a judge reversed the murder conviction of nanny Louise Woodward, who was charged with the murder of one of her young charges.

2-2e Post-trial Procedures

Recovery of Costs/Attorney Fees

Generally, the prevailing party is awarded costs. Costs include filing fees, service-of-process fees, witness fees, deposition transcript costs, and jury fees. Costs do not

ETHICS & THE LAW

Honesty, Lawyers, and BP Claims

Following the Deepwater Horizon oil spill in the Gulf of Mexico, BP established a $20 billion recovery fund. The purpose of the fund was to reimburse businesses and individuals who were affected by the spill, such as fishers, resorts, and boating companies that provided tours and other services.

Several lawyers and accountants were assigned to the Claims Administration Office (CAO) with the responsibilities for the receipt, evaluation, and payment of claims. In 2013, the federal judge overseeing the claims process became concerned about the conduct of those who were administering the trust. As a result, the judge appointed Louis Freeh, a former federal judge and director of the FBI, to investigate.

Among the many findings of the cases were conflicts, such as Lionel Sutton and Christine Reitano, husband and wife, two lawyers working at the CAO who had practiced law together in New Orleans as Sutton & Reitano. They referred a client, Casey Thonn, to Glen Lerner of AndryLerner, a law firm representing claimants to the CAO. Ms. Reitano then requested a referral fee from AndryLerner. The referral arrangement was never disclosed to the client, Casey Thonn,

as Louisiana's code of professional ethics requires, nor the CAO office. Mr. Sutton continued his representation of Casey Thonn in a personal injury case but did not disclose that client relationship to anyone at the CAO. Mr. Sutton also did not disclose that he had a business relationship in a reclamation company, Crown LLC, and that he was one of two equity owners of that company, with Glen Lerner, a partner at AndryLerner, being the other owner. AndryLerner had a total of $7,908,460 in claims before the CAO. Mr. Sutton approved 496 of the claims.

On November 25, 2014, the U.S. Attorney for the Middle District of Florida announced 27 indictments against individuals who are alleged to have submitted fraudulent claims for reimbursement, ranging from $11,000 to $122,000, and totaling over $1,000,000.

BP began running full-page ads in major newspaper around the country with examples of the fraudulent claims. The judge is seeking restitution from many of the claimants.

What should the lawyers have done in their situations? Why did they not do it?

include compensation spent by a party for preparing the case or being present at trial, including the time lost from work because of the case and the fee paid to the attorney, although lost wages from an injury are generally part of damages.

Attorney fees may be recovered by a party who prevails if a statute permits the recovery of attorney fees or if the complaint involves a claim for breach of contract and the contract contains a clause providing for recovery of attorney fees.

Execution of Judgment

execution–the carrying out of a judgment of a court, generally directing that property owned by the defendant be sold and the proceeds first be used to pay the execution or judgment creditor.

garnishment–the name given in some states to attachment proceedings.

After a judgment has been entered or all appeals or appeal rights have ended, the losing party must pay that judgment. The winning party can also take steps to execute, or carry out, the judgment. The **execution** is accomplished by the seizure and sale of the losing party's assets by the sheriff according to a writ of execution or a writ of possession.

Garnishment is a common method of satisfying a judgment. When the judgment debtor is an employee, the appropriate judicial authority in the state garnishes (by written notice to the employer) a portion of the employee's wages on a regular basis until the judgment is paid.

2-3 Alternative Dispute Resolution (ADR)

Parties can use means other than litigation to resolve disagreements or disputes. Litigation takes significant time and money, so many businesses use alternative methods for resolving disputes. Those methods include arbitration, mediation, and several other formats. Figure 2-4 provides an overall view of alternative dispute resolution procedures.

2-3a Arbitration

arbitration–the settlement of disputed questions, whether of law or fact, by one or more arbitrators by whose decision the parties agree to be bound.

In **arbitration,** arbitrators (disinterested persons selected by the parties to the dispute) hear evidence and determine a resolution. Arbitration enables the parties to present the facts before trained experts familiar with the industry practices that may affect the nature and outcome of the dispute. Arbitration first reached extensive use in the field of commercial contracts and was encouraged as a means of avoiding expensive litigation and easing the workload of courts. However, over the past decade the popularity of arbitration has declined because of increasing procedural burdens and longer and more complex hearings. There have been an increasing number of cases in which arbitration clauses have been set aside as too onerous for a consumer or small business party to the agreement.[10]

A number of states have adopted the Uniform Arbitration Act.[11] Under this act and similar statutes, the parties to a contract may agree in advance that all disputes arising under it will be submitted to arbitration. In some instances, the contract will name the arbitrators for the duration of the contract. The uniform act requires a written agreement to arbitrate.[12]

The Federal Arbitration Act[13] provides that an arbitration clause in a contract relating to an interstate transaction is valid, irrevocable, and enforceable. When a contract subject to the Federal Arbitration Act provides for the arbitration of disputes, the parties are

---

[10] *College Park Pentecostal Holiness Church v. General Steel Corp.*, 847 F. Supp. 2d 807 (D. Md. 2012).

[11] On August 3, 2000, the National Conference of Commissioners on Uniform State Laws unanimously passed major revisions to the Uniform Arbitration Act (UAA). These revisions were the first major changes in 45 years to the UAA, which is the basis of arbitration law in 49 states, although not all states have adopted it in its entirety or most current form. Only 18 states and the District of Columbia have adopted the UAA 2000 revisions. John Lande, "A Framework for Advancing Negotiation Theory: Implications from a Study of How Lawyers Reach Agreement in Pretrial Litigation," 16 *Cardozo Journal of Conflict Resolution* 1 (2014).

[12] *Minkowitz v. Israeli*, 77 A.3d 1189 (N.J. Super. 2013).

[13] 9 U.S.C. §§114 *et seq.*

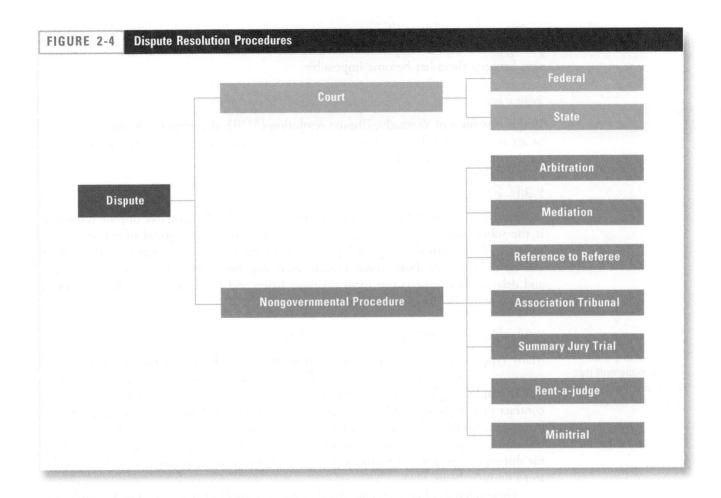

FIGURE 2-4 | **Dispute Resolution Procedures**

bound to arbitrate in accordance with the federal statute even if the agreement to arbitrate would not be binding under state law.

Mandatory Arbitration

In contrast with statutes that merely regulate arbitration when it is selected voluntarily by the parties, some statutes require that certain kinds of disputes be submitted to arbitration. In some states, by rule or statute, the arbitration of small claims is required.

Finality of Arbitration

Most parties provide, within their arbitration agreements, that the decision of the arbitrator will be final. Such a clause is binding on the parties, even when the decision seems to be wrong, and can be set aside only if there is clear proof of fraud, arbitrary conduct, or a significant procedural error.[14]

mediation—the settlement of a dispute through the use of a messenger who carries to each side of the dispute the issues and offers in the case.

2-3b Mediation

In **mediation,** a neutral person acts as a messenger between opposing sides of a dispute, carrying to each side the latest settlement offer made by the other. The mediator has no authority to make a decision, although in some cases the mediator may make suggestions that might ultimately be accepted by the disputing parties.

[14] *PoolRE Ins. Corp. v. Organizational Strategies, Inc.,* 2014 WL 1320188 (S.D. Tex. 2014).

The use of mediation has the advantage of keeping discussions going when the disputing parties have developed such fixed attitudes or personal animosity that direct discussion between them has become impossible.

2-3c MedArb

In this new form of alternative dispute resolution (ADR), the arbitrator is also empowered to act as a mediator. Beyond just hearing a case, the arbitrator acts as a messenger for the parties on unresolved issues.

2-3d Expert Panel

Particularly in the construction industry, one of the tools of alternative dispute resolution is the submission of a case, or perhaps a particular issue, to a panel of experts in the industry. This method has gained popularity in the construction industry where there can be technical questions about breach, including issues related to materials, process, and delays. These experts can focus on these issues and not be caught in the procedural grind of either litigation or arbitration.

2-3e Reference to a Third Person

reference to a third person—settlement that allows a nonparty to resolve the dispute.

Many types of transactions provide for **reference to a third person,** in which a third person or a committee makes an out-of-court determination of the rights of persons. **For Example,** employees and an employer may have agreed as a term of the employment contract that claims of employees under retirement plans will be decided by a designated board or committee. In a sales contract, the seller and buyer can select a third person to determine the price to be paid for goods. Construction contracts often include a provision for disputes to be referred to the architect in charge of the construction with the architect's decision being final.

These referrals often eliminate the disputes or pursuit of remedies. **For Example,** fire insurance policies commonly provide that if the parties cannot agree on the amount of the loss, each will appoint an appraiser, the two appraisers will appoint a third appraiser, and the three will determine the amount of the loss the insurer is required to pay.

2-3f Association Tribunals

association tribunal—a court created by a trade association or group for the resolution of disputes among its members.

Many disputes never reach the courts because both parties to a dispute belong to a group or an association, and the **association tribunal** created by the group or association disposes of the matter. Trade associations commonly require their members to employ out-of-court methods of dispute settlement. **For Example,** the National Association of Home Builders requires its member builders to use arbitration. The National Automobile Dealers Association provides for panels to determine warranty claims of customers. The decision of such panels is final as to the builder or dealer, but the consumer can still bring a regular lawsuit after losing before the panel. Members of an association must use the association tribunal, which means they cannot bypass the association tribunal and go directly to a law court.[15]

2-3g Summary Jury Trial

summary jury trial—a mock or dry-run trial for parties to get a feel for how their cases will play to a jury.

A **summary jury trial** is a dry-run or mock trial in which the lawyers present their claims before a jury of six persons. The object is to get the reaction of a sample jury. No evidence is presented before this jury, and it bases its opinion solely on what the lawyers state. The determination of the jury has no binding effect, but it has value in that it

---

[15] The securities industry follows this process as well.

gives the lawyers some idea of what a jury might think if there were an actual trial. This type of ADR has special value when the heart of a case is whether something is reasonable under all circumstances. When the lawyers and their clients see how the sample jury reacts, they may moderate their positions and reach a settlement.

2-3h Rent-A-Judge

rent-a-judge plan–dispute resolution through private courts with judges paid to be referees for the cases.

Under the **rent-a-judge plan,** the parties hire a judge to hear the case. In many states, the parties voluntarily choose the judge as a "referee," and the judge acts under a statute authorizing the appointment of referees. Under such a statute, the referee hears all evidence just as though there were a regular trial, and the rented judge's determination is binding on the parties unless reversed on appeal if such an appeal (like a court trial) is permitted under the parties' agreement.

2-3i Minitrial

minitrial–a trial held on portions of the case or certain issues in the case.

When only part of a case is disputed, the parties may stay within the framework of a lawsuit but agree that only the disputed issues will be taken to trial and submitted to a jury. **For Example,** if there is no real dispute over who is liable but the parties disagree as to the damages, the issue of damages alone may be submitted to the jury. This shortened trial is often called a **minitrial.** A minitrial may use a retired judge to make a decision on just the disputed issues. The parties may also specify whether this decision will be binding on the parties. As a practical matter, the evaluation of a case by a neutral person often brings the opposing parties together to reach a settlement.

2-3j Contract Provisions

The parties' contract may pave the way for the settlement of future disputes by including clauses that require the parties to use one of the means of ADR. Other provisions in contracts that serve to keep the parties calm with the hope of resolving differences without a lawsuit include waiting periods before a suit can be filed and obligations to continue performing even as they try to resolve differences and issues.

Make the Connection

Summary

Courts have been created to hear and resolve legal disputes. A court's specific power is defined by its jurisdiction. Courts of original jurisdiction are trial courts, and courts that review the decisions of trial courts are appellate courts. Trial courts may have general jurisdiction to hear a wide range of civil and criminal matters, or they may be courts of limited jurisdiction—such as a probate court or the Tax Court—with the subject matter of their cases restricted to certain areas.

The courts in the United States are organized into two different systems: the state and federal court systems.

There are three levels of courts, for the most part, in each system, with trial courts, appellate courts, and a supreme court in each. The federal courts are federal district courts, federal courts of appeals, and the U.S. Supreme Court.

In the states, there may be specialized courts, such as municipal, justice, and small claims courts, for trial courts. Within the courts of original jurisdiction, there are rules for procedures in all matters brought before them. A civil case begins with the filing of a complaint by a plaintiff, which is then answered by a defendant. The parties may be represented by their attorneys. Discovery is the pretrial process used by the parties to find out the evidence in the case. The parties can use depositions, interrogatories, and document requests to uncover relevant information.

The case is managed by a judge and may be tried to a jury selected through the process of *voir dire*, with the parties permitted to challenge jurors on the basis of cause or through the use of their peremptory challenges. The trial begins following discovery and involves opening statements and the presentation of evidence, including the direct examination and cross-examination of witnesses. Once a judgment is entered, the party who has won can collect the judgment through garnishment and a writ of execution.

Alternatives to litigation for dispute resolution are available, including arbitration, mediation, MedArb, reference to a third party, association tribunals, summary jury trials, rent-a-judge plans, minitrials, and expert panels. Court dockets are relieved and cases consolidated using judicial triage, a process in which courts hear the cases involving the most serious medical issues and health conditions first. Triage is a blending of the judicial and alternative dispute resolution mechanisms.

Learning Outcomes

After studying this chapter, you should be able to clearly explain:

2-1 The Court System

LO.1 Explain the federal and state court systems
See Figure 2-1 and accompanying text, page 16.
See Figure 2-3 and accompanying text, page 19.
See the *Stanford* case on page 15 for a discussion of reversible error.

2-2 Court Procedure

LO.2 Describe court procedures
See the discussion of steps in litigation, pages 21–22.
See the *For Example* discussion of the Martha Stewart *voir dire* example, page 22.

See the Google jury issues box on page 23.
See the "Why Do We Require Sworn Testimony" box on page 24.

2-3 Alternative Dispute Resolution (ADR)

LO.3 List the forms of alternative dispute resolution and distinguish among them
See the discussion of arbitration, page 26.
See the discussion of other forms of ADR, mediation, minitrials, rent-a-judge, MedArb, judicial triage, and referral to a third party, pages 27–29.
See the discussion of employee and employer referrals of disputes to a designated board or committee, page 28.

Key Terms

admissibility	expert witness	plaintiff
affirm	federal district courts	pleadings
answer	garnishment	process
appeal	general jurisdiction	prosecutor
appellate jurisdiction	impeach	recross-examination
arbitration	instructions	redirect examination
association tribunal	interrogatories	reference to a third person
attorney-client privilege	judge	remand
complaint	judgment *n.o.v.* or judgment *non*	rent-a-judge plan
counterclaim	*obstante veredicto*	requests for production of documents
court	jurisdiction	reverse
cross-examination	jury	reversible error
defendant	limited (special) jurisdiction	small claims courts
demurrer	mediation	subject matter jurisdiction
deposition	minitrial	summary jury trial
direct examination	mistrial	summations
directed verdict	motion for summary judgment	*voir dire* examination
discovery	motion to dismiss	writ of *certiorari*
en banc	opening statements	
execution	original jurisdiction	

Questions and Case Problems

1. List the steps in a lawsuit. Begin with the filing of the complaint, and explain the points at which there can be a final determination of the parties' rights in the case.

2. Explain why a business person would want to use alternative dispute resolution methods. Discuss the advantages. What disadvantages have you learned?

3. Ralph Dewey has been charged with a violation of the Electronic Espionage Act, a federal statute that prohibits the transfer, by computer or disk or other electronic means, of a company's proprietary data and information. Ralph is curious. What type of court has jurisdiction? Can you determine which court?

4. Jerry Lewinsky was called for jury duty. When *voir dire* began, Jerry realized that the case involved his supervisor at work. Can Jerry remain as a juror on the case? Why or why not?

5. Carolyn, Elwood, and Isabella are involved in a real estate development. The development is a failure, and Carolyn, Elwood, and Isabella want to have their rights determined. They could bring a lawsuit, but they are afraid the case is so complicated that a judge and jury not familiar with the problems of real estate development would not reach a proper result. What can they do?

6. Larketta Randolph purchased a mobile home from Better Cents Home Builders, Inc., and financed her purchase through Green Tree Financial Corporation. Ms. Randolph signed a standard form contract that required her to buy Vendor's Single Interest insurance, which protects the seller against the costs of repossession in the event of default. The agreement also provided that all disputes arising from the contract would be resolved by binding arbitration. Larketta found that there was an additional $15 in finance charges that were not disclosed in the contract. She and other Green Tree customers filed a class-action suit to recover the fees. Green Tree moved to dismiss the suit because Larketta had not submitted the issue to arbitration. Larketta protests, "But I want the right to go to court!" Does she have that right? What are the rights of parties under a contract with an arbitration clause? [*Green Tree Financial Corp. v. Randolph*, 531 U.S. 79]

7. John Watson invested $5,000,000 in SmartRead, Inc., a company that was developing an electronic reading device. Within a few months, the $5,000,000 was spent but SmartRead never developed the reading device. John filed suit against the directors of SmartRead for their failure to supervise SmartRead's CEO in his operation of the company. The directors used an expert on corporate governance to testify that the directors had done all that they could to oversee the company. The expert did not disclose that he had served as a director of a company and had been found to be negligent in his role there and had been required to pay $370,000 to shareholders. The directors won the case. Is there anything Watson can do?

8. Indicate whether the following courts are courts of original, general, limited, or appellate jurisdiction:

   a. Small claims court

   b. Federal bankruptcy court

   c. Federal district court

   d. U.S. Supreme Court

   e. Municipal court

   f. Probate court

   g. Federal court of appeals

9. The Nursing Home Pension Fund filed suit against Oracle Corporation alleging that Larry Ellison, the company's CEO, misled investors in 2001 about the true financial condition of the company. During the time of the alleged misrepresentation, Mr. Ellison was working with a biographer on his life story and there are videotapes of Mr. Ellison's interviews with his biographer as well as e-mails between the two that discuss Oracle. Could the Nursing Home Pension Fund have access to the tapes and e-mails? Explain how. [*Nursing Home Pension Fund, Local 144 v. Oracle Corp.*, 380 F.3d 1226 (9th Cir.)]

10. Mostek Corp., a Texas corporation, made a contract to sell computer-related products to North American Foreign Trading Corp., a New York corporation. North American used its own purchase order form, on which appeared the statement that any dispute arising out of an order would be submitted to arbitration, as provided in the terms set forth on the back of the order. Acting on the purchase order, Mostek delivered almost all of the goods but failed to deliver the final installment. North American then demanded that the matter be arbitrated. Mostek refused to do so. Was arbitration required? [*Application of Mostek Corp.*, 502 N.Y.S.2d 181 (App. Div.)]

11. Ceasar Wright was a longshoreman in Charleston, South Carolina, and a member of the International Longshoremen's Association (AFL-CIO). Wright used the union hiring hall. The collective bargaining agreement (CBA) of Wright's union provides for arbitration of all grievances. Another clause of the CBA states: "It is the intention and purpose of all parties hereto that no provision or part of this Agreement shall be violative of any Federal or State Law."

    On February 18, 1992, while Wright was working for Stevens Shipping and Terminal Company (Stevens), he injured his right heel and back. He sought permanent compensation from Stevens and settled his claims for $250,000 and another $10,000 in attorney fees. Wright was also awarded Social Security disability benefits.

    In January 1995, Wright, whose doctor had approved his return to work, returned to the hiring hall and asked to be referred for work. Wright did work between January 2 and January 11, 1995, but when the companies realized that Wright had been certified as permanently disabled, they deemed him not qualified for longshoreman work under the CBA and refused to allow him to work for them.

    Wright did not file a grievance under the union agreement but instead hired a lawyer and proceeded with a claim under the Americans with Disabilities Act. The district court dismissed the case because Wright had failed to pursue the grievance procedure provided by the CBA. Must Wright pursue the dispute procedure first, or can he go right to court on the basis of his federal rights under the Americans with Disabilities Act? [*Wright v. Universal Maritime Service Corp.*, 525 U.S. 70]

12. Winona Ryder was arrested for shoplifting from Saks Fifth Avenue in California. One of the members of the jury panel for her trial was Peter Guber, a Hollywood executive in charge of the production of three films in which Ms. Ryder starred, including *Bram Stoker's Dracula, The Age of Innocence*, and *Little Women*. If you were the prosecuting attorney in the case, how could you discover such information about this potential juror, and what are your options for excluding him from selection? [Rick Lyman, "For the Ryder Trial, a Hollywood Script," *New York Times*, November 3, 2002, SL-1]

13. Two doctors had a dispute over who was doing how much work at their clinic. Their dispute was submitted to arbitration and the arbitrator held in favor of the less experienced doctor. The senior doctor wants the arbitration set aside. Is it possible for the arbitrator's decision to be set aside?

14. Martha Simms is the plaintiff in a contract suit she has brought against Floral Supply, Inc., for its failure to deliver the green sponge Martha needed in building the floral designs she sells to exclusive home decorators. Martha had to obtain the sponge from another supplier and was late on seven deliveries. One of Martha's customers has been called by Martha's lawyer as a witness and is now on the witness stand, testifying about Martha's late performance and the penalty she charged. The lawyer for Floral Supply knows that Martha's customer frequently waives penalties for good suppliers. How can Floral Supply's lawyer get that information before the jury?

15. Saint Claire Adams was hired by Circuit City as a sales counselor. When he was hired he signed an employment contract that included a mandatory arbitration clause. Two years later he filed a suit against Circuit City for discrimination in the workplace. Circuit City moved to have the suit dismissed because of the arbitration requirement. Mr. Adams responded that he has certain rights under Title VII of the federal anti-discrimination laws that cannot be taken away through an arbitration clause. Is he correct? [*Circuit City Stores, Inc. v. Adams*, 532 U.S. 105]

Chapter 11

Nature and Classes of Contracts: Contracting on the Internet

Learning Outcomes <<<

After studying this chapter, you should be able to

LO.1 Explain the meaning and importance of privity of a contract

LO.2 Describe the way in which a contract arises

LO.3 Distinguish between bilateral and unilateral contracts

LO.4 Explain the reasoning behind quasi-contract recovery

LO.5 Explain how Internet contracts involve the same types of issues as offline contracts

Practically every business transaction affecting people involves a contract.

11-1 Nature of Contracts

This introductory chapter will familiarize you with the terminology needed to work with contract law. In addition, the chapter introduces quasi contracts, which are not true contracts but obligations imposed by law.

11-1a Definition of a Contract

contract—a binding agreement based on the genuine assent of the parties, made for a lawful object, between competent parties, in the form required by law, and generally supported by consideration.

A **contract** is a legally binding agreement.[1] By one definition, "a contract is a promise or a set of promises for the breach of which the law gives a remedy, or the performance of which the law in some way recognizes as a duty."[2] Contracts arise out of agreements, so a contract may be defined as an agreement creating an obligation.

The substance of the definition of a contract is that by mutual agreement or assent, the parties create enforceable duties or obligations. That is, each party is legally bound to do or to refrain from doing certain acts.

11-1b Elements of a Contract

The elements of a contract are (1) an agreement (2) between competent parties (3) based on the genuine assent of the parties that is (4) supported by consideration, (5) made for a lawful objective, and (6) in the form required by law, if any. These elements will be considered in the chapters that follow.

promisor—person who makes a promise.

promisee—person to whom a promise is made.

11-1c Subject Matter of Contracts

The subject matter of a contract may relate to the performance of personal services, such as contracts of employment to work developing computer software or to play professional football. A contract may provide for the transfer of ownership of property, such as a house (real property) or an automobile (personal property), from one person to another.

obligor—promisor.

obligee—promisee who can claim the benefit of the obligation.

11-1d Parties to a Contract

privity—succession or chain of relationship to the same thing or right, such as privity of contract, privity of estate, privity of possession.

privity of contract—relationship between a promisor and the promisee.

The person who makes a promise is the **promisor,** and the person to whom the promise is made is the **promisee.** If the promise is binding, it imposes on the promisor a duty or obligation, and the promisor may be called the **obligor.** The promisee who can claim the benefit of the obligation is called the **obligee.** The parties to a contract are said to stand in **privity** with each other, and the relationship between them is termed **privity of contract. For Example,** when the state of North Carolina and the architectural firm of O'Brien/Atkins Associates executed a contract for the construction of a new building at the University of North Carolina, Chapel Hill, these parties were in privity of contract. However, a building contractor, RPR & Associates, who worked on the project did not have standing to sue on the contract between the architect and the state because the contractor was not in privity of contract.[3]

[1] The Uniform Commercial Code defines *contract* as "the total legal obligation which results from the parties' agreement as affected by [the UCC] and any other applicable rules of law." U.C.C. §1–201(11).

[2] Restatement (Second) of Contracts §1.

[3] *RPR & Associates v. O'Brien/Atkins Associates, PA,* 24 F. Supp. 2d 515 (M.D.N.C. 1998). See also *Roof Techs Int Inc. v. State,* 57 P.3d 538 (Kan. App. 2002), where a layer of litigation was avoided regarding lawsuits involving the renovation of the Farrell Library at Kansas State University. The state was the only party in privity of contract with the architectural firm and would thus have to bring claims against the architectural firm on behalf of all of the contractors. Two subcontractors, the general contractor, and the owner of the library, the state of Kansas, used a settlement and liquidation agreement assigning all of the state's claims against the architect to the general contractor.

In written contracts, parties may be referred to by name. More often, however, they are given special names that better identify each party. For example, consider a contract by which one person agrees that another may occupy a house upon the payment of money. The parties to this contract are called *landlord* and *tenant*, or *lessor* and *lessee*, and the contract between them is known as a *lease*. Parties to other types of contracts also have distinctive names, such as *vendor* and *vendee* for the parties to a sales contract, *shipper* and *carrier* for the parties to a transportation contract, and *insurer* and *insured* for the parties to an insurance policy.

A party to a contract may be an individual, a partnership, a limited liability company, a corporation, or a government.[4] One or more persons may be on each side of a contract. Some contracts are three-sided, as in a credit card transaction, which involves the company issuing the card, the holder of the card, and the business furnishing goods and services on the basis of the credit card.

If a contract is written, the persons who are the parties and who are bound by it can ordinarily be determined by reading what the document says and seeing how it is signed. A contract binds only the parties to the contract. It cannot impose a duty on a person who is not a party to it. Ordinarily, only a party to a contract has any rights against another party to the contract.[5] In some cases, third persons have rights on a contract as third-party beneficiaries or assignees. A person cannot be bound, however, by the terms of a contract to which that person is not a party. **For Example,** in approximately 1995 Jeff and Mark Bass signed Marshall B. Mathers III, better known as rapper Eminem, to an exclusive record deal with FBT Productions LLC (FBT), their production company. In 2000 Aftermath Records entered into a direct contractual relationship with Eminem, transferring Eminem's recording services from FBT directly to Aftermath. Under the contract FBT became a "passive income participant," retaining a right to royalty income from Eminem's recordings. A dispute occurred regarding percentages of royalties due. Aftermath entered into an agreement with Eminem in 2009, setting the royalties for Eminem's *Recovery* and *Relapse* albums, asserting that all royalties, including royalties owed FBT were dictated by this 2009 agreement. FBT was not a party to the 2009 agreement and as such cannot be bound by it. A contract cannot bind a nonparty. Therefore, Aftermath was required to pay FBT royalties for the two albums at a higher rate in accordance with an earlier agreement.[6]

CPA

offeror—person who makes an offer.

offeree—person to whom an offer is made.

11-1e How a Contract Arises

A contract is based on an agreement. An agreement arises when one person, the **offeror**, makes an offer and the person to whom the offer is made, the **offeree,** accepts. There must be both an offer and an acceptance. If either is lacking, there is no contract.

11-1f Intent to Make a Binding Agreement

Because a contract is based on the consent of the parties and is a legally binding agreement, it follows that the parties must have an intent to enter into an agreement that is binding. Sometimes the parties are in agreement, but their agreement does not produce a contract. Sometimes there is merely a preliminary agreement, but the parties never actually make a contract, or there is merely an agreement as to future plans or intentions without any contractual obligation to carry out those plans or intentions.

---

[4] See *Purina Mills, LLC v. Less*, 295 F. Supp. 2d 1017 (N.D. Iowa 2003) in which the pig-seller plaintiff, which converted from a corporation to a limited liability company (LLC) while the contract was in effect, was a proper party in interest and could maintain a contract action against defendant buyers.

[5] *Hooper v. Yakima County*, 904 P.2d 1193 (Wash. App. 1995).

[6] *F.B.T. Productions, LLC v. Aftermath Records*, 2011 WL 5174766 (C.D. Cal. Oct. 31, 2011).

11-1g Freedom of Contract

In the absence of some ground for declaring a contract void or voidable, parties may make such contracts as they choose. The law does not require parties to be fair, or kind, or reasonable, or to share gains or losses equitably.

11-2 Classes of Contracts

formal contracts–written contracts or agreements whose formality signifies the parties' intention to abide by the terms.

Contracts may be classified according to their form, the way in which they were created, their binding character, and the extent to which they have been performed.

CPA

11-2a Formal and Informal Contracts

Contracts can be classified as formal or informal.

Formal Contracts

contract under seal–contract executed by affixing a seal or making an impression on the paper or on some adhering substance such as wax attached to the document.

Formal contracts are enforced because the formality with which they are executed is considered sufficient to signify that the parties intend to be bound by their terms. Formal contracts include (1) **contracts under seal** where a person's signature or a corporation's name is followed by a scroll, the word *seal*, or the letters *L.S.*;[7] (2) contracts of record, which are obligations that have been entered before a court of record, sometimes called a **recognizance;** and (3) negotiable instruments.

recognizance–obligation entered into before a court to do some act, such as to appear at a later date for a hearing. Also called a *contract of record*.

Informal Contracts

All contracts other than formal contracts are called **informal** (or simple) **contracts** without regard to whether they are oral or written. These contracts are enforceable, not because of the form of the transaction but because they represent agreement of the parties.

informal contract–simple oral or written contract.

11-2b Express and Implied Contracts

Simple contracts may be classified as *express contracts* or *implied contracts* according to the way they are created.

Express Contracts

express contract–agreement of the parties manifested by their words, whether spoken or written.

An **express contract** is one in which the terms of the agreement of the parties are manifested by their words, whether spoken or written.

Implied Contracts

implied contract–contract expressed by conduct or implied or deduced from the facts.

An **implied contract** (or, as sometimes stated, a *contract implied in fact*) is one in which the agreement is shown not by words, written or spoken, but by the acts and conduct of the parties.[8] Such a contract arises when (1) a person renders services under circumstances indicating that payment for them is expected and (2) the other person, knowing such circumstances, accepts the benefit of those services. **For Example,** when a building owner requests a professional roofer to make emergency repairs to the roof of a building, an obligation arises to pay the reasonable value of such services, although no agreement has been made about compensation.

---

[7] Some authorities explain L.S. as an abbreviation for *locus sigilium* (place for the seal).
[8] *Lindquist Ford, Inc. v. Middleton Motors, Inc.*, 557 F.3d 469, 481 (7th Cir. 2009). See also *Dynegy Marketing and Trade v. Multiut Corp.*, 648 F.3d 506 (7th Cir. 2011).

An implied contract cannot arise when there is an existing express contract on the same subject.[9] However, the existence of a written contract does not bar recovery on an implied contract for extra work that was not covered by the contract.

To prevail on a cause of action for breach of an implied-in-fact contract based on an idea submission, plaintiffs must show (1) they conditioned the submission of their ideas on an obligation to pay for any use of the ideas; (2) the defendants voluntarily accepted the submission of ideas; and (3) the defendants actually used these ideas, rather than their own ideas with other sources. In an idea submission case where similarities exist, it is a complete defense for the defendants to show that they independently created their product. **For Example,** in 1977, Anthony Spinner a highly regarded television producer and writer, submitted drafts of his script entitled "Lost" to ABC. ABC decided to pass on the proposal for it would be too expensive to produce. In 2004, ABC premiered a pilot for LOST in September, and the series ran for six years. Spinner's subsequent implied-in-fact idea submission lawsuit was unsuccessful because ABC demonstrated that the script for the LOST series was created independently.[10]

<table>
<tr><td>**CPA**</td><td></td></tr>
</table>

11-2c Valid and Voidable Contracts and Void Agreements

Contracts may be classified in terms of enforceability or validity.

valid contract— agreement that is binding and enforceable.

Valid Contracts

A **valid contract** is an agreement that is binding and enforceable.

voidable contract— agreement that is otherwise binding and enforceable but may be rejected at the option of one of the parties as the result of specific circumstances.

Voidable Contracts

A **voidable contract** is an agreement that is otherwise binding and enforceable, but because of the circumstances surrounding its execution or the lack of capacity of one of the parties, it may be rejected at the option of one of the parties. **For Example,** a person who has been forced to sign an agreement that that person would not have voluntarily signed may, in some instances, avoid the contract.

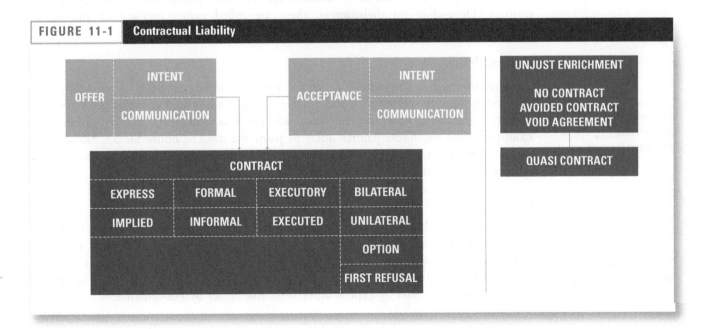

FIGURE 11-1 Contractual Liability

---

[9] *Pepsi-Cola Bottling Co. of Pittsburgh, Inc., v. PepsiCo, Inc.,* 431 F.3d 1241 (10th Cir. 2000).
[10] *Spinner v. American Broadcasting Companies, Inc.,* 155 Cal. Rptr. 3d 32 (Cal. App. 2013).

Void Agreements

void agreement–
agreement that cannot
be enforced.

A **void agreement** is without legal effect. An agreement that contemplates the performance of an act prohibited by law is usually incapable of enforcement; hence it is void. Likewise, it cannot be made binding by later approval or ratification.

11-2d Executed and Executory Contracts

Contracts may be classified as *executed contracts* and *executory contracts* according to the extent to which they have been performed.

Executed Contracts

executed contract–
agreement that has been
completely performed.

An **executed contract** is one that has been completely performed. In other words, an executed contract is one under which nothing remains to be done by either party.[11] A contract may be executed immediately, as in the case of a cash sale, or it may be executed or performed in the future.

Executory Contracts

executory contract–
agreement by which
something remains to be
done by one or both
parties.

In an **executory contract,** something remains to be done by one or both parties.[12] **For Example,** on July 10, Mark agreed to sell to Chris his Pearl drum set for $600, the terms being $200 upon delivery on July 14, with $200 to be paid on July 21, and the final $200 being due July 28. Prior to the July 14 delivery of the drums to Chris, the contract was entirely executory. After the delivery by Mark, the contract was executed as to Mark and executory as to Chris until the final payment was received on July 28.

11-2e Bilateral and Unilateral Contracts

In making an offer, the offeror is in effect extending a promise to do something, such as pay a sum of money, if the offeree will do what the offeror requests. Contracts are classified as *bilateral* or *unilateral*. Some bilateral contracts look ahead to the making of a later contract. Depending on their terms, these are called *option contracts* or *first-refusal contracts*.

CPA
Bilateral Contracts

bilateral contract–
agreement under which
one promise is given in
exchange for another.

If the offeror extends a promise and asks for a promise in return and if the offeree accepts the offer by making the promise, the contract is called a **bilateral contract.** One promise is given in exchange for another, and each party is bound by the obligation. **For Example,** when the house painter offers to paint the owner's house for $3,700 and the owner promises to pay $3,700 for the job, there is an exchange of promises, and the agreement gives rise to a bilateral contract.

Unilateral Contracts

unilateral contract–
contract under which
only one party makes a
promise.

In contrast with a bilateral contract, the offeror may promise to do something or to pay a certain amount of money only when the offeree does an act.[13] Examples of where **unilateral contracts** commonly appear are when a reward is offered, a contest is announced, or changes are made and disseminated in an employee manual. The offeree does not accept the offer by express agreement, but rather by performance.

---

[11] *Marsh v. Rheinecker*, 641 N.E.2d 1256 (Ill. App. 1994).
[12] *DiGennaro v. Rubbermaid, Inc.*, 214 F. Supp. 2d 1354 (S.D. Fla. 2002).
[13] See *Young v. Virginia Birth-Related Neurological Injury Compensation Program*, 620 S.E.2d 131 (Va. App. 2005).

CASE SUMMARY

Unilateral Contract: Pretty Good Bonus!

FACTS: Aon Risk Services, Inc. (ARS Arkansas), and Combined Insurance Companies are subsidiaries of Aon Corporation. The parent corporation issued an "Interdependency Memo" dated February 2000, which encouraged ARS brokerage offices to place insurance business with Aon-affiliated companies. It also set up a bonus pool for revenues generated under the plan, with Combined agreeing to pay "30% of annualized premium on all life products over 15-year term plus 15% 1st year for all other products." John Meadors saw the memo in February 2000, and believed it would entitle him to this compensation over and above his employment contract. Meadors put Combined in touch with Dillard's Department Stores and on March 24, 2000, Dillard's and Combined executed a five-year agreement whereby Dillard's employees could purchase life, disability, and other insurance policies through workplace enrollment. When Meadors did not receive bonus-pool money generated by the transaction, he sued his employer for breach of a unilateral contract. The employer's defense was that the memo was not sufficiently definite to constitute an offer.

DECISION: Judgment for Meadors for $2,406,522.60. A unilateral contract is composed of an offer that invites acceptance in the form of actual performance. For example, in the case of a reward, the offeree accepts by performing the particular task, such as the capture of the fugitive for which the reward is offered. In this case the offer contained in the Interdependency Memo set out specific percentages of provisions that would go into the bonus pool, and required that the pool be distributed annually. It was sufficiently definite to constitute an offer. Meadors was responsible for the production of the Dillard's account, and was entitled to the bonus promised in the memo. [*Aon Risk Services Inc. v. Meadors*, 267 S.W.3d 603 (Ark. App. 2007)]

Option and First-Refusal Contracts

option contract—contract to hold an offer to make a contract open for a fixed period of time.

The parties may make a contract that gives a right to one of them to enter into a second contract at a later date. If one party has an absolute right to enter into the later contract, the initial contract is called an **option contract.** Thus, a bilateral contract may be made today, giving one of the parties the right to buy the other party's house for a specified amount. This is an option contract because the party with the privilege has the freedom of choice, or option, to buy or not buy. If the option is exercised, the other party to the contract must follow the terms of the option and enter into the second contract. If the option is never exercised, no second contract ever arises, and the offer protected by the option contract merely expires.

right of first refusal—right of a party to meet the terms of a proposed contract before it is executed, such as a real estate purchase agreement.

In contrast with an option contract, a contract may merely give a **right of first refusal.** This imposes only the duty to make the first offer to the party having the right of first refusal.

11-2f Quasi Contracts

quasi contract—court-imposed obligation to prevent unjust enrichment in the absence of a contract.

In some cases, a court will impose an obligation even though there is no contract.[14] Such an obligation is called a **quasi contract,** which is an obligation imposed by law.

Prevention of Unjust Enrichment

A quasi contract is not a true contract reflecting all of the elements of a contract set forth previously in this chapter. The court is not seeking to enforce the intentions of the parties contained in an agreement. Rather, when a person or enterprise receives a benefit from another, even in the absence of a promise to pay for the benefit, a court may impose an obligation to pay for the reasonable value of that benefit, to avoid *unjust enrichment.*

[14] *Thayer v. Dial Industrial Sales, Inc.,* 85 F. Supp. 2d 263 (S.D.N.Y. 2000).

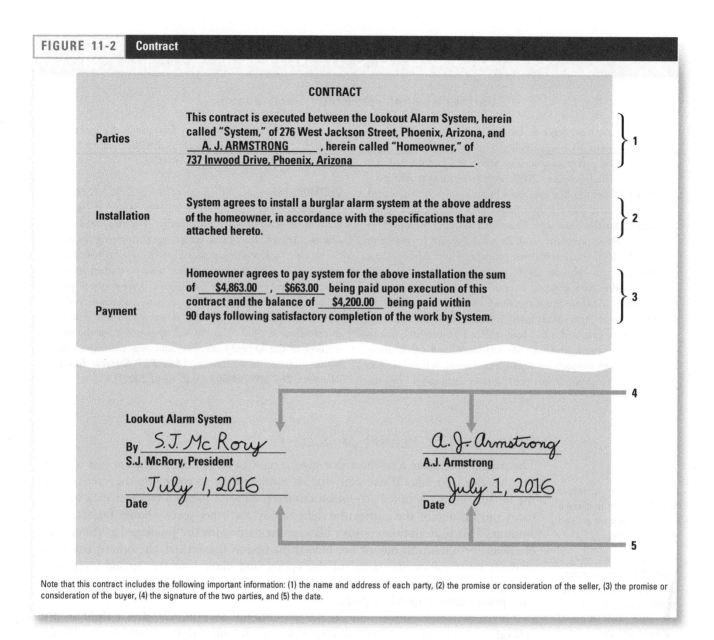

FIGURE 11-2 Contract

CONTRACT

Parties

This contract is executed between the Lookout Alarm System, herein called "System," of 276 West Jackson Street, Phoenix, Arizona, and ___A. J. ARMSTRONG___ , herein called "Homeowner," of 737 Inwood Drive, Phoenix, Arizona _____ .

} 1

Installation

System agrees to install a burglar alarm system at the above address of the homeowner, in accordance with the specifications that are attached hereto.

} 2

Payment

Homeowner agrees to pay system for the above installation the sum of ___$4,863.00___ , ___$663.00___ being paid upon execution of this contract and the balance of ___$4,200.00___ being paid within 90 days following satisfactory completion of the work by System.

} 3

Lookout Alarm System

By *S.J. Mc Rory*
S.J. McRory, President

July 1, 2016
Date

a. J. armstrong
A.J. Armstrong

July 1, 2016
Date

4

5

Note that this contract includes the following important information: (1) the name and address of each party, (2) the promise or consideration of the seller, (3) the promise or consideration of the buyer, (4) the signature of the two parties, and (5) the date.

The spirit behind the law of unjust enrichment is to apply the law "outside the box" and fill in the cracks where common civil law and statutes fail to achieve justice.[15]

A successful claim for unjust enrichment usually requires (1) a benefit conferred on the defendant, (2) the defendant's knowledge of the benefit, and (3) a finding that it would be unjust for the defendant to retain the benefit without payment. The burden of proof is on the plaintiff to prove all of the elements of the claim. **For Example,** Hiram College sued Nicholas Courtad for $6,000 plus interest for tuition and other expenses. Because no evidence of a written contract was produced, the court considered it an unjust enrichment claim by the college. Courtad had attended classes for a few weeks and had not paid his tuition due to a problem with his financial aid package. Because he did not receive any credit hours toward a degree, which is the ultimate benefit

---

[15] *Hernandez v. Lopez,* 103 Cal. Rptr. 3d 376, 381 (Cal. App. 2009).

of attending college, the court found that he did not receive a benefit and that a finding of unjust enrichment was not appropriate.[16]

Sometimes a contract may be unenforceable because of a failure to set forth the contract in writing in compliance with the statute of frauds or a consumer protection act.[17] In other circumstances, no enforceable contract exists because of a lack of definite and certain terms. Yet in both situations, one party may have performed services for the benefit of the other party and the court will require payment of the reasonable value of services to avoid the unjust enrichment of the party receiving the services without paying for them. These damages are sometimes referred to as *restitution damages*. Some courts refer to this situation as an action or recovery in **quantum meruit** (as much as he or she deserved).

quantum meruit—as much as deserved; an action brought for the value of the services rendered the defendant when there was no express contract as to the purchase price.

For Example, Arya Group, Inc. (Arya), sued the entertainer Cher for unjust enrichment. In June 1996, Cher negotiated an oral agreement with Arya to design and construct a house on her Malibu property for $4,217,529. The parties' oral agreement was set forth in a written contract with an August 1997 date and was delivered to Cher in October 1997. She never signed it. Between June 1996 and November 1997, Arya performed and received payment for a number of services discharged under the unsigned contract. In August 1997, Cher requested Arya to meet with a home designer named Bussell who had previously worked with Cher on a Florida project, and Arya showed Bussell the plans and designs for the Malibu property and introduced her to his subcontractors. In November 1997, Cher terminated her agreement with Arya without paying the balance then due, as asserted by Arya, of $415,169.41. Arya claims that Cher and Bussell misappropriated the plans and designs Arya had prepared. Cher and the other defendants demurred to Arya's unjust enrichment complaint, pointing out that construction contracts must be evidenced in a writing signed by both parties under state law in order to be enforceable in a court of law. The appeals court determined that Arya's noncompliance with the state law requiring a signed written contract did not absolutely foreclose Arya from seeking damages for unjust enrichment if he could prove the assertions in the complaint that Cher was a sophisticated homeowner with previous involvement in residential construction who had legal representation in negotiating the agreement with Arya, and that Cher would be unjustly enriched if she were not required to compensate Arya for the reasonable value of the work already performed.[18]

CASE SUMMARY

No Free Rides

FACTS: PIC Realty leased farmland to Southfield Farms. After Southfield harvested its crop, it cultivated the land in preparation for the planting in the following year. However, its lease expired, so it did not plant that crop. It then sued PIC for reimbursement for the reasonable value of the services and materials used in preparing the land because this was a benefit to PIC. There was evidence that it was customary for landlords to compensate tenants for such work.

DECISION: Southfield was entitled to recover the reasonable value of the benefit conferred upon PIC. This was necessary in order to prevent the unjust enrichment of PIC. [*PIC Realty Corp. v. Southfield Farms, Inc.*, **832 S.W.2d 610 (Tex. App. 1992)**]

---

[16] *Hiram College v. Courtad*, 834 N.E.2d 432 (Ohio App. 2005).

[17] See *Shafer Electric & Construction v. Mantia*, 96 A.3d 989 (Pa. 2014) where the Supreme Court of Pennsylvania determined that the state's Home Improvement Consumer Protection Act did not preclude the common law equitable remedy of *quantum meruit* when a contractor fails to fully comply with the Consumer Protection Act.

[18] *Arya Group, Inc. v. Cher*, 91 Cal. Rptr. 2d 815 (Cal. App. 2000). See also *Fischer v. Flax*, 816 A.2d 1 (2003).

A situation may arise over the mistaken conference of a benefit. **For Example,** Nantucket Island has a few approved colors for houses in its historic district. Using the approved gray color, Martin Kane and his crew began painting Sheldon Adams's house in the historic district as the result of a mistaken address. Adams observed the initiation of the work from his office across the street but did nothing to stop the painters. At the end of the day when the work was done, Adams refused to pay for the work, saying, "I signed no contract and never approved this work." The law deems it inequitable that Adams should have received the benefit of this work, having observed the benefit being conferred and knowing that the painters expected payment. Adams would be unjustly enriched if he were allowed to retain the benefit without payment for the reasonable value of the work. If Adams did not have knowledge that the work was being done and thus that payment was expected, quasi-contractual liability would not be imposed.

The mistake that benefits the defendant may be the mistake of a third party.

Preclusion by an Express Contract

Courts award relief based on quasi-contractual principles, implying by law a contract where one did not exist in fact. Thus, where an express contract exists, it precludes an unjust enrichment claim.[19]

CASE SUMMARY

When in Doubt, Write It Out

FACTS: Facing financial turbulence, Philippine Airlines (PAL) sought to renegotiate its aircraft lease contract (ALC) with World Airlines (WA). WA refused to negotiate with PAL. PAL retained John Sununu, the former Governor of New Hampshire and the former Chief of Staff to President George H. W. Bush and Sununu's partner Victor Frank to represent it. Sununu and Frank sent a contract proposal to PAL, which included a proposed "success fee" of $600,000 if they persuaded WA to accept a modification of the lease contract. PAL gave Sununu and Frank a verbal go-ahead but did not sign the proposed contract. Thereafter PAL sent a contract that was different from that proposed by Sununu and Frank, containing a success fee of 4 percent of savings if they were able to reach a settlement to reduce the remaining obligation of PAL to WA in accordance with either of two very specific settlement offers. Caught up in the actual intense settlement negotiations with WA on behalf of PAL Sununu and Frank signed the contract. Thereafter, they were successful in obtaining an amendment to the lease contract, saving PAL $12.8 million. PAL refused to pay a success fee of $520,000 because the actual settlement did not meet the contractual criteria, which was limited to just the two specific settlement offers. Sununu and Frank sued PAL for unjust enrichment and other contract theories.

DECISION: Judgment for PAL. Sununu and Frank conferred a benefit on PAL through their efforts to persuade WA to negotiate with PAL; and PAL accepted and retained the benefit for the renegotiated lease. There can be no claim, however, for unjust enrichment when an express contract exists between two parties. A court awards relief based on quasi-contractual principles, implying by law a contract, only where one did not exist in fact. The court stated:

> To grant PALs summary judgment motion is not to condone its conduct. The airline can rightly be accused of stinginess for enforcing the formalistic terms of the contract in spite of the plaintiffs' earnest efforts on its behalf ... PAL may have violated Sununu and Frank's trust, but it did not violate the law.
>
> ... Sununu and Frank seem to have done their best to serve their client, but they made a reckless bet by trusting PAL. They were accustomed to

---

[19] However, if the parties have abandoned following the written provisions of the contract, it is proper for a court to allow recovery on the basis of *quantum meruit* on an implied contract. See *Geoscience Group Inc. v. Waters Construction Co. Inc.,* 759 S.E.2d 696 (N.C. App. 2014).

Extent of Recovery

When recovery is allowed in quasi contract, the plaintiff recovers the reasonable value of the benefit conferred on the defendant,[20] or the fair and reasonable[21] value of the work performed, depending on the jurisdiction and the circumstances of the case itself. The customary method of calculating damages in construction contract cases is actual job costs plus an allowance for overhead and profits minus amount paid.[22]

THINKING THINGS THROUGH

Twelve Years of Litigation

Brown University accepted the bid of Marshall Contractors, Inc. (Marshall), to build the Pizzitola Sports Facility on its Providence, Rhode Island, campus. The parties intended to execute a formal written contract. Brown decided to pay $7,157,051 for the project, but Marshall sought additional payment for items it deemed extras and not contemplated in its bid. Because the parties were unable to agree on the scope of the project as compared to the price Brown was willing to pay, they never executed the formal written contract. Nevertheless, in the context of this disagreement over terms and price, construction began in May 1987. When the parties could not resolve their disagreements as the project neared completion in January 1989, Marshall sued Brown University, seeking to recover the costs for what it deemed "changes." Brown asserted that an implied-in-fact contract existed for all work at the $7,157,051 figure because the contractor went ahead with the project knowing the money Brown would pay. The litigation ended up in the Supreme Court of Rhode Island, and in 1997, the court concluded that no express or implied-in-fact contract had ever been reached by the parties concerning the scope of the project and what costs were to be included in the price stipulated by Brown. The case was remanded to the trial court for a new trial. After a trial on the theories of *quantum meruit* and unjust enrichment, a jury awarded Marshall $1.2 million dollars, which was some $3.1 million less than Marshall sought. Brown University appealed, and on November 21, 2001, the Supreme Court of Rhode Island affirmed the jury verdict for the contractor, determining that the proper measure of damages on unjust enrichment and *quantum meruit* theories was "the reasonable value of the work done."*

In May 1987 when the parties could not reach agreement enabling the execution of a formal written contract, Thinking Things Through at that point in time should have exposed the potential for significant economic uncertainties to both parties in actually starting the building process under such circumstances. In the spring of 1987 when all parties were unable to reach agreement, mediation or expedited arbitration by construction experts may well have resolved the controversy and yielded an amicable written contract with little or no delay to the project. Instead, the unsettled cost issues during the building process could have had an adverse impact on the "job chemistry" between the contractor and the owner, which may have adversely affected the progress and quality of the job. The 12 years of litigation that, with its economic and human resource costs, yielded just $1.2 million for the contractor was a no-win result for both sides. A primary rule for all managers in projects of this scope is to make sure the written contracts are executed before performance begins! Relying on "implied-in-fact" or quasi-contract legal theories is simply a poor management practice.

*****ADP Marshall, Inc. v. Brown University, 784 A.2d 309 (R.I. 2001).**

---

[20] *Ramsey v. Ellis,* 484 N.W.2d 331 (Wis. 1992).
[21] *ADP Marshall, Inc. v. Brown University,* 784 A.2d 309 (R.I. 2001).
[22] *Miranco Contracting, Inc. v. Pelel,* 871 N.Y.S.2d 310 (A.D. 2008).

11-3 Contracting on the Internet

Doing business online for consumers is very similar to doing business through a catalog purchase or by phone. Before placing an order, a buyer is commonly concerned about the reputation of the seller. The basic purchasing principle of *caveat emptor* still applies: buyer beware! The Internet provides valuable tools to allow a buyer to research the reputation of the seller and its products. Online evaluations of companies and their products can be found at Web sites, such as Consumer Reports (**http://www.consumerreports.org**), Consumers Digest (**http://www.consumersdigest.com**), or the Better Business Bureau (**http://www.bbb.org**). E-consumers may have access to categorized histories of comments by other e-consumers, such as Planet Feedback ratings at **http://www.planetfeedback.com.**

The intellectual property principles set forth in Chapter 9—as well as the contractual principles, the law of sales, and privacy laws you are about to study—all apply to e-commerce transactions. When you are purchasing an item online, you must carefully read all of the terms and conditions set forth on the seller's Web site when assessing whether to make a contemplated purchase. The proposed terms may require that any disputes be litigated in a distant state or be resolved through arbitration with restricted remedies, or there may be an unsatisfactory return policy, warranty limitations, or limitation of liability. Generally, the Web site terms become the contract of the parties and are legally enforceable.

The laws you have studied that prevent deceptive advertising by brick-and-mortar businesses also apply to Internet sites.[23] If an in-state site is engaging in false advertising, you may be able to exercise consumer protection rights through your state's attorney general's office, or you may find some therapeutic relief by reporting the misconduct to the Internet Scambusters site (**http://www.scambusters.com**).

From a seller's perspective, it is exceedingly helpful to have as much information as possible on your potential customers' buying habits. Federal law prohibits the collection of personal information from children without parental consent, and some states restrict the unauthorized collection of personal information. European Union countries have strict laws protecting the privacy of consumers. Sellers intending to collect personal information should obtain the consent of their customers, make certain that children are excluded, and make sure that the information is stored in a secure environment.

Advanced encryption technology has made the use of credit card payments through the Internet very safe. No computer system connected to the Internet is totally secure, however. In the worst-case scenario, credit card issuers will not charge a user for more than the first $50 of unauthorized activity.

Internet contracts involve the same types of issues that are addressed in contracts offline but with certain technology-related nuances. The parties to the e-contracts must still negotiate their obligations in clear and unambiguous language, including such terms as quantity, quality, and price as well as warranties, indemnification responsibilities, limitations on liability, and termination procedures. The federal Electronic Signatures in Global and National Commerce Act (E-Sign) and the Uniform Electronic Transactions Act (UETA) mandate parity between paper and electronic contracts. The basic legal rules that govern contracts offline are the very same rules that govern online contracts, and basic civil procedure rules apply. **For Example,** California buyer Paul Boschetto bought a 1964 Ford Galaxy that had been advertised on eBay to be "in awesome condition" from a Milton, Wisconsin, resident, J. Hansing, for $34,106. On delivery Boschetto discovered

---

[23] See *MADCAP I, LLC v. McNamee*, 712 N.W.2d 16 (Wis. App. 2005) in which the court found genuine issues of material fact as to whether a business Web site falsely represented the size and nature of its business to induce the public to purchase products and services described on its Web site in violation of the state's fraudulent representations statute.

that the car had rust, extensive dents, and would not start. His lawsuit against Hansing in U.S. District Court in California was dismissed for lack of personal jurisdiction.[24] (The formation of a contract with a nonresident defendant was not, standing alone, sufficient to create personal jurisdiction in California.)

Boxes identifying special Internet e-commerce topics are strategically placed throughout these chapters.

Make the Connection

Summary

A contract is a binding agreement between two or more parties. A contract arises when an offer is accepted with contractual intent (the intent to make a binding agreement).

Contracts may be classified in a number of ways according to form, the way in which they were created, validity, and obligations. With respect to form, a contract may be either informal or formal, such as those under seal or those appearing on the records of courts. Contracts may be classified by the way they were created as those that are expressed by words—written or oral—and those that are implied or deduced from conduct. The question of validity requires distinguishing between contracts that are valid, those that are voidable, and those that are not contracts at all but are merely void agreements. Contracts can be distinguished on the basis of the obligations created as executed contracts, in which everything has been performed,

and executory contracts, in which something remains to be done. The bilateral contract is formed by exchanging a promise for a promise, so each party has the obligation of thereafter rendering the promised performance. In the unilateral contract, which is the doing of an act in exchange for a promise, no further performance is required of the offeree who performed the act.

In certain situations, the law regards it as unjust for a person to receive a benefit and not pay for it. In such a case, the law of quasi contracts allows the performing person to recover the reasonable value of the benefit conferred on the benefited person even though no contract between them requires any payment. Unjust enrichment, which a quasi contract is designed to prevent, sometimes arises when there was never any contract between the persons involved or when there was a contract, but for some reason it was avoided or held to be merely a void agreement.

Learning Outcomes

After studying this chapter, you should be able to clearly explain:

11-1 Nature of Contracts

LO.1 Explain the meaning and importance of privity of a contract

See the example of the subcontractor, RPR & Associates, who worked on a project but could not sue the owner for payment, pages 206–207.

See the example involving rapper Eminem, FBT, and Aftermath Records, where FBT was not a party to the contract and thus not bound by it, page 207.

LO.2 Describe the way in which a contract arises

See the discussion on offer and acceptance, page 207.

11-2 Classes of Contracts

LO.3 Distinguish between bilateral and unilateral contracts

See the example of the Nantucket painters, pages 213–214.

See the *AON Risk Services* case where an insurance agent won his case based on a unilateral contract theory, page 211.

---

[24] *Boschetto v. Hansing*, 539 F.3d 1011 (9th Cir. 2008).

LO.4 Explain the reasoning behind quasi-contract recovery

See the example whereby Cher had to pay a home designer for certain work even though there was no contract, page 213.

11-3 Contracting on the Internet

LO.5 Explain how Internet contracts involve the same types of issues as offline contracts

See the eBay example, page 217.

Key Terms

bilateral contract
contract
contract under seal
executed contract
executory contract
express contract
formal contract
implied contract
informal contract

obligee
obligor
offeree
offeror
option contract
privity
privity of contract
promisee
promisor

quantum meruit
quasi contract
recognizance
right of first refusal
unilateral contracts
valid contract
void agreement
voidable contract

Questions and Case Problems

1. What is a contract?

2. Fourteen applicants for a city of Providence, Rhode Island, police academy training class each received from the city a letter stating that it was a "conditional offer of employment" subject to successful completion of medical and psychological exams. The 14 applicants passed the medical and psychological exams. However, these applicants were replaced by others after the city changed the selection criteria. Can you identify an offer and acceptance in this case? Can you make out a bilateral or unilateral contract? [*Ardito et al. v. City of Providence*, 213 F. Supp. 2d 358 (D.R.I.)]

3. Compare an implied contract with a quasi contract.

4. The Jordan Keys law firm represented the Greater Southeast Community Hospital of Washington, D.C., in a medical malpractice suit against the hospital. The hospital was self-insured for the first $1,000,000 of liability and the St. Paul Insurance Co. provided excess coverage up to $4,000,000. The law firm was owed $67,000 for its work on the malpractice suit when the hospital went into bankruptcy. The bankruptcy court ordered the law firm to release its files on the case to St. Paul to defend under the excess coverage insurance, and the Jordan Keys firm sued St. Paul for its legal fees of $67,000 expended prior to the bankruptcy under an "implied-in-fact contract" because the insurance company would have the benefit of all of its work. Decide. [*Jordan Keys v. St. Paul Fire*, 870 A.2d 58 (D.C.)]

5. Beck was the general manager of Chilkoot Lumber Co. Haines sold fuel to the company. To persuade Haines to sell on credit, Beck signed a paper by which he promised to pay any debt the lumber company owed Haines. He signed this paper with his name followed by "general manager." Haines later sued Beck on this promise, and Beck raised the defense that the addition of "general manager" showed that Beck, who was signing on behalf of Chilkoot, was not personally liable and did not intend to be bound by the paper. Was Beck liable on the paper? [*Beck v. Haines Terminal and Highway Co.*, 843 P.2d 1229 (Alaska)]

6. *A* made a contract to construct a house for *B*. Subsequently, *B* sued *A* for breach of contract. *A* raised the defense that the contract was not binding because it was not sealed. Is this a valid defense? [*Cooper v. G. E. Construction Co.*, 158 S.E.2d 305 (Ga. App.)]

7. Edward Johnson III, the CEO and principal owner of the world's largest mutual fund company, Fidelity Investments, Inc., was a longtime tennis buddy of Richard Larson. In 1995, Johnson asked Larson, who had construction experience, to supervise the construction of a house on Long Pond, Mount Desert Island, Maine. Although they had no written contract, Larson agreed to take on the project for $6,700 per month plus lodging. At the end of the project in 1997, Johnson made a $175,000 cash payment to Larson, and he made arrangements for

Larson to live rent-free on another Johnson property in the area called Pray's Meadow in exchange for looking after Johnson's extensive property interests in Maine. In the late summer of 1999, Johnson initiated a new project on the Long Pond property. Johnson had discussions with Larson about doing this project, but Larson asked to be paid his former rate, and Johnson balked because he had already hired a project manager. According to Johnson, at a later date he again asked Larson to take on the "shop project" as a favor and in consideration of continued rent-free use of the Pray's Meadow home. Johnson stated that Larson agreed to do the job "pro bono" in exchange for the use of the house, and Johnson acknowledged that he told Larson he would "take care" of Larson at the end of the project, which could mean as much or as little as Johnson determined. Larson stated that Johnson told him that he would "take care of" Larson if he would do the project and told him to "trust the Great Oracle" (meaning Johnson, the highly successful businessperson). Larson sought payment in March 2000 and asked Johnson for "something on account" in April. Johnson offered Larson a loan. In August during a tennis match, Larson again asked Johnson to pay him. Johnson became incensed, and through an employee, he ended Larson's participation in the project and asked him to vacate Pray's Meadow. Larson complied and filed suit for payment for work performed at the rate of $6,700 per month. Did Larson have an express contract with Johnson? What legal theory or theories could Larson utilize in his lawsuit? How would you decide this case if you believed Larson's version of the facts? How would you decide the case if you believed Johnson's version of the facts? [*Larson v. Johnson*, 196 F. Supp. 2d 38 (D. Me. 2002)]

8. While Clara Novak was sick, her daughter Janie helped her in many ways. Clara died, and Janie then claimed that she was entitled to be paid for the services she had rendered her mother. This claim was opposed by three brothers and sisters who also rendered services to the mother. They claimed that Janie was barred because of the presumption that services rendered between family members are gratuitous. Janie claimed that this presumption was not applicable because she had not lived with her mother but had her own house. Was Janie correct? [In re *Estate of Novak*, 398 N.W.2d 653 (Minn. App.)]

9. Dozier and his wife, daughter, and grandson lived in the house Dozier owned. At the request of the daughter and grandson, Paschall made some improvements to the house. Dozier did not authorize these, but he knew that the improvements were being made and did not object to them. Paschall sued Dozier for the reasonable value of the improvements, but Dozier argued that he had not made any contract for such improvements. Was he obligated to pay for such improvements?

10. When Harriet went away for the summer, Landry, a house painter, painted her house. He had a contract to paint a neighbor's house but painted Harriet's house by mistake. When Harriet returned from vacation, Landry billed her for $3,100, which was a fair price for the work. She refused to pay. Landry claimed that she had a quasi-contractual liability for that amount. Was he correct?

11. Margrethe and Charles Pyeatte, a married couple, agreed that she would work so that he could go to law school and that when he finished, she would go back to school for her master's degree. After Charles was admitted to the bar and before Margrethe went back to school, the two were divorced. She sued Charles, claiming that she was entitled to quasi-contractual recovery of the money that she had paid for Charles's support and law school tuition. He denied liability. Was she entitled to recover for the money she spent for Charles's maintenance and law school tuition? [*Pyeatte v. Pyeatte*, 661 P.2d 196 (Ariz. App.)]

12. Carriage Way was a real estate development of approximately 80 houses and 132 apartments. The property owners were members of the Carriage Way Property Owners Association. Each year, the association would take care of certain open neighboring areas, including a nearby lake, that were used by the property owners. The board of directors of the association would make an assessment or charge against the property owners to cover the cost of this work. The property owners paid these assessments for a number of years and then refused to pay any more. In spite of this refusal, the association continued to take care of the areas in question. The association then sued the property owners and claimed that they were liable for the benefit that had been conferred on them. Were the owners liable? [*Board of Directors of Carriage Way Property Owners Ass n v. Western National Bank*, 487 N.E.2d 974 (Ill. App.)]

13. When improvements or buildings are added to real estate, the real estate tax assessment is usually increased to reflect the increased value of the property. Frank Partipilo and Elmer Hallman owned neighboring tracts of land. Hallman made improvements to his land, constructing a new building and driveway on the tract. The tax assessor made a mistake about the location of the boundary line between Partipilo's and Hallman's land and thought the improvements were made on Partipilo's property. Instead of increasing the taxes on Hallman's land, the assessor wrongly increased the taxes on Partipilo's land. Partipilo paid the increased taxes for three years. When he learned why his taxes had been increased, he sued Hallman for the amount of the increase that Partipilo had been paying. Hallman raised the defense that he had not done anything wrong and that the mistake had been the fault of the tax assessor. Decide. [*Partipilo v. Hallman*, 510 N.E.2d 8 (Ill.App.)]

14. When a college student complained about a particular course, the vice president of the college asked the teacher to prepare a detailed report about the course. The teacher did and then demanded additional compensation for the time spent in preparing the report. He claimed that the college was liable to provide compensation on an implied contract. Was he correct? [*Zadrozny v. City Colleges of Chicago*, 581 N.E.2d 44 (Ill. App.)]

15. Smith made a contract to sell automatic rifles to a foreign country. Because the sale of such weapons to that country was illegal under an act of Congress, the U.S. government prosecuted Smith for making the contract. He raised the defense that because the contract was illegal, it was void and there is no binding obligation when a contract is void; therefore, no contract for which he could be prosecuted existed. Was he correct?

CPA Question

1. Kay, an art collector, promised Hammer, an art student, that if Hammer could obtain certain rare artifacts within two weeks, Kay would pay for Hammer's postgraduate education. At considerable effort and expense, Hammer obtained the specified artifacts within the two-week period. When Hammer requested payment, Kay refused. Kay claimed that there was no consideration for the promise. Hammer would prevail against Kay based on:

   a. Unilateral contract.

   b. Unjust enrichment.

   c. Public policy.

   d. Quasi contract.

Formation of Contracts: Offer and Acceptance

Learning Outcomes ‹‹‹

After studying this chapter, you should be able to

LO.1 Decide whether an offer contains definite and certain terms

LO.2 Explain the exceptions the law makes to the requirement of definiteness

LO.3 Explain all the ways an offer can be terminated

LO.4 Explain what constitutes the acceptance of an offer

LO.5 Explain the implications of failing to read a clickwrap agreement

A *contract* consists of enforceable obligations that have been voluntarily assumed. Thus, one of the essential elements of a contract is an agreement. This chapter explains how the basic agreement arises, when there is a contract, and how there can be merely unsuccessful negotiations without a resulting contract.

12-1 Requirements of an Offer

offer–expression of an offeror's willingness to enter into a contractual agreement.

An **offer** expresses the willingness of the offeror to enter into a contractual agreement regarding a particular subject. It is a promise that is conditional upon an act, a forbearance (a refraining from doing something one has a legal right to do), or a return promise.

CPA

12-1a Contractual Intention

To make an offer, the offeror must appear to intend to create a binding obligation. Whether this intent exists is determined by objective standards.[1] This intent may be shown by conduct. **For Example,** when one party signs a written contract and sends it to the other party, such action is an offer to enter into a contract on the terms of the writing.

There is no contract when a social invitation is made or when an offer is made in obvious jest or excitement. A reasonable person would not regard such an offer as indicating a willingness to enter into a binding agreement. The test for a valid, binding offer is whether it induces a reasonable belief in the offeree that he or she can, by accepting it, bind the offeror, as developed in the *Wigod* case.

CASE SUMMARY

A Valid Offer!

FACTS: The U.S. Department of the Treasury implemented the federal Home Affordable Mortgage Program (HAMP) to help homeowners avoid foreclosure amidst the sharp decline in the nation's housing market in 2008. In 2009, Wells Fargo Bank issued Lori Wigod a four-month "trial" loan modification under a Trial Period Plan (TPP). After the trial period, if the borrower complied with all of the terms of the TPP agreement, including making all required payments and providing all required documentation, and if the borrower's representations remained true and correct, the servicer, Well Fargo, had to offer a permanent mortgage modification. Wigod alleged that she complied with these requirements and that Wells Fargo refused to grant a permanent modification. Wells Fargo contended that the TPP contained no valid offer.

DECISION: Judgment for Wigod. A person can prevent his submission from being treated as an offer by using suitable language conditioning the formation of a contract on some further step, such as approval by corporate headquarters. It is when the promisor conditions a promise on *his own* future action or approval that there is no binding offer. Here, the TTP spelled out two conditions precedent to Wells Fargo's obligation to offer a permanent modification. Wigod had to comply with the requirements of the TPP, and her financial representations had to be true and accurate. These conditions had to be satisfied by the promisee (Wigod). Here a reasonable person in Wigod's position would read the TPP as a default offer that she could accept so long as she satisfied the two conditions. [*Wigod v. Wells Fargo Bank*, **673 F.3d 547 (7th Cir. 2012)**]

Invitation to Negotiate

The first statement made by one of two persons is not necessarily an offer. In many instances, there may be a preliminary discussion or an invitation by one party to the

[1] *Glass Service Co. v. State Farm Mutual Automobile Ins. Co.*, 530 N.W.2d 867 (Minn. App. 1995).

other to negotiate or to make an offer. Thus, an inquiry by a school as to whether a teacher wished to continue the following year was merely a survey or invitation to negotiate and was not an offer that could be accepted. Therefore, the teacher's affirmative response did not create a contract.

Ordinarily, a seller sending out circulars or catalogs listing prices is not regarded as making an offer to sell at those prices. The seller is merely indicating a willingness to consider an offer made by a buyer on those terms. The reason for this rule is, in part, the practical consideration that because a seller does not have an unlimited supply of any commodity, the seller cannot possibly intend to make a contract with everyone who sees the circular. The same principle is applied to merchandise that is displayed with price tags in stores or store windows and to most advertisements. An advertisement in a newspaper is ordinarily considered an invitation to negotiate and is not an offer that can be accepted by a reader of the paper.[2] However, some court decisions have construed advertisements as offers that called for an act on the part of the customer, thereby forming a unilateral contract, such as the advertisement of a reward for the return of lost property.

Quotations of prices, even when sent on request, are likewise not offers unless the parties have had previous dealings or unless a trade custom exists that would give the recipient of the quotation reason to believe that an offer was being made. Whether a price quotation is to be treated as an offer or merely an invitation to negotiate is a question of the intent of the party giving the quotation.[3]

Agreement to Make a Contract at a Future Date

No contract arises when the parties merely agree that at a future date they will consider making a contract or will make a contract on terms to be agreed on at that time. In such a case, neither party is under any obligation until the future contract is made. Unless an agreement is reached on all material terms and conditions and nothing is left to future negotiations, a contract to enter a contract in the future is of no effect. **For Example,** Hewitt Associates provided employee benefits administrative services to Rollins, Inc., under a contract negotiated in 2001 to run through 2006. Prior to its expiration, the parties negotiated—seeking to agree to a multiyear extension of the 2001 agreement. They agreed to all of the material terms of the contract, except that Rollins balked at a $1.8 million penalty clause. Rollins's employees told Hewitt that the extension "was going to be signed." However, Rollins did not sign and the 2001 agreement expired. Hewitt's contention that the agreement was enforceable at the moment Rollins told Hewitt it was going to sign the new agreement was rejected by the court, stating that an agreement to reach an agreement is a contradiction in terms and imposes no obligation on the parties.[4]

Contracts to Negotiate

Regarding modern transactions involving significant up-front investments in deal structuring and due diligence, compelling reasons exist for parties to exchange binding promises protective of the deal-making process and why the courts may deem it socially beneficial to enforce them. Without any legal protection a counter-party may attempt to hijack the deal. Parties may wish to build in safeguards that operate early in the bargaining process to allow investing resources in a deal, but without inextricably locking themselves into a transaction that is still in a partially formulated state. *Contracts to negotiate* can satisfy this need.[5] **For Example,** David Butler, an inventor of safety technology

---

[2] *Zanakis-Pico v. Cutter, Dodge, Inc.*, 47 P.2d 1222 (Haw. 2002).

[3] Statutes prohibiting false or misleading advertising may require adherence to advertised prices.

[4] *Hewitt Associates, LLC v. Rollins, Inc.*, 669 S.E.2d 551 (Ga. App. 2008).

[5] New York, Illinois, Pennsylvania, California, and Delaware have recognized this doctrine. Mississippi and Washington have repudiated it.

for cutting tools was allowed to pursue his claim of breach of contract to negotiate against Shiraz Balolia.[6]

12-1b Definiteness

An offer, and the resulting contract, must be definite and certain so that it is capable of being enforced.[7]

CASE SUMMARY

Definite and Certain Terms

FACTS: ServiceMaster, as the general contractor hired to restore the Cleveland Brown Stadium in time for the Browns' first pre-season football game, hired subcontractor Novak to perform restoration and construction work. Novak sued for $37,158.82 for work performed on the August 2, 2007, severe rainstorm project, referred to as Loss 2. ServiceMaster contended that Novak was bound by a written but unsigned subcontractor agreement, and that Novak's alleged oral contract was lacking any definite terms to be enforceable. From a judgment for Novak, ServiceMaster appealed.

DECISION: Judgment for Novak. The record contained sufficient evidence of definite terms to enforce the oral contract. Novak V.P. Pinchot credibly testified that Novak's "time and materials" billing on the final invoice contained the hours worked at the published union rate plus the cost of materials, plus 10 percent, which method of pricing is widely understood in the construction industry. Novak is entitled to $37,158.82 plus an 18% penalty for violation of the state Prompt Payment Statute. [*Frank Novak & Sons, Inc. v. A-Team, LLC, dba ServiceMaster*, 6 N.E.3d 1242 (Ohio App. 2014)]

If an offer is indefinite or vague or if an essential provision is lacking,[8] no contract arises from an attempt to accept it. Courts are not in the business of writing contracts and will not supply terms unless the parties' obligations and intents are clearly implied. Thus, an offer to conduct a business for as long as it is profitable is too vague to be a valid offer. The acceptance of such an offer does not result in a contract that can be enforced. Statements by a bank that it was "with" the debtors and would "support" them in their proposed business venture were too vague to be regarded as a promise by the bank to make necessary loans to the debtors.

CASE SUMMARY

What Is the Meaning of an Agreement for a "Damn Good Job"?

FACTS: Larry Browneller made an oral contract with Hubert Plankenhorn to restore a 1963 Chevrolet Impala convertible. The car was not in good condition. Hubert advised the owner that his work would not yield a car of "show" quality because of the condition of the body, and he accordingly

believed that the owner merely wanted a presentable car. Larry, on the other hand, having told Hubert that he wanted a "damn good job," thought this statement would yield a car that would be competitive at the small amateur car shows he attended. When the finished car had what Larry asserted

---

[6] *Butler v. Balolia*, 736 F.3d 609 (1st Cir. 2013).
[7] *Norton v. Correctional Medicare, Inc.*, 2010 WL 4103016 (N.D.N.Y. Oct. 18, 2010).
[8] *Peace v. Doming Holdings Inc.*, 554 S.E.2d 314 (Ga. App. 2001).

What Is the Meaning of an Agreement for a "Damn Good Job"? continued

were "waves" in the paint as a result of an uneven surface on the body, Larry brought suit against Hubert for breach of the oral contract.

DECISION: There was clearly a misunderstanding between the parties over the quality of work that could and would

be obtained. *Quality* was a material term of the oral contract between the parties, on which there was no shared understanding. Accordingly, a court will not find an individual in breach of a term of the contract where the term did not exist. [**In re *Plankenhorn*, 228 B.R. 638 (N.D. Ohio 1998)**]

The fact that minor, ministerial, and nonessential terms are left for future determination does not make an agreement too vague to be a contract.[9] **For Example,** John McCarthy executed an offer to purchase (OTP) real estate from Ana Tobin on a printed form generated by the local Real Estate Board. The OTP stated that "McCarthy hereby offers to buy" and Tobin's signature indicates that "this offer is hereby accepted". The OTP also detailed the amount to be paid and when and described the property title requirements and the time and place for closing. Above the signature line it stated: "NOTICE: This is a legal document that creates binding obligations. If not understood, consult an attorney". The OTP also required the parties to execute a standard form Purchase and Sale Agreement (PSA). Subsequently Tobin received a much higher offer for the property, which she accepted, asserting that she was free to do so because she had not signed the PSA. The court held that the OTP was a firm offer that bound Tobin to sell to McCarthy.[10]

The law does not favor the destruction of contracts because that would go against the social force of carrying out the intent of the parties.[11] Consequently, when it is claimed that a contract is too indefinite to be enforced, a court will do its best to find the intent of the parties and thereby reach the conclusion that the contract is not too indefinite. **For Example,** boxing promoter Don King had both a Promotional Agreement and a Bout Agreement with boxer Miguel Angel Gonzalez. The Bout Agreement for a boxing match with Julio Cesar Chavez gave King the option to promote the next four of Gonzalez's matches. The contract made clear that if Gonzalez won the Chavez match, he would receive at least $75,000 for the next fight unless the parties agreed otherwise, and if he lost, he would receive at least $25,000 for the subsequent fight unless otherwise agreed. The agreement did not explicitly state the purse for the subsequent match in the event of a draw. The Chavez match ended in a draw, and Gonzalez contended that this omission rendered the contract so indefinite that it was unenforceable. The court disagreed, stating that striking down a contract as indefinite and in essence meaningless is at best a last resort. The court held that although the contract was poorly drafted, the Promotional Agreement contained explicit price terms for which a minimum purse for fights following a draw may be inferred.[12] A court may not, however, rewrite the agreement of the parties in order to make it definite.

---

[9] *Hsu v. Vet-A-Mix, Inc.,* 479 N.W.2d 336 (Iowa App. 1991). But see *Ocean Atlantic Development Corp. v. Aurora Christian Schools, Inc.,* 322 F.3d 983 (7th Cir. 2003), where letter offers to purchase (OTP) real estate were signed by both parties, but the offers conditioned the purchase and sale of each property upon the subsequent execution of a purchase and sale agreement. The court held that the parties thus left themselves room to walk away from the deal under Illinois law, and the OTPs were not enforced.

[10] *McCarthy v. Tobin,* 706 N.E.2d 629 (Mass. 1999). But see [FN 9].

[11] *Mears v. Nationwide Mut., Inc. Co.,* 91 F.3d 1118 (8th Cir. 1996).

[12] *Gonzalez v. Don King Productions, Inc.,* 17 F. Supp. 2d 313 (S.D.N.Y. 1998); see also *Echols v. Pelullo,* 377 F.3d 272 (3rd Cir. 2004).

THINKING THINGS THROUGH

The Rules of Negotiations

Business agreements are often reached after much discussion, study, and posturing by both sides. Many statements may be made by both sides about the price or value placed on the subject of the transaction. Withholding information or presenting selective, self-serving information may be perceived by a party to the negotiations as protective self-interest. Does the law of contracts apply a duty of good faith and fair dealing in the negotiation of contracts? Does the Uniform Commercial Code provide for a general duty of good faith in the negotiation of contracts? Are lawyers under an ethical obligation to inform opposing counsel of relevant facts? The answer to all of these questions is no.

The Restatement (Second) of Contracts applies the duty of good faith and fair dealing to the performance and enforcement of contracts, not their negotiation;* so also does the UCC.** The American Bar Association's Model Rules of Professional Conduct, Rule 4.1 Comment 1, requires a lawyer to be "truthful" when dealing with others on a client's behalf, but it also states that generally a lawyer has "no affirmative duty to inform an opposing party of relevant facts."*** Comment 2 to Rule 4.1 contains an example of a "nonmaterial" statement of a lawyer as "estimates of price or value placed on the subject of a transaction."

The legal rules of negotiations state that—in the absence of fraud, special relationships, or statutory or contractual duties—negotiators are not obligated to divulge pertinent information to the other party to the negotiations. The parties to negotiations themselves must demand and analyze pertinent information and ultimately assess the fairness of the proposed transaction. Should a party conclude that the elements of a final proposal or offer are excessive or dishonest, that party's legal option is to walk away from the deal. Generally, the party has no basis to bring a lawsuit for lack of good faith and fair dealing in negotiations.

However, Thinking Things Through, the ethical standards for negotiations set forth in Chapter 3 indicate that establishing a reputation for trustworthiness, candor, and reliability often leads to commercial success for a company's continuing negotiations with its customers, suppliers, distributors, lenders, unions, and employees.****

*Restatement (Second) of Contracts §105, comment (c).
**Uniform Commercial Code §1-203.
***American Bar Association Model Rule of Professional Conduct 4.1(a) Comment 1.
****For a contrary example, consider the following story. The Atlanta Braves baseball team's general manager Frank Wren negotiated with free agent baseball player Rafael Furcal's agent Paul Kinzer. When all terms had been negotiated, Kinzer asked for a written terms-of-agreement sheet signed by the Braves, which to Wren meant an agreement had been reached. Kinzer took the sheet to the L.A. Dodgers, who then reached an agreement to sign the shortstop. Braves President John Schuerholz said, "The Atlanta Braves will no longer do business with that company—ever. I told Arn Tellem that we can't trust them to be honest and forthright." "Braves GM Blasts Furcal's Agents," Associated Press, *The Boston Globe*, December 20, 2008, C-7.

Definite by Incorporation

An offer and the resulting contract that by themselves may appear "too indefinite" may be made definite by reference to another writing. **For Example,** a lease agreement that was too vague by itself was made definite because the parties agreed that the lease should follow the standard form with which both were familiar. An agreement may also be made definite by reference to the prior dealings of the parties and to trade practices.

Implied Terms

Although an offer must be definite and certain, not all of its terms need to be expressed. Some omitted terms may be implied by law. **For Example,** an offer "to pay $400" for a certain Movado timepiece does not state the terms of payment. A court, however, would not condemn this provision as too vague but would hold that it required that cash be paid and that the payment be made on delivery of the watch. Likewise, terms may be implied from conduct. As an illustration, when borrowed money was given to the borrower by a check on which the word *loan* was written, the act of the borrower in endorsing the check constituted an agreement to repay the amount of the check.

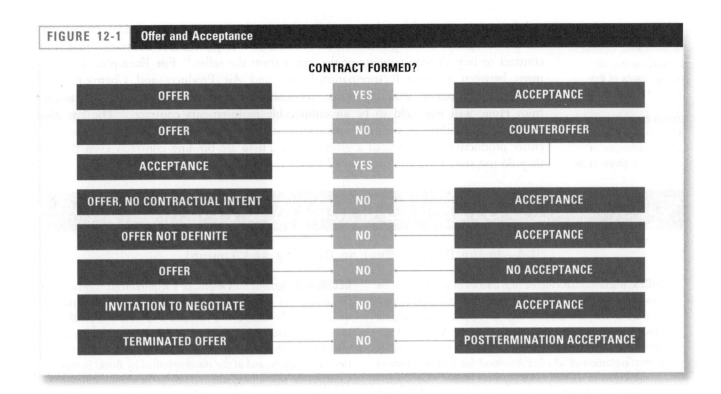

FIGURE 12-1 **Offer and Acceptance**

CONTRACT FORMED?

OFFER	YES	ACCEPTANCE
OFFER	NO	COUNTEROFFER
ACCEPTANCE	YES	
OFFER, NO CONTRACTUAL INTENT	NO	ACCEPTANCE
OFFER NOT DEFINITE	NO	ACCEPTANCE
OFFER	NO	NO ACCEPTANCE
INVITATION TO NEGOTIATE	NO	ACCEPTANCE
TERMINATED OFFER	NO	POSTTERMINATION ACCEPTANCE

"Best Efforts" Clauses

While decades ago it was generally accepted that a duty defined only in terms of "best efforts" was too indefinite to be enforced, such a view is no longer widely held. **For Example,** Thomas Hinc, an inventor, executed a contract with Lime-O-Sol Company (LOS) for LOS to produce and distribute Hinc's secret ingredient Stain Remover. Under the contract, Hinc was to receive $10 per gallon sold. The contract contained a clause obligating both parties to use their "best efforts" to market the product "in a manner that seems appropriate." Ultimately, LOS never produced, marketed, or sold Stain Remover for the duration of the contract. The court rejected the defense that the "best efforts" provision was vague and unenforceable stating "[b]est efforts, as commonly understood, means, at the very least *some* effort. It certainly does not mean *zero* effort—the construction LOS urges here to escape any obligation under its contract."[13]

Divisible Contracts

divisible contract— agreement consisting of two or more parts, each calling for corresponding performances of each part by the parties.

When the agreement consists of two or more parts and calls for corresponding performances of each part by the parties, the agreement is a **divisible contract.** Thus, in a promise to buy several separate articles at different prices at the same time, the agreement may be regarded as separate or divisible promises for the articles.

Exceptions to Definiteness

The law has come to recognize certain situations in which the practical necessity of doing business makes it desirable to have a contract, yet the situation is such that it is impossible to adopt definite terms in advance. In these cases, the indefinite term is often tied to some independent factor that will be definitely ascertainable at some time in the future. The

---

[13] *Hinc v. Lime-O-Sol Company*, 382 F.3d 716 (7th Cir. 2004). See also *Olsenhaus Pure Vegan, LLC v. Electric Wonderland, Inc.*, 983 N.Y.S.2d 506 (A.D. 2014).

requirements contract–contract to buy all requirements of the buyer from the seller.

output contract–contract of a producer to sell its entire production or output to a given buyer.

indefinite term might be tied to market price, production, or sales requirements. Thus, the law recognizes binding contracts in the case of a **requirements contract**—that is, a contract to buy all requirements of the buyer from the seller.[14] **For Example,** an agreement between Honeywell International Inc. and Air Products and Chemicals Inc. whereby Air Products would purchase its total requirements of wet process chemicals from Honeywell was held to be an enforceable requirements contract.[15] The law also recognizes as binding an **output contract**—that is, the contract of a producer to sell the entire production or output to a given buyer. These are binding contracts even though they do not state the exact quantity of goods that are to be bought or sold.

CASE SUMMARY

GM—In the Driver's Seat on Quantity and Timing!

FACTS: Automodular entered into a series of purchase orders that obligated Delphi to purchase and Automodular to provide all of Delphi's requirements deliverable to the original equipment manufacturer (OEM), General Motors. Automodular receives directions from the OEM's final assembly plants, regardless of whether Automodular is under contract to the OEM or Delphi. The purchase orders ("Contracts") incorporated Delphi's terms that the Buyer, GM, could require Automodular to implement changes to the specifications or design of the goods or to the scope of any services covered by the Contracts. GM informed Automodular that it needed fewer components and directed Automodular to, among other requirements, reduce shifts, change the assembly line speed, and change the length of workers' shifts. As a result, Automodular requested a price increase per unit assembled from Delphi because Automodular believed that such an increase was warranted pursuant to the Contract's change-in-scope provision. Delphi, however, refused to negotiate any price increase and the matter was litigated.

DECISION: Judgment for Delphi. In a requirements contract, the parties do not fix a quantity term, but instead, the quantity will be the buyer's needs of a specific commodity over the contract's life. Section 2.5 of the Contract states in relevant part that "[d]eliveries will be made in the quantities, on the dates, and at the times specified by Buyer in this Contract or any subsequent releases or instructions Buyer issues under this Contract," and that "[i]f the requirements of Buyer's customers or market, economic or other conditions require changes in delivery schedules, Buyer may change the rate of scheduled shipments or direct temporary suspension of scheduled shipments without entitling [Automodular] to a price adjustment or other compensation." This provision demonstrates the intent of the parties to allow the buyer to effectively control the timing and quantity of deliveries without entitling Automodular to an adjustment in price. [**In re Delphi Corp., 2009 WL 803598 (S.D.N.Y. 2009)**]

CPA 12-1c **Communication of Offer to Offeree**

An offer must be communicated to the offeree. Otherwise, the offeree cannot accept even though knowledge of the offer has been indirectly acquired. Internal management communications of an enterprise that are not intended for outsiders or employees do not constitute offers and cannot be accepted by them. Sometimes, particularly in the case of unilateral contracts, the offeree performs the act called for by the offeror without knowing of the offer's existence. Such performance does not constitute an acceptance. Thus, without knowing that a reward is offered for information leading to the arrest of a particular criminal, a person may provide information that leads to the arrest of the criminal. In most states, if that person subsequently learns of the reward, the reward cannot be recovered.[16]

---

[14] *Simcala v. American Coal Trade, Inc.,* 821 So. 2d 197 (Ala. 2001).

[15] *Honeywell International Inc. v. Air Products and Chemicals, Inc.,* 872 A.2d 944 (Sup. Ct. Del. 2005).

[16] With respect to the offeror, it should not make any difference, as a practical matter, whether the services were rendered with or without knowledge of the existence of the offer. Only a small number of states have adopted this view, however.

Not only must the offer be communicated but also it must be communicated by the offeror or at the offeror's direction.

CPA 12-2 Termination of Offer

An offeree cannot accept a terminated offer. Offers may be terminated by revocation, counteroffer, rejection, lapse of time, death or disability of a party, or subsequent illegality.

CPA 12-2a Revocation of Offer by Offeror

Ordinarily, an offeror can revoke the offer before it is accepted. If this is done, the offeree cannot create a contract by accepting the revoked offer. **For Example,** Bank of America (BOA) contended that it had reached a valid settlement agreement on December 17, 2010, with Jonathan Davidoff concerning his lawsuit against BOA seeking damages for slander of credit and breach of contract. At 3:08 P.M. on December 17, 2010, Davidoff revoked his offer to settle the matter. A few minutes later BOA counsel sent by e-mail the settlement agreements signed by the defendants and asked if Mr. Davidoff would "rescind his rejection." Davidoff clearly revoked the settlement offer prior to BOA's delivery of acceptance of the offer and no contract was formed.[17]

An ordinary offer may be revoked at any time before it is accepted even though the offeror has expressly promised that the offer will be good for a stated period and that period has not yet expired.

The fact that the offeror expressly promised to keep the offer open has no effect when no consideration was given for that promise.

What Constitutes a Revocation?

No particular form or words are required to constitute a revocation. Any words indicating the offeror's termination of the offer are sufficient. A notice sent to the offeree that the property that is the subject of the offer has been sold to a third person is a revocation of the offer. A customer's order for goods, which is an offer to purchase at certain prices, is revoked by a notice to the seller of the cancellation of the order, provided that such notice is communicated before the order is accepted.

Communication of Revocation

A revocation of an offer is ordinarily effective only when it is made known to the offeree.[18] Until it is communicated to the offeree, directly or indirectly, the offeree has reason to believe that there is still an offer that may be accepted, and the offeree may rely on this belief. A letter revoking an offer made to a particular offeree is not effective until the offeree receives it. It is not a revocation when the offeror writes it or even when it is mailed or dispatched. A written revocation is effective, however, when it is delivered to the offeree's agent or to the offeree's residence or place of business under such circumstances that the offeree may be reasonably expected to be aware of its receipt.

It is ordinarily held that there is a sufficient communication of the revocation when the offeree learns indirectly of the offeror's revocation. This is particularly true in a land sale when the seller-offeror, after making an offer to sell the land to the offeree, sells the land to a third person and the offeree indirectly learns of such sale. The offeree necessarily realizes that the seller cannot perform the original offer and therefore must be considered to have revoked it.

---

[17] *Davidoff v. Bank of America*, 2011 WL 999564 (S.D. Fla. Oct. 18, 2010).
[18] *MD Drilling and Blasting, Inc. v. MLS Construction, LLC*, 889 A.2d 850 (Conn. App. 2006).

If the offeree accepts an offer before it is effectively revoked, a valid contract is created.

Option Contracts

An *option contract* is a binding promise to keep an offer open for a stated period of time or until a specified date. An option contract requires that the promisor receive consideration—that is, something, such as a sum of money—as the price for the promise to keep the offer open. In other words, the option is a contract to refrain from revoking an offer.

Firm Offers

firm offer—offer stated to be held open for a specified time, under the UCC, with respect to merchants.

As another exception to the rule that an offer can be revoked at any time before acceptance, statutes in some states provide that an offeror cannot revoke an offer prior to its expiration when the offeror makes a firm offer. A **firm offer** is an offer that states that it is to be irrevocable, or irrevocable for a stated period of time. Under the Uniform Commercial Code, this doctrine of firm offer applies to a merchant's signed, written offer to buy or sell goods but with a maximum of three months on its period of irrevocability.[19]

12-2b Counteroffer by Offeree

counteroffer—proposal by an offeree to the offeror that changes the terms of, and thus rejects, the original offer.

The offeree rejects the offer when it ignores the original offer and replies with a different offer.[20] If the offeree purports to accept an offer but in so doing makes any change to the terms of the offer, such action is a **counteroffer** that rejects the original offer. An "acceptance" that changes the terms of the offer or adds new terms is a rejection of the original offer and constitutes a counteroffer.[21]

Ordinarily, if *A* makes an offer, such as to sell a used automobile to *B* for $3,000, and *B* in reply makes an offer to buy at $2,500, the original offer is terminated. *B* is in effect indicating refusal of the original offer and in its place is making a different offer. Such an offer by the offeree is known as a *counteroffer*. No contract arises unless the original offeror accepts the counteroffer.

Counteroffers are not limited to offers that directly contradict the original offers. Any departure from or addition to the original offer is a counteroffer even though the original offer was silent on the point added by the counteroffer.

CASE SUMMARY

The Counteroffer Serves as a Rejection

FACTS: While riding her motorcycle Amy Kemper was struck by a vehicle driven by Brown. She suffered serious injuries and Brown was charged with DUI. Kemper sent a demand letter to Brown's insurance claim's administrator Statewide, which stated in part:

Please send all the insurance money that Mr. Brown had under his insurance policy. In exchange, I will agree to sign a limited release.

The release must not have any language saying that I will have to pay Mr. Brown or his insurance company any of their incurred costs.

.... If you fail to meet my demand, I will be forced to hire an attorney and sue Mr. Brown and your company. Please do not contact me, or my friends[,] as this demand is very simple.

Statewide sent a letter to Kemper agreeing to settle her claims for the limits of Brown's liability insurance. Attached

---

[19] U.C.C. §2-205.
[20] *Bourque v. FDIC*, 42 F.3d 704 (1st Cir. 1994).
[21] *Hardy Corp. v. Rayco Industrial, Inc.*, 143 So. 3d 172 (Ala. 2013).

The Counteroffer Serves as a Rejection continued

to the letter was a $25,000 check and a two-page limited liability release form. The letter stated, in part,

> *[i]n concluding the settlement, we are entrusting that you place money in an escrow account in regards to any and all liens pending. This demand is being asserted to protect the lien's interest[.]*

Ms. Kemper rejected Statewide's "counteroffer" and filed suit. Brown filed a motion to enforce the "settlement agreement."

DECISION: Judgment for Kemper. To establish a contract the offer must be accepted unequivocally and without variance of any sort. Statewide demanded that Kemper place the settlements funds into an escrow account to protect against any pending liens. Its response was a counteroffer rather than an unconditional and unequivocal acceptance. No binding settlement agreement was formed. [***Kemper v. Brown*, 754 S.E.2d 141 (Ga. App. 2014)]**

12-2c Rejection of Offer by Offeree

If the offeree rejects the offer and communicates this rejection to the offeror, the offer is terminated. Communication of a rejection terminates an offer even though the period for which the offeror agreed to keep the offer open has not yet expired. It may be that the offeror is willing to renew the offer, but unless this is done, there is no longer any offer for the offeree to accept.

12-2d Lapse of Time

When the offer states that it is open until a particular date, the offer terminates on that date if it has not yet been accepted. This is particularly so when the offeror declares that the offer shall be void after the expiration of the specified time. Such limitations are strictly construed. **For Example,** Landry's Restaurant Minnesota Inc. extended a written, signed offer to Starlite L.P. to lease Starlite's real estate for a period of 20 years. The written offer stated that if a fully executed acceptance of the lease is not returned to Landry's Minnesota Inc. within six days of the written offer dated April 30, 1998, "the offer to lease ... shall be deemed withdrawn and this lease shall be deemed null and void." Starlite signed and returned the lease agreement on May 11, 1998, five days after the May 6 deadline. Landry's Minnesota occupied the property and built a restaurant on it but vacated the property after nine years. Starlite sued the restaurant's parent corporation, Landry's Restaurants Inc., as guarantor of the lease, seeking payment for past due and ongoing rent. Starlite's lawsuit was not successful as no valid lease agreement existed because no contract could be properly formed when acceptance occurred after the written offer had expired.[22]

If the offer contains a time limitation for acceptance, an attempted acceptance after the expiration of that time has no effect and does not give rise to a contract.[23] When a specified time limitation is imposed on an option, the option cannot be exercised after the expiration of that time, regardless of whether the option was exercised within what would have been held a reasonable time if no time period had been specified.

If the offer does not specify a time, it will terminate after the lapse of a reasonable time. What constitutes a reasonable time depends on the circumstances of each case—that is, on the nature of the subject matter, the nature of the market in which it is sold, the time of

---

[22] *Starlite Limited Partnership v. Landry's Restaurants, Inc.*, 780 N.W.2d 396 (Minn. App. 2010).
[23] *Century 21 Pinetree Properties, Inc. v. Cason*, 469 S.E.2d 458 (Ga. App. 1996).

year, and other factors of supply and demand. If a commodity is perishable or fluctuates greatly in value, the reasonable time will be much shorter than if the subject matter is of a stable value. An offer to sell a harvested crop of tomatoes would expire within a very short time. When a seller purports to accept an offer after it has lapsed by the expiration of time, the seller's acceptance is merely a counteroffer and does not create a contract unless the buyer accepts that counteroffer.

12-2e **Death or Disability of Either Party**

If either the offeror or offeree dies or becomes mentally incompetent before the offer is accepted, the offer is automatically terminated. **For Example,** Chet Wilson offers to sell his ranch to Interport, Inc., for $2.5 million. Five days later, Chet is killed in an aviation accident. Interport, Inc., subsequently writes to Chet Wilson Jr., an adult, that his father's offer is accepted. No contract is formed because the offer made by Chet died with him.

CPA

12-2f **Subsequent Illegality**

If the performance of the contract becomes illegal after the offer is made, the offer is terminated. **For Example,** if an offer is made to sell six semiautomatic handguns to a commercial firing range for $550 per weapon but a new law prohibiting such sales is enacted before the offer is accepted, the offer is terminated.

CPA

12-3 **Acceptance of Offer**

acceptance—unqualified assent to the act or proposal of another; as the acceptance of a draft (bill of exchange), of an offer to make a contract, of goods delivered by the seller, or of a gift or deed.

An **acceptance** is the assent of the offeree to the terms of the offer. Objective standards determine whether there has been an agreement of the parties.

12-3a **What Constitutes an Acceptance?**

No particular form of words or mode of expression is required, but there must be a clear expression that the offeree agrees to be bound by the terms of the offer. If the offeree reserves the right to reject the offer, such action is not an acceptance.[24]

12-3b **Privilege of Offeree**

Ordinarily, the offeree may refuse to accept an offer. If there is no acceptance, by definition there is no contract. The fact that there had been a series of contracts between the parties and that one party's offer had always been accepted before by the other does not create any legal obligation to continue to accept subsequent offers.

CPA

12-3c **Effect of Acceptance**

The acceptance of an offer creates a binding agreement or contract,[25] assuming that all of the other elements of a contract are present. Neither party can subsequently withdraw from or cancel the contract without the consent of the other party. **For Example,** James Gang refused to honor an oral stock purchase agreement he made with Moshen Sadeghi under terms he assented to and that were announced on the record to a court as a mutual

---

[24] *Pantano v. McGowan*, 530 N.W.2d 912 (Neb. 1995).
[25] *Ochoa v. Ford*, 641 N.E.2d 1042 (Ind. App. 1994).

settlement of a dispute. Gang was not allowed subsequently to withdraw from the agreement, because it was an enforceable contract.[26]

CPA 12-3d Nature of Acceptance

An *acceptance* is the offeree's manifestation of intent to enter into a binding agreement on the terms stated in the offer. Whether there is an acceptance depends on whether the offeree has manifested an intent to accept. It is the objective or outward appearance that is controlling rather than the subjective or unexpressed intent of the offeree.[27]

In the absence of a contrary requirement in the offer, an acceptance may be indicated by an informal "okay," by a mere affirmative nod of the head, or in the case of an offer of a unilateral contract, by performance of the act called for.

The acceptance must be absolute and unconditional. It must accept just what is offered.[28] If the offeree changes any terms of the offer or adds any new term, there is no acceptance because the offeree does not agree to what was offered.

When the offeree does not accept the offer exactly as made, the addition of any qualification converts the "acceptance" into a counteroffer, and no contract arises unless the original offeror accepts such a counteroffer.

CPA 12-3e Who May Accept?

Only the person to whom an offer is directed may accept it. If anyone else attempts to accept it, no agreement or contract with that person arises.

If the offer is directed to a particular class rather than a specified individual, anyone within that class may accept it. If the offer is made to the public at large, any member of the public at large having knowledge of the existence of the offer may accept it.

When a person to whom an offer was not made attempts to accept it, the attempted acceptance has the effect of an offer. If the original offeror is willing to accept this offer, a binding contract arises. If the original offeror does not accept the new offer, there is no contract.

CASE SUMMARY

There's No Turning Back

FACTS: As a lease was about to expire, the landlord, CRA Development, wrote the tenant, Keryakos Textiles, setting forth the square footage and the rate terms on which the lease would be renewed. Keryakos sent a reply stating that it was willing to pay the proposed rate but wanted different cancellation and option terms in the renewal contract. CRA rejected Keryakos's terms, and on learning this, Keryakos notified CRA that it accepted the terms of its original letter. CRA sought to evict Keryakos from the property, claiming that no lease contract existed between it and Keryakos.

DECISION: The lease contract is governed by ordinary contract law. When the tenant offered other terms in place of those made by the landlord's offer, the tenant made a counteroffer. This had the effect of rejecting or terminating the landlord's offer. The tenant could not then accept the rejected offer after the tenant's counteroffer was rejected. Therefore, there was no contract. [*Keryakos Textiles, Inc. v. CRA Development, Inc.*, **563 N.Y.S.2d 308 (App. Div. 1990)**]

---

[26] *Sadeghi v. Gang*, 270 S.W.3d 773 (Tex. App. 2008).
[27] *Cowan v. Mervin Mewes, Inc.*, 546 N.W.2d 104 (S.D. 1996).
[28] *Jones v. Frickey*, 618 S.E.2d 29 (Ga. App. 2005).

CPA · ## 12-3f Manner and Time of Acceptance

The offeror may specify the manner and time for accepting the offer. When the offeror specifies that there must be a written acceptance, no contract arises when the offeree makes an oral acceptance. If the offeror calls for acceptance by a specified time and date, a late acceptance has no legal effect, and a contract is not formed. Where no time is specified in the offer, the offeree has a reasonable period of time to accept the offer. After the time specified in the offer or a reasonable period of time expires (when no time is specified in the offer), the offeree's power to make a contract by accepting the offer "lapses."

When the offeror calls for the performance of an act or of certain conduct, the performance thereof is an acceptance of the offer and creates a unilateral contract.

When the offeror has specified a particular manner and time of acceptance, generally, the offeree cannot accept in any other way. The basic rule applied by the courts is that the offeror is the master of the offer![29]

CPA · ## Silence as Acceptance

In most cases, the offeree's silence and failure to act cannot be regarded as an acceptance. Ordinarily, the offeror is not permitted to frame an offer in such a way as to make the silence and inaction of the offeree operate as an acceptance. Nor can a party to an existing contract effect a modification of that agreement without the other party's actual acceptance or approval. **For Example,** H. H. Taylor made a contract with Andy Stricker, a civil engineer, to design a small hotel. The parties agreed on an hourly rate with "total price not to exceed $7,200," and required that additional charges be presented to Taylor prior to proceeding with any changes. Andy was required to dedicate more hours to the project than anticipated but could not present the additional charges to Taylor because Taylor would not return his phone calls. He billed Taylor $9,035 for his services. Taylor's failure to act in not returning phone calls is not a substitute for the assent needed to modify a contract. Stricker is thus only entitled to $7,200.[30]

Unordered Goods and Tickets

Sometimes a seller writes to a person with whom the seller has not had any prior dealings, stating that unless notified to the contrary, the seller will send specified merchandise and the recipient is obligated to pay for it at stated prices. There is no acceptance if the recipient of the letter ignores the offer and does nothing. The silence of the person receiving the letter is not an acceptance, and the sender, as a reasonable person, should recognize that none was intended.

This rule applies to all kinds of goods, books, magazines, and tickets sent through the mail when they have not been ordered. The fact that the items are not returned does not mean that they have been accepted; that is, the offeree is required neither to pay for nor to return the items. If desired, the recipient of the unordered goods may write "Return to Sender" on the unopened package and put the package back into the mail without any additional postage. The Postal Reorganization Act provides that the person who receives unordered mailed merchandise from a commercial sender has the right "to retain, use, discard, or dispose of it in any manner the recipient sees fit without any obligation

---

[29] See *1-800 Contacts, Inc. v. Weigner*, 127 P.3d 1241 (Utah App. 2005).
[30] *Stricker v. Taylor*, 975 P.2d 930 (Or. App. 1999).

whatsoever to the sender."[31] It provides further that any unordered merchandise that is mailed must have attached to it a clear and conspicuous statement of the recipient's right to treat the goods in this manner.

CPA 12-3g Communication of Acceptance

Acceptance by the offeree is the last step in the formation of a bilateral contract. Intuitively, the offeror's receipt of the acceptance should be the point in time when the contract is formed and its terms apply. When the parties are involved in face-to-face negotiations, a contract is formed upon the offeror's receipt of the acceptance. When the offeror hears the offeree's words of acceptance, the parties may shake hands, signifying their understanding that the contract has been formed.

E-COMMERCE & CYBERLAW

Contract Formation on the Internet

It is not possible for an online service provider or seller to individually bargain with each person who visits its Web site. The Web site owner, therefore, as offeror, places its proposed terms on its Web site and requires visitors to assent to these terms in order to access the site, download software, or purchase a product or service.

In a written contract, the parties sign a paper document indicating their intention to be bound by the terms of the contract. Online, however, an agreement may be accomplished by the visitor-offeree simply typing the words "I Accept" in an onscreen box and then clicking a "send" or similar button that indicates acceptance. Or the individual clicks an "I Agree" or "I Accept" icon or check box. Access to the site is commonly denied those who do not agree to the terms. Such agreements have come to be known as *clickwrap* agreements and in the case of software license agreements, *SLAs*. The agreements contain fee schedules and other financial terms and may contain terms such as a notice of the proprietary nature of the material contained on the site and of any limitations on the use of the site and the downloading of software. Moreover, the clickwrap agreements may contain limitations on liability, including losses associated with the use of downloaded software or products or services purchased from the site.

To determine whether a clickwrap agreement is enforceable, courts apply traditional principles of contract law and focus on whether the plaintiffs had reasonable notice of and manifested assent to the clickwrap agreement. Failure to read an enforceable clickwrap agreement, as with any binding contract, will not excuse compliance with its terms.

In *Specht v. Netscape Communications Corp.,** the Internet users were urged to click on a button to download free software, but the offer did not make clear to the user that clicking the download button would signify assent to restrictive contractual terms and conditions. The court, in its 2002 decision, declined to enforce this clickwrap agreement. Internet sellers and service providers generally learned from the *Specht* decision, and most clickwrap agreements now provide sufficient notice and means for clear assent. For example, in *Feldman v. Google, Inc.,*** decided in 2007, the user was unsuccessful in challenging the terms of Google's "AdWords" Program clickwrap agreement. In order to activate an AdWords account, the user had to visit a Web page that displayed the agreement in a scrollable text box. The text of the agreement was immediately visible to the user, as was a prominent admonition in boldface to read the terms and conditions carefully, and with instructions to indicate assent if the user agreed to the terms.

Unlike the impermissible agreement in *Specht*, the user here had to take affirmative action and click the "Yes, I agree to the above terms and conditions" button in order to proceed to the next step. Clicking "Continue" without clicking the "Yes" button would have returned the user to the same Web page. If the user did not agree to all of the terms, he could not have activated his account, placed ads, or incurred charges.

*306 F.3d 17 (2d Cir. 2002).
**Feldman v. Google, Inc., 513 F. Supp. 2d 229 (E.D. Pa. 2007). See also A.V. v. Iparadigms, LLC, 554 F. Supp. 2d 473 (E.D. Va. 2008).

---

[31] Federal Postal Reorganization Act §3009.

CPA   Mailbox Rule

When the parties are negotiating at a distance from each other, special rules have developed as to when the acceptance takes effect based on the commercial expediency of creating a contract at the earliest period of time and the protection of the offeree. Under the so-called *mailbox rule*, a properly addressed, postage-paid mailed acceptance takes effect when the acceptance is placed into the control of the U.S. Postal Service[32] or, by judicial extension, is placed in the control of a private third-party carrier such as Federal Express or United Parcel Service.[33] That is, the acceptance is effective upon dispatch even before it is received by the offeror.

CASE SUMMARY

When the Mailbox Bangs Shut

FACTS: The Thoelkes owned land. The Morrisons mailed an offer to the Thoelkes to buy their land. The Thoelkes agreed to this offer and mailed back a contract signed by them. While this letter was in transit, the Thoelkes notified the Morrisons that their acceptance was revoked. Were the Thoelkes bound by a contract?

DECISION: The acceptance was effective when mailed, and the subsequent revocation of the acceptance had no effect. [*Morrison v. Thoelke*, 155 So. 2d 889 (Fla. App. 1963)]

The offeror may avoid the application of this rule by stating in the offer that acceptance shall take effect upon receipt by the offeror.

CPA   Determining the Applicable Means of Communication

The modern rule on the selection of the appropriate medium of communication of acceptance is that unless otherwise unambiguously indicated in the offer, it shall be construed as inviting acceptance in any manner and by any medium reasonable under the circumstances.[34] A medium of communication is normally reasonable if it is one used by the offeror or if it is customary in similar transactions at the time and place the offer is received. Thus, if the offeror uses the mail to extend an offer, the offeree may accept by using the mail. Indeed, acceptance by mail is ordinarily reasonable when the parties are negotiating at a distance even if the offer is not made by mail.

CPA   Telephone and Electronic Communication of Acceptance

Although telephonic communication is very similar to face-to-face communication, most U.S. courts, nevertheless, have applied the mailbox rule, holding that telephoned acceptances are effective where and when dispatched.

---

[32] See *Adams v. Lindsell*, 106 Eng. Rep. 250 (K.B. 1818). Common law jurisdictions have unanimously adopted the mailbox rule, as has the Restatement (Second) of Contracts §63, and the U.C.C. [see U.C.C. §1-201(26),(38)].

[33] But see *Baca v. Trejo*, 902 N.E.2d 1108 (Ill App. 2009) whereby an Illinois court determined that a statute deeming a document to be filed with a state court on the date shown by the U.S. Postal Service cancellation mark—the mailbox rule—does not apply to documents consigned to a private carrier, UPS. The court reasoned that courts should not have the task of deciding which carriers are acceptable.

[34] Restatement (Second) of Contracts §30; U.C.C. §2-206(1) (a).

The courts have yet to address the applicability of the mailbox rule to e-mail. However, when the offeree's server is under the control of an independent entity, such as an online service provider, and the offeree cannot withdraw the message, it is anticipated that the courts will apply the mailbox rule, and acceptance will take effect on proper dispatch. In the case of companies that operate their own servers, the acceptance will take effect when the message is passed onto the Internet.

Facsimile transmissions are substantially instantaneous and could be treated as face-to-face communications. However, it is anticipated that U.S. courts, when called upon to deal with this issue, will apply the mailbox acceptance-upon-dispatch rule as they do with telephoned acceptances.

Effects of the Mailbox Rule

If an offer requires that acceptance be communicated by a specific date and the acceptance is properly dispatched by the offeree on the final date, the acceptance is timely and the contract is formed, even though the offeror actually receives the acceptance well after the specified date has passed. **For Example,** by letter dated February 18, 1999, Morton's of Chicago mailed a certified letter to the Crab House accepting the Crab House's offer to terminate its restaurant lease. The Crab House, Inc., sought to revoke its offer to terminate the lease in a certified letter dated February 18, 1999, and by facsimile transmission to Morton's dated February 19, 1999. On February 22, 1999, the Crab House received Morton's acceptance letter; and on the same date Morton's received Crab House's letter revoking the offer to terminate the lease. Acceptance of an offer is effective upon dispatch to the Postal Service, and the contract springs into existence at the time of the mailing. Offers, revocations, and rejections are generally effective only upon the offeree's receipt. Morton's dispatch of its acceptance letter on February 18 formed an agreement to terminate the lease, and the fax dispatched on February 19 was too late to revoke the offer to terminate the lease.[35]

12-3h **Auction Sales**

At an auction sale, the statements made by the auctioneer to draw forth bids are merely invitations to negotiate. Each bid is an offer, which is not accepted until the auctioneer indicates that a particular offer or bid is accepted. Usually, this is done by the fall of the auctioneer's hammer, indicating that the highest bid made has been accepted.[36] Because a bid is merely an offer, the bidder may withdraw the bid at any time before it is accepted by the auctioneer.

Ordinarily, the auctioneer who is not satisfied with the amounts of the bids that are being made may withdraw any article or all of the property from the sale. Once a bid is accepted, however, the auctioneer cannot cancel the sale. In addition, if it had been announced that the sale was to be made "without reserve," the property must be sold to the person making the highest bid regardless of how low that bid may be.

In an auction "with reserve," the auctioneer takes bids as agent for the seller with the understanding that no contract is formed until the seller accepts the transaction.[37]

---

[35] *Morton's of Chicago v. Crab House Inc.*, 746 N.Y.S.2d 317 (2002). *Kass v. Grais*, 2007 WL 2815498 (N.Y. Sup. Sept. 4, 2007).

[36] *Dry Creek Cattle Co. v. Harriet Bros. Limited Partnership*, 908 P.2d 399 (Wyo. 1995).

[37] *Marten v. Staab*, 543 N.W.2d 436 (Neb. 1996). Statutes regulate auctions and auctioneers in all states. For example, state of Maine law prohibits an auctioneer from conducting an auction without first having a written contract with the consignor of any property to be sold, including (1) whether the auction is with reserve or without reserve, (2) the commission rate, and (3) a description of all items to be sold. See *Street v. Board of Licensing of Auctioneers*, 889 A.2d 319 ([Me.] 2006).

Make the Connection

Summary

Because a contract arises when an offer is accepted, it is necessary to find that there was an offer and that it was accepted. If either element is missing, there is no contract.

An offer does not exist unless the offeror has contractual intent. This intent is lacking if the statement of the person is merely an invitation to negotiate, a statement of intention, or an agreement to agree at a later date. Newspaper ads, price quotations, and catalog prices are ordinarily merely invitations to negotiate and cannot be accepted.

An offer must be definite. If an offer is indefinite, its acceptance will not create a contract because it will be held that the resulting agreement is too vague to enforce. In some cases, an offer that is by itself too indefinite is made definite because some writing or standard is incorporated by reference and made part of the offer. In some cases the offer is made definite by implying terms that were not stated. In other cases, the indefinite part of the offer is ignored when that part can be divided or separated from the balance of the offer.

Assuming that there is in fact an offer that is made with contractual intent and that it is sufficiently definite, it still does not have the legal effect of an offer unless it is communicated to the offeree by or at the direction of the offeror.

In some cases, there was an offer but it was terminated before it was accepted. By definition, an attempted acceptance made after the offer has been terminated has no effect. The offeror may revoke the ordinary offer at any time. All that is required is the showing of the intent to revoke and the communication of that intent to the offeree. The offeror's power to revoke is barred by the existence of an option contract under common law or a firm offer under the Uniform Commercial Code. An offer is also terminated by the express rejection of the offer or by the making of a counteroffer, by the lapse of the time stated in the offer or of a reasonable time when none is stated, by the death or disability of either party, or by a change of law that makes illegal a contract based on the particular offer.

When the offer is accepted, a contract arises. Only the offeree can accept an offer, and the acceptance must be of the offer exactly as made without any qualification or change. Ordinarily, the offeree may accept or reject as the offeree chooses.

The acceptance is any manifestation of intent to agree to the terms of the offer. Ordinarily, silence or failure to act does not constitute acceptance. The recipient of unordered goods and tickets may dispose of the goods or use the goods without such action constituting an acceptance. An acceptance does not exist until the words or conduct demonstrating assent to the offer is communicated to the offeror. Acceptance by mail takes effect at the time and place when and where the letter is mailed or the fax is transmitted.

In an auction sale, the auctioneer asking for bids makes an invitation to negotiate. A person making a bid is making an offer, and the acceptance of the highest bid by the auctioneer is an acceptance of that offer and gives rise to a contract. When the auction sale is without reserve, the auctioneer must accept the highest bid. If the auction is not expressly without reserve, the auctioneer may refuse to accept any of the bids.

Learning Outcomes

After studying this chapter, you should be able to clearly explain:

12-1 Requirements of an Offer

LO.1 Decide whether an offer contains definite and certain terms

See the *Novak* case for an example of an oral contract with definite enforceable terms, page 224.

See the *Plankenhorn* case for the meaning of a "damn good job," page 225.

See the legal impact of a party's statement that the contract "was going to be signed" in the *Hewitt* example, page 223.

See the *Wigod* case that discusses the test for a valid, binding offer, page 222.

12-2 Termination of Offer

LO.2 Explain the exceptions the law makes to the requirement of definiteness

See the *Delphi* case on requirements contracts, page 228.

LO.3 Explain all the ways an offer can be terminated

See the discussion of revocation, counteroffer, rejection, lapse of time, death or disability of a party, or subsequent illegality, pages 229–232.

See the *Davidoff* example of a revocation communicated to the offeree prior to acceptance, page 229.

See the *Landry's Restaurants* example that illustrates the effect of an "acceptance" signed just a few days after the written offer had expired, page 231.

See the *Kemper* case showing that a counteroffer serves as a rejection, page 231.

12-3   Acceptance of Offer

LO.4 Explain what constitutes the acceptance of an offer

See the *Sadeghi* example where acceptance of an offer created a binding contract, pages 232–233.

See the *Keryakos Textiles* case on the impact of a counteroffer, page 233.

LO.5 Explain the implications of failing to read a clickwrap agreement

See the *Feldman* case as an example of an enforceable clickwrap agreement containing notice and manifested assent, page 235.

Key Terms

acceptance	firm offer	requirements contract
counteroffer	offer	
divisible contract	output contract	

Questions and Case Problems

1. Bernie and Phil's Great American Surplus store placed an ad in the *Sunday Times* stating, "Next Saturday at 8:00 A.M. sharp, 3 brand new mink coats worth $5,000 each will be sold for $500 each! First come, first served." Marsha Lufklin was first in line when the store opened and went directly to the coat department, but the coats identified in the ad were not available for sale. She identified herself to the manager and pointed out that she was first in line in conformity with the store's advertised offer and that she was ready to pay the $500 price set forth in the store's offer. The manager responded that a newspaper ad is just an invitation to negotiate and that the store decided to withdraw "the mink coat promotion." Review the text on unilateral contracts in the section titled "Bilateral and Unilateral Contracts" in Chapter 11. Decide.

2. Brown made an offer to purchase Overman's house on a standard printed form. Underneath Brown's signature was the statement: "ACCEPTANCE ON REVERSE SIDE." Overman did not sign the offer on the back but sent Brown a letter accepting the offer. Later, Brown refused to perform the contract, and Overman sued him for breach of contract. Brown claimed there was no contract because the offer had not been accepted in the manner specified by the offer. Decide. [*Overman v. Brown*, 372 N.W.2d 102 (Neb.)]

3. Katherine mailed Paul an offer with definite and certain terms and that was legal in all respects stating that it was good for 10 days. Two days later she sent Paul a letter by certified mail (time stamped by the Postal Service at 1:14 P.M.) stating that the original offer was revoked. That evening Paul e-mailed acceptance of the offer to Katherine. She immediately phoned him to tell him that she had revoked the offer that afternoon, and that he would surely receive it in tomorrow's mail. Was the offer revoked by Katherine?

4. Nelson wanted to sell his home. Baker sent him a written offer to purchase the home. Nelson made some changes to Baker's offer and wrote him that he, Nelson, was accepting the offer as amended. Baker notified Nelson that he was dropping out of the transaction. Nelson sued Baker for breach of contract. Decide. What social forces and ethical values are involved? [*Nelson v. Baker*, 776 S.W.2d 52 (Mo. App.)]

5. Lessack Auctioneers advertised an auction sale that was open to the public and was to be conducted with reserve. Gordon attended the auction and bid $100 for a work of art that was worth much more. No higher bid, however, was made. Lessack refused to sell the item for $100 and withdrew the item from the sale. Gordon claimed that because he was the highest bidder, Lessack was required to sell the item to him. Was he correct?

6. Willis Music Co. advertised a television set at $22.50 in the Sunday newspaper. Ehrlich ordered a set, but the company refused to deliver it on the grounds that the price in the newspaper ad was a mistake. Ehrlich sued the company. Was it liable? Why or why not? [*Ehrlich v. Willis Music Co.*, 113 N.E.2d 252 (Ohio App.)]

7. When a movement was organized to build Charles City College, Hauser and others signed pledges to contribute to the college. At the time of signing, Hauser inquired what would happen if he should die or be unable to pay. The representative of the college stated that the pledge would then not be binding and that it was merely a statement of intent. The college failed financially, and Pappas was appointed receiver to collect and liquidate the assets of the college corporation. He sued Hauser for the amount due on his pledge. Hauser raised the defense that the pledge was not a binding contract. Decide. What ethical values are involved? [*Pappas v. Hauser*, 197 N.W.2d 607 (Iowa)]

8. Maria Cantu was a special education teacher under a one-year contract with the San Benito School district for the 1990–1991 school year. On Saturday, August 18, just weeks before fall-term classes were to begin, she hand delivered a letter of resignation to her supervisor. Late Monday afternoon the superintendent put in the mail a properly stamped and addressed letter to Cantu accepting her offer of resignation. The next morning at 8:00, before the superintendent's letter reached her, Cantu hand delivered a letter withdrawing her resignation. The superintendent refused to recognize the attempted rescission of the resignation. Decide. [*Cantu v. Central Education Agency*, 884 S.W.2d 563 (Tex. App.)]

9. A. H. Zehmer discussed selling a farm to Lucy. After a 40-minute discussion of the first draft of a contract, Zehmer and his wife, Ida, signed a second draft stating: "We hereby agree to sell to W. O. Lucy the Ferguson farm complete for $50,000 title satisfactory to buyer." Lucy agreed to purchase the farm on these terms. Thereafter, the Zehmers refused to transfer title to Lucy and claimed they had made the contract for sale as a joke. Lucy brought an action to compel performance of the contract. The Zehmers claimed there was no contract. Were they correct? [*Lucy v. Zehmer*, 84 S.E.2d 516 (Va. App.)]

10. Wheeler operated an automobile service station, which he leased from W. C. Cornitius, Inc. The lease ran for three years. Although the lease did not contain any provision for renewal, it was in fact renewed six times for successive three-year terms. The landlord refused to renew the lease for a seventh time. Wheeler brought suit to compel the landlord to accept his offer to renew the lease. Decide. [*William C. Cornitius, Inc. v. Wheeler*, 556 P.2d 666 (Or.)]

11. Buster Cogdill, a real estate developer, made an offer to the Bank of Benton to have the bank provide construction financing for the development of an outlet mall, with funds to be provided at prime rate plus two percentage points. The bank's president Julio Plunkett thanked Buster for the proposal and said, "I will start the paperwork." Did Cogdill have a contract with the Bank of Benton? [*Bank of Benton v. Cogdill*, 454 N.E.2d 1120 (Ill. App.)]

12. Ackerley Media Group, Inc., claimed to have a three-season advertising Team Sponsorship Agreement (TSA) with Sharp Electronics Corporation to promote Sharp products at all Seattle Supersonics NBA basketball home games. Sharp contended that a valid agreement did not exist for the third season (2000–2001) because a material price term was missing, thus resulting in an unenforceable "agreement to agree." The terms of the TSA for the 2000–2001 third season called for a base payment of $144,200 and an annual increase "not to exceed 6% [and] to be mutually agreed upon by the parties." No "mutually agreed" increase was negotiated by the parties. Ackerley seeks payment for the base price of $144,200 only. Sharp contends that since no price was agreed upon for the season, the entire TSA is unenforceable, and it is not obligated to pay for the 2000–2001 season. Is Sharp correct? [*Ackerley Media Group, Inc. v. Sharp Electronics Corp.*, 170 F. Supp. 2d 445 (S.D.N.Y.)]

13. L. B. Foster invited Tie and Track Systems Inc. to submit price quotes on items to be used in a railroad expansion project. Tie and Track responded by e-mail on August 11, 2006, with prices for 9 items of steel ties. The e-mail concluded, "The above prices are delivered/Terms of Payment—to be agreed/Delivery—to be agreed/We hope you are successful with your bid. If you require any additional information please call." Just 3 of the 9 items listed in Tie and Track's price quote were "accepted" by the project. L. B. Foster demanded that Tie and Track provide the items at the price listed in the quote. Tie and Track refused. L. B. Foster sued for breach of contract. Did the August 11 e-mail constitute an offer, acceptance of which could bind the supplier to

a contract? If so, was there a valid acceptance? [*L. B. Foster v. Tie and Track Systems, Inc.*, 2009 WL 900993 (N.D. Ill.)]

14. On August 15, 2003, Wilbert Heikkila signed an agreement with Kangas Realty to sell eight parcels of Heikkila's property. On September 8, 2003, David McLaughlin met with a Kangas agent who drafted McLaughlin's offer to purchase three of the parcels. McLaughlin signed the offer and gave the agent checks for each parcel. On September 9 and 10, 2003, the agent for Heikkila prepared three printed purchase agreements, one for each parcel. On September 14, 2003, David's wife, Joanne McLaughlin, met with the agent and signed the agreements. On September 16, 2003, Heikkila met with his real estate agent. Writing on the printed agreements, Heikkila changed the price of one parcel from $145,000 to $150,000, the price of another parcel from $32,000 to $45,000, and the price of the third parcel from $175,000 to $179,000. Neither of the McLaughlins signed an acceptance of Heikkila's changes to the printed agreements before Heikkila withdrew his offer to sell. The McLaughlins learned that Heikkila had withdrawn his offer on January 1, 2004, when the real estate agent returned the checks to them. Totally shocked at Heikkila's conduct, the McLaughlins brought action to compel specific performance of the purchase agreement signed by Joanne McLaughlin on their behalf. Decide. [*McLaughlin v. Heikkila*, 697 N.W.2d 231 (Minn. App.)]

CPA Questions

1. Able Sofa, Inc., sent Noll a letter offering to sell Noll a custom-made sofa for $5,000. Noll immediately sent a telegram to Able purporting to accept the offer. However, the telegraph company erroneously delivered the telegram to Abel Soda, Inc. Three days later, Able mailed a letter of revocation to Noll, which was received by Noll. Able refused to sell Noll the sofa. Noll sued Able for breach of contract. Able:

   a. Would have been liable under the deposited acceptance rule only if Noll had accepted by mail.

   b. Will avoid liability since it revoked its offer prior to receiving Noll's acceptance.

   c. Will be liable for breach of contract.

   d. Will avoid liability due to the telegraph company's error (Law, #2, 9911).

2. On September 27, Summers sent Fox a letter offering to sell Fox a vacation home for $150,000. On October 2, Fox replied by mail agreeing to buy the home for $145,000. Summers did not reply to Fox. Do Fox and Summers have a binding contract?

   a. No, because Fox failed to sign and return Summers's letter.

   b. No, because Fox's letter was a counteroffer.

   c. Yes, because Summers's offer was validly accepted.

   d. Yes, because Summers's silence is an implied acceptance of Fox's letter (Law, #2, 0462).

3. On June 15, Peters orally offered to sell a used lawn mower to Mason for $125. Peters specified that Mason had until June 20 to accept the offer. On June 16, Peters received an offer to purchase the lawn mower for $150 from Bronson, Mason's neighbor. Peters accepted Bronson's offer. On June 17, Mason saw Bronson using the lawn mower and was told the mower had been sold to Bronson. Mason immediately wrote to Peters to accept the June 15 offer. Which of the following statements is correct?

   a. Mason's acceptance would be effective when received by Peters.

   b. Mason's acceptance would be effective when mailed.

   c. Peters's offer had been revoked and Mason's acceptance was ineffective.

   d. Peters was obligated to keep the June 15 offer open until June 20 (Law, #13, 3095).

Capacity and Genuine Assent

A *contract* is a binding agreement. This agreement must be made between parties who have the capacity to do so. They must also truly agree so that all parties have really consented to the contract. This chapter explores the elements of contractual capacity of the parties and the genuineness of their assent.

13-1 Contractual Capacity

Some persons lack contractual capacity, a lack that embraces both those who have a status incapacity, such as minors, and those who have a factual incapacity, such as persons who are insane.

13-1a Contractual Capacity Defined

contractual capacity— ability to understand that a contract is being made and to understand its general meaning.

Contractual capacity is the ability to understand that a contract is being made and to understand its general meaning. However, the fact that a person does not understand the full legal meaning of a contract does not mean that contractual capacity is lacking. Everyone is presumed to have capacity unless it is proven that capacity is lacking or there is status incapacity.[1] **For Example,** Jacqueline, aged 22, entered into a contract with Sunrise Storage Co. but later claimed that it was not binding because she did not understand several clauses in the printed contract. The contract was binding. No evidence supported her claim that she lacked capacity to contract or to understand its subject. Contractual capacity can exist even though a party does not understand every provision of the contract.

Status Incapacity

Over the centuries, the law has declared that some classes of persons lack contractual capacity. The purpose is to protect these classes by giving them the power to get out of unwise contracts. Of these classes, the most important today is the class identified as minors.

Until recent times, some other classes were held to lack contractual capacity in order to discriminate against them. Examples are married women and aliens. Still other classes, such as persons convicted of and sentenced for a felony, were held to lack contractual capacity in order to punish them. Today, these discriminatory and punitive incapacities have largely disappeared. Married women have the same contractual capacity as unmarried persons.

By virtue of international treaties, the discrimination against aliens has been removed.

CASE SUMMARY

We Really Mean Equal Rights

FACTS: An Alabama statute provided that a married woman could not sell her land without the consent of her husband. Montgomery made a contract to sell land she owned to Peddy. Montgomery's husband did not consent to the sale. Montgomery did not perform the contract and Peddy sued her. The defense was raised that the contract was void and could not be enforced because of the statute. Peddy claimed that the statute was unconstitutional.

DECISION: The statute was unconstitutional. Constitutions, both federal and state, guarantee all persons the equal protection of the law. Married women are denied this equal protection when they are treated differently than married men and unmarried women. The fact that such unequal treatment had once been regarded as proper does not justify its modern continuation. [***Peddy v. Montgomery***, 345 So. 2d 988 (Ala. 1991)]

---

[1] In re *Adoption of Smith*, 578 So. 2d 988 (La. App. 1991).

People who has Dimentia

Mental Illness

Avoidable Contract

Factual Incapacity

A *factual incapacity* contrasts with incapacity imposed because of the class or group to which a person belongs. A factual incapacity may exist when, because of a mental condition caused by medication, drugs, alcohol, illness, or age, a person does not understand that a contract is being made or understand its general nature. However, mere mental weakness does not incapacitate a person from contracting. It is sufficient if the individual has enough mental capacity to understand, to a reasonable extent, the nature and effect of what he is doing.[2]

13-1b Minors

Minors may make contracts.[3] To protect them, however, the law has always treated minors as a class lacking contractual capacity.

Who Is a Minor?

At common law, any person, male or female, under 21 years of age was a minor. At common law, minority ended the day before the 21st birthday. The "day before the birthday" rule is still followed, but the age of majority has been reduced from 21 years to 18 years.

CPA Minor's Power to Avoid Contracts

With exceptions that will be noted later, a contract made by a minor is voidable at the election of the minor. **For Example,** Adorian Deck, a minor, created a Twitter feed titled "@OMGFacts." The feed collected and republished interesting and trivial facts from other sources on the Internet. It was subscribed to by over 300,000 Twitter users, including some celebrities. Spatz, Inc., entered into a joint venture with Deck as described in a written contract signed by both parties, under which Spatz would expand the Twitter feed into a suite of Internet products, including a Web site and a Youtube.com video channel. In an "OMG-moment" prior to his 18th birthday, Deck notified Spatz, Inc., that he wished to disaffirm the parties' agreement. This disaffirmation by a minor rescinded the entire contract, rendering it a nullity.[4] The minor may affirm or ratify the contract on attaining majority by performing the contract, by expressly approving the contract, or by allowing a reasonable time to lapse without avoiding the contract.

CPA
What Constitutes Avoidance? A minor may avoid or *disaffirm* a contract by any expression of an intention to repudiate the contract. Any act inconsistent with the continuing validity of the contract is also an avoidance.

CPA
Time for Avoidance. A minor can disaffirm a contract only during minority and for a reasonable time after attaining majority. After the lapse of a reasonable time, the contract is deemed ratified and cannot be avoided by the minor.

CPA
Minor's Misrepresentation of Age. Generally, the fact that the minor has misrepresented his or her age does not affect the minor's power to disaffirm the contract. Some states hold that such fraud of a minor bars contract avoidance. Some states permit the minor

---

[2] *Fisher v. Schefers,* 656 N.W.2d 591 (Minn. App. 2003).
[3] *Buffington v. State Automobile Mut. Ins. Co.,* 384 S.E.2d 873 (Ga. App. 1989).
[4] *Deck v. Spatz, Inc.,* 2011 WL 775067 (E.D. Cal. Sept. 27, 2011).

to disaffirm the contract in such a case but require the minor to pay for any damage to the property received under the contract.

In any case, the other party to the contract may disaffirm it because of the minor's fraud.

CPA Restitution by Minor after Avoidance

When a minor disaffirms a contract, the question arises as to what the minor must return to the other contracting party.

Original Consideration Intact. When a minor still has what was received from the other party, the minor, on avoiding the contract, must return it to the other party or offer to do so. That is, the minor must put things back to the original position or, as it is called, restore the **status quo ante.**

> **status quo ante**–original positions of the parties.

Original Consideration Damaged or Destroyed. What happens if the minor cannot return what has been received because it has been spent, used, damaged, or destroyed? The minor's right to disaffirm the contract is not affected. The minor can still disaffirm the contract and is required to return only what remains. The fact that nothing remains or that what remains is damaged does not bar the right to disaffirm the contract. In states that follow the common law rule, minors can thus refuse to pay for what has been received under a contract or can get back what had been paid or given even though they do not have anything to return or return property in a damaged condition. There is, however, a trend to limit this rule.

Recovery of Property by Minor on Avoidance

When a minor disaffirms a contract, the other contracting party must return the money received. Any property received from the minor must also be returned. If the property has been sold to a third person who did not know of the original seller's minority, the minor cannot get the property back. In such cases, however, the minor is entitled to recover the property's monetary value or the money received by the other contracting party.

CPA Contracts for Necessaries

A minor can disaffirm a contract for necessaries but must pay the reasonable value for furnished necessaries.

> **necessaries**–things indispensable or absolutely necessary for the sustenance of human life.

What Constitutes Necessaries? Originally, **necessaries** were limited to those things absolutely necessary for the sustenance and shelter of the minor. Thus limited, the term would extend only to food, clothing, and lodging. In the course of time, the rule was relaxed to extend generally to things relating to the health, education, and comfort of the minor. Thus, the rental of a house used by a married minor is a necessary.

Liability of Parent or Guardian. When a third person supplies the parents or guardian of a minor with goods or services that the minor needs, the minor is not liable for these necessaries because the third person's contract is with the parent or guardian, not with the minor.

When necessary medical care is provided a minor, a parent is liable at common law for the medical expenses provided the minor child. However, at common law, the child can be held contractually liable for her necessary medical expenses when the parent is unable or unwilling to pay.

CASE SUMMARY

The Concussion and Legal Repercussions

FACTS: Sixteen-year-old Michelle Schmidt was injured in an automobile accident and taken to Prince George's Hospital. Although the identities of Michelle and her parents were originally unknown, the hospital provided her emergency medical care for a brain concussion and an open scalp wound. She incurred hospital expenses of $1,756.24. Ms. Schmidt was insured through her father's insurance company. It issued a check to be used to cover medical expenses. However, the funds were used to purchase a car for Ms. Schmidt. Since she was a minor when the services were rendered, she believed that she had no legal obligation to pay. After Ms. Schmidt attained her eighteenth birthday and failed to pay the hospital, it brought suit against her.

DECISION: Judgment for the hospital. The prevailing modern rule is that minors' contracts are voidable except for necessaries. The doctrine of necessaries states that a minor may be held liable for necessaries, including medical necessaries when parents are unwilling to pay. The court concluded that Ms. Schmidt's father demonstrated a clear unwillingness to pay by using the insurance money to purchase a car rather than pay the hospital. The policy behind the necessaries exception is for the benefit of minors because the procurement of such is essential to their existence, and if they were not permitted to bind themselves, they might not be able to obtain the necessaries. [*Schmidt v. Prince George's Hospital*, 784 A.2d 1112 (Md. 2001)]

CPA ## Ratification of Former Minor's Voidable Contract

A former minor cannot disaffirm a contract that has been ratified after reaching majority.[5]

CPA **What Constitutes Ratification?** Ratification consists of any words or conduct of the former minor manifesting an intent to be bound by the terms of a contract made while a minor.

CPA **Form of Ratification.** Generally, no special form is required for ratification of a minor's voidable contract, although in some states a written ratification or declaration of intention is required.

CPA **Time for Ratification.** A person can disaffirm a contract any time during minority and for a reasonable time after that but, of necessity, can ratify a contract only after attaining majority. The minor must have attained majority, or the ratification would itself be regarded as voidable.

Contracts That Minors Cannot Avoid

Statutes in many states deprive a minor of the right to avoid an educational loan;[6] a contract for medical care; a contract made while running a business; a contract approved by a court; a contract made in performance of a legal duty; and a contract relating to bank accounts, insurance policies, or corporate stock.

Liability of Third Person for a Minor's Contract

The question arises as to whether parents are bound by the contract of their minor child. The question of whether a person cosigning a minor's contract is bound if the contract is avoided also arises.

[5] *Fletcher v. Marshall*, 632 N.E.2d 1105 (Ill. App. 1994).
[6] A Model Student Capacity to Borrow Act makes educational loans binding on minors in Arizona, Mississippi, New Mexico, North Dakota, Oklahoma, and Washington. This act was reclassified from a uniform act to a model act by the Commissioners on Uniform State Law, indicating that uniformity was viewed as unimportant and that the matter was primarily local in character.

Liability of Parent. Ordinarily, a parent is not liable on a contract made by a minor child. The parent may be liable, however, if the child is acting as the agent of the parent in making the contract. Also, the parent is liable to a seller for the reasonable value of necessaries supplied by the seller to the child if the parent had deserted the child.

Liability of Cosigner. When the minor makes a contract, another person, such as a parent or a friend, may sign along with the minor to make the contract more acceptable to the third person.

With respect to the other contracting party, the cosigner is bound independently of the minor. Consequently, if the minor disaffirms the contract, the cosigner remains bound by it. When the debt to the creditor is actually paid, the obligation of the cosigner is discharged.

If the minor disaffirms a sales contract but does not return the goods, the cosigner remains liable for the purchase price.

13-1c Mentally Incompetent Persons

A person with a mental disorder may be so disabled as to lack capacity to make a contract. An individual seeking to avoid the consequences of a contract due to incompetency must demonstrate that at the time the agreement was executed he or she was suffering from a mental illness or defect, which rendered the party incapable of comprehending the nature of the transaction, or that by reason of mental illness the party was unable to control his or her conduct.[7] **For Example,** a guardian established that Ms. Brunson suffered from a mental illness at the time the challenged mortgage documents were executed, and the contract was set aside by the court.[8] However, where a guardian's evidence was insufficient to demonstrate that at the time two mortgage transactions occurred, one in 1999 for $212,000 and a second in 2003 for $7,628.08, that Mr. and Mrs. Haedrich were incompetent or that Washington Mutual Bank knew or was put on notice of their purported incapacity, the court refused to vacate the judgments of foreclosure.[9]

Effect of Incompetency

An incompetent person may ordinarily avoid a contract in the same manner as a minor. Upon the removal of the disability (that is, upon becoming competent), the formerly incompetent person can either ratify or disaffirm the contract.

A mentally incompetent person or his estate is liable for the reasonable value of all necessaries furnished that individual.

A current trend in the law is to treat an incompetent person's contract as binding when its terms and the surrounding circumstances are reasonable and the person is unable to restore the other contracting party to the status quo ante.

CASE SUMMARY

Friends Should Tell Friends about Medical Leaves

FACTS: Wilcox Manufacturing Group, Inc., did business under the name of Superior Automation Co., and Howard Wilcox served as Superior's president. As part of a loan "lease agreement" of $50,000 executed on December 5, 2000, Superior was to repay Marketing Services of Indiana (MSI) $67,213.80 over the course of 60 months. Wilcox gave a

---

[7] *Horrell v. Horrell*, 900 N.Y.S.2d 666 (2d Dept. 2010).

[8] In re *Doar*, 900 N.Y.S.2d 593 (Sup. Ct. Queens Co., Dec. 18, 2009).

[9] *JP Morgan Chase Bank v. Haedrich*, 918 N.Y.S.2d 398 (Sup. Ct. Nassau County, Oct. 15, 2010).

Friends Should Tell Friends about Medical Leaves continued

personal guarantee for full and prompt payment. Wilcox had been a patient of psychiatrist Dr. Shaun Wood since May 21, 1999, and was diagnosed as suffering from bipolar disorder during the period from June 2000 to January 2001. On June 9, 2000, Wilcox told Dr. Wood he was having problems functioning at work, and Dr. Wood determined that Wilcox was experiencing lithium toxicity, which lasted for 10 months, during which time he suffered from impaired cognitive functions that limited his capacity to understand the nature and quality of his actions and judgments. Superior made monthly payments though to October 28, 2003, and the balance owed at that time was $33,031.37. MSI sued Wilcox personally and the corporation for breach of contract. The defendants raised the defense of lack of capacity and contended that they were not liable on the loan signed by the corporate president when he was incapacitated.

DECISION: Judgment for MSI. The acts or deeds of a person of unsound mind whose condition has not been judicially ascertained and who is not under guardianship are voidable and not absolutely void. The acts are subject to ratification or disaffirmance on removal of the disability. The latest Wilcox could have been experiencing the effects of lithium toxicity was October 2001. Wilcox thus regained his capacity by that date. No attempt was made to disaffirm the contract. Rather, monthly payments continued to be made for a year and one-half before the payments ceased. The contract was thus ratified by the conduct of the president of Superior after he recovered his ability to understand the nature of the contract. [*Wilcox Manufacturing, Inc., v. Marketing Services of Indiana, Inc.,* **832 N.E.2d 559 (Ind. App. 2005)**]

Appointment of Guardian

If a court appoints a guardian for the incompetent person, a contract made by that person before the appointment may be ratified or, in some cases, disaffirmed by the guardian. If the incompetent person makes a contract after a guardian has been appointed, the contract is void and not merely voidable.

13-1d **Intoxicated Persons**

The capacity of a party to contract and the validity of the contract are not affected by the party's being impaired by alcohol at the time of making the contract so long as the party knew that a contract was being made.

If the degree of intoxication is such that a person does not know that a contract is being made, the contract is voidable by that person. On becoming sober, the individual may avoid or rescind the contract. However, an unreasonable delay in taking steps to set aside a known contract entered into while intoxicated may bar the intoxicated person from asserting this right.[10]

Excessive intoxication is a viable defense to contracts arising between casinos and their patrons. Thus, when a casino comes to court to enforce a marker debt against a patron, it seeks to enforce a contractual debt, and the patron is entitled to raise the common law defense that his capacity to contract was impaired by voluntary intoxication.[11]

The courts treat impairment caused by the use of drugs the same as impairment caused by the excessive use of alcohol.

CPA 13-2 **Mistake**

The validity of a contract may be affected by the fact that one or both of the parties made a mistake. In some cases, the mistake may be caused by the misconduct of one of the parties.

---

[10] *Diedrich v. Diedrich*, 424 N.W.2d 580 (Minn. App. 1988).
[11] See *Adamar of New Jersey v. Luber*, 2011 WL 1325978 (D. N.J. Mar. 30, 2011).

13-2a Unilateral Mistake

A *unilateral mistake*—that is, a mistake by only one of the parties—as to a fact does not affect the contract when the mistake is unknown to the other contracting party.[12] When a contract is made on the basis of a quoted price, the validity of the contract is not affected by the fact that the party furnishing the quotation made a mathematical mistake in computing the price if there was no reason for the other party to recognize that there had been a mistake.[13] The party making the mistake may avoid the contract if the other contracting party knew or should have known of the mistake.

CASE SUMMARY

Bumper Sticker: "Mistakes Happen!" (or words to that effect)

FACTS: Lipton-U City, LLC (Lipton), and Shurgard Storage Centers discussed the sale of a self-storage facility for approximately $7 million. Lipton became concerned about an existing environmental condition and, as a result, the parties agreed to a lease with an option to buy rather than an outright sale. The contract specified a 10-year lease with an annual rent starting at $636,000 based on a property valuation of $7 million. Section 2.4 of the contract contained the purchase option. Shurgard representatives circulated an e-mail with a copy to Lipton representatives that a purchase option price would be based on six months of *annualized* net operating income. When the lease was submitted to Lipton, inexplicably any language regarding multiplying by 2 or annualizing the net income was omitted. Donn Lipton announced to his attorneys that the lease reflected his successful negotiation of a purchase option based on six months of *unannualized* net operating income. Eight months after signing the lease, Lipton sought to exercise the purchase option under Section 2.4 and stated a price of $2,918,103. Shurgard rejected the offer and filed suit for rescission, citing the misunderstanding about the price terms.

DECISION: Judgment for Shurgard. Under state law, if a material mistake made by one party is known to the other party or is of such a character or circumstances that the other party should know of it, the mistaken party has a right to rescission. Lipton knew or should have known of the mistake of the lessor (Shurgard) in believing that the purchase price would be based on a full year of net operating income rather than six months of net operating income. Lipton was notified by e-mail that the six-month figure was to be annualized and knew that the property was valued at approximately $7 million. [*Shurgard Storage Centers v. Lipton-U City, LLC*, 394 F.3d 1041 (8th Cir. 2005)]

13-2b Mutual Mistake

When both parties enter into a contract under a mutually mistaken understanding concerning a basic assumption of fact or law on which the contract is made, the contract is voidable by the adversely affected party if the mistake has a material effect on the agreed exchange.[14]

A contract based on *a mutual mistake in judgment* is not voidable by the adversely affected party. **For Example,** if both parties believe that a colt is not fast enough to develop into a competitive race horse and effect a sale accordingly, when the animal later develops into the winner of the Preakness as a three-year-old, the seller cannot rescind the contract based on mutual mistake because the mutual mistake was a mistake in judgment. In contrast, when two parties to a contract believe a cow to be barren at the time they contract for its sale, but before delivery of the animal to the buyer, it is discovered that the assumption was mistaken, such is a mutual mistake of fact making the contract void.[15]

---

[12] *Truck South Inc. v. Patel*, 528 S.E.2d 424 (S.C. 2000).
[13] *Procan Construction Co. v. Oceanside Development Corp.*, 539 N.Y.S.2d 437 (App. Div. 2d 1989).
[14] See *Browning v. Howerton*, 966 P.2d 367 (Wash. App. 1998).
[15] See *Sherwood v. Walker*, 66 Mich. 568 (1887).

13-2c Mistake in the Transcription or Printing of the Contract: Reformation

reformation—remedy by which a written instrument is corrected when it fails to express the actual intent of both parties because of fraud, accident, or mistake.

In some instances, the parties make an oral agreement, and in the process of committing it to writing or printing it from a manuscript, a phrase, term, or segment is inadvertently left out of the final, signed document. The aggrieved party may petition the court to **reform** the contract to reflect the actual agreement of the parties. However, the burden of proof is heightened to clear and convincing evidence that such a mistake was made. **For Example,** Jewell Coke Co. used an illustration to explain a complex pricing formula in its negotiations with the ArcelMittal steel mill in Cleveland, Ohio, for a long-term contract for the supply of blast furnace coke. The multiplier in the illustration was the actual intent of the parties, according to ArcelMittal, but during the drafting process the multiplier was accidently inverted, resulting in an overpayment of $100,000,000 when discovered, and which potentially could result in an overpayment of over $1 billion over the life of the contract. If proven, the court will reform the contract to reflect the intentions of the parties at the time the contract was made.[16]

13-3 Deception

One of the parties may have been misled by a fraudulent statement. In such situations, there is no true or genuine assent to the contract, and it is voidable at the innocent party's option.

FIGURE 13-1   Avoidance of Contract

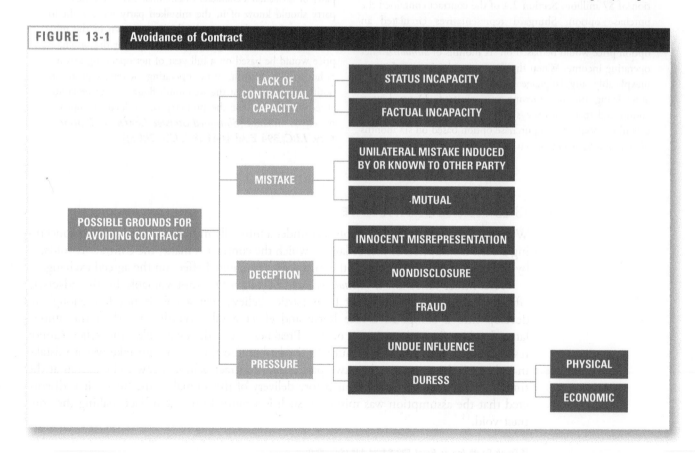

---

[16] *ArcelMittal Cleveland, Inc. v. Jewell Coke Co,* 750 F. Supp. 2d 839 (N.D. Ohio 2010).

13-3a **Intentional Misrepresentation**

Fraud is a generic term embracing all multifarious means that human ingenuity can devise and that are resorted to by one individual to get advantage over another. It is classified in the law as a *tort*. However, where a party is induced into making a contract by a material misrepresentation of fact, this form of fraudulent activity adversely affects the genuineness of the assent of the innocent party, and this type of fraud is the focus of our discussion in the chapters on contracts.

13-3b **Fraud**

fraud–making of a false statement of a past or existing fact, with knowledge of its falsity or with reckless indifference as to its truth, with the intent to cause another to rely thereon, and such person does rely thereon and is harmed thereby.

Fraud is the making of a material misrepresentation (or false statement) of fact with (1) knowledge of its falsity or reckless indifference to its truth, (2) the intent that the listener rely on it, (3) the result that the listener does so rely, and (4) the consequence that the listener is harmed.[17]

To prove fraud, there must be a material misrepresentation of fact. Such a misrepresentation is one that is likely to induce a reasonable person to assent to a contract. **For Example,** Traci Hanson-Suminski purchased a used Honda Civic from Arlington Acura for $10,899. On a test drive with salesperson Mike Dobin, Traci noticed a vibration in the steering wheel and asked if the car had been in an accident. Dobin said, "No, it's fine." The dealer put new tires on the car and Traci bought it. Traci testified that she would not have purchased the car if she had known it had been in an accident. Eight months later when she sought to trade the car for another car, she was shown a Carfax Vehicle History Report, which indicated the car had been in an accident. The dealer testified that all its sales associates are trained to respond to questions about vehicle history with "I don't know." It asserted that Dobin's statement was mere puffery. The court found that Dobin's statement was a material misrepresentation of the car's history, inducing the plaintiff to purchase the car. It rejected outright the dealer's assertion of puffery, which it defined as meaningless superlatives that no reasonable person would take seriously.[18]

Statement of Opinion or Value

Ordinarily, matters of opinion of value or opinions about future events are not regarded as fraudulent. Forecasts about the future state of financial or real estate markets must be regarded not as fact, but as predictions or speculations.

A statement of opinion may be fraudulent when the speaker knows of past or present facts that make the opinion false. **For Example,** Biff Williams, the sales manager of Abrasives International (AI), sold an exclusive dealership selling AI products to Fred Farkas for $100,000 down and a 3 percent royalty on all gross proceeds. Williams told Farkas, "You have the potential to earn $300,000 to $400,000 a year in this territory." He later added, "We have four dealerships making that kind of money today." Farkas was thus persuaded by the business potential of the territory and executed the purchase contract. He later found out that AI had a total of just four distributorships at that time, and that the actual earnings of the highest producer was $43,000. Assertions of opinions about the future profit potential alone may not amount to fraud, but the assertion of present fact—that four dealerships were presently earning $300,000 to $400,000 a year—was a material misstatement of fact that made the forecast sales potential for Farkas's territory a

---

[17] *Maack v. Resource Design & Construction, Inc.*, 875 P.2d 570 (Utah 1994); *Bortz v. Noon*, 729 A.2d 555 (Pa. 1999).
[18] *Hanson-Suminski v. Rohrman Midwest Motors Inc.*, 858 N.E.2d 194 (Ill. App. 2008).

material misstatement of fact as well. Because there were reliance and damages, Farkas can rescind the contract based on fraud and recover all damages resulting from it.[19]

CASE SUMMARY

Remember This One: Mere Opinions Are Not Actionable at All!

FACTS: In approximately July 2005 a loan broker and an appraiser working for a subsidiary of Bank of America appraised the Cansinos home at a fair market value of $620,000. Based on that appraisal and other representations by lending personnel, the Cansinos elected to refinance their home with a $496,000 adjustable rate mortgage. Lending personnel told them their home would appreciate and they would be able to sell or refinance the home at a later date before having to make higher monthly loan payments. In 2010, the Cansinos discovered that their home was valued between $350,000 and $400,000. Soon thereafter they stopped making payments on the 2005 loan. As of March 2012 the monthly payments were approximately $1,960, the balance due on the loan was approximately $626,000, and the fair market value of the home was approximately $350,000. The trial court dismissed the Cansinos fraud action against B of A, and they appealed.

DECISION: Judgment against the Cansinos. Concerning B of A's representation on the future appreciation of the Cansinos' home, such statements or predictions regarding future events are deemed to be mere opinions, which are not actionable. And, any financial market forecast must be regarded not as a fact but as prediction or speculation. While the Casinos state the home was valued between $350,000 and $400,000 in 2010, this does not support their claim that the 2005 appraisal of $620,000 was a misrepresentation. [*Cansinos v. Bank of America,* **169 Cal. Rptr. 3d 619 (Cal. App. 2014)**]

Justifiable Reliance on Statement

A fraudulent statement made by one party has no importance unless the other party relies on the statement's truth. **For Example,** after making thorough tests of Nagel Company's pump, Allstate Services Company ordered 100 pumps. It later sued Nagel on the ground that advertising statements made about the pumps were false. Allstate Services cannot impose fraud liability on Nagel for the advertisements, even if they were false, because it had not relied on them in making the purchase but had acted on the basis of its own tests.

Disclaimer of reliance clauses are common in commerce these days. Trusting the honesty of salespersons or their disarming statements, an individual may knowingly or obliviously agree in a sales agreement containing a disclaimer of reliance clause that no representations have been made to him or her, while at the same time believing and relying upon representations, which in fact have been made and in fact are false and but for which the individual would not have made the agreement. Ordinarily, purchasers cannot assert justifiable reliance on statements made by sellers that directly contradict clear and specific terms of their written contracts.[20]

---

[19] The Federal Trade Commission and state agencies have franchise disclosure rules that will penalize the franchisor in this case. See Chapter 40.

[20] But see *Italian Cowboy Partners, Ltd. v. Prudential Insurance,* 341 S.W.3d 323 (Tex. 2011) where a split decision of the Texas Supreme Court determined that the following contract language was not a disclaimer of reliance to negate the "justifiable reliance" element of a fraud claim.

> *Tenant acknowledges that neither Landlord nor Landlord's agents, employees or contractors have made any representations or promises with respect to the Site, the Shopping Center or this lease except as expressly set forth herein.*

The court determined that the property manager's representations to the future tenant that the building was problem free; no problems had been experienced by the prior tenant; and the building was a perfect restaurant site were false statements of fact known to be false when made. Testimony indicated that the manager herself had personally experienced a sewer gas odor in the prior tenant's restaurant she described as "almost unbearable" and "ungodly."

CASE SUMMARY

Are Disclaimer of Reliance Clauses a License to Lie?

FACTS: David Sarif and seven other purchasers (Purchasers) each bought a unit at the 26-story Twelve Atlantic Station (Twelve) condominiums in 2005 and 2006. They sued the developers and the brokers for fraud in the inducement and negligent misrepresentation. They alleged that at the time of their purchases, the developers were advertising "spectacular city views" of Atlanta while they had already undertaken to develop the 46-story Atlantic Station tower directly across the street, and that their brokers were advising the Purchasers that any future development to the south of Twelve would be low- to mid-rise office buildings. Purchasers allege that they paid substantial premiums for their views of the city from the south side of the building, which is now blocked by the 46-story building. Each Purchaser signed an agreement containing a provision stating that "[t]he views from and natural light available to the Unit may change over time due to, among other circumstances, additional development and the removal or addition of landscaping"; a disclaimer at the top of the first page as required by the Georgia Condominium Act stating that "ORAL REPRESENTATIONS CANNOT BE RELIED UPON AS CORRECTLY STATING THE REPRESENTATIONS OF SELLER"; an express disclaimer in which Purchasers affirmed that they did not rely upon any representations or statements of the brokers; and a comprehensive merger clause.

DECISION: Set forth in the written contract of the parties, all of the Purchasers signed agreements that expressly stated that views may change over time, and oral representations of the sellers could not be relied on. Justifiable reliance is an essential element of a fraud or negligent misrepresentation claim. Since the Purchasers are estopped from relying on representations outside their agreements, they cannot sustain a case that requires justifiable reliance. [***Novare Group, Inc. v. Sarif,*** 718 S.E.2d 304 (Ga. 2011)]

Proof of Harm

For an individual to recover damages for fraud, proof of harm to that individual is required. The injured party may recover the actual losses suffered as a result of the fraud as well as punitive damages when the fraud is gross or oppressive. The injured party has the right to have the court order the rescission or cancellation of the contract that has been induced by fraud.[21]

13-3c Negligent Misrepresentation

While fraud requires the critical element of a known or recklessly made falsity, a claim of negligent misrepresentation contains similar elements except it is predicated on a negligently made false statement. That is, the speaker failed to exercise due care regarding material information communicated to the listener but did not intend to deceive. When the negligent misrepresentation of a material fact that the listener relies on results in harm to the listener, the contract is voidable at the option of the injured party. If fraud is proven, as opposed to misrepresentation, recovery of punitive damages in addition to actual damages can occur. Because it may be difficult to prove the intentional falsity required for fraud, it is common for a lawsuit to allege both a claim of fraud and a claim of negligent misrepresentation. **For Example,** Marshall Armstrong worked for Fred Collins, owner of Collins Entertainment, Inc., a conglomerate that owns and operates video games. Collins Entertainment's core product, video poker, was hurt by a court ruling that prohibited cash payouts, which adversely affected its business and resulted in a debt of $13 to $20 million to SouthTrust bank. Chief operating officer Armstrong, on his

---

[21] *Paden v. Murray,* 523 S.E.2d 75 (Ga. App. 2000).

own time, came up with the idea of modifying bingo machines as a new venture. To exploit this idea, Collins agreed to form a corporation called Skillpins Inc., that was unencumbered by the SouthTrust debt and to give Armstrong a 10 percent ownership interest. After a period, with some 300 Skillpins machines producing income, Armstrong discovered the revenues from the new venture on the debt-laden Collins Entertainment profit and loss statement, not that of Skillpins, Inc. Armstrong's suit for both fraud and intentional misrepresentation was successful. In addition to actual damages, he received $1.8 million in punitive damages for fraud.[22]

13-3d Nondisclosure

Under certain circumstances, nondisclosure serves to make a contract voidable, especially when the nondisclosure consists of active concealment.

General Rule of Nonliability

Ordinarily, a party to a contract has no duty to volunteer information to the other party. **For Example,** if Fox does not ask Tehan any questions, Tehan is not under any duty to make a full statement of material facts. Consequently, the nondisclosure of information that is not asked for does not impose fraud liability or impair the validity of a contract.

CASE SUMMARY

Welcome to the Seesaw: Buyer versus Seller

FACTS: Dalarna Management Corporation owned a building constructed on a pier on a lake. There were repeated difficulties with rainwater leaking into the building, and water damage was visible in the interior of the building. Dalarna made a contract to sell the building to Curran. Curran made several inspections of the building and had the building inspected twice by a licensed engineer. The engineer reported there were signs of water leaks. Curran assigned his contract to Puget Sound Service Corporation, which then purchased the building from Dalarna. Puget Sound spent approximately $118,000 attempting to stop the leaks. Puget Sound then sued Dalarna for damages, claiming that Dalarna's failure to disclose the extent of the water leakage problem constituted fraud.

DECISION: Judgment for Dalarna. Curran was aware there was a water leakage problem, and therefore the burden was on the buyer to ask questions to determine the extent of the problem. There was no duty on the seller to volunteer the extent of the water damage merely because it had been a continuing problem that was more than just a simple leak. The court reached this conclusion because the law "balances the harshness of the former rule of caveat emptor [let the buyer beware] with the equally undesirable alternative of courts standing in loco parentis [in the place of a parent] to parties transacting business." [*Puget Sound Service Corp. v. Dalarna Management Corp.*, 752 P.2d 1353 (Wash. App. 1988)]

Exceptions

The following exceptions to the general rule of nonliability for nondisclosure exist.

Unknown Defect or Condition. A duty may exist in some states for a seller who knows of a serious defect or condition to disclose that information to the other party where the defect or condition is unknown to the other person and is of such a nature that it is unlikely that the other person would discover it. However, a defendant who had no knowledge of the defect cannot be held liable for failure to disclose it.[23]

---

[22] *Armstrong v. Collins*, 621 S.E.2d 368 (S.C. App. 2005).
[23] *Nesbitt v. Dunn*, 672 So. 2d 226 (La. App. 1996).

confidential relationship–
relationship in which, because of the legal status of the parties or their respective physical or mental conditions or knowledge, one party places full confidence and trust in the other.

Confidential Relationship. If parties stand in a **confidential relationship,** failure to disclose information may be regarded as fraudulent. **For Example,** in an attorney-client relationship,[24] the attorney has a duty to reveal anything that is material to the client's interest when dealing with the client. The attorney's silence has the same legal consequence as a knowingly made false statement that there was no material fact to be told the client.

Active Concealment. Nondisclosure may be more than the passive failure to volunteer information. It may consist of a positive act of hiding information from the other party by physical concealment, or it may consist of knowingly or recklessly furnishing the wrong information. Such conduct constitutes fraud. **For Example,** when Nigel wanted to sell his house, he covered the wooden cellar beams with plywood to hide extensive termite damage. He sold the house to Kuehne, who sued Nigel for damages on later discovering the termite damage. Nigel claimed he had no duty to volunteer information about the termites, but by covering the damage with plywood, he committed active fraud as if he had made a false statement that there were no termites.

13-4 Pressure

What appears to be an agreement may not in fact be voluntary because one of the parties entered into it as the result of undue influence or physical or economic duress.

CPA

13-4a Undue Influence

An aged parent may entrust all business affairs to a trusted child; a disabled person may rely on a nurse; a client may follow implicitly whatever an attorney recommends. The relationship may be such that for practical purposes, one person is helpless in the hands of the other. When such a confidential relationship exists, it is apparent that the parent, the disabled person, or the client is not exercising free will in making a contract suggested by the child, nurse, or attorney but is merely following the will of the other person. Because of the great possibility of unfair advantage, the law presumes that the dominating person exerts **undue influence** on the other person whenever the dominating person obtains any benefit from a contract made with the dominated person.[25] The contract is then voidable. It may be set aside by the dominated person unless the dominating person can prove that, at the time the contract was made, no unfair advantage had been taken.

undue influence–
influence that is asserted upon another person by one who dominates that person.

The class of confidential relationships is not well defined. It ordinarily includes the relationships of parent and child, guardian and ward, physician and patient, and attorney and client, and any other relationship of trust and confidence in which one party exercises a control or influence over another.

Whether undue influence exists is a difficult question for courts (ordinarily juries) to determine. The law does not regard every influence as undue.

An essential element of undue influence is that the person making the contract does not exercise free will. In the absence of a recognized type of confidential relationship, such as that between parent and child, courts are likely to take the attitude that the person who claims to have been dominated was merely persuaded and there was therefore no undue influence.

[24] In re *Boss Trust,* 487 N.W.2d 256 (Minn. App. 1992).
[25] *Ayers v. Shaffer,* 748 S.E.2d 83 (Va. 2013).

CASE SUMMARY

Cards and Small Talk Sometimes Make the Sale

FACTS: John Lentner owned the farm adjacent to the Schefers. He moved off the farm to a nursing home in 1999. In the fall of 2000, Kristine Schefers visited Lentner at the nursing home some 15 times, engaging in small talk and watching him play cards. In the spring of 2001, Lentner agreed to sell his farm to Kristine and her husband Thomas for $50,000 plus $10,000 for machinery and tools. Kristine drove Lentner to the bank to get the deed from his safe deposit box. She also took him to the abstractor who drafted the transfer documents. Soon after the sale, Earl Fisher was appointed special conservator of Lentner. Fisher sought to set aside the transaction, asserting that Kristine's repeated visits to the nursing home and her failure to involve Lentner's other family members in the transaction unduly influenced Lentner.

DECISION: Judgment for Thomas and Kristine Schefers. Undue influence is shown when the person making the contract ceased to act of his own free volition and became a mere puppet of the wielder of that influence. Mere speculation alone that Lentner was a "puppet" acting according to the wishes of Schefers is insufficient to set aside the sale. Undue influence was not established. [*Fisher v. Schefers,* **656 N.W.2d 592 (Minn. App. 2003)**]

CPA

13-4b Duress

physical duress—threat of physical harm to person or property.

economic duress—threat of financial loss.

duress—conduct that deprives the victim of free will and that generally gives the victim the right to set aside any transaction entered into under such circumstances.

A party may enter into a contract to avoid a threatened danger. The danger threatened may be a physical harm to person or property, called **physical duress,** or it may be a threat of financial loss, called **economic duress.**

Physical Duress

A person makes a contract under **duress** when there is such violence or threat of violence that the person is deprived of free will and makes the contract to avoid harm. The threatened harm may be directed either at a near relative of the contracting party or against the contracting party. If a contract is made under duress, the resulting agreement is voidable at the victim's election.

Agreements made to bring an end to mass disorder or violence are ordinarily not binding contracts because they were obtained by duress.

One may not void a contract on grounds of duress merely because it was entered into with great reluctance and proves to be very disadvantageous to that individual.[26]

Economic Duress

Economic duress is a condition in which one is induced by a wrongful act or threat of another to make a contract under circumstances that deprive one of the exercise of his own free will.[27] **For Example,** Richard Case, an importer of parts used to manufacture high-quality mountain bicycles, had a contractual duty to supply Katahdin Manufacturing Company's needs for specifically manufactured stainless steel brakes for the 2016 season. Katahdin's president, Bill Read, was in constant contact with Case about the delay in delivery of the parts and the adverse consequences it was having on Katahdin's relationship with its retailers. Near the absolute deadline for meeting orders for the 2016 season, Case called Read and said, "I've got the parts in, but I'm not sure I'll be able to send

---

[26] *Miller v. Calhoun/Johnson Co,* 497 S.E.2d 397 (Ga. App. 1998).
[27] *Hurd v. Wildman, Harrold, Allen, and Dixon,* 707 N.E.2d 609 (Ill. App. 1999).

them to you because I'm working on next year's contracts, and you haven't signed yours yet." Case's 2017 contract increased the cost of parts by 38 percent. Read signed the contract to obtain the delivery but later found a new supplier and gave notice to Case of this action. The defense of economic duress would apply in a breach of contract suit brought by Case on the 2017 contract because Case implicitly threatened to commit the wrongful act of not delivering parts due under the prior contract, and Katahdin Company had no means available to obtain parts elsewhere to prevent the economic loss that would occur if it did not receive those parts.

Make the Connection

Summary

An agreement that otherwise appears to be a contract may not be binding because one of the parties lacks contractual capacity. In such a case, the contract is ordinarily voidable at the election of the party who lacks contractual capacity. In some cases, the contract is void. Ordinarily, contractual incapacity is the inability, for mental or physical reasons, to understand that a contract is being made and to understand its general terms and nature. This is typically the case when it is claimed that incapacity exists because of insanity, intoxication, or drug use. The incapacity of minors arises because society discriminates in favor of that class to protect them from unwise contracts.

The age of majority is 18. Minors can disaffirm most contracts. If a minor received anything from the other party, the minor, on avoiding the contract, must return what had been received from the other party if the minor still has it.

When a minor disaffirms a contract for a necessary, the minor must pay the reasonable value of any benefit received.

Minors only are liable for their contracts. Parents of a minor are not liable on the minor's contracts merely because they are the parents. Frequently, an adult enters into the contract as a coparty of the minor and is then liable without regard to whether the minor has avoided the contract.

The contract of an insane person is voidable to much the same extent as the contract of a minor. An important distinction is that if a guardian has been appointed for the insane person, a contract made by the insane person is void, not merely voidable.

An intoxicated person lacks contractual capacity if the intoxication is such that the person does not understand that a contract is being made.

The consent of a party to an agreement is not genuine or voluntary in certain cases of mistake, deception, or pressure. When this occurs, what appears to be a contract can be avoided by the victim of such circumstances or conduct.

As to mistake, it is necessary to distinguish between unilateral mistakes that are unknown to the other contracting party and those that are known. Mistakes that are unknown to the other party usually do not affect the binding character of the agreement. A unilateral mistake of which the other contracting party has knowledge or has reason to know makes the contract avoidable by the victim of the mistake.

The deception situation may be one of negligent misrepresentation or fraud. The law ordinarily does not attach any significance to nondisclosure. Contrary to this rule, there is a duty to volunteer information when a confidential relationship exists between the possessor of the knowledge and the other contracting party.

When concealment goes beyond mere silence and consists of actively taking steps to hide the truth, the conduct may be classified as fraud. A statement of opinion or value cannot ordinarily be the basis for fraud liability.

The voluntary character of a contract may be lacking because the agreement had been obtained by pressure. This may range from undue influence through the array of threats of extreme economic loss (called *economic duress*) to the threat of physical force that would cause serious personal injury or damage to property (called *physical duress*). When the voluntary character of an agreement has been destroyed by deception, or pressure, the victim may avoid or rescind the contract or may obtain money damages from the wrongdoer.

Learning Outcomes

After studying this chapter, you should be able to clearly explain:

13-1 Contractual Capacity

LO.1 Define contractual capacity

See the example where Jacqueline, age 22, did not understand parts of a storage contract, page 243.

LO.2 Explain the extent and effect of avoidance of a contract by a minor

See the *Adorian Deck* example where the creator of a Twitter feed, a minor, disaffirmed his joint venture contract, page 244.

See the *Prince George's Hospital* case where a minor had to pay for medical necessaries, page 246.

13-2 Mistake

LO.3 Distinguish unilateral mistakes and mutual mistakes

See the *Shurgard Storage* case where the "other party" should have known of the unilateral mistake, page 249.

See the *Jewell Coke Co.* example of a remedy for a billion dollar mistake, page 250.

See the example of the mutual mistake of fact regarding the fertility of a cow, page 249.

13-3 Deception

LO.4 Explain the difference between intentional misrepresentation, negligent misrepresentation, and puffery

See the example of the purchase of the used Honda, where the misrepresentation was found to be fraud, not puffery, page 251.

See the *Novare Group, Inc.*, decision on the enforceability of disclaimer-of-liability clauses, page 253.

13-4 Pressure

LO.5 Explain the difference between undue influence and duress

See the *Fisher v. Schefers* undue influence litigation, page 256.

See the Katahdin bicycle example on economic duress, page 256.

Key Terms

confidential relationship	fraud	status quo ante
contractual capacity	necessaries	undue influence
duress	physical duress	
economic duress	reformation	

Questions and Case Problems

1. Lester purchased a used automobile from MacKintosh Motors. He asked the seller if the car had ever been in a wreck. The MacKintosh salesperson had never seen the car before that morning and knew nothing of its history but quickly answered Lester's question by stating: "No. It has never been in a wreck." In fact, the auto had been seriously damaged in a wreck and, although repaired, was worth much less than the value it would have had if there had been no wreck. When Lester learned the truth, he sued MacKintosh Motors and the salesperson for damages for fraud. They raised the defense that the salesperson did not know the statement was false and had not intended to deceive Lester. Did the conduct of the salesperson constitute fraud?

2. Helen, age 17, wanted to buy a Harley-Davidson "Sportster" motorcycle. She did not have the funds to pay cash but persuaded the dealer to sell the cycle to her on credit. The dealer did so partly because Helen said that she was 22 and showed the dealer an identification card that falsely stated her age as 22. Helen drove the motorcycle away. A few days later, she damaged it and then returned it to the dealer and stated that she disaffirmed the contract because she was a minor. The dealer said that she could not because (1) she had misrepresented her age and (2) the motorcycle was damaged. Can she avoid the contract?

3. Paden signed an agreement dated May 28 to purchase the Murrays' home. The Murrays accepted Paden's offer the following day, and the sale closed on June 27. Paden and his family moved into the home on July 14, 1997. Paden had the home inspected prior to closing. The report listed four minor repairs needed by the home, the cost of which

was less than $500. Although these repairs had not been completed at the time of closing, Paden decided to go through with the purchase. After moving into the home, Paden discovered a number of allegedly new defects, including a wooden foundation, electrical problems, and bat infestation. The sales agreement allowed extensive rights to inspect the property. The agreement provided:

> *Buyer … shall have the right to enter the property at Buyer's expense and at reasonable times … to thoroughly inspect, examine, test, and survey the Property…. Buyer shall have the right to request that Seller repair defects in the Property by providing Seller within 12 days from Binding Agreement Date with a copy of inspection report(s) and a written amendment to this agreement setting forth the defects in the report which Buyer requests to be repaired and/or replaced…. If Buyer does not timely present the written amendment and inspection report, Buyer shall be deemed to have accepted the Property "as is."*

Paden sued the Murrays for fraudulent concealment and breach of the sales agreement. If Mr. Murray told Paden on May 26 that the house had a concrete foundation, would this be fraud? Decide. [*Paden v. Murray*, 523 S.E.2d 75 (Ga. App.)]

4. High-Tech Collieries borrowed money from Holland. High-Tech later refused to be bound by the loan contract, claiming the contract was not binding because it had been obtained by duress. The evidence showed that the offer to make the loan was made on a take-it-or-leave-it basis. Was the defense of duress valid? [*Holland v. High-Tech Collieries, Inc.*, 911 F. Supp. 1021 (N.D. W.Va.)]

5. Thomas Bell, a minor, went to work in the Pittsburgh beauty parlor of Sam Pankas and agreed that when he left the employment, he would not work in or run a beauty parlor business within a 10-mile radius of downtown Pittsburgh for a period of two years. Contrary to this provision, Bell and another employee of Pankas's opened a beauty shop three blocks from Pankas's shop and advertised themselves as Pankas's former employees. Pankas sued Bell to stop the breach of the noncompetition, or restrictive, covenant. Bell claimed that he was not bound because he was a minor when he had agreed to the covenant. Was he bound by the covenant? [*Pankas v. Bell*, 198 A.2d 312 (Pa.)]

6. Aldrich and Co. sold goods to Donovan on credit. The amount owed grew steadily, and finally Aldrich refused to sell any more to Donovan unless Donovan signed a promissory note for the amount due. Donovan did not want to but signed the note because he had no money and needed more goods. When Aldrich brought an action to enforce the note, Donovan claimed that the note was not binding because it had been obtained by economic duress. Was he correct? [*Aldrich & Co. v. Donovan*, 778 P.2d 397 (Mont.)]

7. James Fitl purchased a 1952 Mickey Mantle Topps baseball card from baseball card dealer Mark Strek for $17,750 and placed it in a safe deposit box. Two years later, he had the card appraised, and he was told that the card had been refinished and trimmed, which rendered it valueless. Fitl sued Strek and testified that he had relied on Strek's position as a sports card dealer and on his representations that the baseball card was authentic. Strek contends that Fitl waited too long to give him notice of the defects that would have enabled Strek to contact the person who sold him the card and obtain relief. Strek asserts that he therefore is not liable. Advise Fitl concerning possible legal theories that apply to his case. How would you decide the case? [See *Fitl v. Strek*, 690 N.W.2d 605 (Neb.)]

8. Willingham proposed to obtain an investment property for the Tschiras at a "fair market price," lease it back from them, and pay the Tschiras a guaranteed return through a management contract. Using a shell corporation, The Wellingham Group bought a commercial property in Nashville for $774,000 on December 14, and the very same day sold the building to the Tschiras for $1,985,000. The title insurance policy purchased for the Tschiras property by Willingham was for just $774,000. Willingham believes that the deal was legitimate in that they "guaranteed" a return on the investment. The Tschiras disagree. In a lawsuit against Willingham, what theory will the Tschiras rely on? Decide. [*Tschiras v. Willingham*, 133 F.3d 1077 (6th Cir.)]

9. Blubaugh was a district manager of Schlumberger Well Services. Turner was an executive employee of Schlumberger. Blubaugh was told that he would be fired unless he chose to resign. He was also told that if he would resign and release the company and its employees from all claims for wrongful discharge, he would receive about $5,000 in addition to his regular severance pay of approximately $25,000 and would

be given job-relocation counseling. He resigned, signed the release, and received about $40,000 and job counseling. Some time thereafter, he brought an action claiming that he had been wrongfully discharged. He claimed that the release did not protect the defendants because the release had been obtained by economic duress. Were the defendants protected by the release? [*Blubaugh v. Turner*, 842 P.2d 1072 (Wyo.)]

10. Sippy was thinking of buying Christich's house. He noticed watermarks on the ceiling, but the agent showing the house stated that the roof had been repaired and was in good condition. Sippy was not told that the roof still leaked and that the repairs had not been able to stop the leaking. Sippy bought the house. Some time later, heavy rains caused water to leak into the house, and Sippy claimed that Christich was liable for damages. What theory would he rely on? Decide. [*Sippy v. Christich*, 609 P.2d 204 (Kan. App.)]

11. CEO Bernard Ellis sent a memo to shareholders of his Internet-related services business some four days before the expiration of a lock-up period during which these shareholders had agreed not to sell their stock. In the memo, he urged shareholders not to sell their stock on the release date because in the event of a massive sell-off "our stock could plummet." He also stated *"I think our share price will start to stabilize and then rise as our company's strong performance continues."* Based on Ellis' "strong performance" statement, a major corporate shareholder did not sell. The price of the stock fell from $40 a share to 29 cents a share over the subsequent nine-month period. The shareholder sued Ellis for fraud, seeking $27 million in damages. Analyze the italicized statement to see if it contains an actionable misrepresentation of fact and a basis of fraud liability. [*New Century Communications v. Ellis*, 318 F.3d 1023 (11th Cir.)]

12. Office Supply Outlet, Inc., a single-store office equipment and supply retailer, ordered 100 model RVX-414 computers from Compuserve, Inc. A new staff member made a clerical error on the order form and ordered a quantity that was far in excess of what Office Supply could sell in a year. Office Supply realized the mistake when the delivery trucks arrived at its warehouse. Its manager called Compuserve and explained that it had intended to order just 10 computers. Compuserve declined to accept the return of the extra machines. Is the contract enforceable? What additional facts would allow the store to avoid the contract for the additional machines?

13. The Printers International Union reached agreement for a new three-year contract with a large regional printing company. As was their practice, the union negotiators then met with Sullivan Brothers Printers, Inc., a small specialty shop employing 10 union printers, and Sullivan Brothers and the union agreed to follow the contractual pattern set by the union and the large printing company. That is, Sullivan Brothers agreed to give its workers all of the benefits negotiated for the employees of the large printing company. When the contract was typed, a new benefit of 75 percent employer-paid coverage for a dental plan was inadvertently omitted from the final contract the parties signed. The mistake was not discovered until six months after the contract took effect. Sullivan Brothers Printers, Inc., is reluctant to assume the additional expense. It contends that the printed copy, which does not cover dental benefits, must control. The union believes that clear and convincing evidence shows an inadvertent typing error. Decide.

14. The city of Salinas entered into a contract with Souza & McCue Construction Co. to construct a sewer. City officials knew unusual subsoil conditions (including extensive quicksand) existed that would make performance of the contract unusually difficult. This information was not disclosed when city officials advertised for bids. The advertisement for bids directed bidders to examine carefully the site of the work and declared that the submission of a bid would constitute evidence that the bidder had made an examination. Souza & McCue was awarded the contract, but because of the subsoil conditions, it could not complete on time and was sued by Salinas for breach of contract. Souza & McCue counterclaimed on the basis that the city had not revealed its information on the subsoil conditions and was thus liable for the loss. Was the city liable? [*City of Salinas v. Souza & McCue Construction Co.*, 424 P.2d 921 (Cal. App. 3d)]

15. Vern Westby inherited a "ticket" from Anna Sjoblom, a survivor of the sinking of the *Titanic*, which had been pinned to the inside of her coat. He also inherited an album of postcards, some of which related to the *Titanic*. The ticket was a one-of-a-kind item in good condition. Westby needed cash and went to the biggest antique dealer in Tacoma, operated by Alan Gorsuch and his family, doing business

as Sanford and Sons, and asked about the value of these items. Westby testified that after Alan Gorsuch examined the ticket, he said, "It's not worth nothing." Westby then inquired about the value of the postcard album, and Gorsuch advised him to come back later. On Westby's return, Gorsuch told Westby, "It ain't worth nothing." Gorsuch added that he "couldn't fetch $500 for the ticket." Since he needed money, Westby asked if Gorsuch would give him $1,000 for both the ticket and the album, and Gorsuch did so.

Six months later, Gorsuch sold the ticket at a nationally advertised auction for $110,000 and sold most of the postcards for $1,200. Westby sued Gorsuch for fraud. Testimony showed that Gorsuch was a major buyer in antiques and collectibles in the Puget Sound area and that he would have had an understanding of the value of the ticket. Gorsuch contends that all elements of fraud are not present since there was no evidence that Gorsuch intended that Westby rely on the alleged representations, nor did Westby rely on such. Rather, Gorsuch asserts, it was an arm's-length transaction and Westby had access to the same information as Gorsuch. Decide. [*Westby v. Gorsuch*, 50 P.3d 284 (Wash. App.)]

CPA Questions

1. A building subcontractor submitted a bid for construction of a portion of a high-rise office building. The bid contained material computational errors. The general contractor accepted the bid with knowledge of the errors. Which of the following statements best represents the subcontractor's liability?

   a. Not liable, because the contractor knew of the errors.

   b. Not liable, because the errors were a result of gross negligence.

   c. Liable, because the errors were unilateral.

   d. Liable, because the errors were material (5/95, Law, #17, 5351).

2. Egan, a minor, contracted with Baker to purchase Baker's used computer for $400. The computer was purchased for Egan's personal use. The agreement provided that Egan would pay $200 down on delivery and $200 thirty days later. Egan took delivery and paid the $200 down payment. Twenty days later, the computer was damaged seriously as a result of Egan's negligence. Five days after the damage occurred and one day after Egan reached the age of majority, Egan attempted to disaffirm the contract with Baker. Egan will:

   a. Be able to disaffirm despite the fact that Egan was *not* a minor at the time of disaffirmance.

   b. Be able to disaffirm only if Egan does so in writing.

   c. Not be able to disaffirm because Egan had failed to pay the balance of the purchase price.

   d. Not be able to disaffirm because the computer was damaged as a result of Egan's negligence (11/93, Law, #21, 4318).

Consideration

sec Sales of Good Contract

Will the law enforce every promise? Generally, a promise will not be enforced unless something is given or received for the promise.

14-1 General Principles

As a general rule, one of the elements needed to make an agreement binding is consideration.

14-1a Consideration Defined and Explained

consideration–promise or performance that the promisor demands as the price of the promise.

Consideration is what each party to a contract gives up to the other in making their agreement.

Bargained-for Exchange

Consideration is the bargained-for exchange between the parties to a contract. In order for consideration to exist, something of value must be given or promised in return for the performance or promise of performance of the other.[1] The value given or promised can be money, services, property, or the forbearance of a legal right.

For Example, Beth offers to pay Kerry $100 for her used skis, and Kerry accepts. Beth has promised something of value, $100, as consideration for Kerry's promise to sell the skis, and Kerry has promised Beth something of value, the skis, as consideration for the $100. If Kerry offered to *give* Beth the used skis and Beth accepted, these parties would have an agreement but not an enforceable contract because Beth did not provide any consideration in exchange for Kerry's promise of the skis. There was no *bargained-for exchange* because Kerry was not promised anything of value from Beth.

Benefit-Detriment Approach

Some jurisdictions analyze consideration from the point of view of a *benefit-detriment approach*, defining *consideration* as a benefit received by the promisor or a detriment incurred by the promisee.[2]

As an example of a unilateral contract analyzed from a benefit-detriment approach to consideration, Mr. Scully, a longtime summer resident of Falmouth, states to George Corfu, a college senior, "I will pay you $3,000 if you paint my summer home." George in fact paints the house. The work of painting the house by George, the promisee, was a legal detriment to him. Also, the painting of the house was a legal benefit to Scully, the promisor. There was consideration in this case, and the agreement is enforceable.

14-1b Gifts

Promises to make a gift are unenforceable promises under the law of contracts because of lack of consideration, as illustrated previously in the scenario of Kerry promising to give her used skis to Beth without charge. There was no bargained-for exchange because Kerry was not promised anything of value from Beth. A completed gift, however, cannot be rescinded for lack of consideration.[3]

Charitable subscriptions by which individuals make pledges to finance the construction of a college building, a church, or another structure for charitable purposes are binding to the extent that the donor (promisor) should have reasonably realized that the charity was relying on the promise in undertaking the building program. Some states require proof that the charity has relied on the subscription.[4]

---

[1] *Brooksbank v. Anderson*, 586 N.W.2d 789 (Minn. App. 1998).
[2] *Sullo Investments, LLC v. Moreau*, 95 A.3d 1144 (Ct. 2014).
[3] *Homes v. O'Bryant*, 741 So. 2d 366 (Miss. App. 1999).
[4] *King v. Trustees of Boston University*, 647 N.E.2d 1176 (Ma. 1995).

An agreement to give property for the consideration of love and affection does not transfer the property to the donee nor secure for the donee a right to sue to compel the completion of the contract. Love and affection alone have not been recognized as consideration for a contract.

CASE SUMMARY

What's Love Got to Do With It...

FACTS: Amber Williams and Frederick Ormsby lived together in a nonmarital relationship in a house deeded to Ormsby in 2004. The couple separated and attended couples counseling. Amber refused to move back into the house unless Frederick granted her a one-half interest in the property. On June 2, 2005, they signed a document purportedly making themselves equal partners in the home. Amber ended the relationship in September 2007, and she sought specific performance of the June 2, 2005, contract giving her a half-interest in the property. Frederick defended that "love and affection is insufficient consideration for a contract."

DECISION: Judgment for Ormsby. The only consideration offered by Amber for the June 2, 2005, agreement was her resumption of a romantic relationship with Frederick. Essentially this agreement amounts to a gratuitous promise by Frederick to give Amber an interest in property based solely on the consideration of love and affection. This June 2005 document is not an enforceable contract because it fails for want of consideration. [*Williams v. Ormsby*, 966 N.E.2d 255 (Ohio 2012)]

14-1c **Adequacy of Consideration**

Ordinarily, courts do not consider the adequacy of the consideration given for a promise. The fact that the consideration supplied by one party is slight when compared with the burden undertaken by the other party is immaterial. It is a matter for the parties to decide when they make their contract whether each is getting a fair return. It is not a function of a court to review the amount of the consideration passed unless the amount is so grossly inadequate as to shock the conscience of the court.

CASE SUMMARY

A Good Neighbor Shocks the Conscience of the Court

FACTS: Dr. George Dohrmann made a contract with his very elderly childless neighbor, Mrs. Virginia Rogers, wherein she agreed to transfer to Dr. Dohrmann upon her death her valuable condominium and its contents and $4,000,000 in cash in exchange for Dohrmann incorporating the name of Rogers into the names of his two children to help perpetuate the Rogers names after her death. Dr. Dohrmann performed by taking the legal action necessary to add the Rogers name into the legal names of his two boys. From a judgment against Dohrmann on his breach of contract action against the Rogers estate, he appealed.

DECISION: Judgment against Dohrmann. He did not change the boys' surnames to Rogers, nor even change their middle names to Rogers. He merely added Rogers after their middle names. This can hardly be said to perpetuate the Rogers name after Mrs. Rogers' death. Dohrmann's argument that it is improper for a court to consider the relative value or adequacy of the consideration is rejected in this particular case. While the statement is generally true, in cases such as the one at bar it will not be applied where the consideration is so grossly inadequate as to shock the conscience of the court. [*Dohrmann v. Swaney*, 14 N.E.3d 605 (Ill. App. 2014)]

The fact that the consideration turns out to be disappointing does not affect the binding character of the contract. Thus, the fact that a business purchased by a group of investors proves unprofitable does not constitute a failure of consideration that releases the buyers from their obligation to the seller.

14-1d **Forbearance as Consideration**

forbearance–refraining from doing an act.

In most cases, consideration consists of the performance of an act, such as providing a service, or the making of a promise to provide a service or goods, or paying money.[5] Consideration may also consist of **forbearance,** which is refraining from doing an act that an individual has a legal right to do, or it may consist of a promise of forbearance. In other words, the promisor may desire to buy the inaction or a promise of inaction of the other party.

The giving up of any legal right can be consideration for the promise of the other party to a contract. Thus, the relinquishment of a right to sue for damages will support a promise for the payment of money given in return for the promise to relinquish the right, if such is the agreement of the parties.

The promise of a creditor to forbear collecting a debt is consideration for the promise of the debtor to modify the terms of the transaction.

14-1e **Illusory Promises**

illusory promise–promise that in fact does not impose any obligation on the promisor.

In a bilateral contract, each party makes a promise to the other. For a bilateral contract to be enforceable, there must be *mutuality of obligation.* That is, both parties must have created obligations to the other in their respective promises. If one party's promise contains either no obligation or only an apparent obligation to the other, this promise is an **illusory promise.** The party making such a promise is not bound because he or she has made no real promise. The effect is that the other party, who has made a real promise, is also not bound because he or she has received no consideration. It is said that the contract fails for lack of mutuality.

Consider the example of the Jacksonville Fire soccer team's contract with Brazilian soccer star Edmundo. Edmundo signed a contract to play for the Jacksonville franchise of the new International Soccer League for five years at $25 million. The extensive document signed by Edmundo set forth the details of the team's financial commitment and the details of Edmundo's obligations to the team and its fans. On page 4 of the document, the team inserted a clause reserving the right "to terminate the contract and team obligations at any time in its sole discretion." During the season, Edmundo received a $40 million five-year offer to play for Manchester United of the English Premier League, which he accepted. Because Jacksonville had a free way out of its obligation by the unrestricted cancellation provision in the contract, it thus made its promises to Edmundo illusory. Edmundo was not bound by the Jacksonville contract as a result of a lack of mutuality and was free to sign with Manchester United.

Cancellation Provisions

cancellation provision–crossing out of a part of an instrument or a destruction of all legal effect of the instrument, whether by act of party, upon breach by the other party, or pursuant to agreement or decree of court.

Although a promise must impose a binding obligation, it may authorize a party to cancel the agreement under certain circumstances on giving notice by a certain date. Such a provision does not make this party's promise illusory, for the party does not have a free way out and is limited to living up to the terms of the **cancellation provision. For Example,** actress Zsa Zsa Gabor made a contract with Hollywood Fantasy Corporation to appear at a fantasy vacation in San Antonio, Texas, on May 2–4, for a $10,000 appearance fee plus itemized (extravagant) expenses. The last paragraph of the agreement stated: "It is agreed that if a significant acting opportunity in a film comes up, Ms. Gabor will have the right to cancel her appearance in San Antonio by advising Hollywood Fantasy in writing by April 15, 1991." Ms. Gabor sent a telegram on April 15, 1991, canceling her appearance. During the May 2 through 4 period, Ms. Gabor's only acting activity was a 14-second cameo role during the opening credits of *Naked Gun 2½.* In a lawsuit for breach of

[5] *Prenger v. Baumhoer,* 914 S.W.2d 413 (Mo. App. 1996).

contract that followed, the jury saw this portion of the movie and concluded that Ms. Gabor had not canceled her obligation on the basis of a "significant acting opportunity," and she was held liable for breach of contract.[6]

Conditional Promises

A *conditional promise* is a promise that depends on the occurrence of a specified condition in order for the promise to be binding. **For Example,** Mary Sparks, in contemplation of her signing a lease to take over a restaurant at Marina Bay, wanted to make certain that she had a highly qualified chef to run the restaurant's food service. She made a contract with John "Grumpy" White to serve as executive chef for a one-year period at a salary of $150,000. The contract set forth White's responsibilities and was conditioned on the successful negotiation of the restaurant lease with Marina Bay Management. Both parties signed it. Although the happening of the condition was within Mary's control because she could avoid the contract with Grumpy White by not acquiring the restaurant lease, she limited her future options by the contract with White. Her promise to White was not illusory because after signing the contract with him, if she acquired the restaurant lease, she was bound to hire White as her executive chef. Before signing the contract with White, she was free to sign any chef for the position. The contract was enforceable.

CPA 14-2 Special Situations

The following sections analyze certain common situations in which a lawsuit turns on whether the promisor received consideration for the promise sued on.

14-2a Preexisting Legal Obligation

Ordinarily, doing or promising to do what one is already under a legal obligation to do is not consideration.[7] Similarly, a promise to refrain from doing what one has no legal right to do is not consideration. This preexisting duty or legal obligation can be based on statute, on general principles of law, on responsibilities of an office held, or on a preexisting contract.

For Example, Officer Mary Rodgers is an undercover police officer in the city of Pasadena, California, assigned to weekend workdays. Officer Rodgers promised Elwood Farnsworth that she would diligently patrol the area of the Farnsworth estate on weekends to keep down the noise and drinking of rowdy young persons who gathered in this area, and Mr. Farnsworth promised to provide a $500 per month gratuity for this extra service. Farnsworth's promise is unenforceable because Officer Rodgers has a preexisting official duty as a police officer to protect citizens and enforce the antinoise and public drinking ordinances.

CPA Completion of Contract

Suppose that a contractor refuses to complete a building unless the owner promises a payment or bonus in addition to the sum specified in the original contract, and the owner promises to make that payment. The question then arises as to whether the owner's promise is binding. Most courts hold that the second promise of the owner is without consideration.

---

[6] *Hollywood Fantasy Corp. v. Gabor,* 151 F.2d 203 (5th Cir. 1998).
[7] *Willamette Management Associates, Inc. v. Palczynski,* 38 A.3d 1212 (Conn. App. 2012).

CASE SUMMARY

You're Already Under Contract

FACTS: Crookham & Vessels had a contract to build an extension of a railroad for the Little Rock Port Authority. It made a contract with Larry Moyer Trucking to dig drainage ditches. The ditch walls collapsed because water would not drain off. This required that the ditches be dug over again. Larry Moyer refused to do this unless extra money was paid. Crookham & Vessels agreed to pay the additional compensation, but after the work was done, it refused to pay. Larry Moyer sued for the extra compensation promised.

DECISION: Judgment against Moyer. Moyer was bound by its contract to dig the drainage ditches. Its promise to perform that obligation was not consideration for the promise of Crookham & Vessels to pay additional compensation. Performance of an obligation is not consideration for a promise by a party entitled to that performance. The fact that performance of the contract proved more difficult or costly than originally contemplated does not justify making an exception to this rule. [*Crookham & Vessels, Inc. v. Larry Moyer Trucking, Inc.*, **699 S.W.2d 414 (Ark. App. 1985)**]

If the promise of the contractor is to do something that is not part of the first contract, then the promise of the other party is binding. **For Example,** if a bonus of $5,000 is promised in return for the promise of a contractor to complete the building at a date earlier than that specified in the original agreement, the promise to pay the bonus is binding.

CPA   **Good-Faith Adjustment.** A current trend is to enforce a second promise to pay a contractor a higher amount for the performance of the original contract when there are extraordinary circumstances caused by unforeseeable difficulties and when the additional amount promised the contractor is reasonable under the circumstances.

CASE SUMMARY

"You Had a Preexisting Legal Obligation," Said the Public Guardian, Mr. Angel

FACTS: John Murray was director of finance of the city of Newport. A contract was made with Alfred Maher to remove trash. Later, Maher requested that the city council increase his compensation. Maher's costs were greater than had been anticipated because 400 new dwelling units had been put into operation. The city council voted to pay Maher an additional $10,000 a year. After two such annual payments had been made, Angel and other citizens of the city sued Murray and Maher for a return of the $20,000. They said that Maher was already obligated by his contract to perform the work for the contract sum, and there was, accordingly, no consideration for the payment of the increased compensation. From a decision in favor of the plaintiffs, the city and Maher appealed.

DECISION: Judgment for the city and Maher. When a promise modifying an original contract is made before the contract is fully performed on either side due to unanticipated circumstances that prompt the modification, and the modification is fair and equitable, such a good faith adjustment will be enforced. The unanticipated increase in the number of new units from 20 to 25 per year to 400 units in the third year of this five-year contract, which prompted the additional yearly payments of $10,000, was a voluntary good faith adjustment. It was not a "hold up" by a contractor refusing to complete an unprofitable contract unless paid additional compensation, where the preexisting duty rule would apply. [*Angel v. Murray*, 322 A.2d 630 (R.I. 1974)]

Contract for Sale of Goods. When the contract is for the sale of goods, any modification made in good faith by the parties to the contract is binding without regard to the existence of consideration for the modification.

CPA   Compromise and Release of Claims

The rule that doing or promising to do what one is already legally bound to do is not consideration applies to a part payment made in satisfaction of an admitted or *liquidated debt*. Thus, a promise to pay part of an amount that is admittedly owed is not consideration for a promise to discharge the balance. It will not prevent the creditor from demanding the remainder later. **For Example,** John owes Mark $100,000, which was due on March 1, 2016. On March 15, John offers to pay back $80,000 if Mark will agree to accept this amount as the discharge of the full amount owed. Mark agrees to this proposal, and it is set forth in writing signed by the parties. However, Mark later sues for the $20,000 balance. Mark will be successful in the lawsuit because John's payment of the $80,000 is not consideration for Mark's promise to discharge the full amount owed because John was doing only what he had a preexisting legal duty to do.

If the debtor pays the part payment before the debt is due, there is consideration because, on the day when the payment was made, the creditor was not entitled to demand any payment. Likewise, if the creditor accepts some article (even of slight value) in addition to the part payment, consideration exists.

A debtor and creditor may have a bona fide dispute over the amount owed or whether any amount is owed. Such is called an *unliquidated debt*. In this case, payment by the debtor of less than the amount claimed by the creditor is consideration for the latter's agreement to release or settle the claim. It is generally regarded as sufficient if the claimant believes in the merit of the claim.[8]

Part-Payment Checks

When there is a good-faith dispute about the amount of a debt and the debtor tenders a check that states on its face "paid in full" and references the transaction in dispute, but the amount of the check is less than the full amount the creditor asserts is owed, the cashing of the check by the creditor discharges the entire debt.

Composition of Creditors

composition of creditors—agreement among creditors that each shall accept a part payment as full payment in consideration of the other creditors doing the same.

In a **composition of creditors,** the various creditors of one debtor mutually agree to accept a fractional part of their claims in full satisfaction of the claims. Such agreements are binding and are supported by consideration. When creditors agree to extend the due date of their debts, the promise of each creditor to forbear is likewise consideration for the promise of other creditors to forbear.

14-2b Past Consideration

past consideration—something that has been performed in the past and which, therefore, cannot be consideration for a promise made in the present.

A promise based on a party's past performance lacks consideration.[9] It is said that **past consideration** is no consideration. **For Example,** Fred O'Neal came up with the idea for the formation of the new community bank of Villa Rica and was active in its formation. Just prior to the execution of the documents creating the bank, the organizers discussed that once the bank was formed, it would hire O'Neal, giving him a three-year contract in inflation adjusted figures of $104,000 the first year, $107,000 the second year, and $110,000 the third. In a lawsuit against the bank for breach of contract, O'Neal testified that the consideration he gave in exchange for the three-year contract was his past effort to organize the bank. The court stated that past consideration generally will not support a subsequent promise and that the purported consideration was not rendered to the bank, which had not yet been established when his promotion and

---

[8] *F. H. Prince & Co. v. Towers Financial Corp.,* 656 N.E.2d 142 (Ill. App. 1995).
[9] *Smith v. Locklear,* 906 So. 2d 1273 (Fla. App. 2005).

ETHICS & THE LAW

Alan Fulkins, who owns a construction company that specializes in single-family residences, is constructing a small subdivision with 23 homes. Tretorn Plumbing, owned by Jason Tretorn, was awarded the contract for the plumbing work on the homes at a price of $4,300 per home.

Plumbing contractors complete their residential projects in three phases. Phase one consists of digging the lines for the plumbing and installing the pipes that are placed in the foundation of the house. Phase two consists of installing the pipes within the walls of the home, and phase three is installing of the surface plumbing, such as sinks and tubs. However, industry practice dictates that the plumbing contractor receive one-half of the contract amount after completion of phase one.

Tretorn completed the digs of phase one for Fulkins and received payment of $2,150. Tretorn then went to Fulkins and demanded an additional $600 per house to complete the work.

Fulkins said, "But you already have a contract for $4,300!" Tretorn responded, "I know, but the costs are killing me. I need the additional $600."

Fulkins explained the hardship of the demand, "Look, I've already paid you half. If I hire someone else, I'll have to pay them two-thirds for the work not done. It'll cost me $5,000 per house."

Tretorn responded, "Exactly. I'm a bargain because the additional $600 I want only puts you at $4,900. If you don't pay it, I'll just lien the houses and then you'll be stuck without a way to close the sales. I've got the contract all drawn up. Just sign it and everything goes smoothly."

Should Fulkins sign the agreement? Does Tretorn have the right to the additional $600? Was it ethical for Tretorn to demand the $600? Is there any legal advice you can offer Fulkins?

organization work took place.[10] The presence of a bargained-for exchange is not present when a promise is made in exchange for a past benefit.[11]

14-2c Moral Obligation

In most states, promises made to another based on "moral obligation" lack consideration and are not enforceable.[12] They are considered gratuitous promises and unenforceable. **For Example,** Robert Lewis and his brother Lewis Lester had an agreement under which Robert would provide help for his uncle Floyd and serve as his power of attorney and the brothers would split the uncle's estate equally. Floyd left his estate to Lewis Lester. Robert's suit against his brother to enforce their agreement failed for lack of consideration. Services performed by one family member on behalf of another family member are presumed to have been rendered in obedience to a moral obligation without expectation of compensation.[13]

14-3 Exceptions to the Laws of Consideration

The ever-changing character of law clearly appears in the area of consideration as part of the developing law of contracts.

14-3a Exceptions to Consideration

By statute or decision, traditional consideration is not required in these situations:

---

[10] *O'Neal v. Home Town Bank of Villa Rica*, 514 S.E.2d 669 (Ga. App. 1999); *Lee v. Choi*, 754 S.E.2d 371 (Ga. App. 2013).

[11] But see *United Resource Recovery Corp v. Ranko Venture Management Inc.*, 854 F. Supp. 2d 645 (S.D.N.Y. 2008) where a past work agreement was unenforceable because it was based on past consideration—however, the individual could recover under a signed consulting agreement for which no compensation had been paid. See also *Travis v. Paepke*, 3 So. 3d 131 (Miss. App. 2009).

[12] *Production Credit Ass'n of Manaan v. Rub*, 475 N.W.2d 532 (N.D. 1991). As to the Louisiana rule of moral consideration, see *Thomas v. Bryant*, 596 So. 2d 1065 (La. App. 1992).

[13] *Lewis v. Lester*, 760 N.E.2d 91 (N.C. App. 2014).

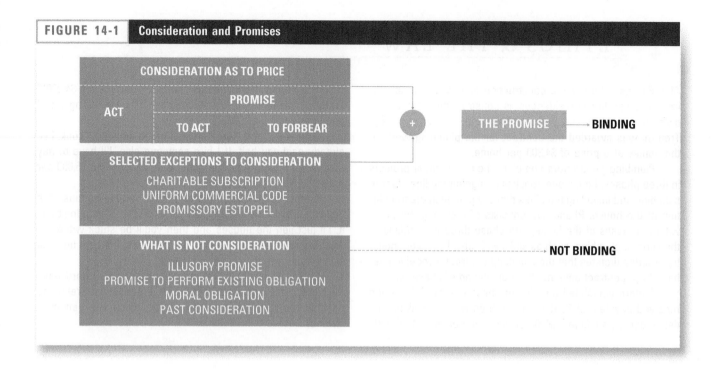

FIGURE 14-1 | **Consideration and Promises**

Charitable Subscriptions

Where individuals made pledges to finance the construction of buildings for charitable purposes, consideration is lacking according to technical standards applied in ordinary contract cases. For public policy reasons, the reliance of the charity on the pledge in undertaking the project is deemed a substitute for consideration.

Uniform Commercial Code

In some situations, the Uniform Commercial Code abolishes the requirement of consideration. **For Example,** under the Code, consideration is not required for (1) a merchant's written, firm offer for goods stated to be irrevocable, (2) a written discharge of a claim for an alleged breach of a commercial contract, or (3) an agreement to modify a contract for the sale of goods.[14]

Promissory Estoppel

promissory estoppels—
doctrine that a promise will be enforced although it is not supported by consideration when the promisor should have reasonably expected that the promise would induce action or forbearance of a definite and substantial character on the part of the promised and injustice can be avoided only by enforcement of the promise.

Under the doctrine of **promissory estoppel,** a promisor may be prevented from asserting that his or her promise is unenforceable because the promisee gave no consideration for the promise.[15] This doctrine, sometimes called the *doctrine of detrimental reliance*, is applicable when (1) the promisor makes a promise that lacks consideration, (2) the promisor intends or should reasonably expect that the promisee will rely on the promise, (3) the promisee in fact relies on the promise in some definite and substantial manner, and (4) enforcement of the promise is the only way to avoid injustice.[16]

Damages recoverable in a case of promissory estoppel are not the profits that the promisee expected, but only the amount necessary to restore the promisee to the position he or she would have been in had the promisee not relied on the promise.[17]

---

[14] U.C.C. §2-209(1).
[15] See *Weiss v. Smulders,* 96 A.3d 1175 (Conn. 2014).
[16] *Neuhoff v. Marvin Lumber and Cedar Co.,* 370 F.3d 197 (1st Cir. 2004).
[17] *Medistar Corp. v. Schmidt,* 267 S.W.3d 150 (Tex. App. 2008).

Legal difficulties often arise because parties take certain things for granted. Frequently, they will be sure that they have agreed to everything and that they have a valid contract. Sometimes, however, they do not. The courts are then faced with the problem of leaving them with their broken dreams or coming to their rescue when promissory estoppel can be established.

CASE SUMMARY

Brits Rescued by Promissory Estoppel

FACTS: Portman Lamborghini, Ltd. (Portman), was owned by Chaplake Holdings, Ltd., a United Kingdom company, which was owned by David Jolliffe and David Lakeman as equal shareholders. Between 1984 and 1987, Portman sold approximately 30 new Lamborghinis each year through its exclusive concession contract with the car maker. It was then the largest Lamborghini dealer in the world since Lamborghini's production was just 250 cars per year. These cars sold at a retail price between $200,000 and $300,000. In 1987, Chrysler Corporation bought Lamborghini, and its chairman, Lee Iacocca, presented a plan to escalate production to 5,000 units within five years. The plan included the introduction of a new model, the P140, with a retail price of $70,000. Between 1987 and 1991, *all* of the Chrysler/Lamborghini top executives with whom Jolliffe and Lakeman and their top advisors came in contact provided the same message to them: Chrysler was committed to the Expansion Plan, and in order for Portman to retain its exclusive U.K. market, it must expand its operational capacity from 35 cars in 1987 to 400 cars by 1992. Accordingly, Portman acquired additional financing, staff, and facilities and built a new distribution center. An economic downturn in the United States and major development and production problems at Lamborghini led Chrysler to reduce its expansion investment by two-thirds. Factory production delays eroded Portman's profitability and success, and it entered into receivership in April 1992. Suit was brought on behalf of the Portman and Chaplake entities on a promissory estoppel theory against Chrysler, a Delaware corporation.

DECISION: Judgment for Portman and Chaplake on the promissory estoppel theory. (1) A promise was made by Chrysler that the Lamborghini line would expand tenfold and that Portman would retain its exclusivity deal *only* if it expanded its operational capacity. (2) The promisor, Chrysler, should have reasonably expected that Portman would rely on this promise. (3) Lakeman and Jolliffe were given the same message and promise by *all* of the top executives involved, and it was therefore not unreasonable for them to rely upon the promises made by these executives and to undertake the detriment of major expansion activity that would have been unnecessary but for the Expansion Plan and the role they were promised. (4) The prevention of injustice is the "fundamental idea" underlying the doctrine of promissory estoppel, and injustice can be avoided in this case only by the enforcement of Chrysler's promise. Portman is entitled to £ 569,321 for its costs to implement its Expansion Plan, and Chaplake is entitled to £ 462,686 for its investment in Portman's expansion. [*Chrysler Corp. v. Chaplake Holdings, Ltd.*, 822 A.2d 1024 (Del. 2003)]

Make the Connection

Summary

A promise is not binding if there is no consideration for the promise. Consideration is what the promisor requires as the price for his promise. That price may be doing an act, refraining from the doing of an act, or merely promising to do or to refrain. In a bilateral contract, it is necessary to find that the promise of each party is supported by consideration. If either promise is not so supported, it is not binding, and the agreement of the parties is not a contract.

Consequently, the agreement cannot be enforced. When a promise is the consideration, it must be a binding promise. The binding character of a promise is not affected by the circumstance that there is a condition precedent to the performance promised. A promise to do what one is already obligated to do is not consideration, although some exceptions are made. Such exceptions include the rendering of a partial performance or a modified performance accepted as a good-faith adjustment to a changed situation, a compromise and release of claims, a part-payment check, and a compromise of creditors. Because consideration is the price that is given to obtain the promise, past benefits conferred on the promisor cannot be consideration.

A promise to refrain from doing an act can be consideration. A promise to refrain from suing or asserting a particular claim can be consideration. When consideration is forbearance to assert a claim, it is immaterial whether the claim is valid as long as the claim has been asserted in the good-faith belief that it was valid.

When the promisor obtains the consideration specified for the promise, the law is not ordinarily concerned with the value or adequacy of that consideration.

Under the doctrine of promissory estoppel a court may enforce a promise lacking consideration where it is the only way to avoid injustice.

Learning Outcomes

After studying this chapter, you should be able to clearly explain:

14-1   General Principles

LO.1   Explain what constitutes consideration

See the *Williams v. Ormsby* case, which determined that love and affection is not recognized as consideration, page 264.

See the "bargained for exchange" example involving Beth and Kerry, page 263.

See the "benefit-detriment" approach to consideration example, page 263.

See the discussion on forbearance as consideration, page 265.

14-2   Special Situations

LO.2   Distinguish between a "preexisting legal obligation" and "past consideration"

See the preexisting duty example involving Officer Rodgers, page 266.

See the *Angel v. Murray* case involving a good-faith adjustment exception to the preexisting duty rule, page 267.

See the example involving Fred O'Neal where he found out the past consideration is no consideration rule, page 268.

LO.3   Explain why promises based on moral obligations lack consideration

See the example of the gratuitous deeds of Robert Lewis, page 269.

14-3   Exceptions to the Laws of Consideration

LO.4   List the exceptions to the requirement of consideration

See the discussion on charitable subscriptions, the UCC, and promissory estoppel, pages 270–271.

LO.5   Explain the "fundamental idea" underlying promissory estoppel

See the *Chaplake Holdings* case where the court enforced Chrysler's promise in order to correct an injustice, page 271.

Key Terms

cancellation provision	forbearance	promissory estoppel
composition of creditors	illusory promise	
consideration	past consideration	

Questions and Case Problems

1. Sarah's house caught on fire. Through the prompt assistance of her neighbor Odessa, the fire was quickly extinguished. In gratitude, Sarah promised to pay Odessa $1,000. Can Odessa enforce this promise?

2. William E. Story agreed to pay his nephew, William E. Story II, a large sum of money (roughly equivalent to $75,000 in 2016 dollars) "if he would refrain from drinking liquor, using tobacco, swearing, and

playing cards or billiards for money until he should come to be 21 years of age." William II had been using tobacco and occasionally drank liquor but refrained from using these stimulants over several years until he was 21 and also lived up to the other requirements of his uncle's offer. Just after William II's 21st birthday, Story acknowledged that William II had fulfilled his part of the bargain and advised that the money would be invested for him with interest. Story died, and his executor, Sidway, refused to pay William II because he believed the contract between Story and William II was without consideration. Sidway asserted that Story received no benefit from William II's performance and William II suffered no detriment (in fact, by his refraining from the use of liquor and tobacco, William II was not harmed but benefited, Sidway asserted). Is there any theory of consideration that William II can rely on? How would you decide this case? [*Hamer v. Sidway*, 124 N.Y. 538]

3. Dale Dyer, who was employed by National By-Products, Inc., was seriously injured at work as the result of a job-related accident. He agreed to give up his right to sue the employer for damages in consideration of the employer's giving him a lifetime job. The employer later claimed that this agreement was not binding because Dyer's promise not to sue could not be consideration for the promise to employ on the ground that Dyer in fact had no right to sue. Dyer's only remedy was to make a claim under workers' compensation. Was the agreement binding? [*Dyer v. National By-Products, Inc.*, 380 N.W.2d 732 (Iowa)]

4. Charles Sanarwari retained Stan Gissel to prepare his income tax return for the year 2014. The parties agreed on a fee of $400. Charles had done a rough estimate based on last year's return and believed he would owe the IRS approximately $2,000. When Stan's work was completed, it turned out that Charles would receive a $2,321 tax refund. Charles paid for Stan's services and was so pleased with the work that he promised to pay Stan an additional $400 for the excellent job on the tax return when he received his tax refund. Thereafter, Charles had a falling out with Stan over a golf tournament snub. Stan was not paid the $400 promised for doing an excellent job on the tax return, and he sued Charles as a matter of principle. Decide.

5. Medistar is a real estate development company specializing in the development of medical facilities.

Dr. Schmidt, the team physician for the San Antonio Spurs basketball team, sought to develop "The Texas Center for Athletes" medical center next to the Spurs facility and urged Medistar to obtain the real estate and develop the project on his group's behalf. Medistar spent more than $1 million and thousands of man-hours on the project from 2000 to July 12, 2004, when Dr. Schmidt's new group of investors purchased the property next to the Spur's facility for the project; subsequently, Medistar was informed that it would have no role in the project. Medistar asserts that it relied on Dr. Schmidt's assurances that it would be the developer of the project—and after four years and the $1 million in time and expenses it spent, it is unconscionable to be excluded from the project. Dr. Schmidt and associates contend that Medistar has presented no contractual agreement tying it to any legal obligation to Medistar. Is there a viable legal theory available to Medistar? If so what is the remedy? [*Medistar v. Schmidt*, 267 S.W.3d 150 (Tex. App.)]

6. While on a fishing trip, Tom Snyder met an elderly couple living in near-destitute conditions in a rural area of Texas. He returned to the area often, and he regularly purchased groceries for the couple and paid for their medical needs. Some two years later, the couple's son, David, discovered what Tom had been doing and promised to reimburse Snyder for what he had furnished his parents. He failed to do so and Tom sued David for breach of his promise to reimburse Snyder. Tom has receipts for most of the purchases. What defense, if any, does David have? Decide.

7. The Aqua Drilling Company made a contract to drill a well for the Atlas Construction Company. It was expected that this would supply water for a home being constructed by Atlas. Aqua did not make any guarantee or warranty that water would be produced. Aqua drilled the well exactly as required by the contract, but no water was produced. Atlas refused to pay. It asserted that the contract was not binding on the theory that there had been a failure of consideration because the well did not produce water. Was the contract binding? [*Atlas Construction Co., Inc. v. Aqua Drilling Co.*, 559 P.2d 39 (Wyo.)]

8. Sears, Roebuck and Co. promised to give Forrer permanent employment. Forrer sold his farm at a loss to take the job. Shortly after beginning work, he was discharged by Sears, which claimed that the contract could be terminated at will. Forrer claimed

that promissory estoppel prevented Sears from terminating the contract. Was he correct? [*Forrer v. Sears, Roebuck & Co.*, 153 N.W.2d 587 (Wis.)]

9. Kemp leased a gas filling station from Baehr. Kemp, who was heavily indebted to Penn-O-Tex Oil Corp., transferred to it his right to receive payments on all claims. When Baehr complained that the rent was not paid, he was assured by the corporation that the rent would be paid to him. Baehr did not sue Kemp for the overdue rent but later sued the corporation. The defense was raised that there was no consideration for the promise of the corporation. Decide. [*Baehr v. Penn-O-Tex Corp.*, 104 N.W.2d 661 (Minn.)]

10. John Blackwell was seriously injured in an auto accident. His wife was Korean and spoke little English and needed help communicating with Blackwell's doctor. The Blackwells hired Choi as an interpreter in 1997 and over time Mr. Choi assisted with the family finances and other matters. In 2010 Blackwell's wife fired Choi and later the parties signed an agreement agreeing to pay Choi $450,000 "for the work Choi had done for Blackwell." Choi sued to obtain payment. Was he successful? [*Lee v. Choi*, 754 S.E.2d 371 (Ga. App.)]

11. Kelsoe worked for International Wood Products, Inc., for a number of years. One day Hernandez, a director and major stockholder of the company, promised Kelsoe that the corporation would give her 5 percent of the company's stock. This promise was never kept, and Kelsoe sued International for breach of contract. Had the company broken its contract? [*Kelsoe v. International Wood Products, Inc.*, 588 So. 2d 877 (Ala.)]

12. Kathy left her classic 1978 Volkswagen convertible at Freddie's Service Station, requesting a "tune-up." When she returned that evening, Freddie's bill was $374. Kathy stated that Firestone and Sears advertise tune-ups for $70, and she asked Freddie, "How can you justify this bill?" Freddie responded, "Carburator work." Kathy refused to pay the bill and left. That evening, when the station closed, she took her other set of keys and removed her car, after placing a check in the station's mail slot. The check was made out to Freddie's Service Station for $200 and stated on its face: "This check is in full payment of my account with you regarding the tune-up today on my 1978 Volkswagen convertible." Freddie cashed the check in order to meet his business expenses and then sued Kathy for the difference owed. What result?

13. On the death of their mother, the children of Jane Smith gave their interests in their mother's estate to their father in consideration of his payment of $1 to each of them and his promise to leave them the property on his death. The father died without leaving them the property. The children sued their father's second wife to obtain the property in accordance with the agreement. The second wife claimed that the agreement was not a binding contract because the amount of $1 and future gifts given for the children's interests were so trivial and uncertain. Decide.

14. Radio Station KSCS broadcast a popular music program. It announced that it would pay $25,000 to any listener who detected that it did not play three consecutive songs. Steve Jennings listened to and heard a program in which two songs were followed by a commercial program. He claimed the $25,000. The station refused to pay on the ground that there was no consideration for its promise to pay that amount. Was the station liable? [*Jennings v. Radio Station KSCS*, 708 S.W.2d 60 (Tex. App.)]

15. Hoffman wanted to acquire a franchise for a Red Owl grocery store. (Red Owl was a corporation that maintained a system of chain stores.) An agent of Red Owl informed Hoffman and his wife that if they would sell their bakery in Wautoma, acquire a certain tract of land in Chilton (another Wisconsin city), and put up $6,000, they would be given a franchise. In reliance on the agent's promise, Hoffman sold his business and acquired the land in Chilton, but he was never granted a franchise. He and his wife sued Red Owl. Red Owl raised the defense that there had been only an assurance that Hoffman would receive a franchise, but because there was no promise supported by consideration, there was no binding contract to give him a franchise. Decide. [*Hoffman v. Red Owl Stores, Inc.*, 133 N.W.2d 267 (Wis.)]

Legality and Public Policy

Learning Outcomes

After studying this chapter, you should be able to

LO.1 Explain the general contract principles on "illegality"

LO.2 Explain the implied obligation on all parties of good faith and fair dealing

LO.3 Understand that it is only in unusual situations that a contract provision will be unenforceable because it is unconscionable

LO.4 Explain the rationale for requiring licenses to carry on as a business, trade, or profession

LO.5 Distinguish between noncompete clauses after the sale of a business and noncompete clauses in employment contracts

A court will not enforce a contract if it is illegal, contrary to public policy, or unconscionable.

15-1 General Principles

An agreement is illegal either when its formation or performance is a crime or a tort or when it is contrary to public policy or unconscionable.

15-1a Effect of Illegality

Ordinarily, an illegal agreement is void. When an agreement is illegal, the parties are usually not entitled to the aid of the courts. Examples of illegal contracts where the courts have left the parties where they found them include a liquor store owner not being allowed to bring suit for money owed for goods (liquor) sold and delivered on credit in violation of statute and an unlicensed home improvement contractor not being allowed to enforce his contract for progress payments due him. If the illegal agreement has not been performed, neither party can sue the other to obtain performance or damages. If the agreement has been performed, neither party can sue the other to obtain damages or to set the agreement aside.[1]

CASE SUMMARY

The Illegal Paralegal

FACTS: Brian Neiman was involved in the illegal practice of law for over seven years. Having been found guilty of illegally practicing law, he sought to collect disability benefits under his disability insurance policy with Provident Life due to an alleged bipolar disorder, the onset of which occurred during the pendency of criminal and bar proceedings against him. Neiman contends that his bipolar disorder prevents him from working as a paralegal. Provident contends that Neiman should not be indemnified for the loss of income generated from his illegal practice of law.

DECISION: Because all of Neiman's income was derived from the unlawful practice of law in the seven years preceding his claim, as a matter of public policy, a court will not enforce a disability benefits policy that compensates him for his loss of income he was not entitled to earn. Neiman's own wrongdoing caused the contract to be void. Accordingly, Neiman was *in pari delicto* [equally guilty], if not more at fault than the insurance company, in causing the contract to be void and will recover neither benefits nor the premiums he paid. The court must leave the parties where it found them. [*Neiman v. Provident Life & Accident Insurance Co.,* **217 F. Supp. 2d 1281 (S.D. Fla. 2002)**]

Even if a contract appears to be legal on its face, it may be unenforceable if it was entered into for an illegal purpose. **For Example,** if zoning regulations in the special-purpose district of Washington, D.C., require that only a professional can lease space in a given building, and the rental agent suggests that two nonprofessionals take out the lease in their attorney's name but all parties realize that the premises will be used only by the nonprofessionals, then the lease in question is illegal and unenforceable.[2]

15-1b Exceptions to Effect of Illegality

To avoid hardship, exceptions are made to the rules stated previously in the section titled "Effect of Illegality."

[1] *Sabia v. Mattituck Inlet Marina, Inc.,* 805 N.Y.S.2d 346 (A.D. 2005).
[2] *McMahon v. A, H, & B,* 728 A.2d 656 (D.C. 1999).

Protection of One Party

When the law that the agreement violates is intended to protect one of the parties, that party may seek relief. **For Example,** when, in order to protect the public, the law forbids the issuance of securities by certain classes of corporations, a person who has purchased them may recover the money paid.

Unequal Guilt

in pari delicto—equally guilty; used in reference to a transaction as to which relief will not be granted to either party because both are equally guilty of wrongdoing.

When the parties are not *in pari delicto*—equally guilty—the least guilty party is granted relief when public interest is advanced by doing so. **For Example,** when a statute is adopted to protect one of the parties to a transaction, such as a usury law adopted to protect borrowers, the person to be protected will not be deemed to be *in pari delicto* with the wrongdoer when entering into a transaction that the statute prohibits.

15-1c Partial Illegality

An agreement may involve the performance of several promises, some of which are illegal and some legal. The legal parts of the agreement may be enforced provided that they can be separated from the parts that are illegal.

When the illegal provision of a contract may be ignored without defeating the contract's basic purpose, a court will merely ignore the illegal provision and enforce the balance of the contract. Consequently, when a provision for the payment of an attorney's fee in a car rental agreement was illegal because a local statute prohibited it, the court would merely ignore the fee provision and enforce the balance of the contract.[3]

Contracts that involve both unlawful and lawful provisions may be enforced if the illegal portion is severable from the legal. **For Example,** where two separate funds were provided to Watkins by Kyablue, one for gambling purposes and the other in the form of a loan for personal expenses, Kyablue was allowed to recover the repayment of the personal loan, which was severable from the arguably illegal portion relating to gambling-related contracts.[4]

15-1d Crimes and Civil Wrongs

An agreement is illegal, and therefore void, when it calls for the commission of any act that constitutes a crime. To illustrate, one cannot enforce an agreement by which the other party is to commit an assault, steal property, burn a house, or kill a person. A contract to obtain equipment for committing a crime is illegal and cannot be enforced. Thus, a contract to manufacture and sell illegal slot machines is void.

An agreement that calls for the commission of a civil wrong is also illegal and void. Examples are agreements to slander a third person; defraud another; infringe another's patent, trademark, or copyright; or fix prices.

15-1e Good Faith and Fairness

good faith—absence of knowledge of any defects or problems.

Every contract has an implied obligation that neither party shall do anything that will have the effect of destroying or injuring the right of the other party to receive the fruits of the contract. This means that in every contract there exists an implied covenant of **good faith** and fair dealing. **For Example,** Katy Lesser entered into a 10-year lease of retail space to operate a natural food store in South Burlington, Vermont. Her business prospered and in April 1999 she signed a lease for additional space. For five years, the

---

[3] *Harbour v. Arelco, Inc.,* 678 N.E.2d 381 (Ind. 1997).
[4] *Kyablue v. Watkins,* 149 Cal. Rptr. 3d 156 (Cal. App. 2012).

landlord continually rebuffed her efforts to meet and discuss plans to renovate the 1999 space to expand the grocery store, motivated solely by a desire to pressure the tenant to pay a portion of his legal fees in an unrelated zoning case. The court found that the landlord breached the obligation of good faith and fair dealing, causing the 1999 space to be essentially unusable from 1999 to 2004. The court awarded the tenant the rent she paid for this period less a storage fee adjustment.[5]

15-1f Unconscionable Clauses

Ordinarily, a court will not consider whether a contract is fair or unfair, is wise or foolish, or operates unequally between the parties. **For Example,** the Kramper Family Farm agreed to sell 17.59 acres of land to Dakota Industrial Development, Inc. (DID), for $35,000 per acre if the buyer constructed a paved road along the property by December 31. The contract also provided that if the road was not completed by the date set forth in the contract, the price per acre would be $45,000. When the road was not completed by the December 31 date, Family Farm sued DID for the additional $10,000 per acre. DID defended that to apply the contract according to its plain language would create an unconscionable result and was an unenforceable penalty provision contrary to public policy. The court refused to allow DID to escape its contractual obligations on the pretext of unconscionability and public policy arguments. The parties are at liberty to contract as they see fit, the court concluded, and, generally, a court will not inquire into the adequacy of consideration inasmuch as the value of property is a matter of personal judgment by the parties to the contract. In this case, the price consisted of either $45,000 per acre, or $35,000 per acre with the road by a certain date.[6]

However, in certain unusual situations, the law may hold a contract provision unenforceable because it is too harsh or oppressive to one of the parties. This principle may be applied to invalidate a clause providing for the payment by one party of an excessive penalty on the breaking of a contract or a provision inserted by the dominant party that it shall not be liable for the consequences of intentional torts, fraud, or gross negligence. This principle is extended in connection with the sale of goods to provide that "if the court ... finds the contract or any clause of the contract to have been unconscionable at the time it was made, the court may refuse to enforce the contract, or it may enforce the remainder of the contract without the unconscionable clause, or it may so limit the application of any unconscionable clause as to avoid any unconscionable result."[7]

What Constitutes Unconscionability?

A provision in a contract that gives what the court believes is too much of an advantage over a buyer may be held void as unconscionable.

Determination of Unconscionability

Some jurisdictions analyze unconscionability as having two separate elements: procedural and substantive. Both elements must be present for a court to refuse to enforce a contract provision. Other jurisdictions analyze unconscionability by considering the doctrine of adhesion and whether the clause in question is unduly oppressive.

Procedural unconscionability has to do with matters of freedom of assent resulting from inequality of bargaining power and the absence of real negotiations and meaningful

---

[5] *Century Partners, LP v. Lesser Goldsmith Enterprises,* 958 A.2d 627 (Vt. 2008).
[6] *Kramper Family Farm v. Dakota Industrial Development, Inc.,* 603 N.W.2d 463 (Neb. App. 1999).
[7] U.C.C. §2-302(1).

contract of adhesion— contract offered by a dominant party to a party with inferior bargaining power on a take-it-or-leave-it basis.

choice or a surprise resulting from hiding a disputed term in an unduly long document or fine print. Companywide standardized form contracts imposed on a take-it-or-leave-it basis by a party with superior bargaining strength are called **contracts of adhesion,** and they may sometimes be deemed procedurally unconscionable.

Substantive unconscionability focuses on the actual terms of the contract itself. Such unconscionability is indicated when the contract terms are so one-sided as to shock the conscience or are so extreme as to appear unconscionable according to the mores and business practices of the time and place.

The U.S. Supreme Court has made clear that arbitration is an acceptable forum for the resolution of employment disputes between employees and their employers, including employment-related claims based on federal and state statutes.[8] The controlling arbitration agreement language is commonly devised and implemented by the employer. Under the Federal Arbitration Act (FAA), the employer can obtain a court order to stay court proceedings and compel arbitration according to the terms of the controlling arbitration agreement. The Supreme Court also made clear that in agreeing to arbitration of a statutory claim, a party does not forgo substantive rights afforded by the statute. In a growing number of court decisions, in effect employers are finding that courts will not enforce arbitration agreements in which the employer has devised an arbitration agreement that functions as a thumb on the employer's side of the scale.[9]

When a court finds that a contract or any clause of a contract was unconscionable at the time it was made, it may enforce the remainder of the contract without the unconscionable clause or refuse to enforce the entire agreement if the agreement is permeated by unconscionability. **For Example,** two provisions of a premarital agreement between Jeffrey and Nancy Facter waiving the right to spousal and child support upon the dissolution of the marriage were found to be unconscionable. The invalid provisions were deleted and the remainder of the agreement was enforced.[10] An arbitration agreement may be substantively unconscionable if fees and costs are so excessive as to deny the litigant the ability to pursue a claim. **For Example,** an arbitration agreement was found to be substantively unconscionable because the plaintiff John Clark, a retired senior citizen

THINKING THINGS THROUGH

Legality and Public Policy

Karl Llewellyn, the principal drafter of the law that governs nearly all sales of goods in the United States—the Uniform Commercial Code (UCC)—once wrote, "Covert tools are never reliable tools." He was referring to unfairness in a contract or between the contracting parties.

The original intent of declaring certain types of contracts void because of issues of imbalance was based in equity. Courts stepped in to help parties who found themselves bound under agreements that were not fair and open in both their written terms and the communications between the parties. One contracts scholar wrote that the original

intent could be described as courts stepping in to help "presumptive sillies like sailors and heirs..." and others who, if not crazy, are "pretty peculiar."

However, as the sophistication of contracts and commercial transactions increased, the importance of accuracy, honesty, and fairness increased. Unconscionability is a contracts defense that permits courts to intervene where contracts, if enforced, would "affront the sense of decency." Unconscionability is a term of ethics or moral philosophy used by courts to prevent exploitation and fraud.

---

[8] *Gilmer v. Interstate/Johnson Lane Corp.,* 500 U.S. 20 (1991); *Circuit City Stores, Inc. v. Adams,* 532 U.S. 105 (2001).
[9] See *Vassi/Kouska v. Woodfield Nissan Inc.,* 830 N.E.2d 619 (Ill. App. 2005).
[10] In re *the Marriage of Facter,* 152 Cal. Rptr. 3d 79 (Cal. App. 2013).

living on a fixed income, could not afford to pay the projected $22,800 in arbitrators' fees to arbitrate his medical negligence and abuse and neglect of a vulnerable adult action against the defendant nursing home, where the arbitration agreement did not provide for a waiver/reduction of fees based on financial hardship.[11]

15-2 Agreements Affecting Public Welfare

Agreements that may harm the public welfare are condemned as contrary to public policy and are not binding. Agreements that interfere with public service or the duties of public officials, obstruct legal process, or discriminate against classifications of individuals may be considered detrimental to public welfare and, as such, are not enforceable.

15-2a Agreements Contrary to Public Policy

A given agreement may not violate any statute but may still be so offensive to society that the courts feel that enforcing the contract would be contrary to public policy.

public policy—certain objectives relating to health, morals, and integrity of government that the law seeks to advance by declaring invalid any contract that conflicts with those objectives even though there is no statute expressly declaring such a contract illegal.

Public policy cannot be defined precisely but is loosely described as protection from that which tends to be injurious to the public or contrary to the public good or which violates any established interest of society. Contracts that may be unenforceable as contrary to public policy frequently relate to the protection of the public welfare, health, or safety; to the protection of the person; and to the protection of recognized social institutions. **For Example,** a woman entered into a services contract with a male in exchange for financial support. The record disclosed, however, that the association between the parties was one founded upon the exchange of money for sex. The court determined that the agreement for financial support in exchange for illicit sexual relations was violative of public policy and thus was unenforceable.[12] Courts are cautious in invalidating a contract on the ground that it is contrary to public policy because courts recognize that, on the one hand, they are applying a very vague standard and, on the other hand, they are restricting the freedom of the contracting parties to contract freely as they choose.[13]

15-2b Gambling, Wagers, and Lotteries

Gambling contracts are illegal. Largely as a result of the adoption of antigambling statutes, wagers or bets are generally illegal. Private **lotteries** involving the three elements of prize, chance, and consideration (or similar affairs of chance) are also generally held illegal. In many states, public lotteries (lotteries run by a state government) have been legalized by statute. Raffles are usually regarded as lotteries. In some states, bingo games, lotteries, and raffles are legalized by statute when the funds raised are used for a charitable purpose.

lottery—any plan by which a consideration is given for a chance to win a prize; it consists of three elements: (1) there must be a payment of money or something of value for an opportunity to win, (2) a prize must be available, and (3) the prize must be offered by lot or chance.

Sales promotion schemes calling for the distribution of property according to chance among the purchasers of goods are held illegal as lotteries without regard to whether the scheme is called a *guessing contest*, a *raffle*, or a *gift*.

Giveaway plans and games are lawful so long as it is not necessary to buy anything or give anything of value to participate. If participation is free, the element of consideration is lacking, and there is no lottery.

An activity is not gambling when the result is solely or predominantly a matter of skill. In contrast, it is gambling when the result is solely a matter of luck. Rarely is any activity 100 percent skill or 100 percent luck.

---

[11] *Clark v. Renaissance West*, LLC, 307 P.3d 77 (Ariz. App. 2013).
[12] *Anonymous v. Anonymous,* 740 N.Y.S.2d 341 (App. Div. 2002).
[13] *Beacon Hill Civic Ass'n v. Ristorante Toscano, Inc.,* 662 N.E.2d 1015 (Mass. 1996).

ETHICS & THE LAW

Public Policy Issues Regarding Surrogacy Contracts

William Stern and his wife were unable to have children. The Sterns entered into a surrogacy contract with Mary Beth Whitehead though the Infertility Center of New York (ICNY). William Stern and the Whiteheads (husband and wife) signed a contract for Mary Beth to be artificially inseminated and carry Stern's child to term, for which Stern was to pay Mary Beth $10,000 and ICNY $7,500.

Mary Beth was successfully artificially inseminated in 1985, and "Baby M" was born on March 27, 1986. On March 30, 1986, Mary Beth turned Baby M over to the Sterns. Subsequently, Mary Beth became so emotionally distraught that the Sterns allowed her to take Baby M for one week to help her adjust. The Whiteheads fled to New Jersey with the baby, and the search and return of Baby M attracted national attention and brought forth the national discussion of the legality of surrogacy contracts. The Supreme Court of New Jersey invalidated the surrogacy contract as against public policy but affirmed the trial court's use of "the best interests of the child" analysis,* and on remand the trial court awarded the Sterns custody and visitation rights to Mary Beth Whitehead.

Assisted Reproductive Technology (ART) has created ways for people to have children regardless of their reproductive capacity, including traditional and gestational categories. The ability to create a family using ART has seemingly outpaced legislative responses to the legal questions presented. In *Rosecky v. Schissel*, the Wisconsin Supreme Court determined that a surrogacy agreement was a valid and largely enforceable contract except for the language requiring the surrogate mother to terminate her parental rights.**

Chief Justice Shirley Abrahamson in her concurring opinion disagreed with the majority opinion's authorization of people to contract out the State's traditional, statutory oversight role in the protection of children. She points out numerous public policy issues regarding the validity of surrogacy agreements including:

*Must the agreement be in writing; should compensated agreements be allowed and what are the limits on compensation; should the availability of surrogacy be limited to married couples or to infertile intended parents; should the age of any party be limited; should a spouse be required either to consent or to be made party to the contract; must each individual involved be represented by counsel; should the State require that information about each individual's legal rights be provided; what provisions are valid regarding who makes decisions about health care and termination of the pregnancy; how and when may the agreement be terminated; and must any party to the agreement be given the opportunity to change his or her mind before or after the birth of the child.****

What is your opinion?

*Matter of Baby M., 537 A.2d 1227 (N.J. 1988).
**Rosecky v. Schissel, 833 N.W.2d 634 (Wis. 2013).
***Id. at 126 FN.2.

15-3 Regulation of Business

Local, state, and national laws regulate a wide variety of business activities and practices.

15-3a Effect of Violation

Whether an agreement made in connection with business conducted in violation of the law is binding or void depends on how strongly opposed the public policy is to the prohibited act. Some courts take the view that the agreement is not void unless the statute expressly specifies this. In some instances, a statute expressly preserves the validity of the contract. **For Example,** if someone fails to register a fictitious name under which a business is conducted, the violator, after registering the name as required by statute, is permitted to sue on a contract made while illegally conducting business.

15-3b Statutory Regulation of Contracts

To establish uniformity or to protect one of the parties to a contract, statutes frequently provide that contracts of a given class must follow a statutory model or must contain specified provisions. **For Example,** statutes commonly specify that particular clauses must be included in insurance policies to protect the persons insured and their beneficiaries. Other statutes require that contracts executed in connection with credit buying and loans contain particular provisions designed to protect the debtor.

Consumer protection legislation gives the consumer the right to rescind the contract in certain situations. Laws relating to truth in lending, installment sales, and home improvement contracts commonly require that an installment-sale contract specify the cash price, the down payment, the trade-in value (if any), the cash balance, the insurance costs, and the interest and finance charges.

CPA ## 15-3c **Licensed Callings or Dealings**

Statutes frequently require that a person obtain a license, certificate, or diploma before practicing certain professions, such as law and medicine.[14] A license may also be required before carrying on a particular business or trade, such as that of a real estate broker, stockbroker, hotel keeper, or pawnbroker.

If a license is required to protect the public from unqualified persons, a contract made by an unlicensed person is unenforceable. **For Example,** a corporation that does not hold a required real estate broker's license cannot sue to recover fees for services as a broker. An unlicensed insurance broker who cannot recover a fee because of the absence of a license cannot evade the statutory requirement by having a friend who is a licensed broker bill for the services and collect the payment for him.

CASE SUMMARY

How Much for a Brokerage License? How Much Commission Was Lost?

FACTS: Thompson Halbach & Associates, Inc., an Arizona corporation, entered into an agreement with Meteor Motors, Inc., the owner of Palm Beach Acura, to find a buyer for the dealership, and Meteor agreed to pay a 5 percent commission based on the closing price of the sale. Working out of Scottsdale, Arizona, Thompson solicited potential Florida purchasers for the Florida business by phone, fax, and e-mail. Among those contacted was Craig Zinn Automotive Group, which ultimately purchased Palm Beach Acura from Meteor Motors for $5,000,000. Thompson was not paid its $250,000 commission and brought suit against Meteor for breach of contract. Meteor defended that Thompson was an unlicensed broker and that a state statute declares a contract for a commission with an unlicensed broker to be invalid. Thompson responded that the Florida state statute did not apply because it worked out of Scottsdale.

DECISION: Judgment for Meteor. The Florida statute clearly applies to a foreign broker who provides brokerage activities in Florida. Thompson solicited potential Florida purchasers for the Florida business and that purchaser was a Florida corporation. [*Meteor Motors v. Thompson Halbach & Associates*, 914 So. 2d 479 (Fla. App. 2005)]

In some states an unlicensed contractor can neither enforce a home improvement contract against an owner nor seek recovery in *quantum meruit*. **For Example,** a contractor who performed work on Adam Gottbetter's apartment in New York City and was not paid for its work was barred from pursuing its claim against the owner.[15]

However, if the statute does not provide expressly that its violation will deprive the parties of their right to sue on the contract, and the denial of relief is wholly out of proportion to the requirements of public policy, the right to recover will not be denied. **For Example,** an unlicensed contractor who installed water pumps on Staten Island little

---

[14] *Hakimi v. Cantwell*, 855 N.Y.S.2d 273 (App. Div. 2008).
[15] *Orchid Construction Corp. v. Gottbetter*, 932 N.Y.S.2d 100 (A.D. 2011).

league fields was not barred from recovering $18,316.59 for the work in question, which was not home improvement work.[16]

CPA 15-3d **Contracts in Restraint of Trade**

An agreement that unreasonably restrains trade is illegal and void on the ground that it is contrary to public policy. Such agreements take many forms, such as a combination to create a monopoly or to obtain a corner on the market or an association of merchants to increase prices. In addition to the illegality of the agreement based on general principles of law, statutes frequently declare monopolies illegal and subject the parties to various civil and criminal penalties.[17]

CPA 15-3e **Agreements Not to Compete**

In the absence of a valid restrictive covenant, the seller of a business may compete with the buyer, or an ex-employee may solicit customers of the former employer. Restrictive covenants not to compete are disfavored (but not prohibited) in many states as a trade restraint because they may prevent an employee from earning a living, adversely restrain the mobility of employees, and may be overly protective of the interests of employers at the expense of employees. A noncompete provision may be enforceable, however, if (1) it is narrowly drawn to protect the employer's legitimate business interests, (2) it is not unduly burdensome on the employee's ability to earn a living, (3) the geographic restriction is not overly broad, and (4) a reasonable time limitation is given. Reasonably necessary noncompete clauses in the sale of a business are enforced in all states.

Sale of Business

When a going business is sold, it is commonly stated in the contract that the seller shall not go into the same or a similar business again within a certain geographic area or for a certain period of time, or both. In early times, such agreements were held void because they deprived the public of the service of the person who agreed not to compete, reduced competition, and exposed the public to monopoly. To modern courts, the question is whether, under the circumstances, the restriction imposed on one party is reasonably necessary to protect the other party. If the restriction is reasonable, it is valid and enforceable. **For Example,** when Scott Gaddy, the majority stockholder of GWC Insurance Brokers sold his business to Alliant for $4.1 million he agreed to refrain from competing in the insurance business in California for five years. Under California law contracts not to compete are void, except for noncompetition covenants in connection with the sale of a business. The reason for the exception is to prevent the seller from depriving the buyer of the full value of the acquisition, including the sold company's goodwill. The court enforced the covenant against Gaddy.[18]

Employment Contract

Employers rely on noncompete clauses to protect their businesses from employees who leave after receiving expensive training or engineers, scientists, or other professionals or

---

[16] *Del Carlo v. Staten Island Little League, Inc.*, 993 N.Y.S.2d 435 (A.D. 2014).

[17] Sherman Antitrust Act, 15 U.S.C. §§1–7; Clayton Act, 15 U.S.C. §§12–27; Federal Trade Commission Act, 15 U.S.C. §§41–58.

[18] Cal. Rptr. 3d 259 (Cal. App. 2008). Aside from the sale of a business, under California law, any "contract by which anyone is restrained from engaging in a lawful profession, trade or business is to that extent void." Cal B&P Code §16600. A noncompete provision is permitted, however, when "necessary to protect the employer's trade secrets." See *Lotono v. Aetna U.S. Healthcare Inc.*, 82 F. Supp. 2d 1089 (C.D. Cal. 1999), where Aetna was liable for wrongful termination when it fired a California employee for refusing to sign a noncompete agreement.

nonprofessionals who leave firms or businesses to join competitors. Employers enforce these clauses by notifying the new employer and threatening litigation,[19] or seeking a preliminary injunction prohibiting the violation of the noncompete agreement.[20] The burden of proof is on the employer to show that the provision is narrowly drawn to protect the employer's legitimate business interests as to time, place, and activities. Employers have legitimate protectable business interests including maintaining their goodwill with existing customers, their confidential information, and trade secrets. If the noncompete provision is overly broad, however, it will be unenforceable. **For Example,** Home Paramount Pest Control's noncompete clause with Justin Shaffer that prohibited him from working in the pest control industry in any capacity, barring him "in any manner whatsoever," was overly broad and unenforceable.[21] Geographic restrictions are also at issue. **For Example,** Illinois manufacturer Arcor's noncompete clause, which had a restricted area of "the United States and Canada" precluding competition by a former employee for a one-year period, was found to be unenforceable as an industry-wide ban that constituted a "blanket prohibition on competition."[22] Overly broad and unreasonable restrictive covenants will not be enforced.

CASE SUMMARY

Unreasonable and Unenforceable

FACTS: On December 12, 2012, Defendants Contreras, Senn, Verduzco, and VanderWeerd, inseminated cows at several dairy farms in Sunnyside, Washington, on behalf of their employer, Genex Cooperative, Inc. ("Genex"). The very next day, they inseminated cows at the same dairy farms—but this time on behalf of CRV USA ("CRV"), a Genex rival. Jilted by its former employees and spurned by its customers, Genex filed suit to enforce non-competition agreements against three of the defendants. Although the individual contracts varied in terms, Contreras, Senn, and Verduzco contended the agreements were unenforceable. Mr. VanderWeerd had not signed an agreement.

DECISION: Judgment against Genex. Verduzco's noncompete covenant prohibited him from contacting any dairy farm, which he had sought either new or increased business from in the last eighteen months. Under Wisconsin law, applicable to Verduzco's agreement, prohibiting an employee from soliciting any customer the employee has

tried but failed to do business with for the former employer is a violation of state law.

Senn's restrictive agreement was governed by Washington law and found to be unreasonable because it was not limited to soliciting or serving former clients. It appeared to the court that Genex actually used restrictive covenants to eliminate legitimate competition or to strong-arm employees to accept ever-dwindling wages and restrict their freedom to work.

Contreras—who cannot read or write English—was a low-level agricultural worker with an employment-at-will relationship with Genex. An at-will employee may be terminated without any cause and then be prohibited from seeking new employment in his line of work. Genex did not meet its burden to establish the reasonableness of its covenant with Contreras, and the noncompete agreement was thus unenforceable. [*Genex Cooperative, Inc. v. Contreras,* **39 IER Cases 294 (E.D. Wash. 2014)**]

---

[19] In *Socko v. Mid-Atlantic Systems of CPA, Inc.,* 99 A.3d 928 (Pa. Super. 2014), the employer notified the new employer and threatened litigation. Socko successfully challenged this action, with the court deciding that the agreement was unenforceable for lack of consideration because it was entered into after the commencement of Socko's employment with Mid-Atlantic.

[20] A motion for a preliminary injunction is heard expeditiously by the court and is ordinarily used to preserve the status quo pending a trial on the merits. However, in noncompete cases, the validity of the time limitation is "clothed with immediacy." Decisions at the preliminary injunction stage become, in effect, a determination on the merits. See *Horner International Co. v. McCoy,* 754 S.E.2d 852 (2014).

[21] *Home Paramount Pest Control Companies, Inc. v. Shaffer,* 718 S.E.2d 762 (Va. 2011).

[22] *Arcor, Inc. v. Haas,* 842 N.E.2d 265 (Ill. App. 2005).

Effect of Invalidity

When a restriction of competition agreed to by the parties is invalid because its scope as to time or geographic area is too great, how does this affect the contract? Some courts trim the restrictive covenant down to a scope they deem reasonable and require the parties to abide by that revision.[23] This rule is nicknamed the "blue-pencil rule." **For Example,** Julie Murray signed a noncompete agreement, which was validly assigned to the purchaser of the Accounting Center of Luca County, Inc. When the new owner changed from an hourly wage to commission pay for her tax preparation work, she objected and was terminated. The court found that the 24-month noncompete restriction exceeded what was reasonable to protect the employer's legitimate business interests and modified the time period to one year.[24] In the *Arcor* case, the court refused to "blue-pencil" the covenant because to render the clause reasonable, the court would in effect be writing a new agreement, which is inappropriate.[25] Other courts refuse to apply the blue-pencil rule and hold that the restrictive covenant is void or that the entire contract is void.[26] There is also authority that a court should refuse to apply the blue-pencil rule when the restrictive covenant is manifestly unfair and would virtually keep the employee from earning a living.

15-3f Usurious Agreements

usury–lending money at an interest rate that is higher than the maximum rate allowed by law.

Usury is committed when money is loaned at a higher rate of interest than the law allows. Most states prohibit by statute charging more than a stated amount of interest. These statutes provide a maximum annual contract rate of interest that can be exacted under the law of a given state. In many states, the usury law does not apply to loans made to corporations.

THINKING THINGS THROUGH

Noncompete Clauses, Cause for Concern?

Several states do not enforce noncompete clauses in employment contracts, according to the research of Matt Marx, who dedicated his doctoral studies at Harvard to this topic. The states are (from west to east): California, Nevada, Montana, North Dakota, Minnesota, Oklahoma, West Virginia, and Connecticut. (New York, Washington, and Oregon have significantly limited their applicability.) Marx had naively signed a two-year noncompete agreement out of MIT at SpeechWorks, a voice recognition start-up, and when he wanted to leave and continue in the voice recognition field, his options were to sit out the two-year noncompete period or go to work at a California firm, which he did. He is now researching whether enforcing noncompetes in a state can spur inventors, engineers, and entrepreneurs to move elsewhere to pursue development of their ideas.*

Does a state's innovation suffer when noncompete clauses handcuff employees to an employer, or force employees to take an unpaid leave for the noncompete period before continuing in their field with a new or start-up employer? Thinking Things Through, prospective employees should carefully consider the impact noncompetes would have on their lives, and if they must sign one, carefully negotiate its duration and scope.**

*See Scott Kirsner, "Why 'Noncompete' Means 'Don't Thrive,'" *Boston Globe,* December 30, 2007, E–1; Scott Kirsner, "Start-ups Stifled by Noncompetes," *Boston Globe,* June 21, 2009, G–1.
**For a comprehensive study of the strength of noncompetition enforcement rankings by state, see Norman D. Bishara, "Fifty Ways to Leave Your Employer: Relative Enforcement of Covenants Not to Compete, Trends and Implications for Employee Mobility Policy," 13 *U. Pa. J. Bus. L.* 751 (2011).

---

[23] *Keeley v. CSA, P.C.,* 510 S.E.2d 880 (Ga. App. 1999).
[24] *Murray v. Accounting Center of Lucas County, Inc.,* 898 N.E.2d 89 (Ohio App. 2008).
[25] *Arcor, Inc. v. Hass* 842 N.E.2d 265 (Ill. App. 2005).
[26] *Volcen Steel Structures, Inc. v. McCarty,* 764 S.E.2d 458 (Ga. App. 2014).

When a lender incurs expenses in making a loan, such as the cost of appraising property or making a credit investigation of the borrower, the lender will require the borrower to pay the amount of such expenses. Any fee charged by a lender that goes beyond the reasonable expense of making the loan constitutes "interest" for the purposes of determining whether the transaction is usurious.[27]

Penalites for violating usury laws vary from state to state, with a number of states restricting the lender to the recovery of the loan but no interest whatsoever; other states allow recovery of the loan principal and interest up to the maximum contract rate. Some states also impose a penalty on the lender such as the payment of double the interest paid on a usurious loan.

CASE SUMMARY

Would You Recommend Karen Canzoneri as an Investment Advisor?

FACTS: Karen Canzoneri entered into two agreements with Howard Pinchuck. Under the first agreement, Canzoneri advanced $50,000 to be repaid at 12 percent per month for 12 consecutive months "as an investment profit." The second agreement required "$36,000 to be repaid on or before 6/1/01 with an investment profit of $36,000, total being $72,000." The annualized rate of return for the first transaction was 144 percent and for the second transaction was 608 percent. The civil penalty for violating the state's maximum interest rate of 25 percent per annum is forfeiture of the entire principal amount. Canzoneri contends that the transactions were investments not subject to the usury law.

DECISION: Judgment for Pinchuck. The four elements of a usurious transaction are present: (1) the transaction was a loan, (2) the money loaned required that it be returned, (3) an interest rate higher than allowed by law was required, and (4) a corrupt intention to take more than the legal rate for the use of the money loaned exists. Even though the terms called for "profit," not "interest," the courts looked to the substance, not the form of the transaction. [*Pinchuck v. Canzoneri*, 920 So. 2d 713 (Fla. App. 2006)]

Make the Connection

Summary

When an agreement is illegal, it is ordinarily void and no contract arises from it. Courts will not allow one party to an illegal agreement to bring suit against the other party. There are some exceptions to this, such as when the parties are not equally guilty or when the law's purpose in making the agreement illegal is to protect the person who is bringing suit. When possible, an agreement will be interpreted as being lawful. Even when a particular provision is held unlawful, the balance of the agreement may be saved so that the net result is a contract minus the clause that was held illegal.

The term *illegality* embraces situations in unconscionable contract clauses in which the courts hold that contract provisions are unenforceable because they are too harsh or oppressive to one of the parties to a transaction. If the clause is part of a standard form contract drafted by the party having superior bargaining power and is presented on a take-it-or-leave-it basis (a contract of adhesion) and the substantive terms of the clause itself are unduly oppressive, the clause will be found to be unconscionable and not enforced.

27 *Lentimo v. Cullen Center Bank and Trust Co.,* 919 S.W.2d 743 (Tex. App. 1996).

Whether a contract is contrary to public policy may be difficult to determine because public policy is not precisely defined. That which is harmful to the public welfare or general good is contrary to public policy. Contracts condemned as contrary to public policy include those designed to deprive the weaker party of a benefit that the lawmaker desired to provide, agreements injuring public service, and wagers and private lotteries. Statutes commonly make the wager illegal as a form of gambling. The private lottery is any plan under which, for a consideration, a person has a chance to win a prize.

Learning Outcomes

After studying this chapter, you should be able to clearly explain:

15-1 General Principles

LO.1 Explain the general contract principles on "illegality"

See the unenforceable illegal lease to nonprofessionals example, page 276.
See the example where a contract to manufacture and sell illegal slot machines is void, page 277.

LO.2 Explain the implied obligation on all parties of good faith and fair dealing

See the example of the Vermont landlord who deprived a tenant of her rights under a lease, page 278.

15-2 Agreements Affecting Public Welfare

LO.3 Understand that it is only in unusual situations that a contract provision will be unenforceable because it is unconscionable

See the *Kramper Family Farm* example where the court refused to consider whether the contract was fair or unfair, wise or foolish, page 278.

Key Terms

contracts of adhesion
good faith

in pari delicto
lotteries

public policy
usury

Questions and Case Problems

1. When are the parties to an illegal agreement *in pari delicto?*

2. John Iwen sued U.S. West Direct because of a negligently constructed yellow pages advertisement. U.S. West Direct moved to stay litigation and compel arbitration under the yellow pages order form, which

Illegality may consist of the violation of a statute or administrative regulation adopted to regulate business. An agreement not to compete may be illegal as a restraint of trade except when reasonable in its terms and when it is incidental to the sale of a business or to a contract of employment.

The charging by a lender of a higher rate of interest than allowed by law is usury. Courts must examine transactions carefully to see whether a usurious loan is disguised as a legitimate transaction.

But see *John Clark's* case, illustrating an unconscionable arbitration clause, page 280.

15-3 Regulation of Business

LO.4 Explain the rationale for requiring licenses to carry on as a business, trade, or profession

See the discussion requiring licenses to protect the public from unqualified persons, page 282.

LO.5 Distinguish between noncompete clauses after the sale of a business and noncompete clauses in employment contracts

See the example where the California court enforced a five-year noncompete clause against the seller of a business, page 283.
See the example involving Julie Murray's noncompete clause and why it was modified from 24 months to one year, page 285.
See the *Genex* case that illustrates a trend barring enforcement of overly broad and unreasonable noncompetition clauses, page 284.

required advertisers to resolve all controversies through arbitration, but allowed U.S. West (the publisher) to pursue judicial remedies to collect amounts due it. Under the arbitration provision, Iwen's sole remedy was a pro rata reduction or refund of the cost of the advertisement. The order form language was drafted by U.S. West Direct on a take-it-or-leave-it basis and stated in part:

Any controversy or claim arising out of or relating to this Agreement, or breach thereof, other than an action by Publisher for the collection of amounts due under this Agreement, shall be settled by final, binding arbitration in accordance with the Commercial Arbitration rules of the American Arbitration Association.

If forced to arbitration, Iwen would be unable to recover damages for the negligently constructed yellow pages ad, nor could he recover damages for infliction of emotional distress and punitive damages related to his many efforts to adjust the matter with the company, which were ignored or rejected. Must Iwen have his case resolved through arbitration rather than a court of law? [*Iwen v. U.S. West Direct*, 977 P.2d 989 (Mont.)]

3. Sutcliffe Banton, dba Nemard Construction, furnished labor and materials (valued at $162,895) for improving Vicky Deafeamkpor's New York City residential property. She paid only $41,718, leaving $121,987 unpaid. Banton sued her and the jury awarded $90,000 in damages. Deafeamkpor moved for an order setting aside the jury's verdict because Banton was not properly licensed by New York City. Under NYC Code an unlicensed contractor may neither enforce a home improvement contract against an owner or recover in *quantum meruit*. The jury heard all the evidence regarding the materials and labor expended on Deafeamkpor's residence and concluded that the plaintiff performed satisfactory work valued at $90,000 for which he was not paid. Should the court allow the owner to take advantage of Banton and his employees and suppliers? What public policy would support such an outcome? Decide. [*Nemard Construction Corp. v. Deafeamkpor*, 863 N.Y.S.2d 846]

4. Eugene McCarthy left his position as director of sales for Nike's Brand Jordan division in June 2003 to become vice president of U.S. footwear sales and merchandising at Reebok, one of Nike's competitors. Nike sought a preliminary injunction to prevent McCarthy from working for Reebok for a year, invoking a noncompete agreement McCarthy had signed in Oregon in 1997 when Nike had promoted him to his earlier position as a regional footwear sales manager. The agreement stated in pertinent part:

During EMPLOYEE'S employment by NIKE... and for one (1) year thereafter, ("the Restriction Period"), EMPLOYEE will not directly or indirectly ... be employed by, consult for, or be connected in any manner with, any business engaged anywhere in the world in the athletic footwear, athletic apparel or sports equipment and accessories business, or any other business which directly competes with NIKE or any of its subsidiaries or affiliated corporations.

McCarty contends that such a contract is a restraint of trade and should not be enforced. Nike contends that the agreement is fair and should be enforced. Decide. [*Nike, Inc. v. McCarthy*, 379 F.3d 576 (9th Cir.)]

5. Ewing was employed by Presto-X-Co., a pest exterminator. His contract of employment specified that he would not solicit or attempt to solicit customers of Presto-X for two years after the termination of his employment. After working several years, his employment was terminated. Ewing then sent a letter to customers of Presto-X stating that he no longer worked for Presto-X and that he was still certified by the state. Ewing set forth his home address and phone number, which the customers did not previously have. The letter ended with the statement, "I thank you for your business throughout the past years." Presto-X brought an action to enjoin Ewing from sending such letters. He raised the defense that he was prohibited only from soliciting and there was nothing in the letters that constituted a seeking of customers. Decide. What ethical values are involved? [*Presto-X-Co. v. Ewing*, 442 N.W.2d 85 (Iowa)]

6. The Minnesota adoption statute requires that any agency placing a child for adoption make a thorough investigation and not give a child to an applicant unless the placement is in the best interests of the child. Tibbetts applied to Crossroads, Inc., a private adoption agency, for a child to adopt. He later sued the agency for breach of contract, claiming that the agency was obligated by contract to supply a child for adoption. The agency claimed that it was required only to use its best efforts to locate a child and was not required to supply a child to Tibbetts unless it found him to be a suitable parent. Decide. [*Tibbetts v. Crossroads, Inc.*, 411 N.W.2d 535 (Minn. App.)]

7. Siddle purchased a quantity of fireworks from Red Devil Fireworks Co. The sale was illegal, however, because Siddle did not have a license to make the purchase, which the seller knew because it had been so informed by the attorney general of the state. Siddle did not pay for the fireworks, and Red Devil

sued him. He defended on the ground that the contract could not be enforced because it was illegal. Was the defense valid? [*Red Devil Fireworks Co. v. Siddle*, 648 P.2d 468 (Wash. App.)]

8. Justin Shaffer, while an employee of the Home Paramount Pest Control Companies Inc., signed an employment agreement providing that:

    > *The Employee will not engage directly or indirectly or concern himself/herself in any manner whatsoever in the carrying on or conducting the business of exterminating, pest control, termite control and/or fumigation services as an owner, agent, servant, representative, or employee, and/or as a member of a partnership and/or as an officer, director or stockholder of any corporation, or in any manner whatsoever, in any city, cities, county or counties in the state(s) in which the Employee works and/or in which the Employee was assigned during the two (2) years next preceding the termination of the Employment Agreement and for a period of two (2) years from and after the date upon which he/she shall cease for any reason whatsoever to be an employee of [Home Paramount].*

    Shaffer resigned from Home Paramount and became an employee of Connor's Termite and Pest Control Inc. Home Paramount sued Shaffer and Connor's, claiming that Shaffer's employment by Connor's violated the contract. The defendants contended that the provision was overboard and unenforceable. Decide. [*Home Paramount Pest Control Companies, Inc. v. Shaffer*, 718 S.E.2d 762 (Va.)]

9. Smith was employed as a salesman for Borden, Inc., which sold food products in 63 counties in Arkansas, 2 counties in Missouri, 2 counties in Oklahoma, and 1 county in Texas. Smith's employment contract prohibited him from competing with Borden after leaving its employ. Smith left Borden and went to work for a competitor, Lady Baltimore Foods. Working for this second employer, Smith sold in 3 counties of Arkansas. He had sold in 2 of these counties while he worked for Borden. Borden brought an injunction action against Smith and Lady Baltimore to enforce the noncompete covenant in Smith's former contract. Was Borden entitled to the injunction? [*Borden, Inc. v. Smith*, 478 S.W.2d 744 (Ark.)]

10. All new employees of Circuit City Stores were required to sign a Dispute Resolution Agreement (DRA) mandating that employees submit all employment-related disputes to arbitration. Under the DRA Circuit City was not obligated to arbitrate its claims against employees and may bring lawsuits against employees. Remedies are limited under the DRA, including a one-year back pay limit and a two-year front pay limit, with cap on punitive damages of an amount up to the greater of the amount of back pay and front pay awarded or $5,000. In a civil lawsuit under state law a plaintiff is entitled to all forms of relief. The DRA requires that employees split the cost of the arbitrator's fees with the employer. An individual is not required to pay for the services of a judge. Adams filed a sexual harassment case against his employer in state court. Circuit City filed a petition in federal court to compel arbitration. Decide. [*Circuit City Stores, Inc. v. Adams*, 274 F.3d 889 (9th Cir.)]

11. Vodra was employed as a salesperson and contracting agent for American Security Services. As part of his contract of employment, Vodra signed an agreement that for three years after leaving this employment, he would not solicit any customer of American. Vodra had no experience in the security field when he went to work for American. To the extent that he became known to American's customers, it was because of being American's representative rather than because of his own reputation in the security field. After some years, Vodra left American and organized a competing company that solicited American's customers. American sued him to enforce the restrictive covenant. Vodra claimed that the restrictive covenant was illegal and not binding. Was he correct? [*American Security Services, Inc. v. Vodra*, 385 N.W.2d 73 (Neb.)]

12. Potomac Leasing Co. leased an automatic telephone system to Vitality Centers. Claudene Cato signed the lease as guarantor of payments. When the rental was not paid, Potomac Leasing brought suit against Vitality and Cato. They raised the defense that the rented equipment was to be used for an illegal purpose—namely, the random sales solicitation by means of an automatic telephone in violation of state statute; that this purpose was known to Potomac Leasing; and that Potomac Leasing could therefore not enforce the lease. Was this defense valid? [*Potomac Leasing Co. v. Vitality Centers, Inc.*, 718 S.W.2d 928 (Ark.)]

13. The English publisher of a book called *Cambridge* gave a New York publisher permission to sell that book any place in the world except in England. The New York publisher made several bulk sales of the book to buyers who sold the book throughout the world, including England. The English publisher

sued the New York publisher and its customers for breach of the restriction prohibiting sales in England. Decide.

14. Sandra Menefee sued Geographic Expeditions, Inc. (GeoEx), for the wrongful death of her son while on a GeoEx expedition up Mount Kilimanjaro. GeoEx moved to compel arbitration under the parties' limitation of liability contract. GeoEx designed its arbitration clause to limit the plaintiffs' recovery and required them to indemnify GeoEx for its legal costs and fees if they unsuccessfully pursued any claim covered by the release agreement. Moreover, GeoEx required that plaintiffs pay half of any mediation fees and arbitrate in San Francisco, GeoEx's choice of venue, as opposed to the plaintiffs' home in Colorado. Should the court require the Menefees to arbitrate? If any component of the arbitration clause is found to be unconscionable, should the court simply sever the objectionable provision and enforce the remainder of the arbitration clause? [*Lhotka v. Geographic Expeditions, Inc.*, 104 Cal. Rptr. 3d 844 (Cal. App. 2010)]

15. Yarde Metals, Inc., owned six season tickets to New England Patriots football games. Gillette Stadium, where the games are played, had insufficient men's restrooms in use for football games at that time, which was the subject of numerous newspaper columns. On October 13, 2002, a guest of Yarde Metals, Mikel LaCroix, along with others, used available women's restrooms to answer the call of nature. As LaCroix left the restroom, however, he was arrested and charged with disorderly conduct. The Patriots organization terminated all six of Yarde's season ticket privileges, incorrectly giving as a reason that LaCroix was ejected "for throwing bottles in the seating section." Yarde sued, contending that "by terminating the plaintiff's season tickets for 2002 and for the future arbitrarily, without cause and based on false information," the Patriots had violated the implicit covenant of good faith and fair dealing of the season tickets contract. The back of each Patriots ticket states:

> *This ticket and all season tickets are revocable licenses. The Patriots reserve the right to revoke such licenses, in their sole discretion, at any time and for any reason.*

How would you decide this case? [*Yarde Metals, Inc. v. New England Patriots Ltd.*, 834 N.E.2d 1233 (Mass. App.)]

CPA Questions

1. West, an Indiana real estate broker, misrepresented to Zimmer that West was licensed in Kansas under the Kansas statute that regulates real estate brokers and requires all brokers to be licensed. Zimmer signed a contract agreeing to pay West a 5 percent commission for selling Zimmer's home in Kansas. West did not sign the contract. West sold Zimmer's home. If West sued Zimmer for nonpayment of commission, Zimmer would be:

   a. Liable to West only for the value of services rendered.

   b. Liable to West for the full commission.

   c. Not liable to West for any amount because West did not sign the contract.

   d. Not liable to West for any amount because West violated the Kansas licensing requirements (5/92, Law, #25).

2. Blue purchased a travel agency business from Drye. The purchase price included payment for Drye's goodwill. The agreement contained a covenant prohibiting Drye from competing with Blue in the travel agency business. Which of the following statements regarding the covenant is *not* correct?

   a. The restraint must be *no* more extensive than is reasonably necessary to protect the goodwill purchased by Blue.

   b. The geographic area to which it applies must be reasonable.

   c. The time period for which it is to be effective must be reasonable.

   d. The value to be assigned to it is the excess of the price paid over the seller's cost of all tangible assets (11/87, Law, #2).

Contract must be in written.

Chapter 16

Writing, Electronic Forms, and Interpretation of Contracts

Mess prove in court!
* Subject matter
* Identity of the parties.

Learning Outcomes <<<

After studying this chapter, you should be able to

LO.1 Explain when a contract must be evidenced by a writing

LO.2 Explain the effect of noncompliance with the statute of frauds

LO.3 Explain the parol evidence rule and the exceptions to this rule

LO.4 Understand the basic rule of contract construction that a contract is enforced according to its terms

LO.5 State the rules for interpreting ambiguous terms in a contract

When must a contract be written? What is the effect of a written contract? These questions lead to the statute of frauds and the parol evidence rule.

16-1 Statute of Frauds

A *contract* is a legally binding agreement. Must the agreement be evidenced by a writing?

16-1a Validity of Oral Contracts

In the absence of a statute requiring a writing, a contract may be oral or written. Managers and professionals should be more fully aware that their oral communications, including telephone conversations and dinner or breakfast discussions, may be deemed legally enforceable contracts. **For Example,** suppose that Mark Wahlberg, after reviewing a script tentatively entitled *The Bulger Boys*, meets with Steven Spielberg to discuss Mark's playing mobster James "Whitey" Bulger in the film. Steven states, "You *are* Whitey, Marky! The nuns at Gate of Heaven Grammar School in South Boston—or maybe it was St. Augustine's—they don't send for the Boston Police when they are troubled about drug use in the schools; they send for you to talk to the kids. Nobody messes with you, and the kids know it. This is true stuff, I think, and this fugitive's brother Bill comes out of the Southie projects to be president of U Mass." Mark likes the script. Steven and Mark block out two months of time for shooting the film this fall. They agree on Mark's usual fee and a "piece of the action" based on a set percentage of the net income from the film. Thereafter, Mark's agent does not like the deal. He believes there are better scripts for Mark. And with Hollywood accounting, a percentage of the "net" take is usually of little value. However, all of the essential terms of a contract have been agreed on, and such an oral agreement would be legally enforceable. As set forth in the following text, no writing is required for a services contract that can be performed within one year after the date of the agreement.

Certain contracts, on the other hand, must be evidenced by a writing to be legally enforceable. These contracts are covered by the **statute of frauds.**[1]

Because many oral contracts are legally enforceable, it is a good business practice in the preliminary stages of discussions to stipulate that no binding agreement is intended to be formed until a written contract is prepared and signed by the parties.

statute of frauds–statute that, in order to prevent fraud through the use of perjured testimony, requires that certain kinds of transactions be evidenced in writing in order to be binding or enforceable.

16-1b Contracts That Must Be Evidenced by a Writing

The statute of frauds requires that certain kinds of contracts be evidenced by a writing or they cannot be enforced. This means that either the contract itself must be in writing and signed by both parties or there must be a sufficient written memorandum of the oral contract signed by the person being sued for breach of contract. A *part performance* doctrine

---

[1] The name is derived from the original Statute of Frauds and Perjuries, which was adopted in 1677 and became the pattern for similar legislation in America. The 17th section of that statute governed the sale of goods, and its modern counterpart is §2-201 of the UCC. The 4th section of the English statute provided the pattern for U.S. legislation with respect to contracts other than for the sale of goods described in this section of the chapter. The English statute was repealed in 1954 except as to land sale and guarantee contracts. The U.S. statutes remain in force, but the liberalization by U.C.C. §2-201 of the pre-Code requirements with respect to contracts for the sale of goods lessens the applicability of the writing requirement. Additional movement away from the writing requirement is seen in the 1994 Revision of Article 8, Securities, which abolishes the statute of frauds provision of the original U.C.C. §8-319 and goes beyond by declaring that the one-year performance provision of the statute of frauds is not applicable to contracts for securities. U.C.C. §8-113 [1994 Revision].

or exception to the statute of frauds may exist when the plaintiff's part performance is "unequivocally referable" to the oral agreement.[2]

Agreement That Cannot Be Performed within One Year After the Contract Is Made

A writing is required when the contract, by its terms or subject matter, cannot be performed within one year after the date of the agreement. An oral agreement to supply a line of credit for two years cannot be enforced because of the statute of frauds.

CASE SUMMARY

Not a Good Move, Doctor

FACTS: Despite not having an executed employment agreement, Dr. William Bithoney sold his home in New York and moved to Atlanta in early October in anticipation of his October 15 start work date as an executive at Grady Memorial Hospital. But the night before his anticipated start, he was informed that Grady's governing body, the Fulton-DeKalb Hospital Authority, did not approve his hiring and would not permit him to commence work. He sued the Authority for breach of an oral contract for severance, claiming that he and Grady's CEO, Otis Story, had agreed that he would receive "a severance payment of 15 months salary if Grady terminated his employment without cause." Bithoney had received a draft employment contract from Grady, which included a provision that, in the event Bithoney was terminated without cause, he would receive "full severance payment," which would be "payable for 15 months from the effective date of said termination."

DECISION: Judgment for the hospital. If the oral severance agreement were to be paid in a lump sum after termination, the oral agreement would not fall within the statute of frauds. Because the draft employment agreement provided that the severance "shall be payable for 15 months from the effective date of said termination," it was found to be a 15-month payment term barred by the statute of frauds. [*Bithoney v. Fulton-DeKalb Hospital Authority*, 721 S.E.2d 577 (Ga. App. 2011)]

The year runs from the time the oral contract is made rather than from the date when performance is to begin. In computing the year, the day on which the contract was made is excluded.

No *part performance* exception exists to validate an oral agreement not performable within one year. **For Example,** Babyback's Foods negotiated a multiyear oral agreement to comarket its barbecue meat products with the Coca-Cola Co. nationwide and arranged to have several coolers installed at area grocery stores in Louisville under the agreement. Babyback's faxed to Coca-Cola a contract that summarized the oral agreement but Coca-Cola never signed it. Because Coca-Cola did not sign and no part performance exception exists for an oral agreement not performable within one year, Babyback's lawsuit was unsuccessful.[3]

When no time for performance is specified by the oral contract and complete performance could "conceivably occur" within one year, the statute of frauds is not applicable to the oral contract.[4]

When a contract may be terminated at will by either party, the statute of frauds is not applicable because the contract may be terminated within a year. **For Example,** David Ehrlich was hired as manager of Gravediggaz pursuant to an oral management agreement that was terminable at will by either Ehrlich or the group. He was entitled to

[2] *Carey & Associates v. Ernst*, 802 N.Y.S.2d 160 (A.D. 2005).
[3] *Coca-Cola Co. v. Babyback's International Inc.*, 841 N.E.2d 557 (Ind. 2006).
[4] *De John v. Speech Language & Communication Assoc.*, 974 N.Y.S.2d 725 (A.D. 2013).

FIGURE 16-1	Hurdles in the Path of a Contract

WRITING REQUIRED

STATUTE OF FRAUDS	EXCEPTIONS
MORE THAN ONE YEAR TO PERFORM SALE OF LAND ANSWER FOR ANOTHER'S DEBT OR DEFAULT PERSONAL REPRESENTATIVE TO PAY DEBT OF DECEDENT FROM PERSONAL FUNDS PROMISE IN CONSIDERATION OF MARRIAGE SALE OF GOODS FOR $500 OR MORE MISCELLANEOUS	PART PERFORMANCE PROMISOR BENEFIT DETRIMENTAL RELIANCE

PAROL EVIDENCE RULE	EXCEPTIONS
EVERY COMPLETE, FINAL WRITTEN CONTRACT	INCOMPLETE CONTRACT AMBIGUOUS TERMS FRAUD, ACCIDENT, OR MISTAKE TO PROVE EXISTENCE OR NONBINDING CHARACTER OF CONTRACT MODIFICATION OF CONTRACT ILLEGALITY

receive 15 percent of the gross earnings of the group and each of its members, including rap artist Robert Diggs, professionally known as RZA, for all engagements entered into while he was manager under this oral agreement. Such an at-will contract is not barred by the statute of frauds.[5]

Agreement to Sell or a Sale of an Interest in Land

All contracts to sell land, buildings, or interests in land, such as mortgages, must be evidenced by a writing.[6] Leases are also interests in land and must be in writing, except in some states where leases for one year or less do not have to be in writing.[7] **For Example,**

---

[5] See *Ehrlich v. Diggs*, 169 F. Supp. 2d 124 (E.D.N.Y. 2001). See also *Sterling v. Sterling*, 800 N.Y.S.2d 463 (A.D. 2005), in which the statute of frauds was no bar to an oral partnership agreement, deemed to be at will, that continued for an indefinite period of time.

[6] *Magnum Real Estate Services, Inc. v. Associates, LLC*, 874 N.Y.S.2d 435 (A.D. 2009).

[7] See, however, *BBQ Blues Texas, Ltd. v. Affiliated Business*, 183 S.W.3d 543 (Tex. App. 2006), in which Eddie Calagero of Affiliated Business and the owners of BBQ Blues Texas, Ltd., entered an oral commission agreement to pay a 10 percent commission if he found a buyer for the restaurant, and he did so. The oral agreement was held to be outside the statute of frauds because the activity of finding a willing buyer did not involve the transfer of real estate. The second contract between the buyer and seller of the restaurant, which involved the transfer of a lease agreement, was a separate and distinct agreement over which Calagero had no control.

Letter agreement can be...
agreement
Kac Defendant
Name et Plentiff

if Mrs. O'Toole orally agrees to sell her house to the Gillespies for $250,000 and, thereafter, her children convince her that she could obtain $280,000 for the property if she is patient, Mrs. O'Toole can raise the defense of the statute of frauds should she be sued for breach of the oral agreement. Under the *part performance doctrine*, an exception exists by which an oral contract for the sale of land will be enforced by a court of equity in a suit for specific performance if the buyer has taken possession of the land under an oral contract and has made substantial improvements, the value of which cannot easily be ascertained, or has taken possession and paid part of the purchase price.

Promise to Answer for the Debt or Default of Another

If an individual *I* promises a creditor *C* to pay the debt of *D* if *D* does not do so, *I* is promising to answer for the debt of another. Such a promise is sometimes called a **suretyship** contract, and it must be in writing to be enforceable. *I*, the promisor, is obligated to pay only if *D* does not pay. *I*'s promise is a *collateral* or *secondary* promise, and such promises must be in writing under the statute of frauds.[8]

> suretyship—undertaking to pay the debt or be liable for the default of another.

Main Purpose of Exception. When the main purpose of the promisor's promise to pay the debt of another is to benefit the promisor, the statute of frauds is not applicable, and the oral promise to pay the debt is binding.

For Example, an individual *I* hires a contractor *C* to repair *I*'s building, and the supplier *S* is unwilling to extend credit to *C*. In an oral promise by *I* to pay *S* what is owed for the supplies in question if *C* does not pay, *I* is promising to pay for the debt of another, *C*. However, the *main purpose* of *I*'s promise was not to aid *C* but to get his own house repaired. This promise is not within the statute of frauds.[9]

CASE SUMMARY

"I Personally Guarantee" Doesn't Mean I'm Personally Liable, Does It?

FACTS: Joel Burgower owned Material Partnerships Inc. (MPI), which supplied Sacos Tubulares del Centro, S.A. de C.V. (Sacos), a Mexican bag manufacturer, essential materials to make its products. When MPI was not paid for shipments, it insisted that Jorge Lopez, Sacos's general manager, personally guarantee all past and future obligations to MPI. In a letter to Burgower dated September 25, 1998, Lopez wrote:

> *I ... want to certify you [sic] that I, personally, guaranty all outstanding [sic] and liabilities of Sacos Tubulares with Material Partnerships as well as future shipments.*

Lopez drafted the letter himself and signed it over the designation "Jorge Lopez Venture, General Manager."

After receiving the September 25th letter, MPI resumed shipping product to Sacos, sending additional shipments valued at approximately $200,000. MPI subsequently received one payment of approximately $60,000 from Sacos. When Sacos did not pay for the additional shipments, MPI stopped shipping to it. The Sacos plant closed, and MPI brought suit in a Texas court against Lopez, claiming he was individually liable for the corporate debt of more than $900,000 under the terms of the personal guarantee. Lopez contended that he signed the letter in his capacity as general manager of Sacos as a corporate guarantee and that it was not an enforceable personal guarantee. MPI contended that the letter was a clear personal guarantee.

---

[8] See *Martin Printing, Inc. v. Sone*, 873 A.2d 232 (Conn. App. 2005), in which James Kuhe, in writing, personally guaranteed Martin Printing, Inc., to pay for printing expenses of *Pub Links Golfer Magazine*, if his corporation, Abbey Inc., failed to do so. When Abbey, Inc., failed to pay, the court enforced Kuhe's promise to pay.

[9] See *Christian v. Smith*, 759 N.W.2d 447 (Neb. 2008).

"I Personally Guarantee" Doesn't Mean I'm Personally Liable, Does It? continued

DECISION: The essential terms of a guarantee agreement required by the statute of frauds were present in this case. Lopez stated in his September 25th letter that "I, personally, guaranty," manifesting an intent to guarantee, and described the obligation being guaranteed as "all outstandings and liabilities of Sacos," as well as "future shipments." Lopez's signature over his corporate office does not render the document ambiguous because the clear intent was expressed in the word "personally." [*MPI v. Jorge Lopez Ventura*, **102 S.W.2d 252 (Tex. App. 2003)**]

Promise by the Executor or Administrator of a Decedent's Estate to Pay a Claim Against the Estate from Personal Funds

personal representative—administrator or executor who represents decedents under UPC.

executor, executrix—person (man, woman) named in a will to administer the estate of the decedent.

administrator, administratrix—person (man, woman) appointed to wind up and settle the estate of a person who has died without a will.

decedent—person whose estate is being administered.

The **personal representative (executor** or **administrator)** has the duty of handling the affairs of a deceased person, paying the debts from the proceeds of the estate and distributing any balance remaining. The executor or administrator is not personally liable for the claims against the estate of the **decedent.** If the personal representative promises to pay the decedent's debts with his or her own money, the promise cannot be enforced unless it is evidenced by a writing.

If the personal representative makes a contract on behalf of the estate in the course of administering the estate, a writing is not required. The representative is then contracting on behalf of the estate. Thus, if the personal representative employs an attorney to settle the estate or makes a burial contract with an undertaker, no writing is required.

Promises Made in Consideration of Marriage

Promises to pay a sum of money or give property to another in consideration of marriage must be in writing under the statute of frauds.

For Example, if Mr. John Bradley orally promises to provide Karl Radford $20,000 on Karl's marriage to Mr. Bradley's daughter Michelle—and Karl and Michelle marry—the agreement is not enforceable under the statute of frauds because it was not in writing.

Prenuptial or *antenuptial* agreements are entered into by the parties before their marriage. After full disclosure of each party's assets and liabilities, and in some states, income,[10] the parties set forth the rights of each partner regarding the property and, among other things, set forth rights and obligations should the marriage end in a separation or divorce. Such a contract must be in writing.

For Example, when Susan DeMatteo married her husband M. J. DeMatteo in 1990, she had a 1977 Nova and $5,000 in the bank. M. Joseph DeMatteo was worth as much as $112 million at that time, and he insisted that she sign a prenuptial agreement before their marriage. After full disclosure of each party's assets, the prenuptial agreement was signed and videotaped some five days before their marriage ceremony. The agreement gave Susan $35,000 a year plus cost-of-living increases, as well as a car and a house, should the marriage dissolve. After the couple divorced, Susan argued before the state's highest court that the agreement was not "fair or reasonable" because it gave her less than 1 percent of her former husband's wealth. The court upheld the agreement, however, pointing out that Susan was fully informed about her fiancé's net worth and was represented by counsel.[11] When there is full disclosure and representation, prenuptial agreements, like other contracts, cannot be set aside unless they are unconscionable, which in a domestic relations setting means leaving a former spouse unable to support herself or himself.

---

[10] See FLA. STAT. §732–702 (2).

[11] *DeMatteo v. DeMatteo*, 762 N.E.2d 797 (Mass. 2002). See also *Waton v. Waton*, 887 So. 2d 419 (Fla. App. 2004).

Sale of Goods

As will be developed in Chapter 22, Nature and Form of Sales, contracts for the sale of goods priced at $500 or more must ordinarily be in writing under U.C.C. §2-201.[12]

Promissory Estoppel

The statute of frauds may be circumvented when the party seeking to get around the statute of frauds is able to prove an enhanced promissory estoppel. While one element of a routine promissory estoppel case requires that the promisee rely on the promise in some definite and substantial manner, an enhanced level of reasonable reliance is necessary in order to have enhanced promissory estoppel, along with proof of an unconscionable injury or unjust enrichment. **For Example,** an Indiana bakery, Classic Cheesecake Inc., was able to interest several hotels and casinos in Las Vegas in buying its products. On July 27, 2004, its principals sought a loan from a local branch office of J. P. Morgan Chase Bank in order to establish a distribution center in Las Vegas. On September 17, local bank officer Dowling told Classic that the loan was a "go." When credit quality issues surfaced, Dowling continued to make assurances that the loan would be approved. On October 12, however, she told Classic that the loan had been turned down. Classic claimed that the bank's breach of its oral promise to make the loan and Classic's detrimental reliance on the promise caused it to lose more than $1 million. The Indiana statute of frauds requires agreements to lend money to be in writing. Classic contended that the oral agreement in this case must be enforced on the basis of promissory estoppel and the company's unconscionable injury. Judge Posner of the Seventh Circuit upheld the dismissal of the claim, writing (in part):

> ... *For the plaintiff to treat the bank loan as a certainty because they were told by the bank officer whom they were dealing with that it would be approved was unreasonable, especially if, as the plaintiffs' damages claim presupposes, the need for the loan was urgent. Rational businessmen know that there is many a slip "twixt cup and lips," that a loan is not approved until it is approved, that if a bank's employee tells you your loan application will be approved that is not the same as telling you it has been approved, and that if one does not have a loan commitment in writing yet the need for the loan is urgent one had better be negotiating with other potential lenders at the same time....*[13]

CPA 16-1c Note or Memorandum

The statute of frauds requires a writing to evidence those contracts that come within its scope. This writing may be a note or memorandum as distinguished from a contract.[14] The statutory requirement is, of course, satisfied if there is a complete written contract signed by both parties.

Signing

The note or memorandum must be signed by the party sought to be bound by the contract. **For Example,** in the previous scenario involving Mark Wahlberg and Steven Spielberg, suppose the parties agreed to do the film according to the same terms but agreed to begin shooting the film a year from next April, and Mark wrote the essential terms on a napkin, dated it, and had Steven sign it "to make sure I got it right." Mark

---

[12] As will be presented in Chapter 22, under Revised Article 2, §2-201, the $500 amount is increased to $5,000. This revision has not yet been adopted by any state.

[13] *Classic Cheesecake Co. Inc. v. J. P. Morgan Chase Bank*, 546 F.3d 839 (7th Cir. 2008).

[14] *McLinden v. Coco*, 765 N.E.2d 606 (Ind. App. 2002).

then placed the napkin in his wallet for his records. Because the contract could not be performed within one year after the date of the agreement, a writing would be required. If Steven thereafter decided not to pursue the film, Mark could enforce the contract against him because the napkin-note had been signed by the party to be bound or "sought to be charged," Steven. However, if Mark later decided not to appear in the film, the agreement to do the film could not be enforced against Mark because no writing existed signed by Mark, the party sought to be charged. The signature may be an ordinary one or any symbol that is adopted by the party as a signature. It may consist of initials, figures, or a mark. In the absence of a local statute that provides otherwise, a signature may be made by pencil, pen, typewriter, print, or stamp. It is unlikely that a logo can constitute a legal signature. **For Example,** University of South Carolina sports fans claimed that a university brochure contained a signed writing sufficient to satisfy the statute of frauds supportive of their rights to continued premium seating at the new basketball arena. The presence or absence of the university's signature turned on whether the university logo on the brochures suffices for a legal signature. The court majority found that the logo did not constitute a legal signature. However, Justice Pleicones admonished the court majority to be more circumspect in holding that a logo can never constitute a signature for the purposes of the statute of frauds.[15]

Electronic Signature. Electronic signatures have parity with on-paper signatures under the Uniform Electronic Transactions Act (UETA).[16] The act treats e-signatures and e-records as if they were handwritten. The parties themselves determine how they will determine each other's identity such as by a credit card, a password or pin, or other secure means. Certain documents and records are exempt under the act, such as wills, trusts, and commercial law matters.

Content

The note or memorandum must contain all of the essential terms of the contract so the court can determine just what was agreed. If any essential term is missing, the writing is not sufficient. A writing evidencing a sale of land that does not describe the land or identify the buyer does not satisfy the statute of frauds. The subject matter must be identified either within the writing itself or in other writings to which it refers. A deposit check given by the buyer to the seller does not take an oral land sales contract out of the statute of frauds. This is so because the check does not set forth the terms of the sale. The note or memorandum may consist of one writing or of separate papers, such as letters, or a combination of such papers. Separate writings cannot be considered together unless they are linked. Linkage may be by express reference in each writing to the other or by the fact that each writing clearly deals with the same subject matter. An exchange of e-mails may constitute an enforceable agreement if the writings include all of the agreement's essential terms. **For Example,** three e-mails were determined to be a binding integrated fee agreement limiting the Kasowitz law firm to a flat $1 million fee and rejecting a higher success fee sought from the client. On September 8, 2006, Kasowitz (by attorney Goldberg) e-mailed a proposed fee arrangement to the client's in-house counsel, Bergman, which provided in relevant part:

> *We can do the Cardtronics case for a flat $1 million, payable over 10 months as you suggested (exclusive of disbursements), plus 20% of amounts recovered above some number, as opposed to a percentage payable from dollar one.*

---

[15] *Springolo v. University of South Carolina,* 757 S.E.2d 384 (S.C. 2014).

[16] Forty-seven states and the District of Columbia have adopted the UETA. The remaining three states, Illinois, New York, and Washington, are subject to the federal Electronic Signatures in Global and National Commerce Act (E-Sign), 15 U.S.C.§7001, which is consistent with the UETA in many respects.

Based on the numbers we have, which obviously are approximations, we actually think the damages could be between $10 and $11 million over the life of the contract. So I'm thinking of 20% of everything above $4 million as the success fee portion…

On September 19, 2006, Goldberg sent an e-mail to Bergman in which he stated, in relevant part,

I would love to have our fee arrangement in place by then so I can just tear into these guys.

In an e-mail response to Kasowitz that same day, Bergman wrote:

Go.

The recovery amounted to $1.75 million, and no success fee was called for under the agreement evident from the e-mails.[17]

16-1d Effect of Noncompliance

The majority of states hold that a contract that does not comply with the statute of frauds is not enforceable.[18] If an action is brought to enforce the contract, the defendant can raise the defense that the alleged contract is not enforceable because it is not evidenced by a writing, as required by the statute of frauds.

Recovery of Value Conferred

In most instances, a person who is prevented from enforcing a contract because of the statute of frauds is nevertheless entitled to recover from the other party the value of any services or property furnished or money given under the oral contract. Recovery is not based on the terms of the contract but on a quasi-contractual obligation. The other party is to restore to the plaintiff what was received in order to prevent unjust enrichment at the plaintiff's expense. **For Example,** when an oral contract for services cannot be enforced because of the statute of frauds, the person performing the work may recover the reasonable value of the services rendered.

Who May Raise the Defense of Noncompliance?

Only a party to the oral contract may raise a defense that it is not binding because there is no writing that satisfies the statute of frauds. Third persons, such as an insurance company or the Internal Revenue Service, cannot claim that a contract is void because the statute of frauds was not satisfied.

16-2 Parol Evidence Rule

When the contract is evidenced by a writing, may the contract terms be changed by the testimony of witnesses?

16-2a Exclusion of Parol Evidence

The general rule is that parol or extrinsic evidence will not be allowed into evidence to add to, modify, or contradict the terms of a written contract that is fully integrated

---

[17] *Kasowitz, Benson, Torres & Friedman, LLP v. Reade*, 950 N.Y.S.2d 8 (A.D. 2012); but see *Dahan v. Weiss*, 991 N.Y.S.2d 119 (A.D. 2014), where e-mail messages failed to express the full intentions of the parties.

[18] The UCC creates several statutes of frauds of limited applicability, in which it uses the phrase "not enforceable": §1-206 (sale of intangible personal property); §2-201 (sale of goods); and §8-319 (sale of securities).

or complete on its face.[19] Evidence of an alleged earlier oral or written agreement within the scope of the fully integrated written contract or evidence of an alleged contemporaneous oral agreement within the scope of the fully integrated written contract is inadmissible as *parol evidence.*

Parol evidence is admissible, however, to show fraud, duress, or mistake and under certain other circumstances to be discussed in the following paragraphs.

The **parol evidence rule** is based on the theory that either there never was an oral agreement or, if there was, the parties abandoned it when they reached the stage in negotiations of executing their written contract. The social objective of the parol evidence rule is to give stability to contracts and to prevent the assertion of terms that did not exist or did not survive the bargaining of the parties so as to reach inclusion in the final written contract.

For Example, L (landlord), the owner of a new development containing a five-store mall, discusses leasing one of the stores to T (tenant), who is viewing the property with his sister S, a highly credible poverty worker on leave from her duties in Central America. L, in the presence of S, agrees to give T the exclusive right to sell coffee and soft drinks in the five-store mall. Soon L and T execute a detailed written lease for the store, which makes no provision for T's exclusive right to sell soft drinks and coffee in the mall. Subsequently, when two of the mall's new tenants begin to sell soft drinks and coffee, T brings suit against L for the breach of the oral promise granting him exclusive rights to sell soft drinks and coffee. T calls S as his first witness to prove the existence of the oral promise. L, through his attorney, will object to the admission of any evidence of a prior oral agreement that would add to or amend the fully integrated written lease, which set forth all restrictions on the landlord and tenant as to uses of the premises. After study of the matter, the court, based on the parol evidence rule, will not hear testimony from either S or T about the oral promise L made to T. In order to preserve his exclusive right to sell the drinks in question, T should have made certain that this promise was made part of the lease. His lawsuit will not be successful.

16-2b   When the Parol Evidence Rule Does Not Apply

The parol evidence rule will not apply in certain cases. The most common of these are discussed in the following paragraphs.

Ambiguity

If a written contract is **ambiguous** or may have two or more different meanings, parol evidence may generally be admitted to clarify the meaning.[20]

Parol evidence may also be admitted to show that a word used in a contract has a special trade meaning or a meaning in the particular locality that differs from the common meaning of that word.

Fraud, Duress, or Mistake

A contract apparently complete on its face may have omitted a provision that should have been included. Parol evidence may be admitted to show that a provision was omitted as the result of fraud, duress, or mistake and to further show what that provision stated. Parol evidence is admissible to show that a provision of the written contract was a mutual mistake even though the written provision is unambiguous. When one party claims to

parol evidence rule—rule that prohibits the introduction into evidence of oral or written statements made prior to or contemporaneously with the execution of a complete written contract, deed, or instrument, in the absence of clear proof of fraud, accident, or mistake causing the omission of the statement in question.

ambiguous—having more than one reasonable interpretation.

---

[19] *Mayday v. Grathwohl,* 805 N.W.2d 285 (Minn. App. 2011).

[20] *Berg v. Hudesman,* 801 P.2d 222 (Wash. 1990). This view is also followed by U.C.C. §2-202(a), which permits terms in a contract for the sale of goods to be "explained or supplemented by a course of dealing or usage of trade … or by course of performance." Such evidence is admissible not because there is an ambiguity but "in order that the true understanding of the parties as to the agreement may be reached." Official Code Comment to §2-202.

have been fraudulently induced by the other to enter into a contract, the parol evidence rule does not bar proof that there was a fraud. **For Example,** the parol evidence rule does not bar proof that the seller of land intentionally misrepresented that the land was zoned to permit use as an industrial park. Such evidence does not contradict the terms of the contract but shows that the agreement is unenforceable.[21]

Modification of Contract

The parol evidence rule prohibits only the contradiction of a complete written contract. It does not prohibit proof that the contract was thereafter modified or terminated.

CASE SUMMARY

All Sail and No Anchor

FACTS: On April 2, 1990, Christian Bourg hired Bristol Boat Co., Inc., and Bristol Marine Co. (defendants) to construct and deliver a yacht on July 1, 1990. However, the defendants did not live up to their promises and the contract was breached. On October 22, 1990, the defendants executed a written settlement agreement whereby Bourg agreed to pay an additional sum of $135,000 for the delivery of the yacht and to provide the defendants a loan of $80,000 to complete the construction of the vessel. Referencing the settlement agreement, the defendants at the same time executed a promissory note obliging them to repay the $80,000 loan plus interest in annual installments due on November 1 of each year, with the final payment due on November 1, 1994. The court stated in presenting the facts: "However, like the yacht itself, the settlement agreement soon proved to be just another hole in the water into which the plaintiff threw his money." Bourg sued the defendants after they failed to make certain payments on the note, and the court granted a motion for summary judgment in favor of Bourg for $59,081. The defendants appealed.

DECISION: Judgment for Bourg. Because the defendants' affidavit recites that an alleged oral side agreement was entered into at the same time as the settlement agreement and promissory note—the oral side agreement allegedly stated "that the note would be paid for by services rendered by the defendants"—the oral side agreement would have constituted a contemporaneous modification that would merge into the integrated promissory note and settlement agreement and thus be barred from admission into evidence under the parol evidence rule. Although parties to an integrated written contract can modify their understanding by a subsequent oral pact, to be legally effective, there must be evidence of mutual assent to the essential terms of the modification and adequate consideration. Here the defendants adduced no competent evidence of either mutual assent to particular terms or a specific consideration that would be sufficiently definite to constitute an enforceable subsequent oral modification to the parties' earlier written agreements. Thus, legally this alleged oral agreement was all sail and no anchor. [*Bourg v. Bristol Boat Co.*, 705 A.2d 969 (R.I. 1998)]

16-3 Rules of Construction and Interpretation

In interpreting contracts, courts are aided by certain rules.

16-3a Intention of the Parties

When persons enter into an agreement, it is to be presumed that they intend for their agreement to have some effect. A court will strive to determine the intent of the parties and to give effect to it. A contract, therefore, is to be enforced according to its terms.[22] A court cannot remake or rewrite the contract of the parties under the pretense of interpreting.[23]

---

[21] *Edwards v. Centrex Real Estate Corp.*, 61 Cal. Rptr. 518 (Cal. App. 1997).
[22] See *Greenwald v. Kersh*, 621 S.E.2d 463 (Ga. App. 2005).
[23] *Abbot v. Schnader, Harrison, Segal & Lewis, LLP*, 805 A.2d 547 (Pa. Super. 2002).

No particular form of words is required, and any words manifesting the intent of the parties are sufficient. In the absence of proof that a word has a peculiar meaning or that it was employed by the parties with a particular meaning, a common word is given its ordinary meaning.

Meaning of Words

Ordinary words are to be interpreted according to their ordinary meaning.[24] **For Example,** when a contract requires the gasoline dealer to pay the supplier for "gallons" supplied, the term *gallons* is unambiguous and does not require that an adjustment of the gallonage be made for the temperature.[25] When a contract calls for a businessperson to pay a builder for the builder's "costs," the term *costs* is unambiguous, meaning actual costs, not a lesser amount based on the builder's bid.[26]

If there is a common meaning to a term, that meaning will be followed even though the dictionary may contain additional meanings. If technical or trade terms are used in a contract, they are to be interpreted according to the area of technical knowledge or trade from which the terms are taken.

Incorporation by Reference

The contract may not cover all of the agreed terms. The missing terms may be found in another document. Frequently, the parties executing the contract for storage will simply state that a storage contract is entered into and that the contract applies to the goods listed in the schedule attached to and made part of the contract. Likewise, a contract for the construction of a building may involve plans and specifications on file in a named city office. The contract will simply state that the building is to be constructed according to those plans and specifications that are "incorporated herein and made part of this contract." When there is such an **incorporation by reference,** the contract consists of both the original document and the detailed statement that is incorporated in it.

When a contract refers to another document, however, the contract must sufficiently describe the document or so much of it as is to be interpreted as part of the contract.

incorporation by reference—contract consisting of both the original or skeleton document and the detailed statement that is incorporated in it.

16-3b Whole Contract

The provisions of a contract must be construed as a whole in such a way that every part is given effect.

Every word of a contract is to be given effect if reasonably possible. The contract is to be construed as a whole, and if the plain language of the contract thus viewed solves the dispute, the court is to make no further analysis.[27]

CASE SUMMARY

When You Permanently Reduced the Shipping Spots to Zero, You "Terminated" the Contract, Silly

FACTS: C.A. Acquisition Newco LLC is a successor in interest to Cyphermint, Inc. ("CI"), a New York corporation specializing in software development for self-service kiosks. DHL Express (USA), Inc., is an Ohio corporation with a principal place of business in Florida. It is a division of DHL International GmBH, a Deutsche Post Company and express carrier

---

[24] *Thorton v. D.F.W. Christian Television, Inc.,* 925 S.W.2d 17 (Tex. App. 1995).
[25] *Hopkins v. BP Oil, Inc.,* 81 F.3d 1070 (11th Cir. 1996).
[26] *Batzer Construction, Inc. v. Boyer,* 125 P.3d 773 (Or. App. 2006).
[27] *Covensky v. Hannah Marine Corp.,* 903 N.E.2d 422 (Ill. App. 2009).

When You Permanently Reduced the Shipping Spots to Zero, You "Terminated" the Contract, Silly continued

of documents and freight. Until 2008, DHL provided express pick-up and delivery, including same-day air delivery of letters and packages throughout the United States.

DHL entered into an agreement with Cyphermint, hoping to expand its customer base by offering domestic shipping services in retail locations, such as Walgreens and OfficeMax, via kiosks, or "Shipping Spots." Customers were able to use the kiosks' touch screen to pay for shipping costs and print shipping labels. The contract provided for an initial three-year term (August 1, 2006, through July 31, 2009) that automatically renewed for two more years unless either party gave notice of its election not to renew 90 days before the end of the initial contract. Under the contract, Cyphermint agreed to provide interactive software, enabling customers to use DHL's services from the shipping spots. Section 10.5 of the contract governs termination fees:

There shall be no termination fees for any termination by either party, irrespective of the reason for such termination, except for a "Material Breach" or as provided pursuant to the "Statement of Work" (SOW).

The SOW contains the following provision concerning termination fees:

Should DHL terminate this agreement for any reason other than a material breach by Cyphermint

before its termination date DHL agrees to compensate CI in the amount of $50,000 per month for each month remaining in the initial term.

In November 2008, DHL decided to end all domestic delivery service within the United States. CI requested early termination fees under Section 10.5 of the contract of $413,333.33. DHL refused to pay, contending that Section 2.8 of the contract gave DHL the discretion to control the number and placement of the shipping spots, and when it ended U.S. domestic operations, it exercised its discretion to reduce shipping spots to zero.

DECISION: Judgment for CI. In reviewing a document, a court must consider the document as a whole, rather than attempting to isolate certain parts of it. Even if the court were to accept DHL's argument that Section 2.8 gave it blanket authority to reduce or eliminate the shipping spot project altogether, the outcome would remain the same. The relevant provision in the contract provides for termination fees without regard to whether the termination was authorized. The only restriction placed on the recovery of such fees is that they will not be available in the case of a material breach by Cyphermint. DHL failed to explain how reducing the shipping spots to zero was in any way different from "terminating" the contract. [*C.A. Acquisition Newco, LLC v. DHL Express (USA), Inc.*, 795 F. Supp. 2d 140 (D. Mass. 2011)]

16-3c Contradictory and Ambiguous Terms

One term in a contract may conflict with another term, or one term may have two different meanings. It is then necessary for the court to determine whether there is a contract and, if so, what the contract really means.

CASE SUMMARY

Who Pays the Piper?

FACTS: Olander Contracting Co., developer Gail Wachter, and the City of Bismarck, North Dakota, entered into a water and sewer construction contract including, among other things, connecting a 10-inch sewer line from Wachter's housing development to the city's existing 36-inch concrete sewer main and installing a manhole at the connection, to be paid for by Wachter. Olander installed the manhole,

but it collapsed within a few days. Olander installed a second manhole, with a large base supported by pilings, but it too failed a few days after it was installed. Olander then placed a rock bedding under the city's sewer main, replaced 78 feet of the existing concrete pipe with PVC pipe, and installed a manhole a third time on a larger base. Olander sued Wachter and the City of Bismarck for damages of

Who Pays the Piper? continued

$456,536.25 for extra work it claims it was required to perform to complete its contract. Both defendants denied they were responsible for the amount sued under the contract. The jury returned a special verdict, finding that Olander performed "extra work/unforeseen work … for which it is entitled to be compensated in excess of the contract price" in the amount of $220,849.67, to be paid by the City of Bismarck. Appeals were taken.

DECISION: Judgment for Olander. The trial judge properly made the initial determination that the contract language was ambiguous. That is, the language used by the parties could support good arguments for the positions of both parties. This resolved a question of law. Once this determination had been made, the judge allowed extrinsic evidence from all parties as to what they meant when they negotiated the contract. This evidence related to the questions of fact, which were left to the jury. Testimony was taken from the parties who negotiated the contract, and testimony was also heard about the role of each of the parties in the actual construction of the manhole, the cause for the collapses, and why the contractor had to replace the city's existing concrete pipe with PVC pipe and the city's role in making this determination. The jury then fulfilled its role answering the question whether or not Olander had performed extra work in the affirmative, concluding that the city was required to pay for it. [*Olander Contracting v. Wachter*, 643 N.W.2d 29 (2002)]

If the language within the four corners of the contract is unambiguous, the parties' intentions are determined from the plain meaning of the words, used in the contract, as a matter of law, by the judge. A contract term or provision is *ambiguous* if it is capable of more than one reasonable interpretation because of the uncertain meaning of terms or missing terms. A finding of ambiguity is justified only if the language of the contract reasonably supports the competing interpretations.[28] It is the role of the judge—a question of law—to initially determine whether a contract is ambiguous. If the contract is ambiguous, it is the role of the jury—a question of fact—to determine which party's position is correct with the aid of extrinsic evidence.

Nature of Writing

When a contract is partly a printed form or partly typewritten and partly handwritten and the written part conflicts with the printed or typewritten part, the written part prevails. When there is a conflict between a printed part and a typewritten part, the latter prevails. Consequently, when a clause typewritten on a printed form conflicts with what is stated by the print, the conflicting print is ignored and the typewritten clause controls. This rule is based on the belief that the parties had given greater thought to what they typed or wrote for the particular contract as contrasted with printed words already in a form designed to cover many transactions. Thus, a typewritten provision to pay 90 cents per unit overrode a preprinted provision setting the price as 45 cents per unit.

When there is a conflict between an amount or quantity expressed both in words and figures, as on a check, the amount or quantity expressed in words prevails. Words control because there is less danger that a word will be wrong than a number.

Ambiguity

A contract is ambiguous when the intent of the parties is uncertain and the contract is capable of more than one reasonable interpretation.[29] The background from which the contract and the dispute arose may help in determining the intention of the parties. **For Example,** when suit was brought in Minnesota on a Canadian insurance policy, the

---

[28] *QEP Energy Co. v. Sullivan*, 444 Fed. Appx. 284 (10th Cir. 2011).
[29] *Kaufman & Stewart v. Weinbrenner Shoe Co.*, 589 N.W.2d 499 (Minn. App. 1999).

question arose whether the dollar limit of the policy referred to Canadian or U.S. dollars. The court concluded that Canadian dollars were intended. Both the insurer and the insured were Canadian corporations; the original policy, endorsements to the policy, and policy renewals were written in Canada; over the years, premiums had been paid in Canadian dollars; and a prior claim on the policy had been settled by the payment of an amount computed on the basis of Canadian dollars.

Strict Construction Against Drafting Party

An ambiguous contract is interpreted strictly against the party who drafted it.[30] **For Example,** an insurance policy containing ambiguous language regarding coverage or exclusions is interpreted against the insurer and in favor of the insured when two interpretations are reasonably possible. This rule is a secondary rule that may be invoked only after all of the ordinary interpretive guides have been exhausted. The rule basically assigns the risk of an unresolvable ambiguity to the party creating it.[31]

16-3d Implied Terms

In some cases, a court will imply a term to cover a situation for which the parties failed to provide or, when needed, to give the contract a construction or meaning that is reasonable.

The court often implies details of the performance of a contract not expressly stated in the contract. In a contract to perform work, there is an implied promise to use such skill as is necessary to properly perform the work.

CASE SUMMARY

Read the Contract Your Honor. Where Did We Promise the Holguins That Their Satellite Dish Would Be Properly Installed?

FACTS: The Holguins ordered a bundle of services from AT&T and affiliates DISH California and EchoStar consisting of telephone, Internet, and satellite television services, with Deborah Holguin signing up with the AT&T sales agents. The installation process did not go as planned. The DISH technician drilled through a sewer pipe in the Holguins' wall, fed a satellite television cable through it, and patched the wall without repairing the sewer pipe. The improper installation was not discovered until 14 months later, and the damaged pipe leaked sewer water into the surrounding wall cavity and caused mold buildup in the Holguins' home. As a result, the Holguins suffered respiratory problems and other health issues. The repair efforts were a nightmare causing the Holguins to hire their own contractor to complete the remediation work. The Holguins sued AT&T, DISH, and EchoStar for breach of contract. From a judgment for the Holguins for $109,000 in compensatory damages and attorney fees, the defendants appealed. AT&T, DISH, and EchoStar contend that the trial court erred in interpreting the Holguins' contract to contain an implied term requiring the Holguins' satellite television equipment to be properly installed.

DECISION: Judgment for the Holguins. It is a well-settled principle that express contractual terms give rise to implied duties, violations of which may themselves constitute breaches of contract. Accompanying every contract is a common-law duty to perform with care, skill, reasonable expedience, and faithfulness the thing agreed to be done, and a negligent failure to observe any of these conditions is a tort, as well as a breach of the contract. There was no error applying the implied contractual term that the equipment be properly installed. [**Holguin v. Dish Network, LLC,** 178 Cal. Rptr. 3d 100 (Cal. App. 2014)]

---

[30] *Idaho Migrant Council, Inc. v. Warila*, 89 P.2d 39 (Wyo. 1995).
[31] *Premier Title Co. v. Donahue*, 765 N.E.2d 513 (Ill. App. 2002).

In every contract, there is an implied obligation that neither party shall do anything that will have the effect of destroying or injuring the right of the other party to receive the fruits of the contract. This means that in every contract there exists an implied covenant of **good faith** and fair dealing. When a contract may reasonably be interpreted in different ways, a court should make the interpretation that is in harmony with good faith and fair dealing. **For Example,** when a contract is made subject to the condition that one of the parties obtain financing, that party must make reasonable, good-faith efforts to obtain financing. The party is not permitted to do nothing and then claim that the contract is not binding because the condition has not been satisfied. Likewise, when a contract requires a party to obtain government approval, the party must use all reasonable means to obtain it.[32]

good faith—absence of knowledge of any defects or problems.

The Uniform Commercial Code imposes an obligation of good faith in the performance or enforcement of every contract.[33]

16-3e Conduct and Custom

The conduct of the parties and the customs and usages of a particular trade may give meaning to the words of the parties and thus aid in the interpretation of their contract.

Conduct of the Parties

The conduct of the parties in carrying out the terms of a contract is the best guide to determine the parties' intent. When performance has been repeatedly tendered and accepted without protest, neither party will be permitted to claim that the contract was too indefinite to be binding. **For Example,** a travel agent made a contract with a hotel to arrange for trips to the hotel. After some 80 trips had already been arranged and paid for by the hotel at the contract price without any dispute about whether the contract obligation was satisfied, any claim by the travel agent that it could charge additional fees must be rejected.

Custom and Usage of Trade

usage of trade—language and customs of an industry.

The customs and **usages of trade** or commercial activity to which the contract relates may be used to interpret the terms of a contract.[34] **For Example,** when a contract for the construction of a building calls for a "turn-key construction," industry usage is admissible to show what this means: a construction in which all the owner needs to do is to turn the key in the lock to open the building for use and in which all construction risks are assumed by the contractor.[35]

Custom and usage, however, cannot override express provisions of a contract that are inconsistent with custom and usage.

16-3f Avoidance of Hardship

As a general rule, a party is bound by a contract even though it proves to be a bad bargain. If possible, a court will interpret a contract to avoid hardship. Courts will, if possible, interpret a vague contract in a way to avoid any forfeiture of a party's interest.

When hardship arises because the contract makes no provision for the situation that has occurred, the court will sometimes imply a term to avoid the hardship.

---

[32] *Kroboth v. Brent,* 625 N.Y.S.2d 748 (A.D. 1995).
[33] U.C.C. §§1-201(19), 1-203.
[34] *Affiliated FM Ins. Co. v. Constitution Reinsurance Corp.,* 626 N.E.2d 878 (Mass. 1994).
[35] *Blue v. R.L. Glossen Contracting, Inc.,* 327 S.E.2d 582 (Ga. App. 1985).

Make the Connection

Summary

An oral agreement may be a contract unless it is the intention of the parties that they should not be bound by the agreement without a writing executed by them. Certain contracts must be evidenced by a writing, however, or else they cannot be enforced. The statutes that declare this exception are called *statutes of frauds*. Statutes of frauds commonly require that a contract be evidenced by writing in the case of (1) an agreement that cannot be performed within one year after the contract is made, (2) an agreement to sell any interest in land, (3) a promise to answer for the debt or default of another, (4) a promise by the executor or administrator of a decedent's estate to pay a claim against the estate from personal funds, (5) a promise made in consideration of marriage, and (6) a contract for the sale of goods for a purchase price of $500 or more.

To evidence a contract to satisfy a statute of frauds, there must be a writing of all essential terms. The writing must be signed by the defendant against whom suit is brought for enforcement of the contract.

If the applicable statute of frauds is not satisfied, the oral contract cannot be enforced. To avoid unjust enrichment, a plaintiff barred from enforcing an oral contract may in most cases recover from the other contracting party the reasonable value of the benefits conferred by the plaintiff on the defendant.

When there is a written contract, the question arises whether that writing is the exclusive statement of the parties' agreement. If the writing is the complete and final statement of the contract, parol evidence as to matters agreed to before or at the time the writing was signed is not admissible to contradict the writing. This is called the *parol evidence*

rule. In any case, the parol evidence rule does not bar parol evidence when (1) the writing is ambiguous, (2) the writing is not a true statement of the agreement of the parties because of fraud, duress, or mistake, or (3) the existence, modification, or illegality of a contract is in controversy.

Because a contract is based on the agreement of the parties, courts must determine the intent of the parties manifested in the contract. The intent that is to be enforced is the intent as it reasonably appears to a third person. This objective intent is followed.

In interpreting a contract, ordinary words are to be given their ordinary meanings. If trade or technical terms have been used, they are interpreted according to their technical meanings. The court must consider the whole contract and not read a particular part out of context. When different writings are executed as part of the same transaction, or one writing refers to or incorporates another, all of the writings are to be read together as the contract of the parties.

When provisions of a contract are contradictory, the court will try to reconcile or eliminate the conflict. If this cannot be done, the conclusion may be that there is no contract because the conflict makes the agreement indefinite as to a material matter. In some cases, conflict is solved by considering the form of conflicting terms. Handwriting prevails over typing and a printed form, and typing prevails over a printed form. Ambiguity will be eliminated in some cases by the admission of parol evidence or by interpreting the provision strictly against the party preparing the contract, particularly when that party has significantly greater bargaining power.

Learning Outcomes

After studying this chapter, you should be able to clearly explain:

16-1 Statute of Frauds

LO.1 Explain when a contract must be evidenced by a writing

See the discussion and examples illustrated throughout this chapter beginning on page 292.

LO.2 Explain the effect of noncompliance with the statute of frauds

See the *Bithoney* case where a doctor's oral contract for severance was barred by the statute of frauds, page 293. See the example in which an oral contract cannot be enforced because it is not in writing, but the plaintiff may recover the reasonable value of the services rendered, page 299.

16-2 Parol Evidence Rule

LO.3 Explain the parol evidence rule and the exceptions to this rule

See the example in which the tenant is not allowed to call a witness to testify about a prior oral agreement that would add to and alter the written lease, page 300. See the exceptions based on ambiguity, fraud, duress, and mistake, pages 300–301.

16-3 Rules of Construction and Interpretation

LO.4 Understand the basic rule of contract construction that a contract is enforced according to its terms

See the example of the interpretation of the word "costs," page 302.

See the *DHL Express* case that illustrates the judicial common sense of interpreting the contract as a whole rather than a strained construction contrary to the contract's intent, pages 302–303.

LO.5 State the rules for interpreting ambiguous terms in a contract

See the discussion on the nature of the writing, page 304.

Key Terms

administrator	good faith	statute of frauds
ambiguous	incorporation by reference	suretyship
decedent	parol evidence rule	usages of trade
executor	personal representative	

Questions and Case Problems

1. Kelly made a written contract to sell certain land to Brown and gave Brown a deed to the land. Thereafter, Kelly sued Brown to get back a 20-foot strip of the land. Kelly claimed that before making the written contract, it was agreed that Kelly would sell all of his land to Brown to make it easier for Brown to get a building permit, but after that was done, the 20-foot strip would be reconveyed to Kelly. Was Kelly entitled to the 20-foot strip? What ethical values are involved? [*Brown v. Kelly*, 545 So. 2d 518 (Fla. App.)]

2. Martin made an oral contract with Cresheim Garage to work as its manager for two years. Cresheim wrote Martin a letter stating that the oral contract had been made and setting forth all of its terms. Cresheim later refused to recognize the contract. Martin sued Cresheim for breach of the contract and offered Cresheim's letter in evidence as proof of the contract. Cresheim claimed that the oral contract was not binding because the contract was not in writing and the letter referring to the contract was not a contract but only a letter. Was the contract binding?

3. Lawrence loaned money to Moore, who died without repaying the loan. Lawrence claimed that when he mentioned the matter to Moore's widow, she promised to pay the debt. She did not pay it, and Lawrence sued her on her promise. Does she have any defense? [*Moore v. Lawrence*, 480 S.W.2d 941 (Ark.)]

4. Jackson signed an agreement to sell 79 acres of land to Devenyns. Jackson owned 80 acres and was apparently intending to keep for himself the acre on which his home was located. The written agreement also stated that "Devenyns shall have the option to buy on property ___," but nothing was stated in the blank space. Devenyns sued to enforce the agreement. Was it binding? [In re *Jackson's Estate*, 892 P.2d 786 (Wyo.)]

5. Boeing Airplane Co. contracted with Pittsburgh–Des Moines Steel Co. for the latter to construct a supersonic wind tunnel. R.H. Freitag Manufacturing Co. sold materials to York-Gillespie Co., which subcontracted to do part of the work. To persuade Freitag to keep supplying materials on credit, Boeing and the principal contractor both assured Freitag that he would be paid. When Freitag was not paid by the subcontractor, he sued Boeing and the contractor. They defended on the ground that the assurances given Freitag were not written. Decide. What ethical values are involved? [*R.H. Freitag Mfg. Co. v. Boeing Airplane Co.*, 347 P.2d 1074 (Wash.)]

6. Louise Pulsifer owned a farm that she wanted to sell and ran an ad in the local newspaper. After Russell Gillespie agreed to purchase the farm, Pulsifer wrote him a letter stating that she would not sell it. He

sued her to enforce the contract, and she raised the defense of the statute of frauds. The letter she had signed did not contain any of the terms of the sale. Gillespie, however, claimed that the newspaper ad could be combined with her letter to satisfy the statute of frauds. Was he correct? [*Gillespie v. Pulsifer*, 655 S.W.2d 123 (Mo.)]

7. In February or March, Corning Glass Works orally agreed to retain Hanan as management consultant from May 1 of that year to April 30 of the next year for a present value fee of $200,000. Was this agreement binding? Is this decision ethical? [*Hanan v. Corning Glass Works*, 314 N.Y.S.2d 804 (A.D.)]

8. Catherine (wife) and Peter (husband) Mallen had lived together unmarried for some four years when Catherine got pregnant and a marriage was arranged. Peter asked Catherine to sign a prenuptial agreement. Although his financial statement attached to the agreement did not state his income at $560,000 per year, it showed he was wealthy, and she had lived with him for four years and knew from their standard of living that he had significant income. Catherine contends that failure to disclose Peter's income was a nondisclosure of a material fact when the agreement was drawn up and that accordingly the agreement is not valid. Peter contends that he fully disclosed his net worth and that Catherine was well aware of his significant income. Further, he contends that disparities in the parties' financial status and business experience did not make the agreement unconscionable. Decide. [*Mallen v. Mallen*, 622 S.E.2d 812 (Ga. Sup. Ct.)]

9. Panasonic Industrial Co. (PIC) created a contract making Manchester Equipment Co., Inc. (MECI), a nonexclusive wholesale distributor of its products. The contract stated that PIC reserved the unrestricted right to solicit and make direct sales of the products to anyone, anywhere. The contract also stated that it contained the entire agreement of the parties and that any prior agreement or statement was superseded by the contract. PIC subsequently began to make direct sales to two of MECI's established customers. MECI claimed that this was a breach of the distribution contract and sued PIC for damages. Decide. What ethical values are involved? [*Manchester Equipment Co. Inc. v. Panasonic Industrial Co.*, 529 N.Y.S.2d 532 (App. Div.)]

10. A contract made for the sale of a farm stated that the buyer's deposit would be returned "if for any reason the farm cannot be sold." The seller later stated that she had changed her mind and would not sell, and she offered to return the deposit. The buyer refused to take the deposit back and brought suit to enforce the contract. The seller contended that the "any reason" provision extended to anything, including the seller's changing her mind. Was the buyer entitled to recover? [*Phillips v. Rogers*, 200 S.E.2d 676 (W. Va.)]

11. Integrated, Inc., entered into a contract with the state of California to construct a building. It then subcontracted the electrical work to Alec Fergusson Electrical Contractors. The subcontract was a printed form with blanks filled in by typewriting. The printed payment clause required Integrated to pay Fergusson on the 15th day of the month following the submission of invoices by Fergusson. The typewritten part of the contract required Integrated to pay Fergusson "immediately following payment" (by the state) to the general contractor. When was payment required? [*Integrated, Inc. v. Alec Fergusson Electrical Contractors*, 58 Cal. Rptr. 503 (Cal. App.)]

12. Consolidated Credit Counseling Services, Inc. (Consolidated), sued Affinity Internet, Inc., doing business as SkyNetWEB (Affinity), for breach of its contract to provide computer and Web hosting services. Affinity moved to compel arbitration, and Consolidated argued that the contract between the parties did not contain an arbitration clause. The contract between the parties stated in part: "This contract is subject to all of SkyNetWEB's terms, conditions, user and acceptable use policies located at **http://www.skynetweb.com/company/legal/legal. php.**" An arbitration provision can be found by going to the Web site and clicking to paragraph 17 of the User Agreement. The contract itself makes no reference to an agreement to arbitrate, nor was paragraph 17 expressly referred to or described in the contract. Nor was a hard copy of the information on the Web site either signed by or furnished to Consolidated. Was Consolidated obligated to arbitrate under the clear language of paragraph 17? [*Affinity Internet v. Consolidated Credit*, 920 So. 2d 1286 (Fla. App.)]

13. Physicians Mutual Insurance Co. issued a policy covering Brown's life. The policy declared that it did not cover any deaths resulting from "mental disorder, alcoholism, or drug addiction." Brown was killed when she fell while intoxicated. The insurance company refused to pay because of the quoted provision. Her executor, Savage, sued the insurance company.

Did the insurance company have a defense? [*Physicians Mutual Ins. Co. v. Savage*, 296 N.E.2d 165 (Ind. App.)]

14. The Dickinson Elks Club conducted an annual Labor Day golf tournament. Charbonneau Buick-Pontiac offered to give a new car as a prize to anyone making "a hole in one on hole no. 8." The golf course of the club was only nine holes. To play 18 holes, the players would go around the course twice, although they would play from different tees or locations for the second nine holes. On the second time around, what was originally the eighth hole became the seventeenth hole. Grove was a contestant in the tournament. He scored 3 on the no. 8 hole, but on approaching it for the second time as the seventeenth hole, he made a hole in one. He claimed the prize car from Charbonneau. The latter claimed

that Grove had not won the prize because he did not make the hole in one on the eighth hole. Decide. [*Grove v. Charbonneau Buick-Pontiac, Inc.*, 240 N.W.2d 8533 (N.D.)]

15. Tambe Electric Inc. entered into a written agreement with Home Depot to provide copper wire to Tambe at a price set forth in the writing, and allowing the contractor the option of paying for the wire over a period of time. Home Depot did not fulfill this written agreement and Tambe sued for $68,598, the additional cost it had to subsequently pay to obtain copper wire for its work. Home Depot defended that it had made an oral condition precedent requiring payment in full by Tambe at the time it accepted the price quoted in the written agreement. Decide. [*Tambe Electric v. Home Depot*, 856 N.Y.S.2d 373]

CPA Questions

1. Which of the following statements is true with regard to the statute of frauds?

   a. All contracts involving consideration of more than $500 must be in writing.

   b. The written contract must be signed by all parties.

   c. The statute of frauds applies to contracts that can be fully performed within one year from the date they are made.

   d. The contract terms may be stated in more than one document.

2. With regard to an agreement for the sale of real estate, the statute of frauds:

   a. Requires that the entire agreement be in a single writing.

   b. Requires that the purchase price be fair and adequate in relation to the value of the real estate.

   c. Does *not* require that the agreement be signed by all parties.

   d. Does *not* apply if the value of the real estate is less than $500.

3. In negotiations with Andrews for the lease of Kemp's warehouse, Kemp orally agreed to pay one-half of the

cost of the utilities. The written lease, later prepared by Kemp's attorney, provided that Andrews pay all of the utilities. Andrews failed to carefully read the lease and signed it. When Kemp demanded that Andrews pay all of the utilities, Andrews refused, claiming that the lease did not accurately reflect the oral agreement. Andrews also learned that Kemp intentionally misrepresented the condition of the structure of the warehouse during the negotiations between the parties. Andrews sued to rescind the lease and intends to introduce evidence of the parties' oral agreement about sharing the utilities and the fraudulent statements made by Kemp. Will the parol evidence rule prevent the admission of evidence concerning each of the following?

	Oral agreement regarding who pays the utilities	Fraudulent statements by Kemp
a.	Yes	Yes
b.	No	Yes
c.	Yes	No
d.	No	No

Third Persons and Contracts

Learning Outcomes ⟨⟨⟨

After studying this chapter, you should be able to

LO.1 Explain the two types of intended third-party beneficiaries

LO.2 Explain why an incidental beneficiary does not have the right to sue as a third-party beneficiary

LO.3 Define an assignment

LO.4 Explain the general rule that a person entitled to receive money under a contract may generally assign that right to another person

LO.5 List the nonassignable rights to performance

17-1 Third-Party Beneficiary Contracts

Generally, only the parties to a contract may sue on it. However, in some cases a third person who is not a party to the contract may sue on the contract.

CPA

17-1a Definition

third-party beneficiary— third person whom the parties to a contract intend to benefit by the making of the contract and to confer upon such person the right to sue for breach of contract.

When a contract is intended to benefit a third person, such a person is an intended **third-party beneficiary** and may bring suit on and enforce the contract.

Creditor Beneficiary

The intended beneficiary is sometimes classified as a *creditor beneficiary* when the promisee's primary intent is to discharge a duty owed to the third party.[1] **For Example,** when Max Giordano sold his business, Sameway Laundry, to Harry Phinn, he had three years of payments totaling $14,500 owing to Davco, Inc., on a commercial Davco shirt drying and pressing machine purchased in 2006. Max (the promisee) made a contract with Harry to sell the business for a stipulated sum. A provision in this contract selling the business called for Harry (the promisor) to make the Davco machine payments when due over the next three years. Should Harry fail to make payments, Davco, Inc., as an intended creditor beneficiary under the contract between Max and Harry, would have standing to sue Harry for breach of the payment provision in the contract.

CPA ### Donee Beneficiary

The second type of intended beneficiary is a *donee beneficiary* to whom the promisee's primary intent in contracting is to give a benefit. A life insurance contract is such an intended third-party beneficiary contract. An individual third-party beneficiary has a right to sue under a broad range of insurance policies.

CASE SUMMARY

Peyton Manning Can't Get the Nationwide Insurance Jingle Out of His Head
What's Prudential's Jingle, Sagarnaga?

FACTS: Dr. Garcia purchased a Prudential (Pruco) life insurance policy for a death benefit of $750,000, with his wife Margarita as the primary beneficiary and his three children as contingent beneficiaries. After Margarita's death in 2005, Dr. Garcia married Sagarnaga in 2007. In 2008, Dr. Garcia contacted Pruco and in a recorded conversation advised Pruco that he wanted to designate his wife Sagarnaga as a 50 percent beneficiary. Pruco sent him a partially completed change of beneficiary [COB] form. Dr. Garcia completed the remaining information and returned the COB request to Pruco. Thereafter the signed COB form, dated April 3, 2008, and received by Pruco on April 10, 2008, listed the beneficiaries as follows: the primary beneficiary designation stated Sagarnaga was to receive 50 percent of the Policy proceeds, 12 percent to Arturo Garcia, Jr., 13 percent to Eloisa, and 25 percent to Cecilia. Contingent beneficiaries were also listed. According to the terms of the Policy, if Pruco received a COB request,

---

[1] The Restatement (Second) of Contracts §302 substitutes "intended beneficiary" for the terms "creditor" and "donee" beneficiary. However, some courts continue to use the classifications of creditor and donee third-party beneficiaries. Regardless of the terminology, the law continues to be the same. See *Continental Casualty v. Zurich American Insurance*, 2009 WL 455285 (D.C. Or. 2009).

Pruco would record the change and file it. The change of beneficiary would be effective as of the date the request was signed.

Dr. Garcia died in Brazil on September 22, 2009. It was discovered that Dr. Garcia's COB form received on April 10, 2008, had not been accepted or recorded because a Pruco employee saw an ambiguity regarding the contingent beneficiaries section, which had not been resolved prior to Dr. Garcia's death. Pruco stated that Sagarnaga was thus not a beneficiary under the policy. The children filed a lawsuit against Pruco seeking the entire death benefit. Pruco contended that Sagarnaga had no standing to sue and asserted that it had not breached the insurance contract. From a judgment for Sagarnaga, Prudential appealed.

DECISION: Judgment of Sagarnaga. An insurance policy is a contract between the insurer and the insured/owner of the policy. A beneficiary under such a policy has no standing to sue under the policy unless his or her interest has vested, such as the insured dies. The policy defined the right of the owner to change beneficiaries, and Dr. Garcia's primary beneficiary designation was clear and unambiguous. With the signed COB form received by Pruco on April 10, 2008, Sagarnaga became the intended beneficiary of the policy, which vested on Dr. Garcia's death. Pruco's failure to tender the 50 percent death benefit to Sagarnaga was a breach of contract. She was entitled to interest penalties and attorney's fees. [*Prudential Insurance Co. v. Durante*, 443 S.W.2d 499 (Tex. App. 2014)]

Necessity of Intent

A third person does not have the status of an intended third-party beneficiary unless it is clear at the time the contract was formed that the parties intended to impose a direct obligation with respect to the third person.[2] In determining whether there is intent to benefit a third party, the surrounding circumstances as well as the contract may be examined.[3] There is a strong presumption that the parties to a contract intend to benefit only themselves.[4]

CASE SUMMARY

The Pest Control Case

FACTS: Admiral Pest Control had a standing contract with Lodging Enterprises to spray its motel every month to exterminate pests. Copeland, a guest in the motel, was bitten by a spider. She sued Admiral on the ground that she was a third-party beneficiary of the extermination contract.

DECISION: Judgment against Copeland. There was no intent manifested in the contract that guests of the motel were beneficiaries of the contract. The contract was made by the motel to protect itself. The guests were incidental beneficiaries of that contract and therefore could not sue for its breach. [*Copeland v. Admiral Pest Control Co.*, 933 P.2d 937 (Okla. App. 1996)]

---

[2] *American United Logistics, Inc. v. Catellus*, 319 F.3d 921 (7th Cir. 2003).

[3] See *Becker v. Crispell-Snyder, Inc.*, 763 N.W.2d 192 (Wis. App. 2009) for an example of complex circumstances surrounding a third-party beneficiary contract. The town of Somers, Wisconsin, entered into a contract with engineering firm Crispell-Synder (C-S) because it needed an engineering firm to oversee a new subdivision to be developed by the Beckers. Under this contract C-S would submit bills to the town for overseeing the development, and the town would pay C-S through a line of credit from the Beckers. The court held that the Beckers were third-party beneficiaries entitled to sue C-S for overcharging change orders.

[4] *Barney v. Unity Paving, Inc.*, 639 N.E.2d 592 (Ill. App. 1994).

Description

It is not necessary that the intended third-party beneficiary be identified by name. The beneficiary may be identified by class, with the result that any member of that class is a third-party beneficiary. **For Example,** a contract between the promoter of an automobile stock car race and the owner of the racetrack contains a promise by the owner to pay specified sums of money to each driver racing a car in certain races. A person driving in one of the designated races is a third-party beneficiary and can sue the owner on the contract for the promised compensation.

17-1b Modification or Termination of Intended Third-Party Beneficiary Contract

Can the parties to the contract modify or terminate it so as to destroy the right of the intended third-party beneficiary? If the contract contains an express provision allowing a change of beneficiary or cancellation of the contract without the consent of the intended third-party beneficiary, the parties to the contract may destroy the rights of the intended beneficiary by acting in accordance with that contract provision.[5]

For Example, Roy obtained a life insurance policy from Phoenix Insurance Company that provided the beneficiary could be changed by the insured. Roy named his son, Harry, as the beneficiary. Later, Roy had a falling out with Harry and removed him as beneficiary. Roy could do this because the right to change the beneficiary was expressly reserved by the contract that created the status of the intended third-party beneficiary.

In addition, the rights of an intended third-party beneficiary are destroyed if the contract is discharged or ended by operation of law, for example, through bankruptcy proceedings.

17-1c Limitations on Intended Third-Party Beneficiary

Although the intended third-party beneficiary rule gives the third person the right to enforce the contract, it obviously gives no more rights than the contract provides. That is, the intended third-party beneficiary must take the contract as it is. If there is a time limitation or any other restriction in the contract, the intended beneficiary cannot ignore it but is bound by it.

If the contract is not binding for any reason, that defense may be raised against the intended third-party beneficiary suing on the contract.[6]

CPA 17-1d Incidental Beneficiaries

Not everyone who benefits from the performance of a contract between other persons is entitled to sue as a third-party beneficiary. If the benefit was intended, the third person is an intended beneficiary with the rights described in the preceding sections. If the benefit was not intended, the third person is an *incidental beneficiary.* **For Example,** real estate developer Ocean Atlantic Corp. purchased a series of bonds from American Southern Insurance Co. for the purpose of guaranteeing the performance of public improvement in a subdivision it was developing in Yorkville, Illinois. The bonds representing the surety contract between Ocean Atlantic and American Southern were issued in favor of the City

---

[5] A common form of reservation is the life insurance policy provision by which the insured reserves the right to change the beneficiary. Section 142 of the Restatement (Second) of Contracts provides that the promisor and the promisee may modify their contract and affect the right of the third-party beneficiary thereby unless the agreement expressly prohibits this or the third-party beneficiary has changed position in reliance on the promise or has manifested assent to it.

[6] *XL Disposal Corp. v. John Sexton Contractors Co.*, 659 N.E.2d 1312 (Ill. App. 1995).

right—legal capacity to require another person to perform or refrain from an action.

duty—obligation of law imposed on a person to perform or refrain from performing a certain act.

of Yorkville. Ocean Atlantic hired subcontractor Aurora Blacktop, Inc., to perform several improvements, but the project stalled and Aurora was never paid for its work. Aurora lacked standing as a third-party beneficiary to enforce the subdivision bonds against American Southern because the contractual obligations ran only to the city. Aurora was deemed an incidental beneficiary rather than a third-party beneficiary.[7]

Whether or not a third party is an *intended* or *incidental* beneficiary, therefore, comes down to determining whether or not a reasonable person would believe that the promisee intended to confer on the beneficiary an enforceable benefit under the contract in question. The intent must be clear and definite or expressed in the contract itself or in the circumstances surrounding the contract's execution.[8]

CASE SUMMARY

Third Party Must Be Identified in the Four Corners of the Contract

FACTS: Novus International, Inc., manufactures a poultry-feed supplement named Alimet at its plant in Chocolate Bayou, Texas. A key component of Alimet is the chemical MMP. Novus contracted with Union Carbide to secure MMP from Carbide's plant in Taft, Louisiana. Sometime later, Carbide entered into a major rail-transportation contract with the Union Pacific Railroad (UP). The rail contract consisted of nearly 100 pages. Exhibit 2 of the contract delineated inbound and outbound shipments to and from all of Carbide's Texas and Louisiana facilities. Among the hundreds of shipments listed in Exhibit 2 were three outbound MMP shipments from Taft, Louisiana, to Chocolate Bayou, Texas. These shipments were described as "Taft outbound liquid chemicals." Due to difficulties that arose from its merger with the Southern Pacific Railroad, UP experienced severe disruptions in its rail service over parts of two years and was unable to transport sufficient MMP to Chocolate Bayou. As a result, Novus had to utilize more expensive methods of transportation to obtain Alimet. It sued UP to recover the increased costs of premium freight resulting from UP's breach of its rail contract with Carbide. UP asserts that Novus did not have standing to sue; and Novus contends that it had standing to sue as an intended third-party beneficiary.

DECISION: Judgment for UP. Third-party beneficiary claims succeed or fail according to the provisions of the contact upon which suit is brought. The intention to confer a direct benefit on a third party must be clearly and fully spelled out in the four corners of the contract. Otherwise, enforcement of the contract by a third party must be denied. After reviewing the rail contract, no intent to confer a direct benefit on Novus is evident. Novus is never named in the contract, and all obligations flow between UP and Carbide. Nor is it stated anywhere in the contract that the parties are contracting for the benefit of Carbide's customers. Novus, thus, is an incidental beneficiary without standing to sue. [*Union Pacific Railroad v. Novus International, Inc.*, 113 S.W.3d 418 (Tex. App. 2003)]

assignment—transfer of a right; generally used in connection with personal property rights, as rights under a contract, commercial paper, an insurance policy, a mortgage, or a lease. (Parties—assignor, assignee.)

17-2 Assignments

The parties to a contract have both rights and duties. Can rights be transferred or sold to another person or entity? Can duties be transferred to another person?

17-2a Definitions

Contracts create **rights** and **duties** between the parties to the contract. An **assignment** is a transfer of contractual rights to a third party. The party owing a duty or debt under the

---

[7] *City of Yorkville v. American Southern Insurance Co.*, 654 F.3d 713 (7th Cir. 2011).
[8] See *Entire Energy & Renewables, LLC v. Duncan*, 999 N.E.2d 214 (Ohio App. 2013).

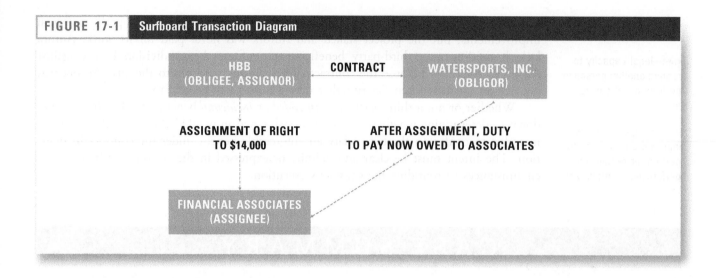

FIGURE 17-1 Surfboard Transaction Diagram

obligor—promisor.

debtor—buyer on credit (i.e., a borrower).

obligee—promisee who can claim the benefit of the obligation.

assignor—party who assigns contract rights to a third party.

assignee—third party to whom contract benefits are transferred.

contract is the **obligor** or **debtor,** and the party to whom the obligation is owed is the **obligee.** The party making the assignment is the **assignor.** The third party to whom the assignment is made is the **assignee. For Example,** Randy Marshall and Marilee Menendez own Huntington Beach Board (HBB) Company, LLC, a five-employee start-up company making top-of-the line surfboards. Marilee was able to sell 100 Duke Kahanamoku–inspired "longboards" to Watersports, Inc., a large retail sporting goods chain, for $140 per board. However, the best payment terms she could obtain were payment in full in 90 days. A contract containing these terms was executed, and the goods were delivered. To meet internal cash flow needs, HBB assigned its right to receive the $14,000 payment from the buyer to West Coast Financial Associates (Associates) and received $12,800 cash from Associates on execution of the assignment documents. Notice was given at that time to Watersports, Inc., of the assignment. The right to receive the payment due in 90 days under the sales contract has thus been transferred by the seller HBB (assignor) to the third party, Associates (the assignee), to whom the buyer, Watersports, Inc. (obligor), now owes the duty of payment. Under the law of assignments, Associates, the assignee, now has direct rights against the obligor, Watersports, Inc. (See Figure 17-1.)

17-2b Form of Assignment

Generally, an assignment may be in any form. Statutes, however, may require that certain kinds of assignments be in writing or be executed in a particular form. Any words, whether written or spoken, that show an intention to transfer or assign will be given the effect of an assignment.[9]

17-2c Notice of Assignment

An assignment, if otherwise valid, takes effect the moment it is made. The assignee should give immediate notice of the assignment to the obligor, setting forth the obligor's duty to the assignee, in order to prevent improper payment.[10]

---

[9] *JBM Investments, LLC v. Callahan Industries, Inc.,* 667 S.E.2d 429 (Ga. App. 2008).

[10] In some cases, an assignee will give notice of the assignment to the obligor in order to obtain priority over other persons who claim the same right or in order to limit the defenses that the obligor may raise against the assignee. U.C.C. §9-318.

CASE SUMMARY

When You Find Yourself in a Hole, NationsBank, Stop Digging

FACTS: L & S General Contractors, LLC (L & S), purchased a book-entry certificate of deposit (CD 005) in the principal amount of $100,000 from NationsBank, N.A. L & S later assigned CD 005 to Credit General Insurance Company (Credit General) as collateral security for performance and payment bonds on a Howard Johnson construction project. Credit General forwarded to NationsBank a written notice of the assignment that stated, "Please hold this account as assigned to use until demanded or released by us." NationsBank recorded the assignment and executed a written acknowledgment. When CD 005 matured, L & S rolled over the proceeds into a short-term certificate of deposit (CD 058) and, upon maturity, rolled over the proceeds of CD 058 into another short-term certificate of deposit (CD 072).

The bank book entries of CD 058 and CD 072 recorded L & S as the only principal/payee and did not reflect Credit General's assignment interest. NationsBank admitted its failure to show Credit General as assignee on the rollover book entries for CD 058 and CD 072 was a mistake.

Upon maturity, L & S withdrew the proceeds of CD 072 without the knowledge or consent of Credit General. Later Credit General made written demand on NationsBank for the proceeds of CD 005, and NationsBank informed Credit General that CD 005 had been redeemed and refused payment. Credit General sued NationsBank for wrongful payment of proceeds. NationsBank argues that the assignment was limited in time to the completion of the Howard Johnson project.

DECISION: Judgment for the assignee, Credit General. Upon notice and acknowledgment of the assignment, NationsBank incurred a legal duty to pay the account proceeds only to the assignee, Credit General, in whom the account was vested by the terms of the assignment. The assignment was absolute and unambiguous on its face and clearly was not limited as NationsBank proposes. The assignment language controls. [*Credit General Insurance Co. v. NationsBank*, 299 F.3d 943 (8th Cir. 2002)]

If the obligor is notified in any manner that there has been an assignment and that any money due must be paid to the assignee, the obligor's obligation can be discharged only by making payment to the assignee.

If the obligor is not notified that there has been an assignment and that the money due must be paid to the assignee, any payment made by the obligor to the assignor reduces or cancels that portion of the debt. The only remedy for the assignee is to sue the assignor to recover the payments that were made by the obligor.

The Uniform Consumer Credit Code (UCCC) protects consumer-debtors making payments to an assignor without knowledge of the assignment[11] and imposes a penalty for using a contract term that would destroy this protection of consumers.[12]

17-2d Assignment of Right to Money

claim–right to payment.

cause of action–right to damages or other judicial relief when a legally protected right of the plaintiff is violated by an unlawful act of the defendant.

Assignments of contracts are generally made to raise money. **For Example,** an automobile dealer assigns a customer's credit contract to a finance company and receives cash for it. Sometimes assignments are made when an enterprise closes and transfers its business to a new owner.

A person entitled to receive money, such as payment for goods sold to a buyer or for work done under a contract, may generally assign that right to another person.[13] A **claim** or **cause of action** against another person may be assigned. Isaac Hayes, an Academy Award®–winning composer, producer, and the original voice of Chef in the television series South Park, assigned his copyright interests in several musical works in exchange for

---

[11] U.C.C.C. §2.412.
[12] U.C.C.C. §5.202.
[13] *Pravin Banker Associates v. Banco Popular del Peru*, 109 F.3d 850 (2d Cir. 1997).

royalties from Stax Records.[14] A contractor entitled to receive payment from a building's owner can assign that right to a bank as security for a loan or can assign it to anyone else.

For Example, Celeste owed Roscoe Painters $5,000 for painting her house. Roscoe assigned this claim to the Main Street Bank. Celeste later refused to pay the bank because she had never consented to the assignment. The fact that Celeste had not consented is irrelevant. Roscoe was the owner of the claim and could transfer it to the bank. Celeste, therefore, is obligated to pay the assignee, Main Street Bank.

Future Rights

By the modern rule, future and expected rights to money may be assigned. Thus, prior to the start of a building, a building contractor may assign its rights to money not yet due under an existing contract's payment on completion-phase schedule.

Purpose of Assignment

The assignment of the right to money may be a complete transfer of the right that gives the assignee the right to collect and keep the money. In contrast, the assignment may be held for security. In this case, the assignee may hold the money only as a security for some specified obligation.

Prohibition of Assignment of Rights

A clear and specific contractual prohibition against the assignment of rights is enforceable at common law. However, the UCC favors the assignment of contracts, and express contractual prohibitions on assignments are ineffective against (1) the assignment of rights to payment for goods or services, including accounts receivable,[15] and (2) the assignment of the rights to damages for breach of sales contracts.[16]

17-2e Nonassignable Rights

If the transfer of a right would materially affect or alter a duty or the rights of the obligor, an assignment is not permitted.[17]

Assignment Increasing Burden of Performance

When the assignment of a right would increase the burden of the obligor in performing, an assignment is ordinarily not permitted. To illustrate, if the assignor has the right to buy a certain quantity of a stated article and to take such property from the seller's warehouse, this right can be assigned. However, if the sales contract stipulates that the seller should deliver to the buyer's premises and the assignee's premises are a substantial distance from the assignor's place of business, the assignment would not be given effect. In this case, the seller would be required to give a different performance by providing greater transportation if the assignment were permitted.

Personal Services

Contracts for personal services are generally not assignable. **For Example,** were golf instructor David Ledbetter to sign a one-year contract to provide instruction for professional golfer Davis Love III, David Ledbetter could not assign his first assistant to provide the instruction, nor could Davis Love assign a protégé to receive instruction from Ledbetter.

---

[14] *Hayes v. Carlin America, Inc.*, 168 F. Supp. 2d 154 (S.D.N.Y. 2001).
[15] U.C.C. §9-318(4). This section of the UCC is applicable to most common commercial assignments.
[16] U.C.C. §2-210(2).
[17] *Aslakson v. Home Savings Ass'n*, 416 N.W.2d 786 (Minn. App. 1987) (increase of credit risk).

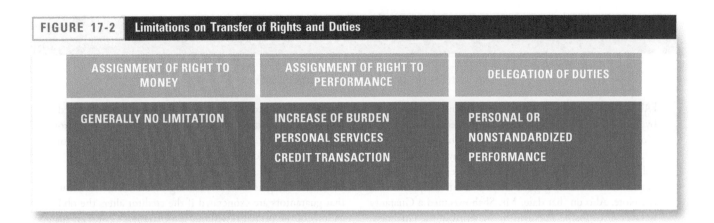

FIGURE 17-2 | Limitations on Transfer of Rights and Duties

ASSIGNMENT OF RIGHT TO MONEY	ASSIGNMENT OF RIGHT TO PERFORMANCE	DELEGATION OF DUTIES
GENERALLY NO LIMITATION	INCREASE OF BURDEN PERSONAL SERVICES CREDIT TRANSACTION	PERSONAL OR NONSTANDARDIZED PERFORMANCE

Professional athletes and their agents commonly deal with assignment or trading rights of the athletes in their contracts with professional sports franchises.

There is a split among jurisdictions regarding whether employee noncompetition covenants are assignable to the new owner of a business absent employee consent. That is, some courts permit a successor employer to enforce an employee's noncompetition agreement as an assignee of the original employer. However, a majority of states that have considered this issue have concluded that restrictive covenants are personal in nature and not assignable. **For Example,** in September 2000, Philip Burkhardt signed a non-competition agreement with his employer, NES Trench Shoring. On June 30, 2002, United Rentals Purchased NES with all contracts being assigned to United Rentals. Burkhardt stayed on with the new owner for five weeks and thereafter went to work for Traffic Control Services, a direct competitor of United. United was unsuccessful in its action to enforce the noncompetition covenant Burkhardt had signed with NES. Burkhardt's covenant with NES did not contain a clause allowing the covenant to be assigned to a new owner, and the court refused to enforce it, absent an express clause permitting assignment.[18]

Credit Transaction

When a transaction is based on extending credit, the person to whom credit is extended cannot assign any rights under the contract to another. **For Example,** Jack Aldrich contracted to sell his summer camp on Lake Sunapee to Pat Norton for $200,000, with $100,000 in cash due at the closing and the balance due on an installment basis secured by a mortgage on the property to be executed by Norton. Several days later, Norton found a more desirable property, and her sister Meg was very pleased to take over the Sunapee contract. Pat assigned her rights to Meg. Jack Aldrich, having received a better offer after contracting with Pat, refused to consent to the assignment. In this situation, the assignment to Meg is prohibited because the assignee, Meg, is a different credit risk even though the property to serve as security remained unchanged.

CPA 17-2f **Rights of Assignee**

Unless restricted by the terms of the assignment or applicable law, the assignee acquires all the rights of the assignor.[19]

---

[18] *Traffic Control Sources, Inc. v. United Rentals Northwest, Inc.,* 87 P.3d 1054 (Nev. 2004).
[19] *Puget Sound National Bank v. Washington Department of Revenue,* 868 P.2d 127 (Wash. 1994).

CASE SUMMARY

An Example of An "Ironclad Contract"

FACTS: On July 7, 2006, Riviera Plaza Investments, LLC, by Haresh Shah, for value received, executed and delivered a Note by which it promised to pay Citibank the sum of $2,925,000.00 in monthly installment payments of principal plus interest. On the same date, Riviera, again by Mr. Shah, executed a Mortgage in order to secure the payment of the Note. Also on that date, Mr. Shah executed a Guaranty in favor of Citibank. Pursuant to the terms of the Guaranty, Shah guaranteed the prompt, complete, and full payment and performance of Riviera's obligations in accordance with the terms of the Note. Riviera failed to make its monthly payments and foreclosure proceedings were initiated in 2010. On February 9, 2011, Wells Fargo Bank was assigned the rights, title, and interest in the loan document and was substituted as the plaintiff in the foreclosure proceedings against Riviera and Shah in the trial court. As guarantor Shah contested litigation. From a judgment against Shah on his obligations under the Guaranty, Shah appealed.

DECISION: Judgment for Wells Fargo Bank. While it is true that guarantors are exonerated if the creditor alters the obligations of the principal without the guarantor's consent, the Guaranty expressly provided that: "this Guaranty shall follow the note and Security Instrument"… and "the holder of this Guaranty may enforce this Guaranty just as if said holder had been originally named as lender hereunder." [*Riviera Plaza Investments, LLC v. Wells Fargo Bank, N.A.,* **10 N.E.3d 541 (Ind. App. 2014)**]

An assignee stands exactly in the position of the assignor. The assignee's rights are no more or less than those of the assignor. If the assigned right to payment is subject to a condition precedent, that same condition exists for the assignee. **For Example,** when a contractor is not entitled to receive the balance of money due under the contract until all bills of suppliers of materials have been paid, the assignee to whom the contractor assigns the balance due under the contract is subject to the same condition.

17-2g Continuing Liability of Assignor

The making of an assignment does not relieve the assignor of any obligation of the contract. In the absence of a contrary agreement, an assignor continues to be bound by the obligations of the original contract. **For Example,** boatbuilder Derecktor NY's assignment of obligations to a Connecticut boatbuilder did not release it from all liabilities under its boatbuilding contract with New York Water Taxi (NYWT); and NYWT was allowed to proceed against Derecktor NY for breach of contract–design and breach of contract–workmanship.[20]

When a lease is assigned, the assignee becomes the principal obligor for rent payments, and the leasee becomes a surety toward the lessor for the assignee's performance. **For Example,** Tri-State Chiropractic (TSC) held a five-year lease on premises at 6010 East Main Street in Columbus, Ohio. Without the leasor's consent, TSC assigned that lease to Dr. T. Wilson and Buckeye Chiropractic, LLC, prior to the expiration of the lease. TSC continues to be liable for rent as surety during the term of the lease, even if the leasor (owner) had consented to the assignment or accepted payment from the assignee.[21] In order to avoid liability as a surety, TSC would have to obtain a discharge of the lease by **novation,** in which all three parties agree that the original contract (the lease) would be discharged and a new lease between Dr. Wilson and the owner would

novation–substitution for an old contract with a new one that either replaces an existing obligation with a new obligation or replaces an original party with a new party.

---

[20] *New York Trans Harbor, LLC v. Derecktor Shipyards,* 841 N.Y.S.2d 821 (2007).
[21] *Schottenstein Trustees v. Carano,* 2000 WL 1455425 (Ohio App. 2000).

take effect. A novation allows for the discharge of a contractual obligation by the substitution of a new contract involving a new party.[22]

17-2h Liability of Assignee

It is necessary to distinguish between the question of whether the obligor can assert a particular defense against the assignee and the question of whether any person can sue the assignee. Ordinarily, the assignee is not subject to suit by virtue of the fact that the assignment has been made.

Consumer Protection Liability of Assignee

The assignee of the right to money may have no direct relationship to the original debtor except with respect to receiving payments. Consumer protection laws in most states, however, may subject the assignee to some liability for the assignor's misconduct.

Defenses and Setoffs

The assignee's rights are no greater than those of the assignor.[23] If the obligor could successfully defend against a suit brought by the assignor, the obligor will also prevail against the assignee.

The fact that the assignee has given value for the assignment does not give the assignee any immunity from defenses that the other party, the obligor, could have asserted against the assignor. The rights acquired by the assignee remain subject to any limitations imposed by the contract. Moreover, an assumption of obligations may be implied from an acceptance of benefits. **For Example,** Missouri Breaks, LLC, an entity formed under a bankruptcy reorganization plan that received assignment of the oil and gas leases of the now defunct entity Athens/Alpha Gas Corporation (Alpha), received the revenue from operation of the well under the leases and assumed the obligation to pay creditors. The court determined that Mission Breaks implicitly agreed to assume the liability to certain owners for unpaid royalties that were not discharged in the bankruptcy proceedings.[24]

17-2i Warranties of Assignor

When the assignment is made for a consideration, the assignor is regarded as providing an **implied warranty** that the right assigned is valid. The assignor also warrants that the assignor is the owner of the claim or right assigned and that the assignor will not interfere with the assignee's enforcement of the obligation.

17-2j Delegation of Duties

A **delegation of duties** is a transfer of duties by a contracting party to another person who is to perform them. Under certain circumstances, a contracting party may obtain someone else to do the work. When the performance is standardized and nonpersonal, so that it is not material who performs, the law will permit the **delegation** of the performance of the contract. In such cases, however, the contracting party remains liable in the case of default of the person doing the work just as though no delegation had been made.[25]

implied warranty–warranty that was not made but is implied by law.

delegation of duties–transfer of duties by a contracting party to another person who is to perform them.

delegation–transfer to another of the right and power to do an act.

[22] *Willamette Management Association, Inc. v. Palczynski,* 38 A.3d 1212 (Conn. App. 2012).
[23] *Shoreline Communications, Inc. v. Norwich Taxi, LLC,* 797 A.2d 1165 (Conn. App. 2002).
[24] *Van Sickle v. Hallmark & Associates, Inc.,* 840 N.W.2d 92, 105 (N.D. 2013).
[25] *Orange Bowl Corp. v. Warren,* 386 S.E.2d 293 (S.C. App. 1989).

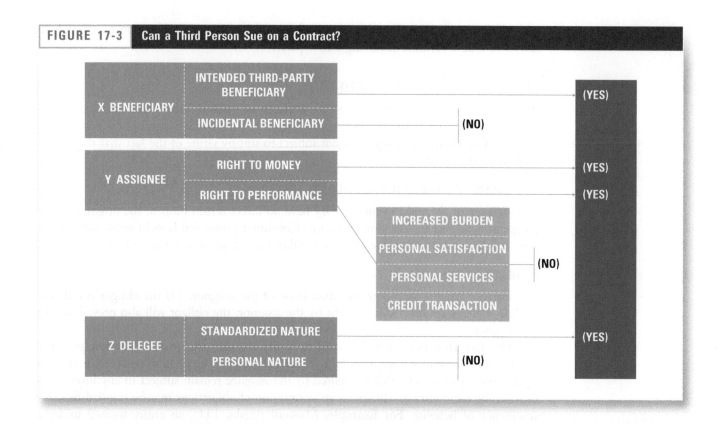

FIGURE 17-3 Can a Third Person Sue on a Contract?

CASE SUMMARY

Who's Liable for $871,069 In Damages? Not Me. I Wasn't Even There!

FACTS: The Emersons contracted with Martin Winters, the owner of Winters Roofing Company, to install a new roof on their home. When the new roof leaked, Winters agreed to fix the problems. Without the knowledge of the Emersons, Winters hired a subcontractor, Bruce Jacobs, to perform the repair work. Jacobs's use of a propane torch in repairing the roof resulted in a fire that caused $871,069 in damages to the house and personal property. Federal Insurance Co. sued Winters to recover sums it paid the Emersons for damages resulting from the fire. Winters defended that Federal had sued the wrong party because

Winters did not participate in the repair work but had subcontracted the work out to Jacobs and was neither at the job site nor supervised Jacobs's work.

DECISION: Judgment for the plaintiff. Winters, based on his contract with the Emersons, had an implied duty under the contract to install the roof properly, skillfully, diligently, and in a workmanlike manner. The delegation of these duties to Jacobs did not serve to release Winters from liability implicit in the original content. [*Federal Insurance Co. v. Winters*, **354 S.W.3d 287 (Tenn. 2011)**]

A contract may prohibit a party owing a duty of performance under a contract from delegating that duty to another.[26] **For Example,** Tom Joyce of Patriot Plumbing Co. contracts to install a new heating system for Mrs. Lawton. A notation on the sales contract that Tom Joyce will do the installation prohibits Patriot Plumbing from delegating the installation to another equally skilled plumber or to another company if a backlog of work occurs at Patriot Plumbing.

[26] See *Physical Distribution Services, Inc. v. R. R. Donnelley*, 561 F.3d 792 (8th Cir. 2009).

If the performance of a party to a contract involves personal skill, talents, judgment, or trust, the delegation of duties is barred unless consented to by the person entitled to the performance. Examples include performance by professionals such as physicians, dentists, lawyers, consultants, celebrities, artists, and craftpersons with unusual skills.

Intention to Delegate Duties

An assignment of rights does not in itself delegate the performance of duties to the assignee. In the absence of clear language in the assignment stating that duties are or are not delegated, all circumstances must be examined to determine whether there is a delegation. When the total picture is viewed, it may become clear what was intended. The fact that an assignment is made for security of the assignee is a strong indication that there was no intent to delegate to the assignee the performance of any duty resting on the assignor.[27]

Delegation of Duties under the UCC

With respect to contracts for the sale of goods, "an assignment of 'the contract' or of 'all my rights under the contract' or an assignment in similar general terms is an assignment of rights and, unless the language or the circumstances (as in an assignment for security) indicate the contrary, it is a delegation of performance of the duties of the assignor, and its acceptance by the assignee constitutes a promise … to perform those duties. This promise is enforceable by either the assignor or the other party to the original contract."[28]

Make the Connection

Summary

Ordinarily, only the parties to contracts have rights and duties with respect to such contracts. Exceptions are made in the case of third-party beneficiary contracts and assignments.

When a contract shows a clear intent to benefit a third person or class of persons, those persons are called *intended third-party beneficiaries*, and they may sue for breach of the contract. A third-party beneficiary is subject to any limitation or restriction found in the contract. A third-party beneficiary loses all rights when the original contract is terminated by operation of law or if the contract reserves the right to change the beneficiary and such a change is made.

In contrast, an incidental beneficiary benefits from the performance of a contract, but the conferring of this benefit was not intended by the contracting parties. An incidental beneficiary cannot sue on the contract.

An assignment is a transfer of a right; the assignor transfers a right to the assignee. In the absence of a local statute, there are no formal requirements for an assignment. Any words manifesting the intent to transfer are sufficient to constitute an assignment. No consideration is required. Any right to money may be assigned, whether the assignor is entitled to the money at the time of the assignment or will be entitled or expects to be entitled at some time in the future.

A right to a performance may be assigned except when (1) it would increase the burden of performance, (2) the contract involves the performance of personal services, or (3) the transaction is based on extending credit.

When a valid assignment is made, the assignee has the same rights—and only the same rights—as the assignor. The assignee is also subject to the same defenses and set-offs as the assignor had been.

---

[27] *City National Bank of Fort Smith v. First National Bank and Trust Co. of Rogers*, 732 S.W.2d 489 (Ark. App. 1987).
[28] U.C.C. §2-210(4).

The performance of duties under a contract may be delegated to another person except when a personal element of skill or judgment of the original contracting party is involved. The intent to delegate duties may be expressly stated. The intent may also be found in an "assignment" of "the contract" unless the circumstances make it clear that only the right to money was intended to be transferred. The fact that there has been a delegation of duties does not release the assignor from responsibility for performance. The assignor is liable for breach of the contract if the assignee does not properly perform the delegated duties. In the absence of an effective delegation or the formation of a third-party beneficiary contract, an assignee of rights is not liable to the obligee of the contract for its performance by the assignor.

Notice is not required to effect an assignment. When notice of the assignment is given to the obligor together with a demand that future payments be made to the assignee, the obligor cannot discharge liability by payment to the assignor.

When an assignment is made for a consideration, the assignor makes implied warranties that the right assigned is valid and that the assignor owns that right and will not interfere with its enforcement by the assignee.

Learning Outcomes

After studying this chapter, you should be able to clearly explain:

17-1   Third-Party Beneficiary Contracts

LO.1   Explain the two types of intended third-party beneficiaries

See the Sameway Laundry example that illustrates how the "intended creditor beneficiary" can sue the buyer, page 312.

See the *Prudential Insurance Co.* case, involving a life insurance contract and an "intended" donee third-party beneficiary's right to sue, pages 312–313.

LO.2   Explain why an incidental beneficiary does not have the right to sue as a third-party beneficiary

See the *City of Yorkville* example, in which a subcontractor was an incidental beneficiary with no standing to sue on performance bonds because the obligation ran only to the city, pages 314–315.

17-2   Assignments

LO.3   Define an assignment

See the text discussion explaining that an assignment is the transfer of contractual rights to a third party, page 315.

See the *Huntington Beach Board* example that discusses the assignee's direct rights against the obligor, page 316.

LO.4   Explain the general rule that a person entitled to receive money under a contract may generally assign that right to another person

See the example of an automobile dealer assigning a customer's credit contract to a finance company in order to raise cash to buy more inventory, page 317.

LO.5   List the nonassignable rights to performance

See the text discussion regarding increase of burden, personal services, and credit transactions, pages 318–319.

Key Terms

assignee	debtor	novation
assignment	delegation	obligee
assignor	delegation of duties	obligor
cause of action	duties	rights
claim	implied warranty	third-party beneficiary

Questions and Case Problems

1. Give an example of a third-party beneficiary contract.

2. A court order required John Baldassari to make specified payments for the support of his wife and child. His wife needed more money and applied for Pennsylvania welfare payments. In accordance with the law, she assigned to Pennsylvania her right to the support payments from her husband. Pennsylvania then increased her payments. Pennsylvania obtained a court order directing John, in accordance with the terms of the assignment from his wife, to make the support-order payments directly

to the Pennsylvania Department of Public Welfare. John refused to pay on the ground that he had not been notified of the assignment or the hearing directing him to make payment to the assignee. Was he correct? [*Pennsylvania v. Baldassari*, 421 A.2d 306 (Pa. Super.)]

3. Lee contracts to paint Sally's two-story house for $2,500. Sally realizes that she will not have sufficient money, so she transfers her rights under this agreement to her neighbor Karen, who has a three-story house. Karen notifies Lee that Sally's contract has been assigned to her and demands that Lee paint Karen's house for $2,500. Is Lee required to do so?

4. Assume that Lee agrees to the assignment of the house-painting contract to Karen as stated in question 3. Thereafter, Lee fails to perform the contract to paint Karen's house. Karen sues Sally for damages. Is Sally liable?

5. Jessie borrows $1,000 from Thomas and agrees to repay the money in 30 days. Thomas assigns the right to the $1,000 to Douglas Finance Co. Douglas sues Jessie. Jessie argues that she had agreed to pay the money only to Thomas and that when she and Thomas had entered into the transaction, there was no intention to benefit Douglas Finance Co. Are these objections valid?

6. Washington purchased an automobile from Smithville Motors. The contract called for payment of the purchase price in installments and contained the defense preservation notice required by the Federal Trade Commission regulation. Smithville assigned the contract to Rustic Finance Co. The car was always in need of repairs, and by the time it was half paid for, it would no longer run. Washington canceled the contract. Meanwhile, Smithville had gone out of business. Washington sued Rustic for the amount she had paid Smithville. Rustic refused to pay on the grounds that it had not been at fault. Decide.

7. Helen obtained an insurance policy insuring her life and naming her niece Julie as beneficiary. Helen died, and about a year later the policy was found in her house. When Julie claimed the insurance money, the insurer refused to pay on the ground that the policy required that notice of death be given to it promptly following the death. Julie claimed that she was not bound by the time limitation because she had never agreed to it, as she was not a party to the insurance contract. Is Julie entitled to recover?

8. Lone Star Life Insurance Co. agreed to make a long-term loan to Five Forty Three Land, Inc., whenever that corporation requested one. Five Forty Three wanted this loan to pay off its short-term debts. The loan was never made, as it was never requested by Five Forty Three, which owed the Exchange Bank & Trust Co. on a short-term debt. Exchange Bank then sued Lone Star for breach of its promise on the theory that the Exchange Bank was a third-party beneficiary of the contract to make the loan. Was the Exchange Bank correct? [*Exchange Bank & Trust Co. v. Lone Star Life Ins. Co.*, 546 S.W.2d 948 (Tex. App.)]

9. The New Rochelle Humane Society made a contract with the city of New Rochelle to capture and impound all dogs running at large. Spiegler, a minor, was bitten by some dogs while in her schoolyard. She sued the school district of New Rochelle and the Humane Society. With respect to the Humane Society, she claimed that she was a third-party beneficiary of the contract that the Humane Society had made with the city. She claimed that she could therefore sue the Humane Society for its failure to capture the dogs that had bitten her. Was she entitled to recover? [*Spiegler v. School District of the City of New Rochelle*, 242 N.Y.S.2d 430]

10. Zoya operated a store in premises rented from Peerless. The lease required Zoya to maintain liability insurance to protect Zoya and Peerless. Caswell entered the store, fell through a trap door, and was injured. She then sued Zoya and Peerless on the theory that she was a third-party beneficiary of the lease requirement to maintain liability insurance. Was she correct? [*Caswell v. Zoya Intl*, 654 N.E.2d 552 (Ill. App.)]

11. Henry was owed $10,000 by Jones Corp. In consideration of the many odd jobs performed for him over the years by his nephew, Henry assigned the $10,000 claim to his nephew Charles. Henry died, and his widow claimed that the assignment was ineffective so that the claim was part of Henry's estate. She based her assertion on the ground that the past performance rendered by the nephew was not consideration. Was the assignment effective?

12. Ibberson Co., the general contractor hired by AgGrow Oils, LLC, to design and build an oilseed processing plant, contracted with subcontractor Anderson International Corp. to supply critical seed

processing equipment for the project. Anderson's formal proposal to Ibberson identified the AgGrow Oils Project, and the proposal included drawings of the planned AgGrow plant. The project was a failure. Does AgGrow Oils have standing to sue Anderson under the Anderson-Ibberson contract? Explain. [*AgGrow Oils, LLC v. National Union Fire Inc.*, 420 F.2d 751 (8th Cir.)]

CPA Questions

1. On August 1, Neptune Fisheries contracted in writing with West Markets to deliver to West 3,000 pounds of lobster at $4.00 a pound. Delivery of the lobsters was due October 1, with payment due November 1. On August 4, Neptune entered into a contract with Deep Sea Lobster Farms that provided as follows: "Neptune Fisheries assigns all the rights under the contract with West Markets dated August 1 to Deep Sea Lobster Farms." The best interpretation of the August 4 contract would be that it was:

   a. Only an assignment of rights by Neptune.

   b. Only a delegation of duties by Neptune.

   c. An assignment of rights and a delegation of duties by Neptune.

   d. An unenforceable third-party beneficiary contract.

2. Graham contracted with the city of Harris to train and employ high school dropouts residing in Harris. Graham breached the contract. Long, a resident of Harris and a high school dropout, sued Graham for damages. Under the circumstances, Long will:

   a. Win, because Long is a third-party beneficiary entitled to enforce the contract.

   b. Win, because the intent of the contract was to confer a benefit on all high school dropouts residing in Harris.

   c. Lose, because Long is merely an incidental beneficiary of the contract.

   d. Lose, because Harris did not assign its contract rights to Long.

3. Union Bank lent $200,000 to Wagner. Union required Wagner to obtain a life insurance policy naming Union as beneficiary. While the loan was outstanding, Wagner stopped paying the premiums on the policy. Union paid the premiums, adding the amounts paid to Wagner's loan. Wagner died, and the insurance company refused to pay the policy proceeds to Union. Union may:

   a. Recover the policy proceeds because it is a creditor beneficiary.

   b. Not recover the policy proceeds because it is a donee beneficiary.

   c. Not recover the policy proceeds because it is not in privity of contract with the insurance company.

   d. Not recover the policy proceeds because it is only an incidental beneficiary.

13. The Ohio Department of Public Welfare made a contract with an accountant to audit the accounts of health care providers who were receiving funds under the Medicaid program. Windsor House, which operated six nursing homes, claimed that it was a third-party beneficiary of that contract and could sue for its breach. Was it correct? [*Thornton v. Windsor House, Inc.*, 566 N.E.2d 1220 (Ohio)]

Discharge of Contracts

Learning Outcomes ‹‹‹

After studying this chapter, you should be able to

LO.1 List the three types of conditions that affect a party's duty to perform

LO.2 Explain the on-time performance rule

LO.3 Explain the adequacy of performance rules

LO.4 Explain four ways a contract can be discharged by agreement of the parties

LO.5 State the effect on a contract of the death or disability of one of the contracting parties

LO.6 Explain when impossibility or impracticability may discharge a contract

In the preceding chapters, you studied how a contract is formed, what a contract means, and who has rights under a contract. In this chapter, attention is turned to how a contract is ended or discharged. In other words, what puts an end to the rights and duties created by a contract?

18-1 Conditions Relating to Performance

As developed in the body of this chapter, the ordinary method of discharging obligations under a contract is by performance. Certain promises may be less than absolute and instead come into effect only upon the occurrence of a specified event, or an existing obligation may be extinguished when an event happens. These are conditional promises.

18-1a Classifications of Conditions

condition–stipulation or prerequisite in a contract, will, or other instrument.

When the occurrence or nonoccurrence of an event, as expressed in a contract, affects the duty of a party to the contract to perform, the event is called a **condition.** Terms such as *if, provided that, when, after, as soon as, subject to,* and *on the condition that* indicate the creation of a condition.[1] Conditions are classified as *conditions precedent, conditions subsequent,* and *concurrent conditions.*

Condition Precedent

condition precedent–event that if unsatisfied would mean that no rights would arise under a contract.

A **condition precedent** is a condition that must occur before a party to a contract has an obligation to perform under the contract. **For Example,** a condition precedent to a contractor's (MasTec's) obligation to pay a subcontractor (MidAmerica) under a "pay-if-paid" by the owner (PathNet) clause in their subcontract agreement is the receipt of payment by MasTec from PathNet. The condition precedent—payment by the owner—did not occur due to bankruptcy, and, therefore, MasTec did not have an obligation to pay MidAmerica.[2]

CASE SUMMARY

A Blitz on Offense?

FACTS: Richard Blitz owns a piece of commercial property at 4 Old Middle Street. On February 2, 1998, Arthur Subklew entered into a lease with Blitz to rent the rear portion of the property. Subklew intended to operate an auto sales and repair business. Paragraph C of the lease was a zoning contingency clause that stated, "Landlord [plaintiff] will use Landlord's best efforts to obtain a written verification that Tenant can operate [an] Auto Sales and Repair Business at the demised premises. If Landlord is unable to obtain such commitment from the municipality, then this agreement shall be deemed null and void and Landlord shall immediately return deposit monies to Tenant." The zoning board approved the location only as a general repair business. When Subklew refused to occupy the premises, Blitz sued him for breach of contract.

[1] *Harmon Cable Communications v. Scope Cable Television, Inc.,* 468 N.W.2d 350 (Neb. 1990).
[2] *MidAmerica Construction Management, Inc. v. MasTec North America, Inc.,* 436 F.3d 1257 (10th Cir. 2006). But see *International Engineering Services, Inc. v. Scherer Construction Co.,* 74 So. 3d 53 (Fla. App. 2011), where a "pay-when-paid" provision was found to be ambiguous, resulting in the general contractor being liable for the payment to the subcontractor.

A Blitz on Offense? continued

DECISION: Judgment for Subklew. A condition precedent is a fact or event that the parties intend must exist before there is right to a performance. If the condition is not fulfilled, the right to enforce the contract does not come into existence.

Blitz's obligation to obtain written approval of a used car business was a condition precedent to the leasing agreement. Since it was not obtained, Blitz cannot enforce the leasing agreement. [**Blitz v. Subklew, 810 A.2d 841 (Conn. App. 2002)**]

Condition Subsequent

condition subsequent— event whose occurrence or lack thereof terminates a contract.

The parties to a contract may agree that a party is obligated to perform a certain act or pay a certain sum of money, but the contract contains a provision that relieves the obligation on the occurrence of a certain event. That is, on the happening of a **condition subsequent,** such an event extinguishes the duty to thereafter perform. **For Example,** Chad Newly served as the weekend anchor on *Channel 5 News* for several years. The station manager, Tom O'Brien, on reviewing tapes in connection with Newly's contract renewal, believed that Newly's speech on occasion was slightly slurred, and he suspected that it was from alcohol use. In the parties' contract discussions, O'Brien expressed his concerns about an alcohol problem and offered help. Newly denied there was a problem. O'Brien agreed to a new two-year contract with Newly at $190,000 for the first year and $220,000 for the second year with other benefits subject to "the condition" that the station reserved the right to make four unannounced drug-alcohol tests during the contract term; and should Newly test positive for drugs or alcohol under measurements set forth in the contract, then all of Channel 5's obligations to Newly under the contract would cease. When Newly subsequently failed a urinalysis test three months into the new contract, the happening of this event extinguished the station's obligation to employ and pay him under the contract. Conditions subsequent are strictly construed, and where ambiguous, are construed against forfeiture.[3]

SPORTS & ENTERTAINMENT LAW

Endorsement Contracts

Sports marketing involves the use of famous athletes to promote the sale of products and services in our economy. Should an athlete's image be tarnished by allegations of immoral or illegal conduct, a company could be subject to financial losses and corporate embarrassment. Endorsement contracts may extend for multiyear periods, and should a "morals" issue arise, a company would be well served to have had a broad morals clause in its contract that would allow the company at its sole discretion to summarily terminate the endorsement contract. Representatives of athletes, on the other hand, seek narrow contractual language that allows for termination of endorsement contracts only upon the indictment for a crime, and they seek the right to have an arbitrator, as opposed to the employer, make the determination as to whether the morals clause was violated. John Daly's endorsement contract with Callaway Golf was terminated by the company when he violated his good conduct clause that restricted gambling and drinking activities; and NFL running back Adrian Peterson's endorsement contracts were canceled after he injured his four-year-old son by spanking him with a wooden switch. Nike, RadioShack, and other sponsors ended their relationships (with an estimated value of $10 million a year) with cyclist Lance Armstrong after he admitted taking performance enhancing drugs.

Can the courts be utilized to resolve controversies over whether a "morals clause" has been violated? If so, is the occurrence of a morals clause violation a condition precedent or a condition subsequent?

---

[3] *Cardone Trust v. Cardone*, 8 A.3d 1 (N.H. 2010).

Concurrent Condition

In most bilateral contracts, the performances of the parties are *concurrent conditions.* That is, their mutual duties of performance under the contract are to take place simultaneously. **For Example,** concerning a contract for the sale and delivery of certain goods, the buyer must tender to the seller a certified check at the time of delivery as set forth in the contract, and the seller must tender the goods to the buyer at the same time.

18-2 Discharge by Performance

When it is claimed that a contract is discharged by performance, questions arise as to the nature, time, and sufficiency of the performance.

18-2a Normal Discharge of Contracts

A contract is usually discharged by the performance of the terms of the agreement. In most cases, the parties perform their promises and the contract ceases to exist or is thereby discharged. A contract is also discharged by the expiration of the time period specified in the contract.[4]

18-2b Nature of Performance

Performance may be the doing of an act or the making of payment.

Tender

tender–goods have arrived, are available for pickup, and the buyer is notified.

An offer to perform is known as a **tender.** If performance of the contract requires the doing of an act, the refusal of a tender discharges the party offering to perform and is a basis for that party to bring a lawsuit.

A valid tender of payment consists of an unconditional offer of the exact amount due on the date when due. A tender of payment is not just an expression of willingness to pay; it must be an actual offer to perform by making payment of the amount owed.

Payment

When the contract requires payment, performance consists of the payment of money.

Application of Payments. If a debtor owes more than one debt to the creditor and pays money, a question may arise as to which debt has been paid. If the debtor specifies the debt to which the payment is to be applied and the creditor accepts the money, the creditor is bound to apply the money as specified.[5] Thus, if the debtor specifies that a payment is to be made for a current purchase, the creditor may not apply the payment to an older balance.

Payment by Check. Payment by commercial paper, such as a check, is ordinarily a conditional payment. A check merely suspends the debt until the check is presented for payment. If payment is then made, the debt is discharged; if not paid, the suspension terminates, and suit may be brought on either the debt or the check. Frequently, payment must be made by a specified date. It is generally held that the payment is made on time if it is mailed on or before the final date for payment.

---

[4] *Washington National Ins. Co. v. Sherwood Associates,* 795 P.2d 665 (Utah App. 1990).
[5] *Oakes Logging, Inc. v. Green Crow, Inc.,* 832 P.2d 894 (Wash. App. 1992).

Foreseeable Risk

CASE SUMMARY

The Mailed-Check Payment

FACTS: Thomas Cooper was purchasing land from Peter and Ella Birznieks. Cooper was already in possession of the land but was required to pay the amount owed by January 30; otherwise, he would have to vacate the property. The attorney handling the transaction for the Birznieks told Cooper that he could mail the payment to him. On January 30, Cooper mailed to the attorney a personal check drawn on an out-of-state bank for the amount due. The check arrived at the Birznieks' attorney's office on February 1. The Birznieks refused to accept the check on the grounds that it was not a timely payment and moved to evict Cooper from the property.

DECISION: Because of the general custom to regard a check mailed to a creditor as paying the bill that is owed, payment was made by Cooper on January 30 when he mailed the check. Payment was therefore made within the required time even though received after the expiration of the required time. [*Birznieks v. Cooper*, 275 N.W.2d 221 (Mich. 1979)]

18-2c Time of Performance

When the date or period of time for performance is specified in the contract, performance should be made on that date or within that time period.

No Time Specified

When the time for performance is not specified in the contract, an obligation to perform within a reasonable time is implied.[6] The fact that no time is specified neither impairs the contract on the ground that it is indefinite nor allows an endless time in which to perform. What constitutes a reasonable time is determined by the nature of the subject matter of the contract and the facts and circumstances surrounding the making of the contract.

When Time Is Essential

If performance of the contract on or within the exact time specified is vital, it is said that "time is of the essence." Time is of the essence when the contract relates to property that is perishable or that is fluctuating rapidly in value. When a contract fixes by unambiguous language a time for performance and where there is no evidence showing that the parties did not intend that time should be of the essence, failure to perform within the specified time is a breach of contract entitling the innocent party to damages. **For Example,** Dixon and Gandhi agreed that Gandhi would close on the purchase of a motel as follows: "Closing Date. The closing shall be held … on the date which is within twenty (20) days after the closing of Nomura Financing." Gandhi did not close within the time period specified, and Dixon was allowed to retain $100,000 in prepaid closing costs and fees as liquidated damages for Gandhi's breach of contract.[7]

When Time Is Not Essential

Unless a contract so provides, time is ordinarily not of the essence, and performance within a reasonable time is sufficient. In the case of the sale of property, time is not

---

[6] *First National Bank v. Clark,* 447 S.E.2d 558 (W. Va. 1994).
[7] *Woodhull Corp. v. Saibaba Corp.,* 507 S.E.2d 493 (Ga. App. 1998).

regarded as of the essence when there has not been any appreciable change in the market value or condition of the property and when the person who delayed does not appear to have done so for the purpose of speculating on a change in market price.

Waiver of Essence of Time Limitation

A provision that time is of the essence may be waived. It is waived when the specified time has expired but the party who could complain requests the delaying party to take steps necessary to perform the contract.

18-2d Adequacy of Performance

When a party renders exactly the performance called for by the contract, no question arises as to whether the contract has been performed. In other cases, there may not have been a perfect performance, or a question arises as to whether the performance satisfies the standard set by the contract.

CPA

Substantial Performance

substantial performance—equitable rule that if a good-faith attempt to perform does not precisely meet the terms of the agreement, the agreement will still be considered complete if the essential purpose of the contract is accomplished.

Perfect performance of a contract is not always possible when dealing with construction projects. A party who in good faith has provided **substantial performance** of the contract may sue to recover the payment specified in the contract.[8] However, because the performance was not perfect, the performing party is subject to a counterclaim for the damages caused the other party. When a building contractor has substantially performed the contract to construct a building, the contractor is responsible for the cost of repairing or correcting the defects as an offset from the contract price.[9]

The measure of damages under these circumstances is known as "cost of completion" damages.[10] If, however, the cost of completion would be unreasonably disproportionate to the importance of the defect, the measure of damages is the diminution in value of the building due to the defective performance.

Whether there is substantial performance is a question of degree to be determined by all of the facts, including the particular type of structure involved, its intended purpose, and the nature and relative expense of repairs.

For Example, a certain building contractor (BC) and a certain owner (O) made a contract to construct a home overlooking Vineyard Sound on Martha's Vineyard according to plans and specifications that clearly called for the use of General Plumbing Blue Star piping. The contract price was $1,100,000. Upon inspecting the work before making the final $400,000 payment and accepting the building, O discovered that BC had used Republic piping throughout the house. O explained to BC that his family had made its money by investing in General Plumbing, and he, therefore, would not make the final payment until the breach of contract was remedied. BC explained that Republic pipes were of the same industrial grade and quality as the Blue Star pipes. Moreover, BC estimated that it would cost nearly $300,000 to replace all of the pipes because of the destruction of walls and fixtures necessary to accomplish such a task. BC may sue O for $400,000 for breach of contract, claiming he had substantially performed the contract, and O may counterclaim for $300,000, seeking an offset for the cost of remedying the breach. The court will find in favor of the contractor and will not allow the $300,000 offset but will allow a "nominal" offset of perhaps $100 to $1,000 for the amount by

[8] *Gala v. Harris,* 77 So. 3d 1065 (La. App. 2012).

[9] Substantial performance is not a defense to a breach of contract claim, however. See *Bentley Systems Inc. v. Intergraph Corp.,* 922 So. 2d 61 (Ala. 2005).

[10] *Hammer Construction Corp. v. Phillips,* 994 So. 2d 1135 (Fla. App. 2008).

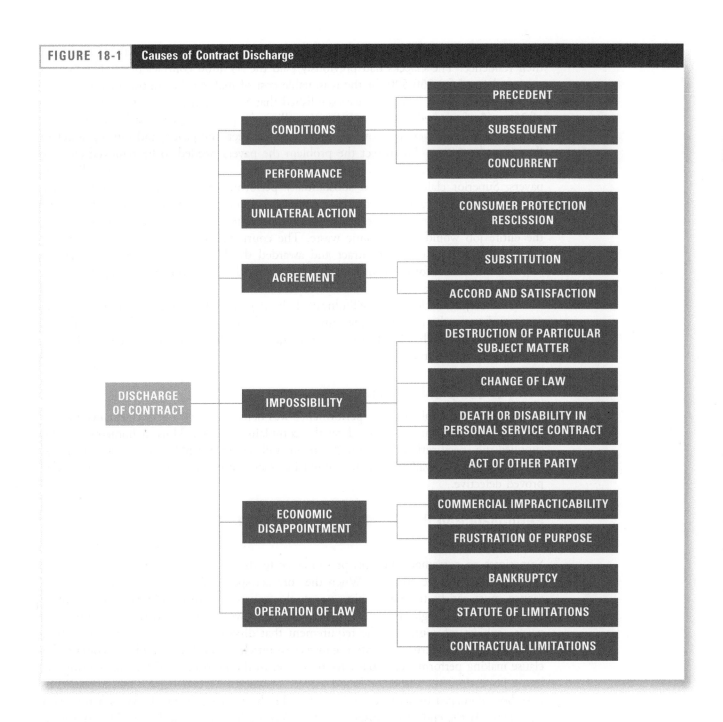

FIGURE 18-1 | Causes of Contract Discharge

which the Republic pipes diminished the value of the building. To have required the pipes to be replaced would amount to economic waste.[11]

When a contractor does not substantially perform its obligations under a contract, not only will the contractor not prevail in a breach of contract claim against a homeowner for extra work beyond the contract price but the contractor is liable for the reasonable cost of making the contractor's work conform to the contract. **For Example,** Superior Wall and Paver, LLC, sued homeowners Pamela and Mark Gacek for $14,350 it claimed

---

[11] See *Jacob & Youngs, Inc. v. Kent,* 230 N.Y. 239 (1921).

was still owed Superior as extra work, for concrete pavers it installed in the driveway of their residence. The Gaceks had previously paid the $45,000 contract price. The Gaceks counterclaimed for $60,500 for the reasonable cost of making the contractor's work conform to the contract. The evidence established that Superior did not install a proper base of 3″ to 4″ of crushed limestone before installing the pavers as required by the contract, which caused the pavers to move, creating gaps between the pavers and causing water to flow into the garage. To correct the problem the pavers needed to be removed and the area excavated and replaced with a crushed limestone base before again installing the pavers. Superior claimed it had substantially performed the contract as a fully usable driveway, and the proper remedy, if any, was the diminution of the market value of the Gaceks' property due to any defective performance. Superior asserted the cost of redoing the entire job would be economic waste. The court determined that Superior had not substantially performed the contract and awarded the homeowners the cost of making Superior's work conform to the contract by having the job redone, rejecting Superior's assertion of economic waste.[12]

In most jurisdictions, the willfulness of the departure from the specifications of the contract does not by itself preclude some recovery for the contractor on the "cost of completion" basis but rather is a factor in consideration of whether there was substantial performance by the contractor.[13]

Fault of Complaining Party

A party cannot complain that a performance was defective when the performance follows the terms of the contract required by the complaining party. Thus, a homeowner who supplied the specifications for poured cement walls could not hold a contractor liable for damages when the walls that were poured in exact compliance with those specifications proved defective.

Performance to the Satisfaction of the Contracting Party or a Third Party

Sometimes an agreement requires performance to the satisfaction, taste, or judgment of the other party to the contract. When the contract specifically stipulates that the performance must satisfy the contracting party, the courts will ordinarily enforce the plain meaning of the language of the parties and the work must satisfy the contracting party—subject, of course, to the requirement that dissatisfaction be made in good faith. **For Example,** the Perrones' written contract to purchase the Hills' residence contained a clause making performance subject to inspection to the Perrones' satisfaction. During the house inspection, the inspector found a piece of wood in a crawl space that appeared to have been damaged by termites and had possibly been treated some 18 years before with chlordane. At the end of the inspection Mr. Perrone indicated that he would perform on the contract. Thereafter, he went on the Internet and found that chlordane is a highly toxic pesticide now banned from use as a termite treatment. As a result, the Perrones rescinded the contract under the buyer satisfaction clause. The Hills sued, believing that speculation about a pesticide treatment 18 years ago was absurd. They contended that the Perrones had breached the contract without a valid reason. The court decided for the

---

[12] *Superior Wall and Paver, LLC v. Gacek,* 73 So. 3d (Ala. App. 2011).
[13] But see *USX Corp. v. M. DeMatteo Construction Co.,* 315 F.3d 43 (1st Cir. 2002), for application of a common law rule that prohibits a construction contractor guilty of a willful breach of contract from maintaining any suit on the contract against the other party.

Perrones, since they exercised the "satisfaction clause" in good faith.[14] Good-faith personal satisfaction is generally required when the subject matter of the contract is personal, such as interior design work, tailoring, or the painting of a portrait.

With respect to things mechanical or routine performances, courts require that the performance be such as would satisfy a reasonable person under the circumstances.

When work is to be done subject to the approval of an architect, an engineer, or another expert, most courts apply the reasonable person test of satisfaction.

18-3 Discharge by Action of Parties

Contracts may be discharged by the joint action of both contracting parties or, in some cases, by the action of one party alone.

18-3a Discharge by Unilateral Action

rescission–action of one party to a contract to set the contract aside when the other party is guilty of a breach of the contract.

Ordinarily, a contract cannot be discharged by the action of either party alone. In some cases, however, the contract gives one of either party the right to cancel the contract by unilateral action, such as by notice to the other party. Insurance policies covering loss commonly provide that the insurer may cancel the policy upon giving a specified number of days' notice.

Consumer Protection Rescission

substitution–substitution of a new contract between the same parties.

accord and satisfaction–agreement to substitute for an existing debt some alternative form of discharging that debt, coupled with the actual discharge of the debt by the substituted performance.

A basic principle of contract law is that once made, a contract between competent persons is a binding obligation. Consumer protection legislation introduces into the law a contrary concept—that of giving the consumer a chance to think things over and to rescind the contract. Thus, the federal Consumer Credit Protection Act (CCPA) gives the debtor the right to rescind a credit transaction within three business days when the transaction would impose a lien on the debtor's home. **For Example,** a homeowner who mortgages his or her home to obtain a loan may cancel the transaction for any reason by notifying the lender before midnight of the third full business day after the loan is made.[15]

A Federal Trade Commission regulation gives the buyer three business days in which to cancel a home-solicited sale of goods or services costing more than $25.[16]

release–an instrument by which the signing party (releasor) relinquishes claims or potential claims against one or more persons (releasees) who might otherwise be subject to liability to the releasor.

18-3b Discharge by Agreement

A contract may be discharged by the operation of one of its provisions or by a subsequent agreement. Thus, there may be a discharge by (1) the terms of the original contract, such as a provision that the contract should end on a specified date; (2) a mutual cancellation, in which the parties agree to end their contract; (3) a mutual **rescission,** in which the parties agree to annul the contract and return both parties to their original positions before the contract had been made; (4) the **substitution** of a new contract between the same parties; (5) a novation or substitution of a new contract involving a new party;[17] (6) an **accord and satisfaction;** (7) a **release;** or (8) a **waiver.**

waiver–release or relinquishment of a known right or objection.

---

[14] *Hill v. Perrones,* 42 P.3d 210 (Kan. App. 2002).

[15] If the owner is not informed of this right to cancel, the three-day period does not begin until that information is given. Consumer Credit Protection Act §125, 15 U.S.C. §1635(a), (e), (f).

[16] C.F.R. §429.1.

[17] *Eagle Industries, Inc. v. Thompson,* 900 P.2d 475 (Or. 1995). In a few jurisdictions, the term *novation* is used to embrace the substitution of any new contract, whether between the original parties or not.

Substitution

The parties may decide that their contract is not the one they want. They may then replace it with another contract. If they do, the original contract is discharged by substitution.[18]

Accord and Satisfaction

When the parties have differing views as to the performance required by the terms of a contract, they may agree to a different performance. Such an agreement is called an *accord.* When the accord is performed or executed, there is an accord and satisfaction, which discharges the original obligation. To constitute an accord and satisfaction, there must be a bona fide dispute, a proposal to settle the dispute, and performance of the agreement.

CASE SUMMARY

A Full Court Press to No Avail

FACTS: In September 2002, La Crosse Litho Supply, LLC (La Crosse), entered into a distribution agreement with MKL Pre-Press Electronics (MKL) for the distribution of a printing system. La Crosse purchased a 7000 System unit from MKL for its end user Printing Plus. MKL technicians were to provide service and training for the unit. The 7000 System at Printing Plus failed on three occasions, and ultimately repairs were unsuccessful. On September 30, 2003, La Crosse canceled the distribution agreement. On October 2, 2003, La Crosse sent a letter to MKL's sales vice president Bill Landwer setting forth an itemized accounting of what it owed MKL Pre-Press with deductions for the purchase price of the failed 7000 System and other offsets. MKL sent a subsequent bill for repairs and services, to which La Crosse objected and stated that it would not pay. MKL's attorney sent a demand letter for $26,453.31. La Crosse's president, Randall Peters, responded by letter dated December 30, 2003, explaining that with an offset for training and warranty work it had performed, "we are sending you the final payment in the amount of $1,696.47." He added, "[w]ith this correspondence, we consider all open issues between La Crosse Litho Supply and MKL Pre-Press closed." Enclosed

with the letter was a check for $1,696.47 payable to MKL Pre-Press. In the remittance portion of the check, under the heading "Ref," was typed "FINAL PAYM." The check was endorsed and deposited on either January 26 or 27, 2004. MKL sued La Crosse for $24,756.84. La Crosse defended that the tender and subsequent deposit of the check for $1,696.47 constituted an accord and satisfaction. Jill Fleming, MKL's office manager, stated that it was her duty to process checks and that she did not read Peters' letter. From a judgment for La Crosse, MKL appealed.

DECISION: Judgment for La Crosse. There was an honest dispute as to the amount owed, as evident from the exchange of letters. La Crosse tendered an amount with the explicit understanding that it was the "final payment" of all demands, and the creditor MKL's acceptance and negotiation of a check for that amount constitutes an accord and satisfaction. Ms. Fleming had the authority to endorse checks and deposit them, and her doing so can and should be imputed to her employer, thereby constituting an accord and satisfaction. [*MKL Pre-Press Electronics v. La Crosse Litho Supply, LLC,* **840 N.E.2d 687 (Ill. App. 2005)**]

Release

A release is an instrument by which the signing party (releasor) relinquishes claims or potential claims against one or more persons (releasees) who might otherwise be subject to liability to the releasor. The existence of a valid release is a complete defense to a tort action against the releasee. **For Example,** Heriberto Rodriguez, while driving a Hertz rental car, was injured in a collision with a vehicle operated by Takeshi Oto, who was

---

[18] See *Foti Fuels, Inc. v. Kurrle Corp.,* 90 A.3d 885 (Vt. 2013).

on company related business for his employer Toshiba of America. Heriberto settled with Hertz for $25,000.00, the limit of the Hertz coverage of the vehicle and signed a written release in favor of Hertz and Oto "and all other persons, firms, corporations, associations or partnerships." Later, Rodriquez filed a negligence action against Oto and Toshiba of America. The settlement releasing "all persons ... and corporations" applied to Oto and Toshiba and was a complete defense in this case.[19]

18-4   Discharge by External Causes

Circumstances beyond the control of the contracting parties may discharge the contract.

18-4a   Discharge by Impossibility

To establish impossibility a party must show (1) the unexpected occurrence of an intervening act; (2) that the risk of the unexpected occurrence was not allocated by agreement or custom; and (3) that the occurrence made performance impossible. The doctrine of impossibility relieves nonperformance only in extreme circumstances.[20] The party asserting the defense of impossibility bears the burden of proving "a real impossibility and not a mere inconvenience or unexpected difficulty."[21] Moreover, courts will generally only excuse nonperformance where performance is objectively impossible—that is, incapable performance by anyone. Financial inability to perform a contract that a party voluntarily entered into will rarely, if ever, excuse nonperformance. **For Example,** Ms. Robinson was employed by East Capital Community Development Group under a written employment contract for one year but was terminated early for lack of funding. The contract did not reference that her continued employment was contingent on continued grant funding. The contract was objectively capable of performance. The defense of impossibility was rejected by the court.[22]

Destruction of Particular Subject Matter

When parties contract expressly for, or with reference to, a particular subject matter, the contract is discharged if the subject matter is destroyed through no fault of either party. When a contract calls for the sale of a wheat crop growing on a specific parcel of land, the contract is discharged if that crop is destroyed by blight.

On the other hand, if there is merely a contract to sell a given quantity of a specified grade of wheat, the seller is not discharged when the seller's crop is destroyed by blight. The seller had made an unqualified undertaking to deliver wheat of a specified grade. No restrictions or qualifications were imposed as to the source. If the seller does not deliver the goods called for by the contract, the contract is broken, and the seller is liable for damages.

Change of Law

A contract is discharged when its performance is made impossible, impractical, or illegal by a subsequent change in the law. A contract to construct a nonfireproof building at a particular place is discharged by the adoption of a zoning law prohibiting such a building within that area. Mere inconvenience or temporary delay caused by the new law, however, does not excuse performance.

[19] *Rodriquez v. Oto*, 151 Cal. Rptr. 3d 667 (Cal. App. 2013).
[20] *Island Development Corp. v. District of Columbia*, 933 A.2d 340, 350 (D.C. 2007).
[21] *Bergmann v. Parker*, 216 A.2d 581 (D.C. 1966).
[22] *East Capital View Community Development Corp. v. Robinson*, 941 A.2d 1036 (D.C. 2008).

CASE SUMMARY

If you're fond of sand dunes, and salty air...
... served by a window with an ocean view
You're not at the Petrozzi's house in Ocean City

FACTS: To rectify seashore protection problems, the City of Ocean City in 1989 participated in a beach replenishment and sand dunes restoration program. The Army Corps of Engineers required Ocean City to have access rights where sand was to be placed. To ease property owners' concerns over their beach front views, Ocean City proposed easements under which it would construct and maintain the dune system with height limitations of no greater than three feet above the average elevation of block bulkheads. From May 1992 to December 1995 Ocean City acquired the necessary easements. Between 1992 and 2000 natural accretion caused the dunes to grow in height and width. After 1994 the Coastal Area Facilities Review Act (CAFRA) required municipalities to receive written authorization from the Department of Environmental Protection (DEP) for dunes maintenance. Ocean City's permit applications to reduce the height of existing sand dunes was denied by the DEP. Owners of the beach front properties sued for breach of its easement agreements. From the dismissal of their claims by the trial court, certain owners appealed.

DECISION: Decision for the property owners. The 1994 CAFRA amendments rendered impossible Ocean City's performance under the easement agreements in question. Impossibility or impracticability of performance are compete defenses where a fact essential to performance is assumed by the parties but does not exist at the time of performance. Yet the fact remains that the plaintiffs gave up their rights to compensation in reliance on Ocean City's promise to protect their ocean views. The owners are entitled to damages for the loss of their ocean views. [*Petrozzi v. City of Ocean City*, 433 N.J. Super. 290 (App. Div. 2013)]

Death or Disability

When the contract obligates a party to render or receive personal services requiring peculiar skill, the death, incapacity, or illness of the party that was either to render or receive the personal services excuses both sides from a duty to perform. It is sometimes said that "the death of either party is the death of the contract."

The rule does not apply, however, when the acts called for by the contract are of such a character that (1) the acts may be as well performed by others, such as the promisor's personal representatives, or (2) the contract's terms contemplate continuance of the obligations after the death of one of the parties. **For Example,** Lynn Jones was under contract to investor Ed Jenkins to operate certain Subway sandwich shops and to acquire new franchises with funding provided by Jenkins. After Jenkins's death, Jones claimed that he was no longer bound under the contract and was free to pursue franchise opportunities on his own. The contract between Jones and Jenkins expressed that it was binding on the parties' "heirs and assigns" and that the contract embodied property rights that passed to Jenkins's widow. The agreement's provisions thus established that the agreement survived the death of Jenkins, and Jones was therefore obligated to remit profits from the franchise he acquired for himself after Jenkins's death.[23]

Act of Other Party

Every contract contains "an implied covenant of good faith and fair dealing." As a result of this covenant, a promisee is under an obligation to do nothing that would interfere with the promisor's performance. When the promisee prevents performance or otherwise makes performance impossible, the promisor is discharged from the contract. Thus, a

---

[23] *Jenkins Subway, Inc. v. Jones,* 990 S.W.2d 713 (Tenn. App. 1998).

subcontractor is discharged from any obligation when it is unable to do the work because the principal contractor refuses to deliver the material, equipment, or money required by the subcontract. When the default of the other party consists of failing to supply goods or services, the duty may rest on the party claiming a discharge of the contract to show that substitute goods or services could not be obtained elsewhere.

18-4b Developing Doctrines

Commercial impracticability and frustration of purpose may excuse performance.

Commercial Impracticability

The doctrine of *commercial impracticability* was developed to deal with the harsh rule that a party must perform its contracts unless it is absolutely impossible. However, not every type of impracticability is an excuse for nonperformance. **For Example,** I. Patel was bound by his franchise agreement with Days Inn, Inc., to maintain his 60-room inn on old Route 66 in Lincoln, Illinois, to at least minimum quality assurance standards. His inn failed five consecutive quality inspections over two years, with the inspector noting damaged guest rooms, burns in the bedding, and severely stained carpets. Patel's defense when his franchise was canceled after the fifth failed inspection was that bridge repairs on the road leading from I-55 to his inn had adversely affected his business and made it commercially impractical to live up to the franchise agreement. The court rejected his defense, determining that while the bridge work might have affected patronage, it had no effect on his duty to comply with the quality assurance standards of his franchise agreement.[24] Commercial impracticability is available only when the performance is made impractical by the subsequent occurrence of an event whose nonoccurrence was a basic assumption on which the contract was made.[25]

The defense of commercial impracticability will not relieve sophisticated business entities from their contractual obligations due to an economic downturn, even one as drastic and severe as the recent recession. **For Example,** real estate developer Beemer Associates was not excused under this doctrine of commercial impracticability from performance of its construction loan payment obligation of $5,250,000 plus interest and fees where unanticipated changes in the financial and real estate markets made it unable to secure tenants at the expected rate.[26] Economic downturns and other market shifts do not constitute unanticipated circumstances in a market economy.[27]

Frustration of Purpose Doctrine

Because of a change in circumstances, the purpose of the contract may have no value to the party entitled to receive performance. In such a case, performance may be excused if both parties were aware of the purpose and the event that frustrated the purpose was unforeseeable.[28]

For Example, National Southern Bank rents a home near Willowbend Country Club on the southeastern shore of North Carolina for $75,000 a week to entertain business guests at the Ryder Cup matches scheduled for the week in question. Storm damage

---

[24] *Days Inn of America, Inc. v. Patel,* 88 F. Supp. 2d 928 (C.D. Ill. 2000).

[25] See Restatement (Second) of Contracts §261; U.C.C. §2-615.

[26] *LSREF2 Baron, LLC v. Beemer,* 2011 WL 6838163 (M.D. Fla. Dec. 29, 2011).

[27] *Flathead-Michigan I, LLC v. Peninsula Dev., LLC,* 2011 WL 940048 (E.D. Mich. March 16, 2011).

[28] The defense of frustration of purpose, or commercial frustration, is very difficult to invoke because the courts are extremely reluctant to allow parties to avoid obligations to which they have agreed. See *Wal-Mart Stores, Inc. v. AIG Life Insurance Co.,* 872 A.2d 611 (Del. Ch. 2005), denying application of the commercial frustration doctrine when the supervening event, the invalidation of hundreds of millions in tax deductions by the IRS, was reasonably foreseeable and could have been provided for in the contract.

from Hurricane David the week before the event caused the closing of the course and the transfer of the tournament to another venue in a different state. The bank's duty to pay for the house may be excused by the doctrine of *frustration of purpose*, because the transfer of the tournament fully destroyed the value of the home rental, both parties were aware of the purpose of the rental, and the cancellation of the golf tournament was unforeseeable.

Comparison to Common Law Rule

The traditional common law rule refuses to recognize commercial impracticability or frustration of purpose. By the common law rule, the losses and disappointments against which commercial impracticability and frustration of purpose give protection are merely the risks that one takes in entering into a contract. Moreover, the situations could have been guarded against by including an appropriate condition subsequent in the contract. A condition subsequent declares that the contract will be void if a specified event occurs.[29] The contract also could have provided for a readjustment of compensation if there was a basic change of circumstances. The common law approach also rejects these developing concepts because they weaken the stability of a contract.

An indication of a wider recognition of the concept that "extreme" changes of circumstances can discharge a contract is found in the Uniform Commercial Code (UCC). The UCC provides for the discharge of a contract for the sale of goods when a condition that the parties assumed existed, or would continue, ceases to exist.[30]

Force Majeure

To avoid litigation over impossibility and impracticability issues, modern contracting parties often contract around the doctrine of impossibility, specifying the failures that will excuse performance in their contracts. The clauses in which they do this are called *force majeure*—uncontrollable event—clauses. And they are enforced by courts as written.

18-4c Temporary Impossibility

Ordinarily, a temporary impossibility suspends the duty to perform. If the obligation to perform is suspended, it is revived on the termination of the impossibility. If, however, performance at that later date would impose a substantially greater burden on the party obligated to perform, some courts discharge the obligor from the contract.

After the September 11, 2001, terrorist attack on the World Trade Center, New York City courts followed wartime precedents that had developed the law of temporary impossibility. Such impossibility, when of brief duration, excuses performance until it subsequently becomes possible to perform rather than excusing performance altogether. Thus, an individual who was unable to communicate her cancellation of travel 60 days prior to her scheduled travel as required by her contract, which needed to occur on or before September 14, 2001, could expect relief from a cancellation penalty provision in the contract based on credible testimony of attempted phone calls to the travel agent on and after September 12, 2001, even though the calls did not get through due to communication problems in New York City.[31]

Weather

Acts of God, such as tornadoes, lightning, and floods, usually do not terminate a contract even though they make performance difficult. Thus, weather conditions constitute a risk

---

[29] *Wermer v. ABI*, 10 S.W.3d 575 (Mo. App. 2000).
[30] U.C.C. §2-615.
[31] See *Bugh v. Protravel International, Inc.*, 746 N.Y.S.2d 290 (Civ. Ct. N.Y.C. 2002).

Foreseeable Risk

that is assumed by a contracting party in the absence of a contrary agreement. Consequently, extra expense sustained by a contractor because of weather conditions is a risk that the contractor assumes in the absence of an express provision for additional compensation in such a case. **For Example,** Danielo Contractors made a contract to construct a shopping mall for the Rubicon Center, with construction to begin November 1. Because of abnormal cold and blizzard conditions, Danielo was not able to begin work until April 1 and was five months late in completing the construction of the project. Rubicon sued Danielo for breach of contract by failing to perform on schedule. Danielo is liable. Because the contract included no provision covering delay caused by weather, Danielo bore the risk of the delay and resulting loss.

Modern contracts commonly contain a "weather clause" and reflect the parties' agreement on this matter. When the parties take the time to discuss weather issues, purchasing insurance coverage is a common resolution.

18-4d Discharge by Operation of Law

A contract is discharged by **operation of law** by (1) an alteration or a material change made by a party, (2) the destruction of the written contract with intent to discharge it, (3) bankruptcy, (4) the operation of a statute of limitations, or (5) a contractual limitation.

Bankruptcy

As set forth in the chapter on bankruptcy, even though all creditors have not been paid in full, a discharge in **bankruptcy** eliminates ordinary contract claims against the debtor.

Statute of Limitations

A **statute of limitations** provides that after a certain number of years have passed, a contract claim is barred. The time limitation provided by state statutes of limitations varies widely. The time period for bringing actions for breach of an oral contract is two to three years. The period may differ with the type of contract—ranging from a relatively short time for open accounts (ordinary customers' charge accounts) to four years for sales of goods.[32] A somewhat longer period exists for bringing actions for breach of written contracts (usually 4 to 10 years). **For Example,** Prate Installations, Inc., sued homeowners Richard and Rebecca Thomas for failure to pay for a new roof installed by Prate. Prate had sent numerous invoices to the Thomases over a four-year period seeking payment to no avail. The Thomases moved to dismiss the case under a four-year limitation period. However, the court concluded that the state's 10-year limitations period on written contracts applied.[33] The maximum period for judgments of record is usually 10 to 20 years.

A breach of contract claim against a builder begins to run when a home's construction is substantially complete. **For Example,** a breach of contract claim against home builder Stewart Brockett was time barred under a state's six-year statute of limitations for breach of contract actions inasmuch as the home in question was substantially completed in September 2001 and the breach of contract action commenced on June 17, 2008.[34] A breach of contract claim not founded upon an instrument of writing may be governed by a two-year statute of limitations.

---

operation of law— attaching of certain consequences to certain facts because of legal principles that operate automatically as contrasted with consequences that arise because of the voluntary action of a party designed to create those consequences.

bankruptcy—procedure by which one unable to pay debts may surrender all assets in excess of any exemption claim to the court for administration and distribution to creditors, and the debtor is given a discharge that releases him from the unpaid balance due on most debts.

C P A

statute of limitations— statute that restricts the period of time within which an action may be brought.

---

[32] U.C.C. §2-725(1).
[33] *Prate Installations, Inc. v. Thomas,* 842 N.E.2d 1205 (Ill. App. 2006).
[34] *New York Central Mutual Fire Insurance Co. v. Gilder Oil Co.,* 936 N.Y.S.2d 815 (Sup. Ct. A.D. 2011).

CASE SUMMARY

Tempus Fugit: File It on Time or Loose It!

FACTS: Larry Montz and Daena Smoller, the real parties in interest (RPIs) in this case pitched a concept for a television program entitled *Ghost Expeditions Haunted* (Concepts) to NBCUniversal Media, LLC (NBC) from 1996 to 2001. The RPIs claim that, after NBC informed them they were not interested in Concepts, NBC teamed up with another company to misappropriate and exploit their concepts by producing the hit series *Ghost Hunters* without permission or compensation. The *Ghost Hunters* show premiered on the Syfy cable channel on October 6, 2004. The RPIs filed their first lawsuit on November 8, 2006. The Superior Court denied NBC's motion for summary judgment, which asserted the claims were time-barred by the applicable two-year statute of limitations, and NBC appealed this decision.

DECISION: Judgment for NBC. The statute of limitations for implied contracts in California is two years from the time the last element of a cause of action is complete. In this case a suit for breach of an implied contract not to exploit an idea without paying for it arises with the sale or exploitation of the idea. Here, the accrual date is the date on which the work is released to the general public on television on October 6, 2004. Thus RPIs had until October 5, 2006, to file their lawsuit. They did not do so until November 8, 2006, resulting in the action being time-barred. While the "discovery rule" may operate to delay accrual of a cause of action where professionals such as a doctor or lawyer breaches a duty of care, for a layperson would lack ability to observe, evaluate or detect the wrongdoing; but such a rule is inapplicable here because the offending work was publicly televised. [*NBCUniversal Media, LLC v. Superior Court*, 171 Cal. Rptr. 3d 1 (Cal. App. 2014)]

Contractual Limitations

Some contracts, particularly insurance contracts, contain a time limitation within which suit must be brought. This is in effect a private statute of limitations created by the agreement of the parties.

A contract may also require that notice of any claim be given within a specified time. A party who fails to give notice within the time specified by the contract is barred from suing on the contract.

A contract provision requiring that suit be brought within one year does not violate public policy, although the statute of limitations would allow two years in the absence of such a contract limitation.[35]

Make the Connection

Summary

A party's duty to perform under a contract can be affected by a condition precedent, which must occur before a party has an obligation to perform; a condition subsequent, that is, a condition or event that relieves the duty to thereafter perform; and concurrent conditions, which require mutual and often simultaneous performance.

Most contracts are discharged by performance. An offer to perform is called a *tender of performance*. If a tender of performance is wrongfully refused, the duty of the tenderer to perform is terminated. When the performance called for by the contract is the payment of money, it must be legal tender that is offered. In actual practice, it is

---

[35] *Keiting v. Skauge,* 543 N.W.2d 565 (Wis. App. 1995).

common to pay and to accept payment by checks or other commercial paper.

When the debtor owes the creditor on several accounts and makes a payment, the debtor may specify which account is to be credited with the payment. If the debtor fails to specify, the creditor may choose which account to credit.

When a contract does not state when it is to be performed, it must be performed within a reasonable time. If time for performance is stated in the contract, the contract must be performed at the time specified if such time is essential (is of the essence). Ordinarily, a contract must be performed exactly in the manner specified by the contract. A less-than-perfect performance is allowed if it is a substantial performance and if damages are allowed the other party.

A contract cannot be discharged by unilateral action unless authorized by the contract itself or by statute, as in the case of consumer protection rescission.

Because a contract arises from an agreement, it may also be terminated by an agreement. A contract may also be discharged by the substitution of a new contract for the original contract; by a novation, or making a new contract with a new party; by accord and satisfaction; by release; or by waiver.

A contract is discharged when it is impossible to perform. Impossibility may result from the destruction of the subject matter of the contract, the adoption of a new law that prohibits performance, the death or disability of a party whose personal action was required for performance of the contract, or the act of the other party to the contract. Some courts will also hold that a contract is discharged when its performance is commercially impracticable or there is frustration of purpose. Temporary impossibility, such as a labor strike or bad weather, has no effect on a contract. It is common, though, to include protective clauses that excuse delay caused by temporary impossibility.

A contract may be discharged by operation of law. This occurs when (1) the liability arising from the contract is discharged by bankruptcy, (2) suit on the contract is barred by the applicable statute of limitations, or (3) a time limitation stated in the contract is exceeded.

Learning Outcomes

After studying this chapter, you should be able to clearly explain:

18-1 Conditions Relating to Performance

LO.1 List the three types of conditions that affect a party's duty to perform

See the "pay-if-paid" condition-precedent example in the section titled "Condition Precedent," page 328. See the TV anchor's "failed urinalysis test" condition subsequent example, page 329.

18-2 Discharge by Performance

LO.2 Explain the on-time performance rule

See the "mailed-check payment" example, page 331. See the "time is of the essence" example, page 331.

LO.3 Explain the adequacy of performance rules

See the application of the substantial performance rule to the nonconforming new home piping example, page 332.

See the effect of failure to substantially perform a contract in the *Superior Wall and Paver* case, pages 333–334.

18-3 Discharge by Action of Parties

LO.4 Explain four ways a contract can be discharged by agreement of the parties

See the text discussion on rescission, cancellation, substitution, and novation in the section titled "Discharge by Agreement," page 335.

18-4 Discharge by External Causes

LO.5 State the effect on a contract of the death or disability of one of the contracting parties

See the Subway sandwich shops example, page 338.

LO.6 Explain when impossibility or impracticability may discharge a contract

See the Ryder Cup frustration-of-purpose example, pages 339–340.

See the *Ocean City* impossibility case, which provided a remedy, page 338.

Key Terms

accord and satisfaction
bankruptcy
condition
condition precedent
condition subsequent

operation of law
release
rescission
statute of limitations
substantial performance

substitution
tender
waiver

Questions and Case Problems

1. CIT entered into a sale/leaseback contract with Condere Tire Corporation for 11 tire presses at Condere's tire plant in Natchez, Mississippi. Condere ceased making payments on these presses owned by CIT, and Condere filed for Chapter 11 bankruptcy. CIT thereafter contracted to sell the presses to Specialty Tires Inc. for $250,000. When the contract was made, CIT, Condere, and Specialty Tire believed that CIT was the owner of the presses and was entitled to immediate possession. When CIT attempted to gain access to the presses to have them shipped, Condere changed its position and refused to allow the equipment to be removed from the plant. When the presses were not delivered, Specialty sued CIT for damages for nondelivery of the presses, and CIT asserted the defense of impracticability. Decide. [*Specialty Tires, Inc. v. CIT*, 82 F. Supp. 2d 434 (W.D. Pa.)]

2. Lymon Mitchell operated a Badcock Home Furnishings dealership, under which as dealer he was paid a commission on sales and Badcock retained title to merchandise on display. Mitchell sold his dealership to another and to facilitate the sale, Badcock prepared a summary of commissions owed with certain itemized offsets it claimed that Mitchell owed Badcock. Mitchell disagreed with the calculations, but he accepted them and signed the transfer documents, closing the sale on the basis of the terms set forth in the summary, and was paid accordingly. After pondering the offsets taken by Badcock and verifying the correctness of his position, he brought suit for the additional funds owed. What defense would you expect Badcock to raise? How would you decide the case? Explain fully. [*Mitchell v. Badcock Corp.*, 496 S.E.2d 502 (Ga. App.)]

3. American Bank loaned Koplik $50,000 to buy equipment for a restaurant about to be opened by Casual Citchen Corp. The loan was not repaid, and Fast Foods, Inc., bought out the interest of Casual Citchen. As part of the transaction, Fast Foods agreed to pay the debt owed to American Bank, and the parties agreed to a new schedule of payments to be made by Fast Foods. Fast Foods did not make the payments, and American Bank sued Koplik. He contended that his obligation to repay $50,000 had been discharged by the execution of the agreement providing for the payment of the debt by Fast Foods.

Was this defense valid? [*American Bank & Trust Co. v. Koplik*, 451 N.Y.S.2d 426 (A. D.)]

4. Metalcrafters made a contract to design a new earth-moving vehicle for Lamar Highway Construction Co. Metalcrafters was depending on the genius of Samet, the head of its research department, to design a new product. Shortly after the contract was made between Metalcrafters and Lamar, Samet was killed in an automobile accident. Metalcrafters was not able to design the product without Samet. Lamar sued Metalcrafters for damages for breach of the contract. Metalcrafters claimed that the contract was discharged by Samet's death. Is it correct?

5. The Tinchers signed a contract to sell land to Creasy. The contract specified that the sales transaction was to be completed in 90 days. At the end of the 90 days, Creasy requested an extension of time. The Tinchers refused to grant an extension and stated that the contract was terminated. Creasy claimed that the 90-day clause was not binding because the contract did not state that time was of the essence. Was the contract terminated? [*Creasy v. Tincher*, 173 S.E.2d 332 (W. Va.)]

6. Christopher Bloom received a medical school scholarship created by the U.S. Department of Health and Human Services to increase the number of doctors serving rural areas. In return for this assistance, Bloom agreed to practice four years in a region identified as being underserved by medical professionals. After some problem with his postgraduation assignment, Bloom requested a repayment schedule from the agency. Although no terms were offered, Bloom tendered to the agency two checks totaling $15,500 and marked "Final Payment." Neither check was cashed, and the government sued Bloom for $480,000, the value of the assistance provided. Bloom claimed that by tendering the checks to the agency, his liability had been discharged by an accord and satisfaction. Decide. [*United States v. Bloom*, 112 F.3d 200 (7th Cir.)]

7. Dickson contracted to build a house for Moran. When it was approximately 25 percent to 40 percent completed, Moran would not let Dickson work anymore because he was not following the building plans and specifications and there were many defects. Moran hired another contractor to correct the defects and finish the building. Dickson sued Moran for

breach of contract, claiming that he had substantially performed the contract up to the point where he had been discharged. Was Dickson correct? [*Dickson v. Moran*, 344 So. 2d 102 (La. App.)]

8. A lessor leased a trailer park to a tenant. At the time, sewage was disposed of by a septic tank system that was not connected with the public sewage system. The tenant knew this, and the lease declared that the tenant had examined the premises and that the landlord made no representation or guarantee as to the condition of the premises. Sometime thereafter, the septic tank system stopped working properly, and the county health department notified the tenant that he was required to connect the septic tank system with the public sewage system or else the department would close the trailer park. The tenant did not want to pay the additional cost involved in connecting with the public system. The tenant claimed that he was released from the lease and was entitled to a refund of the deposit that he had made. Was he correct? [*Glen R. Sewell Street Metal v. Loverde*, 451 P.2d 721 (Cal. App.)]

9. Oneal was a teacher employed by the Colton Consolidated School District. Because of a diabetic condition, his eyesight deteriorated so much that he offered to resign if he would be given pay for a specified number of "sick leave" days. The school district refused to do this and discharged Oneal for nonperformance of his contract. He appealed to remove the discharge from his record. Decide. What ethical values are involved? [*Oneal v. Colton Consolidated School District*, 557 P.2d 11 (Wash. App.)]

10. Northwest Construction, Inc., made a contract with the state of Washington for highway construction. Part of the work was turned over under a subcontract to Yakima Asphalt Paving Co. The contract required that any claim be asserted within 180 days. Yakima brought an action for damages after the expiration of 180 days. The defense was that the claim was too late. Yakima replied that the action was brought within the time allowed by the statute of limitations and that the contractual limitation of 180 days was therefore not binding. Was Yakima correct?

11. Farmer William Weber sued the North Loup Irrigation District for breach of contract because North Loup failed to deliver water to his farm during the 2010 season as a result of the destruction of a diversion dam caused by catastrophic flooding in June 2010. The contract between the parties stated that irrigation charges must be paid by December of the year preceding the irrigation season. At the time of the flood Weber had not yet paid his 2010 irrigation charges; and he paid the 2010 charge under protest on April 13, 2011. Weber explained, "I've never wrote a check for $10,000 in my life that I didn't get something for." Did North Loup breach its contractual duties to Weber? Was payment by December 2009 a condition precedent to North Loup's duty to deliver water? Decide. [*Weber v. North Loup River Power and Irrigation District*, 854 N.W.2d 263 (Neb.)]

12. Suburban Power Piping Corp., under contract to construct a building for LTV Steel Corp., made a subcontract with Power & Pollution Services, Inc., to do some of the work. The subcontract provided that the subcontractor would be paid when the owner (LTV) paid the contractor. LTV went into bankruptcy before making the full payment to the contractor, who then refused to pay the subcontractor on the ground that the "pay-when-paid" provision of the subcontract made payment by the owner a condition precedent to the obligation of the contractor to pay the subcontractor. Was the contractor correct? [*Power & Pollution Services, Inc. v. Suburban Power Piping Corp.*, 598 N.E.2d 69 (Ohio App.)]

13. Union Pacific Railroad's long-term coal-hauling contract with electric utility WEPCO provided that if the railroad is prevented by "an event of Force Majeure" from reloading empty coal cars (after it has delivered coal to WEPCO) with iron ore destined for Geneva, Utah, it can charge the higher rate that the contract makes applicable to shipments that do not involve backhauling. The iron ore that the railroad's freight trains would have picked up in Minnesota was intended for a steel mill in Utah. The steel company was bankrupt in 1999 when the parties signed the contract. In November 2001 the steel mill shut down and closed for good in February 2004. Thereafter, the railroad wrote WEPCO to declare "an event of Force Majeure," and that henceforth it would be charging WEPCO the higher rate applicable to shipments without a backhaul. WEPCO sued the railroad for breach of the force majeure provision in the contract, contending that the railroad waited over two plus years to increase rates. The railroad contends that the clause should be interpreted as written. Decide. [*Wisconsin Electric Power Co. v. Union Pacific Railroad Co.*, 557 F.3d 504 (7th Cir.)]

14. Beeson Company made a contract to construct a shopping center for Sartori. Before the work was

fully completed, Sartori stopped making the payments to Beeson that the contract required. The contract provided for liquidated damages of $1,000 per day if Beeson failed to substantially complete the project within 300 days of the beginning of construction. The contract also provided for a bonus of $1,000 for each day Beeson completed the project ahead of schedule. Beeson stopped working and sued Sartori for the balance due under the contract, just as though it had been fully performed. Sartori defended on the ground that Beeson had not substantially completed the work. Beeson proved that Sartori had been able to rent most of the stores in the center. Was there substantial performance of the contract? If so, what would be the measure of damages? [*J.M. Beeson Co. v. Sartori*, 553 So. 2d 180 (Fla. App.)]

15. New Beginnings provides rehabilitation services for alcohol and drug abuse to both adults and adolescents. New Beginnings entered into negotiation with Adbar for the lease of a building in the city of St. Louis and subsequently entered into a three-year lease. The total rent due for the three-year term was $273,000. After the lease was executed, the city denied an occupancy permit because Alderman Bosley and residents testified at a hearing in vigorous opposition to the presence of New Beginnings in the neighborhood. A court ordered the permit issued. Alderman Bosley thereafter contacted the chair of the state's appointment committee and asked her to pull the agency's funding. He received no commitment from her on this matter. After a meeting with the state director of Alcohol and Drug Abuse where it was asserted that the director said the funding would be pulled if New Beginnings moved into the Adbar location, New Beginnings' board decided not to occupy the building. Adbar brought suit for breach of the lease, and New Beginnings asserted that it was excused from performance because of commercial impracticability and frustration of purpose. Do you believe the doctrine of commercial impracticability should be limited in its application so as to preserve the certainty of contracts? What rule of law applies to this case? Decide. [*Adbar v. New Beginnings*, 103 S.W.2d 799 (Mo. App.)]

CPA Questions

1. Parc hired Glaze to remodel and furnish an office suite. Glaze submitted plans that Parc approved. After completing all the necessary construction and painting, Glaze purchased minor accessories that Parc rejected because they did not conform to the plans. Parc refused to allow Glaze to complete the project and refused to pay Glaze any part of the contract price. Glaze sued for the value of the work performed. Which of the following statements is correct?

   a. Glaze will lose because Glaze breached the contract by not completing performance.

   b. Glaze will win because Glaze substantially performed and Parc prevented complete performance.

   c. Glaze will lose because Glaze materially breached the contract by buying the accessories.

   d. Glaze will win because Parc committed anticipatory breach.

2. Ordinarily, in an action for breach of a construction contract, the statute of limitations time period would be computed from the date the contract is:

   a. Negotiated.

   b. Breached.

   c. Begun.

   d. Signed.

3. Which of the following will release all original parties to a contract but will maintain a contractual relationship?

	Novation	Substituted contract
a.	Yes	Yes
b.	Yes	No
c.	No	Yes
d.	No	No

Breach of Contract and Remedies

Learning Outcomes ⟨⟨⟨

After studying this chapter, you should be able to

LO.1 Explain what constitutes a breach of contract and an anticipatory breach of contract

LO.2 Describe the effect of a waiver of a breach

LO.3 Explain the range of remedies available for breach of contract

LO.4 Explain when liquidated damages clauses are valid and invalid

LO.5 State when liability-limiting clauses and releases are valid

What can be done when a contract is broken?

19-1 What Constitutes a Breach of Contract?

The question of remedies does not become important until it is first determined that a contract has been violated or breached.

19-1a Definition of Breach

breach–failure to act or perform in the manner called for in a contract.

A **breach** is the failure to act or perform in the manner called for by the contract. When the contract calls for performance, such as painting an owner's home, the failure to paint or to paint properly is a *breach of contract*. If the contract calls for a creditor's forbearance, the creditor's action in bringing a lawsuit is a breach of the contract.

19-1b Anticipatory Breach

When the contract calls for performance, a party may make it clear before the time for performance arrives that the contract will not be performed. This is referred to as an **anticipatory breach.**

Anticipatory Repudiation

anticipatory breach–promisor's repudiation of the contract prior to the time that performance is required when such repudiation is accepted by the promisee as a breach of the contract.

anticipatory repudiation–repudiation made in advance of the time for performance of the contract obligations.

When a party expressly declares that performance will not be made when required, this declaration is called an **anticipatory repudiation** of the contract. To constitute such a repudiation, there must be a clear, absolute, unequivocal refusal to perform the contract according to its terms. **For Example,** Procter & Gamble (P&G) sought payment on four letters of credit issued by a Serbian bank, Investbanka. P&G presented two letters by June 8, prior to their expiration dates, with the necessary documentation for payment to Beogradska Bank New York, Investbanka's New York agent. A June 11 letter from Beogradska Bank broadly and unequivocally stated that the bank would not pay the letters of credit. Two additional letters of credit totaling $20,000 issued by Investbanka that expired by June 30 were not thereafter submitted to the New York agent bank by P&G. However, a court found that the bank had anticipatorily breached its obligations under those letters of credit by its broad renouncements in the June 11 letter, and judgments were rendered in favor of P&G.[1]

CASE SUMMARY

Splitting Tips—Contract Price Less Cost of Completion

FACTS: Hartland Developers, Inc., agreed to build an airplane hangar for Robert Tips of San Antonio for $300,000, payable in three installments of $100,000, with the final payment due upon the completion of the building and the issuance of a certificate of completion by the engineer representing Tips. The evidence shows that Tips's representative, Mr. Lavelle, instructed Hartland to cease work on the building because Tips could no longer afford to make payments. Hartland ceased work as instructed before final completion of the building, having been paid $200,000 at the time. He sued Tips for breach of contract. On May 6, 1996, the trial court allowed Hartland the amount owing on the contract, $100,000, less the cost of completing the building according to the contract, $65,000, plus attorney fees and prejudgment interest. Tips appealed, pointing out, among other assertions, that he was required to

---

[1] *Procter & Gamble v. Investbanka*, 2000 WL 520630 (S.D.N.Y. 2000).

Splitting Tips—Contract Price Less Cost of Completion continued

spend $23,000 to provide electrical outlets for the hangar, which were contemplated in the contract.

DECISION: Judgment for Tips, subject to offsets. The trial judge based his damages assessment on anticipatory repudiation of contract. The evidence that Tips's representative,

Lavelle, instructed Hartland to cease work on the project because Tips no longer could afford to make payments was sufficient to support this finding. However, Tips is entitled to an offset for electrical connections of $23,000 under a breach of contract theory. [*Tips v. Hartland Developers, Inc.*, 961 S.W.2d 618 (Tex. App. 1998)]

A refusal to perform a contract that is made before performance is required, unless the other party to the contract does an act or makes a concession that is not required by the contract, is an anticipatory repudiation of the contract.[2] However, a firmly stated request for additional payment under an existing contract without refusal to perform until the additional payment is made is not a repudiation of a contract. **For Example,** Sunesis Trucking Company's August 14, 2009, letter to Thistledown Racetrack seeking additional payment for hauling straw and manure from the raceway's horse stalls stating "accept this as notice that we will haul your manure at the following fees" was held not to be a notice of termination and did not establish an anticipatory breach excusing Thistledown from its obligations under the contract.[3]

Anticipatory Repudiation by Conduct

The anticipatory repudiation may be expressed by conduct that makes it impossible for the repudiating party to perform subsequently. **For Example,** while the Town of Mammoth Lakes, California, was claiming a willingness to move forward with a hotel/condominium project under its contract with the developer, in actuality, the evidence established that town officials refused to move forward and actively sought to undermine the developer's rights under the development contract. The court affirmed a judgment of $30 million in damages and attorneys' fees.[4]

19-2 Waiver of Breach

The breach of a contract may have no importance because the other party to the contract waives the breach.

19-2a Cure of Breach by Waiver

waiver–release or relinquishment of a known right or objection.

The fact that one party has broken a contract does not necessarily mean that there will be a lawsuit or a forfeiture of the contract. For practical business reasons, one party may be willing to ignore or waive the breach. When it is established that there has been a **waiver** of a breach, the party waiving the breach cannot take any action on the theory that the contract was broken. The waiver, in effect, erases the past breach. The contract continues as though the breach had not existed.

The waiver may be express or it may be implied from the continued recognition of the existence of the contract by the aggrieved party.[5] When the conduct of a party shows an intent to give up a right, it waives that right.[6]

---

[2] See *Black Diamond Energy, Inc. v. Encana Oil and Gas (USA) Inc.*, 326 P.3d 904 (Wyo. 2014).
[3] *Sunesis Trucking Co. v. Thistledown Racetrack, LLC*, 13 N.E.3d 727 (Ohio App. 2014).
[4] *Mammoth Lakes Land Acquisition, LLC v. Town of Mammoth Lakes*, 120 Cal. Rptr. 3d 797 (Cal. Ct. of App. 3d Dist. 2010).
[5] *Huger v. Morrison*, 809 So. 2d 1140 (La. App. 2002).
[6] *Stronghaven Inc. v. Ingram*, 555 S.E.2d 49 (Ga. App. 2001).

19-2b Existence and Scope of Waiver

It is a question of fact whether there has been a waiver.

CASE SUMMARY

Have You Driven a Ford Lately, Jennifer?

FACTS: In 1995, Northland Ford Dealers, an association of dealerships, offered to sponsor a "hole in one" contest at Moccasin Creek Country Club. A banner announced that a hole in one would win a car but gave no other details, and the local dealer parked a Ford Explorer near the banner. Northland paid a $4,602 premium to Continental Hole-In-One, Inc., to ensure the award of the contest prize. The insurance application stated in capital letters that "ALL AMATEUR MEN AND WOMEN WILL UTILIZE THE SAME TEE." And Continental established the men/women yardage for the hole to be 170 yards but did not make this known to the participants. Jennifer Harms registered for the tournament and paid her entrance fee. At the contest hole, she teed off from the amateur women's red marker, which was a much shorter distance to the pin than the 170 yards from the men's marker—and she made a hole in one. When she inquired about the prize, she was told that because of insurance requirements, all amateurs had to tee off from the amateur men's tee box, and because she had not done so, she was disqualified. Harms, a collegiate golfer at Concordia College, returned there to complete her last year of athletic eligibility and on graduation sued Northland for breach of contract. Northland contends that under NCAA rules, accepting a prize or agreeing to accept a prize would have disqualified Harms from NCAA competition. It also asserts that her continuation of her NCAA competition evinced intent to waive acceptance of the car.

DECISION: Judgment for Harms. Northland must abide by the rules it announced, not by the ones it left unannounced that disqualified all amateur women from the contest. This was a vintage unilateral contract with performance by the offeree as acceptance. Harms earned the prize when she sank her winning shot. Waiver is a volitional relinquishment, by act or word, of a known existing right conferred in law or contract. Harms could not disclaim the prize; it was not hers to refuse. She was told her shot from the wrong tee disqualified her. One can hardly relinquish what was never conferred. Northland's waiver defense is devoid of merit. [*Harms v. Northland Ford Dealers*, 602 N.W.2d 58 (S.D. 1999)]

Existence of Waiver

A party may express or declare that the breach of a contract is waived. A waiver of a breach is more often the result of an express forgiving of a breach. Thus, a party allowing the other party to continue performance without objecting that the performance is not satisfactory waives the right to raise that objection when sued for payment by the performing party.

For Example, a contract promising to sell back a parcel of commercial property to Jackson required Jackson to make a $500 payment to Massey's attorney on the first of the month for five months, December through April. It was clearly understood that the payments would be "on time without fail." Jackson made the December payment on time. New Year's Day, a holiday, fell on a Friday, and Jackson made the second payment on January 4. He made $500 payments on February 1, March 1, and March 31, respectively, and the payments were accepted and a receipt issued on each occasion. However, Massey refused to convey title back to Jackson because "the January 4 payment was untimely and the parties' agreement had been breached." The court held that the doctrine of waiver applied due to Massey's acceptance of the late payment and the three subsequent payments without objection, and the court declared that Jackson was entitled to possession of the land.[7]

---

[7] *Massey v. Jackson*, 726 So. 2d 656 (Ala. App. 1998).

Scope of Waiver

The waiver of a breach of contract extends only to the matter waived. It does not show any intent to ignore other provisions of the contract.

Antimodification Clause

Modern contracts commonly specify that the terms of a contract shall not be deemed modified by waiver as to any breaches. This means that the original contract remains as agreed to. Either party may therefore return to, and insist on, compliance with the original contract.

In the example involving Jackson and Massey's contract, the trial court reviewed the contract to see whether the court was restricted by the contract from applying the waiver. It concluded: "In this case, the parties' contract did not contain any terms that could prevent the application of the doctrine of waiver to the acceptance of late payments."[8]

19-2c Reservation of Rights

> **reservation of rights**—assertion by a party to a contract that even though a tendered performance (e.g., a defective product) is accepted, the right to damages for nonconformity to the contract is reserved.

It may be that a party is willing to accept a defective performance but does not wish to surrender any claim for damages for the breach. **For Example,** Midwest Utilities, Inc., accepted 20 carloads of Powder River Basin coal (sometimes called *Western coal*) from its supplier, Maney Enterprises, because its power plants were in short supply of coal. Midwest's requirements contract with Maney called for Appalachian coal, a low-sulfur, highly efficient fuel, which is sold at a premium price per ton. Midwest, in accepting the tendered performance with a **reservation of rights,** gave notice to Maney that it reserved all rights to pursue damages for the tender of a nonconforming shipment.

19-3 Remedies for Breach of Contract

> **remedy**—action or procedure that is followed in order to enforce a right or to obtain damages for injury to a right.

One or more **remedies** may be available to the innocent party in the case of a breach of contract. There is also the possibility that arbitration or a streamlined out-of-court alternative dispute resolution procedure is available or required for determining the rights of the parties.

19-3a Remedies Upon Anticipatory Repudiation

When an anticipatory repudiation of a contract occurs, the aggrieved person has several options. The individual may (1) do nothing beyond stating that performance at the proper time will be required, (2) regard the contract as having been definitively broken and bring a lawsuit against the repudiating party without waiting to see whether there will be proper performance when the performance date arrives, or (3) regard the repudiation as an offer to cancel the contract. This offer can be accepted or rejected. If accepted, there is a discharge of the original contract by the subsequent cancellation agreement of the parties.

19-3b Remedies in General and the Measure of Damages

Courts provide a *quasi-contractual* or *restitution* remedy in which a contract is unenforceable because it lacked definite and certain terms or was not in compliance with the statute of frauds, yet one of the parties performed services for the other. The measure of damages in these and other quasi-contract cases is the reasonable value of the services performed, not an amount derived from the defective contract.

[8] *Id.* at 659.

[Handwritten margin notes: "asking to:", "Dismal r", "Damages must be Reasonably Foreseeable", "what damges can collect from", "Prove with Reasonable Certinty.", "liquidated damage clause.", "Non Breaching Party ask court to order specific performance. Specific Performance Appropiate when matter unige.", "Subject matter is unige"]

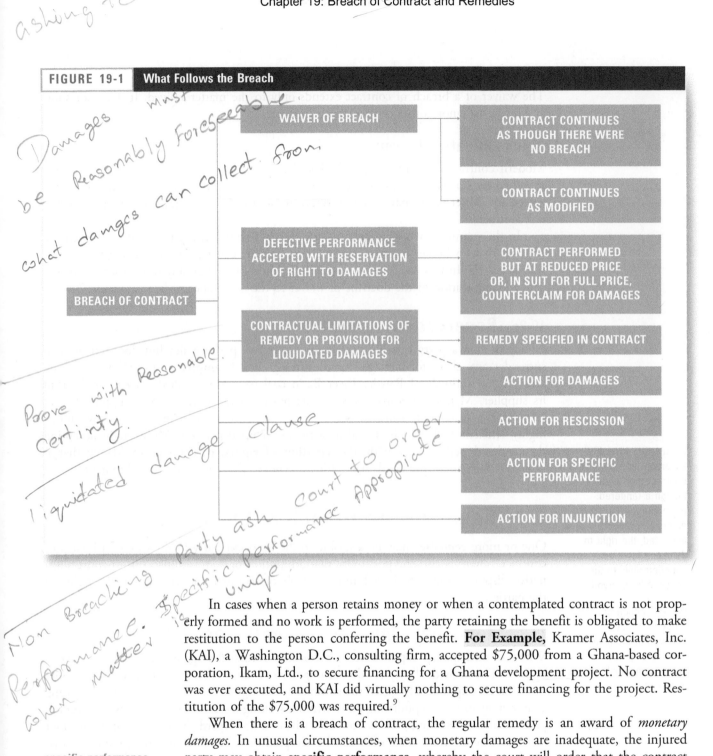

FIGURE 19-1   What Follows the Breach

- WAIVER OF BREACH
  - CONTRACT CONTINUES AS THOUGH THERE WERE NO BREACH
  - CONTRACT CONTINUES AS MODIFIED
- BREACH OF CONTRACT
- DEFECTIVE PERFORMANCE ACCEPTED WITH RESERVATION OF RIGHT TO DAMAGES
  - CONTRACT PERFORMED BUT AT REDUCED PRICE OR, IN SUIT FOR FULL PRICE, COUNTERCLAIM FOR DAMAGES
- CONTRACTUAL LIMITATIONS OF REMEDY OR PROVISION FOR LIQUIDATED DAMAGES
  - REMEDY SPECIFIED IN CONTRACT
  - ACTION FOR DAMAGES
  - ACTION FOR RESCISSION
  - ACTION FOR SPECIFIC PERFORMANCE
  - ACTION FOR INJUNCTION

In cases when a person retains money or when a contemplated contract is not properly formed and no work is performed, the party retaining the benefit is obligated to make restitution to the person conferring the benefit. **For Example,** Kramer Associates, Inc. (KAI), a Washington D.C., consulting firm, accepted $75,000 from a Ghana-based corporation, Ikam, Ltd., to secure financing for a Ghana development project. No contract was ever executed, and KAI did virtually nothing to secure financing for the project. Restitution of the $75,000 was required.[9]

When there is a breach of contract, the regular remedy is an award of *monetary damages*. In unusual circumstances, when monetary damages are inadequate, the injured party may obtain **specific performance,** whereby the court will order that the contract terms be carried out.

specific performance—
action brought to compel the adverse party to perform a contract on the theory that merely suing for damages for its breach will not be an adequate remedy.

The measure of monetary damages when there has been a breach of contract is the sum of money that will place the injured party in the same position that would have been attained if the contract had been performed.[10] That is, the injured party will be given the *benefit of the bargain* by the court. As seen in the *Tips v. Hartland Developers* case, the nonbreaching party, Hartland, was awarded the contract price less the cost of completion of the project, which had the effect of giving the builder the benefit of the bargain.

[9] *Kramer Associates, Inc. v. Ikam, Ltd.,* 888 A.2d 247 (D.C. 2005).
[10] *Leingang v. City of Mandan,* 468 N.W.2d 397 (N.D. 1991).

[handwritten notes in top margin: "12:00" "9:15" "Contract was properly executed" "Damages were compensate for the losses ever caused" "Gain's that prevented"]

19-3c Monetary Damages

Monetary damages are commonly classified as compensatory damages, nominal damages, and punitive damages. **Compensatory damages** compensate the injured party for the damages incurred as a result of the breach of contract. Compensatory damages have two branches, *direct damages* and *consequential* (or *special*) *damages*.

Injured parties that do not sustain an actual loss because of a breach of contract are entitled to a judgment of a small sum of money such as $1; these damages are called **nominal damages.**

Damages in excess of actual loss, imposed for the purpose of punishing or making an example of the defendant, are known as **punitive damages** or *exemplary damages*. In contract actions, punitive damages are not ordinarily awarded.[11]

Direct and Consequential Damages

Direct damages (sometimes called *general damages*) are those that naturally flow from the given type of breach of contract involved and include *incidental damages*, which are extra expenditures made by the injured party to rectify the breach or mitigate damages.[12] **Consequential damages** (sometimes called *special damages*) are those that do not necessarily flow from the type of breach of contract involved but happen to do so in a particular case as a result of the injured party's particular circumstances.[13]

CASE SUMMARY

Who Pays the Expenses?

FACTS: Jerry Birkel was a grain farmer. Hassebrook Farm Service, Inc., made a contract with Jerry to sell to him and install a grain storage and drying bin. Jerry traded in his old dryer to the seller. The new equipment did not work properly, and Jerry had to pay other persons for drying and storing his grain. Jerry sued Hassebrook for damages and claimed the right to be repaid what he had paid to others for drying and storage.

DECISION: Jerry was entitled to recover what he had paid others for drying and storage. Because Jerry had traded in his old dryer to the seller, it was obvious to the seller that if the new equipment did not work properly, Jerry would be forced to pay for alternative drying and storage to prevent the total loss of his crops. The cost of such an alternative was therefore within the seller's contemplation when the contract was made, and so the buyer could recover this cost as an element of damages for the seller's breach of contract. [*Birkel v. Hassebrook Farm Service, Inc.*, 363 N.W.2d 148 (Neb. 1985)]

Consequential damages may be recovered only if it was reasonably foreseeable to the defendant that the kind of loss in question could be sustained by the nonbreaching party if the contract were broken.

For Example, in early August, Spencer Adams ordered a four-wheel-drive GMC truck with a rear-end hydraulic lift for use on his Aroostook County, Maine, potato farm. The contract price was $63,500. He told Brad Jones, the owner of the dealership, that he had to have the truck by Labor Day so he could use it to bring in his crop from the fields before the first frost, and Brad nodded that he understood. The truck did not arrive by

---

[11] A party who is not awarded actual damages but wins nominal damages can be considered a "prevailing party" for the purposes of a contractual attorney fee-shifting provision. *Brock v. King*, 629 S.E.2d 829 (Ga. App. 2006).

[12] In New York State, the courts utilize the terms *general* and *special* damages as opposed to the terms *direct* and *consequential* damages. See *Biotronik A.G. v. Connor Medsystems Ireland, Ltd.*, 988 N.Y.S.2d 527 (Ct. App. 2014).

[13] See *Powell Electrical Systems, Inc. v. Hewlett Packard Co.*, 356 S.W.3d 113 (Tex. App. 2011).

direct damages—losses that are caused by breach of a contract.

consequential damages—damages the buyer experiences as a result of the seller's breach with respect to a third party; also called *special damages*.

Labor Day as promised in the written contract. After a two-week period of gradually escalating recriminations with the dealership, Adams obtained the same model GMC truck at a dealership 40 minutes away in Houlton but at the cost of $65,500. He was also able to rent a similar truck from the Houlton dealer for $250 for the day while the new truck was being prepared. Farmhands had used other means of harvesting, but because of the lack of the truck, their work was set back by five days. As a result of the delays, 30 percent of the crop was still in the fields when the first frost came, causing damages expertly estimated at $320,000. The *direct damages* for the breach of contract in this case would be the difference between the contract price for the truck of $63,500 and the market price of $65,500, or $2,000. These direct damages naturally flow from the breach of contract for the purchase of a truck. Also, the *incidental damages* of $250 for the truck rental are recoverable direct damages. The $320,000 loss of the potato crop was a consequence of not having the truck, and this sum is arguably recoverable by Spencer Adams as *consequential* or *special damages*. Adams notified Brad Jones of the reason he needed to have the truck by Labor Day, and it should have been reasonably foreseeable to Jones that loss of a portion of the crop could occur if the truck contract was breached. However, because of Spencer Adams's obligation to mitigate damages (as discussed next), it is unlikely that Adams will recover the full consequential damages. Truck rental availability or the lack of availability within the rural area, alternative tractor usage, and the actual harvesting methods used by Adams all relate to the mitigation issue to be resolved by the jury.

Mitigation of Damages

The injured party is under the duty to mitigate damages if reasonably possible.[14] In other words, damages must not be permitted to increase if an increase can be prevented by reasonable efforts. This means that the injured party must generally stop any performance under the contract to avoid running up a larger bill. The duty to mitigate damages may require an injured party to buy or rent elsewhere the goods that the wrongdoer was obligated to deliver under the contract. In the case of breach of an employment contract by the employer, the employee is required to seek other similar employment. The wages earned from other employment must be deducted from the damages claimed. The discharged employee, however, is not required to take employment of less-than-comparable work.

Effect of Failure to Mitigate Damages. The effect of the requirement of mitigating damages is to limit recovery by the nonbreaching party to the damages that would have been sustained had this party mitigated the damages where it was possible to do so.

CASE SUMMARY

The Opposite of a Win-Win Situation

FACTS: On February 4, 2006, the Heymanns agreed to buy a condominium from Gayle Fischer for $315,000. Both parties signed a purchase and sale agreement. The Agreement authorized the Heymanns to terminate if Fischer refused to fix any "major defect" discovered upon inspection but did not permit them to terminate if Fischer refused to perform "routine maintenance" or make "minor repair[s]." On February 10, 2006, the Heymanns demanded Fischer fix an electrical problem after an inspection report revealed that electricity was not flowing to three power outlets. The Heymanns thought this was a "major defect" under the Agreement and conditioned their purchase on Fischer's timely response. Fischer failed to timely respond to their demand—even though she eventually fixed the problem

---

[14] *West Pinal Family Health Center, Inc. v. McBryde*, 785 P.2d 66 (Ariz. App. 1989).

The Opposite of a Win-Win Situation continued

for $117 on February 20 by having an electrician push the reset button on three outlets and change a light bulb. The Heymanns tendered a mutual release to void the Agreement. Fischer refused to sign the release and sued for specific performances or damages. The case progressed to the trial court, the court of appeals, back to the trial court, and ultimately to the Supreme Court of Indiana.

After the deal fell through in 2006 Fischer attempted to mitigate damages by selling the condo but the housing market entered a major downturn. On February 13, 2007, she received an offer to purchase the condo for $240,000 but her counter-offer of $286,000 was rejected. She eventually sold the condo in November 2011 for $180,000. Fischer seeks damages for the difference between the Heymann purchase price of $315,000 and the sale in 2011 of $180,000, plus the cost of maintaining the condo from 2006 through 2011, and attorney's fees for a total of $306,616.

DECISION: Fischer's failure to respond to the Heymann's demand for electrical repairs was not a basis to void the contract. Rather the $117 repair consisting of pushing the reset button on three outlets and the change of a light bulb was not a "major defect" which would allow for the voiding of a contract. Accordingly, the Heymanns were in breach of the Purchase Agreement. The duty to mitigate damages is a common law duty independent of contract terms requiring the non-breaching party to make a reasonable effort to decrease the damage caused by the breach. Fischer acted unreasonably when she could have mitigated damages and sold the condo for $240,000, in 2007, instead of waiting until 2011. Accordingly, her compensatory damages are $75,000, the difference between $315,000 and $240,000 plus $15,109 in carrying cost to the 2007 offer date and reasonable attorney fees of $3,862 incurred up to the 2007 date for a total of $93,977. [*Fischer v. Heymann*, 12 N.E.3d 867 (Ind. 2014)]

19-3d Rescission

When one party commits a material breach of the contract, the other party may rescind the contract; if the party in default objects, the aggrieved party may bring an action for rescission. A breach is *material* when it is so substantial that it defeats the object of the parties in making the contract.[15]

CASE SUMMARY

The Buck Doesn't Stop Here (at Slip B1)

FACTS: Edgar Buck owns *Rookie IV*, a $6 million 61-foot boat requiring a dock slip 20 feet in width. Buck's daughter Susanne owns ZAN, LCC, and Buck has authority to act on behalf of ZAN. Susanne wanted a waterfront lot to build a home, and Buck wanted a boat slip out of the Intercoastal Waterway where the boat regularly sustained damage. ZAN (Buck) agreed to purchase a slip for Buck's boat and lot 3 for Susanne. Just prior to the closing, Buck discovered that the slip designated as B1 was actually two slips, B1 and B2 and *Rookie IV* would not fit into B1. Buck was informed by Ripley Cove's agent and later its closing attorney Dan David that the sellers owned B2 and that it would be no problem to give Buck the 20 foot clearance he needed and to place two pilings in the adjoining slip. Buck then agreed to close on the property. It was later discovered that at the time of the closing, Ripley Cove no longer owned B2. Since *Rookie IV* could not fit into the slip, ZAN sued for rescission of the contract for the lot and slip and damages. The trial court determined that ZAN proved its claims, awarded $10,000 for breach of contract and negligent misrepresentation but refused to rescind the contract. ZAN appealed.

DECISION: Judgment for ZAN. The main purpose of the contract was to provide Buck with a slip for *Rookie IV*. Thus ZAN was entitled to rescission of the contract *in toto*, both the slip and the land, despite the parties' lack of dispute regarding the upland parcel. A breach of contract claim warranting rescission of the contract must be so substantial and fundamental as to defeat the purpose of the contract. Such was the nature of the breach in this case. [*ZAN, LLC v. Ripley Cove, LLC*, 751 S.E.2d 664 (S.C. App. 2013)]

[15] *Greentree Properties, Inc. v. Kissee*, 92 S.W.3d 289 (Mo. App. 2003).

An injured party who rescinds a contract after having performed services may recover the reasonable value of the performance rendered under restitutionary or quasi-contractual damages. Money paid by the injured party may also be recovered. **For Example,** the Sharabianlous signed a purchase agreement to buy a building owned by Berenstein Associates for $2 million. Thereafter the parties learned of environmental contamination on the property. Faced with uncertainty about the scope of the problem and the cost of the cleanup, the deal fell through and litigation ensued. The trial court rescinded the agreement based on mutual mistake of fact because neither party knew the full extent of the environmental hazard at the property. Damages available to parties upon mistake are more limited than those available in cases in which rescission is based on fault. The Sharabianlous were awarded $61,423.82 in expenses and an order returning their $115,000 deposit.[16]

The purpose of rescission is to restore the injured party to the position occupied before the contract was made. However, the party seeking restitutionary damages must also return what this party has received from the party in default.

For Example, Pedro Morena purchased real estate from Jason Alexander after Alexander had assured him that the property did not have a flooding problem. In fact, the property regularly flooded after ordinary rainstorms. Morena was entitled to the return of the purchase price and payment for the reasonable value of the improvements he made to the property. Alexander was entitled to a setoff for the reasonable rental value of the property during the time Morena was in possession of this property.

19-3e Action for Specific Performance

Under special circumstances, an injured party may obtain the equitable remedy of specific performance, which compels the other party to carry out the terms of a contract. Specific performance is ordinarily granted only if the subject matter of the contract is "unique," thereby making an award of money damages an inadequate remedy. Contracts for the purchase of land will be specifically enforced.[17]

Specific performance of a contract to sell personal property can be obtained only if the article is of unusual age, beauty, unique history, or other distinction. **For Example,** Maurice owned a rare Revolutionary War musket that he agreed to sell to Herb. Maurice then changed his mind because of the uniqueness of the musket. Herb can sue and win, requesting the remedy of specific performance of the contract because of the unique nature of the goods.

When the damages sustained by the plaintiff can be measured in monetary terms, specific performance will be refused. Consequently, a contract to sell a television station will not be specifically enforced when the buyer had made a contract to resell the station to a third person; the damages caused by the breach of the first contract would be the loss sustained by being unable to make the resale, and such damages would be adequate compensation to the original buyer.[18]

Ordinarily, contracts for the performance of personal services are not specifically ordered. This is because of the difficulty of supervision by the court and the restriction of the U.S. Constitution's Thirteenth Amendment prohibiting involuntary servitude except as criminal punishment.

19-3f Action for an Injunction

injunction—order of a court of equity to refrain from doing (negative injunction) or to do (affirmative or mandatory injunction) a specified act.

When a breach of contract consists of doing an act prohibited by the contract, a possible remedy is an **injunction** against doing the act. **For Example,** when the obligation in an employee's contract is to refrain from competing after resigning from the company and

---

[16] *Sharabianlou v. Karp,* 105 Cal. Rptr. 3d 300 (Cal. App. 2010).
[17] *English v. Muller,* 514 S.E.2d 195 (Ga. 1999).
[18] *Miller v. LeSea Broadcasting, Inc.,* 87 F.3d 224 (7th Cir. 1996).

the obligation is broken by competing, a court may order the former employee to stop competing. Similarly, when a vocalist breaks a contract to record exclusively for a particular label, she may be enjoined from recording for any other company. This may have the indirect effect of compelling the vocalist to record for the plaintiff.

19-3g Reformation of Contract by a Court

At times, a written contract does not correctly state the agreement already made by the parties. When this occurs, either party may seek to have the court reform or correct the writing to state the agreement actually made.

A party seeking reformation of a contract must clearly prove both the grounds for reformation and what the agreement actually was.[19] This burden is particularly great when the contract to be reformed is written. This is so because the general rule is that parties are presumed to have read their written contracts and to have intended to be bound by them when they signed the contracts.

When a unilateral mistake is made and it is of such consequence that enforcing the contract according to its terms would be unconscionable, a court may reform the contract to correct the mistake.

CASE SUMMARY

Will a Court Correct a Huge Mistake?

FACTS: New York Packaging Corp. (NYPC) manufactured plastic sheets used by Owens Corning (OC) at its asphalt plants throughout the country as dividers to separate asphalt containers and prevent them from sticking to one another. Janet Berry, a customer service representative at Owens Corning, called and received a price from NYPC of "$172.50 per box," with a box containing 200 plastic sheets. Ms. Berry put the information into OC's computer systems, which in turn generated a purchase order. She mistakenly believed that the unit of measurement designated as "EA" on the purchase order was per box when it in fact was per sheet. As a result, the purchase orders likewise reflected a price of $172.50 per sheet rather than per box. The computer automatically calculated the total price of the purchase order and faxed it to NYPC as $1,078,195, without Ms. Berry seeing the huge total price. NYPC filled the order, which included overrun sheets, and billed OC $1,414,605.60. NYPC sought payment at the contract price of $172.50 per sheet. It points out that the purchase order contained a "no oral modification" clause and, by its terms, the order was binding when NYPC accepted. The buyer contends that NYPC is attempting to take advantage of this huge and obvious mistake and that the contract should be reformed.

DECISION: Ms. Berry made a unilateral mistake that was, or should have been, known by NYPC. OC used the sheets after its offer to return them to NYPC was refused. Therefore, the contract could not be rescinded. The drafting error in this case was so huge that to enforce the written contract would be unconscionable. Accordingly, the unit of measurement is amended to read "per box" rather than "EA"; the "Order Qty" is amended to read "41 boxes of 200 sheets per box"; and the overall price is modified to read $7,072.50, not $1,078,195. [**In re Owens Corning et al., Debtors in Possession, 291 B.R. 329 (2003)**]

19-4 Contract Provisions Affecting Remedies and Damages

The contract of the parties may contain provisions that affect the remedies available or the recovery of damages.

---

[19] The evidence must be "clear, unequivocal and decisive," *First Chatham Bank v. Liberty Capital, LLC*, 755 S.E.2d 219 (Ga. App. 2014).

19-4a Limitation of Remedies

The contract of the parties may limit the remedies of the aggrieved parties. **For Example,** the contract may give one party the right to repair or replace a defective item sold or to refund the contract price. The contract may require both parties to submit any dispute to arbitration or another streamlined out-of-court dispute resolution procedure.

19-4b Liquidated Damages

liquidated damages–provision stipulating the amount of damages to be paid in the event of default or breach of contract.

The parties may stipulate in their contract that a certain amount should be paid in case of a breach. This amount is known as liquidated damages and may be variously measured by the parties. When delay is possible, **liquidated damages** may be a fixed sum, such as $1,000 for each day of delay. When there is a total default, damages may be a percentage of the contract price or the amount of the down payment.

Validity

liquidated damages clause–specification of exact compensation in case of a breach of contract.

To be valid, a **liquidated damages clause** must satisfy two requirements: (1) The situation must be one in which it is difficult or impossible to determine the actual damages and (2) the amount specified must not be excessive when compared with the probable damages that would be sustained.[20] The validity of a liquidated damages clause is determined on the basis of the facts existing when the clause was agreed to.

Effect

When a liquidated damages clause is held valid, the injured party cannot collect more than the amount specified by the clause. The defaulting party is bound to pay such damages once the fact is established that there has been a default. The injured party is not required to make any proof as to damages sustained, and the defendant is not permitted to show that the damages were not as great as the liquidated sum.

Invalid Clauses

If the liquidated damages clause calls for the payment of a sum that is clearly unreasonably large and unrelated to the possible actual damages that might be sustained, the clause will be held to be void as a penalty. **For Example,** a settlement agreement between 27 plaintiffs seeking recovery for injuries resulting from faulty breast implants and the implants' manufacturer, Dow Corning Corp., called for seven $200,000 payments to each plaintiff. The agreement also called for a $100 per day payment to each plaintiff for any time when the payments were late as "liquidated damages." The court held that the $100 per day figure was not a reasonable estimate of anticipated damages. Rather, it was an unenforceable "penalty" provision.[21]

When a liquidated damages clause is held invalid, the effect is merely to erase the clause from the contract, and the injured party may proceed to recover damages for breach of the contract. Instead of recovering the liquidated damages amount, the injured party will recover whatever actual damages he can prove. **For Example,** Richard Goldblatt and his wife Valerie breached a five-year restrictive covenant in a settlement agreement with the medical devices corporation that Goldblatt had cofounded, C.P. Motion, Inc. A liquidated damages provision in the settlement agreement that obligated Goldblatt and his wife to pay $250,000 per breach of the restrictive covenant was unenforceable as a penalty clause. The appeals court set aside a $4,969,339 judgment against the Goldblatts, determining that the parties could have agreed to arrive at actual damages by

---

[20] *Southeast Alaska Construction Co. v. Alaska,* 791 P.2d 339 (Alaska 1990).

[21] *Bear Stearns v. Dow Corning Corp.,* 419 F.3d 543 (6th Or. 2005). See *Boone Coleman Construction, Inc. v. Village of Piketon,* 13 N.E.3d 1190 (Ohio App. 2014).

calculating a percentage of lost profits of specific lost clients or reclaiming any profits gained by the breaching parties. Because the liquidated damages clause was a penalty provision, C.P. Motion, Inc., may only recover the actual damages filed and proven at trial.[22]

19-4c Attorneys' Fees

Attorneys' fees are a very significant factor in contract litigation. In Medistar Corporation's suit against Dr. David Schmidt, the jury awarded it $418,069 in damages under its promissory estoppel claim and in addition thereto the trial court judge allowed Medistar to recover $408,412 for its attorneys' fees. A state statute allows recovery of attorneys' fees for the prevailing party in a breach of partnership claim. On appeal the recovery of $408,412 in attorneys' fees was reversed since the jury awarded zero damages on Medistars' breach of partnership claim. The net result after payment of attorneys' fees—and not counting attorneys' fees for the appeal—was $9,657 for Medistar, after four years of "successful" litigation.[23]

The so-called American rule states that each party is responsible for its own attorneys' fees in the absence of an express contractual or statutory provision to the contrary.[24] Even in the event of a valid contractual provision for attorneys' fees, a trial court has the discretion to exercise its equitable control to allow only such sum as is reasonable, or the court may properly disallow attorneys' fees altogether on the basis that such recovery would be inequitable. **For Example,** although Evergreen Tree Care Services was awarded some monetary damages in its breach of contract suit against JHL, Inc., it was unsuccessful in its claim for attorneys' fees under a provision for attorneys' fees in the contract because the trial court exercised its equitable discretion, finding that both parties to the litigation came to court with "unclean hands," and that Evergreen failed to sufficiently itemize and exclude fees to discovery abuses.[25]

19-4d Limitation of Liability Clauses

A contract may contain a provision stating that one of the parties shall not be liable for damages in case of breach. Such a provision is called an **exculpatory clause,** or when a monetary limit to damages for breach of contract is set forth in the contract, it may be referred to as a **limitation-of-liability clause.**

Content and Construction

If an exculpatory clause or a limitation-of-liability clause limits liability for damages caused only by negligent conduct, liability is neither excluded nor limited if the conduct alleged is found to be grossly negligent, willful, or wanton. **For Example,** Security Guards Inc. (SGI) provided services to Dana Corporation, a truck frame manufacturer under a contract that contained a limitation-of-liability clause capping losses at $50,000 per occurrence for damages "caused solely by the negligence" of SGI or its employees. When a critical alarm was activated by a fire in the paint shop at 5:39 P.M., the SGI guard on duty did not follow appropriate procedures, which delayed notification to the fire department for 15 minutes. Royal Indemnity Co., Dana's insurer, paid Dana $16,535,882 for the fire loss and sued SGI for $7 million, contending that the SGI guard's actions were grossly negligent and caused the plant to suffer increased damages. The court held that if SGI were to be found grossly negligent, the liability would not be limited to $50,000, and a jury could find damages far exceeding that amount.[26]

exculpatory clause–provision in a contract stating that one of the parties shall not be liable for damages in case of breach; also called a *limitation-of-liability clause.*

limitation-of-liability clause–provision in a contract stating that one of the parties is not liable for damages in case of breach; also called *exculpatory clause.*

---

[22] *Goldblatt v. C. P. Motion, Inc.,* 77 So. 3d 798 (Fla. App. 2011).

[23] *Medistar Corp. v. Schmidt,* 267 S.W.3d 150 (Tex. App. 2008).

[24] *Centimark v. Village Manor Associates, Ltd.,* 967 A.2d 550 (Conn. App. 2009).

[25] *Stafford v. JHL, Inc.,* 194 P.3d 315 (Wyo. 2008). See also *FNBC v. Jennessey Group, LLC,* 759 N.W.2d 808 (Iowa App. 2008).

[26] *Royal Indemnity Co. v. Security Guards, Inc,* 255 F. Supp. 2d 497 (E.D. Pa. 2003).

Validity

While contracts that exculpate persons from liability are not favored by the court because they encourage lack of care and are therefore strictly construed against the person or entity seeking to escape liability, nevertheless when the language of the contract and the intent of the parties are clearly exculpatory, the contract will be upheld. This principle arises out of the broad policy of the law, which accords to contracting parties' freedom to bind themselves as they see fit. **For Example,** the exculpatory clause in a rental contract that David Hyatt signed with Mini Storage On the Green, which was clearly exculpatory, relieved Mini Storage of liability for injuries Hyatt suffered when the unit door he was pulling down with some extra force came off its tracks and injured him.[27]

Releases

Release forms signed by participants in athletic and sporting events declaring that the sponsor, proprietor, or operator of the event shall not be liable for injuries sustained by participants because of its negligence are generally binding.[28]

CASE SUMMARY

How to Handle a Risky Business

FACTS: Chelsea Hamill attended Camp Cheley for three years. Before attending camp each summer her parents signed a liability/risk release form. In July 2004, when Hamill was 15 years old, she fell off a Cheley horse and broke her arm. Chelsea brought a negligence and gross negligence lawsuit against the summer camp. Hamill's mother testified at her deposition that she voluntarily signed the release after having "skimmed" it. At her deposition, the mother testified as follows:

Attorney: And, you know, you knew that someone such as Christopher Reeve had been tragically injured falling off a horse?

Ms. Hamill: Yes.

Attorney: Did you personally know Mr. Reeve?

Ms. Hamill: Yes.

Attorney: And so you were aware that there were significant risks associated with horseback riding?

Ms. Hamill: Yes.

Attorney: And you were aware that your daughter was going to be doing a significant amount of horseback riding?

Ms. Hamill: Yes.

Hamill's mother's interpretation of the release was that prospective negligent claims were not waived. The camp disagreed. The release stated in part:

I, on behalf of myself and my child, hereby release and waive any claim of liability against Cheley ... occurring to my child while he/she participates in any and all camp programs and activities.

I give my permission for my child to participate in all camp activities, including those described above. I acknowledge and assume the risks involved in these activities, and for any damages, illness, injury or death ... resulting from such risks for myself and my child.

(*Emphasis Added.*)

DECISION: Judgment for Camp Cheley. The release did not need to include an exhaustive list of particularized injury scenarios to be effective. Hamill's mother had more than sufficient information to allow her to assess the extent of injury possible in horseback riding and to make an "informed" decision before signing the release. The mother was informed of the intent to release "all claims," including prospective negligence claims. While exculpatory agreements are not a bar to civil liability for gross negligence, the record is devoid of evidence of gross negligence. [*Hamill v. Cheley Colorado Camps, Inc.*, 262 P.3d 945 (Colo. App. 2011)]

---

[27] *Hyatt v. Mini Storage On the Green*, 763 S.E.2d 166 (N.C. App. 2014).

[28] But see *Woodman v. Kera, LLC*, 760 N.W.2d 641 (Mich. App. 2008) where the Court of Appeals of Michigan held that a preinjury waiver signed by a parent on behalf of a five-year-old child was invalid. See also *Brooten v. Hickok Rehabilitation Services, LLC*, 831 N.W.2d 445 (Wis. App. 2013) where the court held that the release was impermissibly broad, well beyond negligence claims.

Make the Connection

Summary

When a party fails to perform a contract or performs improperly, the other contracting party may sue for damages caused by the breach. What may be recovered by the aggrieved person is stated in terms of being direct or consequential damages. Direct damages are those that ordinarily will result from the breach. Direct damages may be recovered on proof of causation and amount. Consequential damages can be recovered only if, in addition to proving causation and amount, it is shown that they were reasonably within the contemplation of the contracting parties as a probable result of a breach of the contract. The right to recover consequential damages is lost if the aggrieved party could reasonably have taken steps to avoid such damages. In other words, the aggrieved person has a duty to mitigate or reduce damages by reasonable means.

In any case, the damages recoverable for breach of contract may be limited to a specific amount by a liquidated damages clause.

In a limited number of situations, an aggrieved party may bring an action for specific performance to compel the other contracting party to perform the acts called for by the contract. Specific performance by the seller is always obtainable for the breach of a contract to sell land or real estate on the theory that such property has a unique value. With respect to other contracts, specific performance will not be ordered unless it is shown that there was some unique element present so that the aggrieved person would suffer a damage that could not be compensated for by the payment of money damages.

The aggrieved person also has the option of rescinding the contract if (1) the breach has been made concerning a material term and (2) the aggrieved party returns everything to the way it was before the contract was made.

Although there has been a breach of the contract, the effect of this breach is nullified if the aggrieved person by word or conduct waives the right to object to the breach. Conversely, an aggrieved party may accept a defective performance without thereby waiving a claim for breach if the party makes a reservation of rights. A reservation of rights can be made by stating that the defective performance is accepted "without prejudice," "under protest," or "with reservation of rights."

Learning Outcomes

After studying this chapter, you should be able to clearly explain:

19-1   What Constitutes a Breach of Contract?

LO.1   Explain what constitutes a breach of contract and an anticipatory breach of contract

See the illustration of a painting contractor's failure to properly paint a house, page 348.

See the *Tips* case in which damages are assessed for anticipatory repudiation of a contract, pages 348–349.

See the racetrack example of a "request," not an anticipatory breach, page 349.

See the *Mammoth Lakes* example involving anticipatory repudiation by conduct, page 349.

19-2   Waiver of Breach

LO.2   Describe the effect of a waiver of a breach

See the application of the waiver doctrine as applied in the Massey example, page 350.

19-3   Remedies for Breach of Contract

LO.3   Explain the range of remedies available for breach of contract

See Figure 19-1, "What Follows the Breach," page 352.

See the Spencer Adams example involving a range of monetary damages, pages 353–354.

See the boat slip for *Rookie IV* case involving rescission of a contract, page 355.

See the rare Revolutionary War musket example of specific performance, page 356.

19-4   Contract Provisions Affecting Remedies and Damages

LO.4   Explain when liquidated damages clauses are valid and invalid

See the Dow Corning faulty breast implants settlement agreement example in which liquidated damages of a $100 per day late payment were found to be unenforceable penalty provision, page 358.

LO.5   State when liability-limiting clauses and releases are valid

See the *Cheley Camps* case that illustrates how the camp successfully raised a signed parental exculpatory release as a defense in a horseback riding injury case, page 360.

Key Terms

anticipatory breach
anticipatory repudiation
breach
compensatory damages
consequential damages
direct damages

exculpatory clause
injunction
limitation-of-liability clause
liquidated damages
liquidated damages clause
nominal damages

punitive damages
remedies
reservation of rights
specific performance
waiver

Questions and Case Problems

1. The Forsyth School District contracted with Textor Construction, Inc., to build certain additions and alter school facilities, including the grading of a future softball field. Under the contract, the work was to be completed by August 1. Various delays occurred at the outset of the project attributable to the school district, and the architect's representative on the job, Mr. Hamilton, told Textor's vice president, William Textor, not to be concerned about a clause in the contract of $250 per day liquidated damages for failure to complete the job by August 1. Textor sued the school district for breach of contract regarding payment for the grading of the softball field, and the District counterclaimed for liquidated damages for 84 days at $250 per day for failure to complete the project by the August 1 date. What legal basis exists for Textor to defend against the counterclaim for failure to complete the job on time? Was it ethical for the school district to bring this counterclaim based on the facts before you? [*Textor Construction, Inc. v. Forsyth R-III School District*, 60 S.W.3d 692 (Mo. App.)]

2. Self-described "sports nut" Gary Baker signed up for a three-year club-seat "package" that entitled him and a companion to tickets for 41 Boston Bruin hockey games and 41 Boston Celtic basketball games at the New Boston Garden Corporation's Fleet Center for approximately $18,000 per year. After one year, Baker stopped paying for the tickets thinking that he would simply lose his $5,000 security deposit. New Boston sued Baker for breach of contract, seeking the balance due on the tickets of $34,866. At trial, Baker argued to the jury that although he had breached his contract, New Boston had an obligation to mitigate damages, for example, by treating his empty seats and those of others in the same situation as "rush seats" shortly before game time and selling them at a discount. New Boston argued that just as a used luxury car cannot be

returned for a refund, a season ticket cannot be canceled without consequences. Decide.

3. Rogers made a contract with Salisbury Brick Corp. that allowed it to remove earth and sand from land he owned. The contract ran for four years with provision to renew it for additional four-year terms up to a total of 96 years. The contract provided for compensation to Rogers based on the amount of earth and sand removed. By an unintentional mistake, Salisbury underpaid Rogers the amount of $863 for the months of November and December 1986. Salisbury offered this amount to Rogers, but he refused to accept it and claimed that he had been underpaid in other months. Rogers claimed that he was entitled to rescind the contract. Was he correct? [*Rogers v. Salisbury Brick Corp.*, 882 S.E.2d 915 (S.C.)]

4. Manny Fakhimi agreed to buy an apartment complex for $697,000 at an auction from David Mason. Fakhimi was obligated to put up 10 percent of the agreed-to price at the auction as a deposit. The agreement allowed Mason to keep this deposit should Fakhimi fail to come up with the remaining 90 percent of the auction price as liquidated damages for the default. Shortly after the auction, Fakhimi heard a rumor that the military base located near the apartment complex might be closing. Fakhimi immediately stopped payment on the check and defaulted on the agreement. Mason sued Fakhimi for the liquidated damages specified in the sales contract. Decide. [*Mason v. Fakhimi*, 865 P.2d 333 (Neb.)]

5. Protein Blenders, Inc., made a contract with Gingerich to buy from him the shares of stock of a small corporation. When the buyer refused to take and pay for the stock, Gingerich sued for specific performance of the contract on the ground that the value of the stock was unknown and could not be readily ascertained because it was not sold on the general market. Was he entitled to specific performance? [*Gingerich v. Protein Blenders, Inc.*, 95 N.W.2d 522 (Iowa)]

6. The buyer of real estate made a down payment. The contract stated that the buyer would be liable for damages in an amount equal to the down payment if the buyer broke the contract. The buyer refused to go through with the contract and demanded his down payment back. The seller refused to return it and claimed that he was entitled to additional damages from the buyer because the damages that he had suffered were more than the amount of the down payment. Decide. [*Waters v. Key Colony East, Inc.*, 345 So. 2d 367 (Fla. App.)]

7. Kuznicki made a contract for the installation of a fire detection system by Security Safety Corp. for $498. The contract was made one night and canceled at 9:00 the next morning. Security then claimed one-third of the purchase price from Kuznicki by virtue of a provision in the contract that "in the event of cancellation of this agreement … the owner agrees to pay 33⅓ percent of the contract price, as liquidated damages." Was Security Safety entitled to recover the amount claimed? [*Security Safety Corp. v. Kuznicki*, 213 N.E.2d 866 (Mass.)]

8. FNBC is a business brokerage firm that assists in the purchase and sale of businesses. Jennings and Hennessey were independent contractors working for FNBC. They left FNBC, and FNBC sued them for breach of their contracts with FNBC. The trial court issued a permanent injunction prohibiting the former contractors from using proprietary information and the court awarded attorneys' fees under a clause in the contract that would obligate Jennings and Hennessey to indemnify FNBC against claims "brought by persons not a party to the provision." Jennings and Hennessey appealed the decision on attorneys' fees. Decide. [*FNBC v. Jennessey Group, LLC*, 759 N.W.2d 808 (Iowa App.)]

9. Melodee Lane Lingerie Co. was a tenant in a building that was protected against fire by a sprinkler and alarm system maintained by the American District Telegraph Co. (ADT). Because of the latter's fault, the controls on the system were defective and allowed the discharge of water into the building, which damaged Melodee's property. When Melodee sued ADT, its defense was that its service contract limited its liability to 10 percent of the annual service charge made to the customer. Was this limitation valid? [*Melodee Lane Lingerie Co. v. American District Telegraph Co.*, 218 N.E.2d 661 (N.Y.)]

10. JRC Trading Corp (JRC) bought computer software and hardware from Progressive Data Systems (PDS) for $167,935, which it paid in full, to track movement of its trucks with inventory and to process transactions. The purchase agreement also called for a $7,500 per year licensing fee for an 18-year period, and it stated that in the event of default PDS could "accelerate and declare all obligations of Customer as a liquidated sum." A dispute arose between the parties, and when the case was litigated the only actual contract charges owed PDS were the license fees of $7,500 for two years. The application of the liquidated damages clause would yield an additional $120,000 cash for PDS for the future fees for 16 years without any reduction for expenses or the present cash value for the not-yet-earned fees. JRC contends that actual damages were clearly ascertainable and that the liquidated damages clause was a penalty provision that should not be enforced. Progressive argued that the court must interpret the contract as written, stating that the court has no power to rewrite the contract. Decide. [*Jefferson Randolf Corp. v. PDS*, 553 S.E.2d 304 (Ga. App.)]

11. Ken Sulejmanagic, aged 19, signed up for a course in scuba diving taught by Madison at the YMCA. Before the instruction began, Ken was required to sign a form releasing Madison and the YMCA from liability for any harm that might occur. At the end of the course, Madison, Ken, and another student went into deep water. After Ken made the final dive required by the course program, Madison left him alone in the water while he took the other student for a dive. When Madison returned, Ken could not be found, and it was later determined that he had drowned. Ken's parents sued Madison and the YMCA for negligence in the performance of the teaching contract. The defendants raised the defense that the release Ken signed shielded them from liability. The plaintiffs claimed that the release was invalid. Who was correct? [*Madison v. Superior Court*, 250 Cal. Rptr. 299 (Cal. App.)]

12. Wassenaar worked for Panos under a three-year contract stating that if the contract were terminated wrongfully by Panos before the end of the three years, he would pay as damages the salary for the remaining time that the contract had to run. After three months, Panos terminated the contract, and Wassenaar sued him for pay for the balance of the contract term. Panos claimed that this amount could not be recovered because the contract provision for the payment was a void penalty. Was this provision valid? [*Wassenaar v. Panos*, 331 N.W.2d 357 (Wis.)]

13. Soden, a contractor, made a contract to build a house for Clevert. The sales contract stated that "if either party defaults in the performance of this contract," that party would be liable to the other for attorneys' fees incurred in suing the defaulter. Soden was 61 days late in completing the contract, and some of the work was defective. In a suit by the buyer against the contractor, the contractor claimed that he was not liable for the buyer's attorneys' fees because he had made only a defective performance and because "default" in the phrase quoted meant "nonperformance of the contract." Was the contractor liable for the attorneys' fees? [*Clevert v. Soden*, 400 S.E.2d 181 (Va.)]

14. Protection Alarm Co. made a contract to provide burglar alarm security for Fretwell's home. The contract stated that the maximum liability of the alarm company was the actual loss sustained or $50, whichever was the lesser, and that this provision was agreed to "as liquidated damages and not as a penalty." When Fretwell's home was burglarized, he sued for the loss of approximately $12,000, claiming that the alarm company had been negligent.

The alarm company asserted that its maximum liability was $50. Fretwell claimed that this was invalid because it bore no relationship to the loss that could have been foreseen when the contract was made or that in fact "had been sustained." Decide.

15. Shepherd-Will made a contract to sell Emma Cousar:

> *5 acres of land adjoining property owned by the purchaser and this being formerly land of Shepherd-Will, Inc., located on north side of Highway 223. This 5 acres to be surveyed at earliest time possible at which time plat will be attached and serve as further description on property.*

Shepherd-Will owned only one 100-acre tract of land that adjoined Emma's property. This tract had a common boundary with her property of 1,140 feet. Shepherd-Will failed to perform this contract. Emma sued for specific performance of the contract. Decide. [*Cousar v. Shepherd-Will, Inc.*, 387 S.E.2d 723 (S.C. App.)]

CPA Questions

1. Master Mfg., Inc., contracted with Accur Computer Repair Corp. to maintain Master's computer system. Master's manufacturing process depends on its computer system operating properly at all times. A liquidated damages clause in the contract provided that Accur pay $1,000 to Master for each day that Accur was late responding to a service request. On January 12, Accur was notified that Master's computer system had failed. Accur did not respond to Master's service request until January 15. If Master sues Accur under the liquidated damages provision of the contract, Master will:

a. Win, unless the liquidated damage provision is determined to be a penalty.

b. Win, because under all circumstances liquidated damages provisions are enforceable.

c. Lose, because Accur's breach was *not* material.

d. Lose, because liquidated damage provisions violate public policy (5/93, Law, #25).

2. Jones, CPA, entered into a signed contract with Foster Corp. to perform accounting and review services. If Jones repudiates the contract prior to the date performance is due to begin, which of the following is *not* correct?

a. Foster could successfully maintain an action for breach of contract after the date performance was due to begin.

b. Foster can obtain a judgment ordering Jones to perform.

c. Foster could successfully maintain an action for breach of contract prior to the date performance is due to begin.

d. Foster can obtain a judgment for the monetary damages it incurred as a result of the repudiation (5/89, Law, #35).

3. Which of the following concepts affect(s) the amount of monetary damages recoverable by the nonbreaching party when a contract is breached?

	Forseeability of damages	Mitigation of damages
a.	Yes	Yes
b.	Yes	No
c.	No	Yes
d.	No	No

The Constitution of the United States

We the people of the United States of America, in order to form a more perfect union, establish justice, insure domestic tranquility, provide for the common defense, promote the general welfare, and secure the blessings of liberty to ourselves and our posterity, do ordain and establish this Constitution for the United States of America.

Article I

SECTION 1

All legislative powers herein granted shall be vested in a Congress of the United States, which shall consist of a Senate and House of Representatives.

SECTION 2

1. The House of Representatives shall be composed of members chosen every second year by the people of the several States, and the electors in each State shall have the qualifications requisite for electors of the most numerous branch of the State legislature.

2. No person shall be a representative who shall not have attained to the age of twenty-five years, and been seven years a citizen of the United States, and who shall not, when elected, be an inhabitant of that State in which he shall be chosen.

3. Representatives and direct taxes shall be apportioned among the several States which may be included within this Union, according to their respective numbers, which shall be determined by adding to the whole number of free persons, including those bound to service for a term of years, and excluding Indians not taxed, three fifths of all other persons.[1] The actual enumeration shall be made within three years after the first meeting of the Congress of the United States, and within every subsequent term of ten years, in such manner as they shall by law direct. The number of representatives shall not exceed one for every thirty thousand, but each State shall have at least one representative; and until such enumeration shall be made, the State of New Hampshire shall be entitled to choose three, Massachusetts eight, Rhode Island and Providence Plantations one, Connecticut five, New York six, New Jersey four, Pennsylvania eight, Delaware one, Maryland six, Virginia ten, North Carolina five, South Carolina five, and Georgia three.

4. When vacancies happen in the representation from any State, the executive authority thereof shall issue writs of election to fill such vacancies.

5. The House of Representatives shall choose their speaker and other officers; and shall have the sole power of impeachment.

SECTION 3

1. The Senate of the United States shall be composed of two senators from each State, chosen by the legislature thereof, for six years; and each senator shall have one vote.

2. Immediately after they shall be assembled in consequence of the first election, they shall be divided as equally as may be into three classes. The seats of the senators of the first class shall be vacated at the expiration of the second year, of the second class at the expiration of the fourth year, and of the third class at the expiration of the sixth year, so that one third may be chosen every second year; and if vacancies happen by resignation, or otherwise, during the recess of the legislature of any State, the executive thereof may make temporary appointments until the next meeting of the legislature, which shall then fill such vacancies.[2]

3. No person shall be a senator who shall not have attained to the age of thirty years, and been nine years a citizen of the United States, and who shall not, when elected, be an inhabitant of that State for which he shall be chosen.

4. The Vice President of the United States shall be President of the Senate, but shall have no vote, unless they be equally divided.

---

[1] See the 14th Amendment.

[2] See the 17th Amendment.

5. The Senate shall choose their other officers, and also a president pro tempore, in the absence of the Vice President, or when he shall exercise the office of the President of the United States.

6. The Senate shall have the sole power to try all impeachments. When sitting for that purpose, they shall be on oath or affirmation. When the President of the United States is tried, the chief justice shall preside: and no person shall be convicted without the concurrence of two thirds of the members present.

7. Judgment in cases of impeachment shall not extend further than to removal from office, and disqualification to hold and enjoy any office of honor, trust or profit under the United States: but the party convicted shall nevertheless be liable and subject to indictment, trial, judgment and punishment, according to law.

SECTION 4

1. The times, places, and manner of holding elections for senators and representatives, shall be prescribed in each State by the legislature thereof; but the Congress may at any time by law make or alter such regulations, except as to the places of choosing senators.

2. The Congress shall assemble at least once in every year, and such meeting shall be on the first Monday in December, unless they shall by law appoint a different day.

SECTION 5

1. Each House shall be the judge of the elections, returns and qualifications of its own members, and a majority of each shall constitute a quorum to do business; but a smaller number may adjourn from day to day, and may be authorized to compel the attendance of absent members, in such manner, and under such penalties as each House may provide.

2. Each House may determine the rules of its proceedings, punish its members for disorderly behavior, and, with the concurrence of two thirds, expel a member.

3. Each House shall keep a journal of its proceedings, and from time to time publish the same, excepting such parts as may in their judgment require secrecy; and the yeas and nays of the members of either House on any question shall, at the desire of one fifth of those present, be entered on the journal.

4. Neither House, during the session of Congress, shall, without the consent of the other, adjourn for more than three days, nor to any other place than that in which the two Houses shall be sitting.

SECTION 6

1. The senators and representatives shall receive a compensation for their services, to be ascertained by law, and paid out of the Treasury of the United States. They shall in all cases, except treason, felony, and breach of the peace, be privileged from arrest during their attendance at the session of their respective Houses, and in going to and returning from the same; and for any speech or debate in either House, they shall not be questioned in any other place.

2. No senator or representative shall, during the time for which he was elected, be appointed to any civil office under the authority of the United States, which shall have been created, or the emoluments whereof shall have been increased during such time; and no person holding any office under the United States shall be a member of either House during his continuance in office.

SECTION 7

1. All bills for raising revenue shall originate in the House of Representatives; but the Senate may propose or concur with amendments as on other bills.

2. Every bill which shall have passed the House of Representatives and the Senate, shall, before it becomes a law, be presented to the President of the United States; if he approves he shall sign it, but if not he shall return it, with his objections to that House in which it shall have originated, who shall enter the objections at large on their journal, and proceed to reconsider it. If after such reconsideration two thirds of that House shall agree to pass the bill, it shall be sent, together with the objections, to the other House, by which it shall likewise be reconsidered, and if approved by two thirds of that House, it shall become a law. But in all such cases the votes of both Houses shall be determined by yeas and nays, and the names of the persons voting for and against the bill shall be entered on the journal of each House respectively. If any bill shall not be returned by the President within ten days (Sundays excepted) after it shall have been presented to him, the same shall be a law, in like manner as if he had signed it, unless the Congress by their adjournment prevent its return, in which case it shall not be a law.

3. Every order, resolution, or vote to which the concurrence of the Senate and the House of Representatives may be necessary (except on a question of adjournment) shall be presented to the President of the United States; and before the same shall take effect, shall be approved

by him, or being disapproved by him, shall be repassed by two thirds of the Senate and House of Representatives, according to the rules and limitations prescribed in the case of a bill.

SECTION 8

The Congress shall have the power

1. To lay and collect taxes, duties, imposts, and excises, to pay the debts and provide for the common defense and general welfare of the United States; but all duties, imposts, and excises shall be uniform throughout the United States;

2. To borrow money on the credit of the United States;

3. To regulate commerce with foreign nations, and among the several States, and with the Indian tribes;

4. To establish a uniform rule of naturalization, and uniform laws on the subject of bankruptcies throughout the United States;

5. To coin money, regulate the value thereof, and of foreign coin, and fix the standard of weights and measures;

6. To provide for the punishment of counterfeiting the securities and current coin of the United States;

7. To establish post offices and post roads;

8. To promote the progress of science and useful arts, by securing for limited times to authors and inventors the exclusive rights to their respective writings and discoveries;

9. To constitute tribunals inferior to the Supreme Court;

10. To define and punish piracies and felonies committed on the high seas, and offenses against the law of nations;

11. To declare war, grant letters of marque and reprisal, and make rules concerning captures on land and water;

12. To raise and support armies, but no appropriation of money to that use shall be for a longer term than two years;

13. To provide and maintain a navy;

14. To make rules for the government and regulation of the land and naval forces;

15. To provide for calling forth the militia to execute the laws of the Union, suppress insurrections and repel invasions;

16. To provide for organizing, arming, and disciplining the militia, and for governing such part of them as may be employed in the service of the United States, reserving to the States respectively, the appointment of the officers, and the authority of training the militia according to the discipline prescribed by Congress;

17. To exercise exclusive legislation in all cases whatsoever, over such district (not exceeding ten miles square) as may, by cession of particular States, and the acceptance of Congress, become the seat of the government of the United States, and to exercise like authority over all places purchased by the consent of the legislature of the State in which the same shall be, for the erection of forts, magazines, arsenals, dockyards, and other needful buildings; and

18. To make all laws which shall be necessary and proper for carrying into execution the foregoing powers, and all other powers vested by this Constitution in the government of the United States, or in any department or officer thereof.

SECTION 9

1. The migration or importation of such persons as any of the States now existing shall think proper to admit, shall not be prohibited by the Congress prior to the year one thousand eight hundred and eight, but a tax or duty may be imposed on such importation, not exceeding ten dollars for each person.

2. The privilege of the writ of habeas corpus shall not be suspended, unless when in cases of rebellion or invasion the public safety may require it.

3. No bill of attainder or ex post facto law shall be passed.

4. No capitation, or other direct, tax shall be laid, unless in proportion to the census or enumeration hereinbefore directed to be taken.[3]

5. No tax or duty shall be laid on articles exported from any State.

6. No preference shall be given by any regulation of commerce or revenue to the ports of one State over those of another: nor shall vessels bound to, or from, one State be obliged to enter, clear, or pay duties in another.

7. No money shall be drawn from the treasury, but in consequence of appropriations made by law; and a regular statement and account of the receipts and expenditures of all public money shall be published from time to time.

[3] See the 16th Amendment.

8. No title of nobility shall be granted by the United States: and no person holding any office of profit or trust under them, shall, without the consent of the Congress, accept of any present, emolument, office, or title, of any kind whatever, from any king, prince, or foreign State.

SECTION 10

1. No State shall enter into any treaty, alliance, or confederation; grant letters of marque and reprisal; coin money; emit bills of credit; make anything but gold and silver coin a tender in payment of debts; pass any bill of attainder, ex post facto law, or law impairing the obligation of contracts, or grant any title of nobility.

2. No State shall, without the consent of the Congress, lay any imposts or duties on imports or exports, except what may be absolutely necessary for executing its inspection laws: and the net produce of all duties and imposts laid by any State on imports or exports, shall be for the use of the treasury of the United States; and all such laws shall be subject to the revision and control of the Congress.

3. No State shall, without the consent of the Congress, lay any duty of tonnage, keep troops, or ships of war in time of peace, enter into any agreement or compact with another State, or with a foreign power, or engage in war, unless actually invaded, or in such imminent danger as will not admit of delay.

Article II

SECTION 1

1. The executive power shall be vested in a President of the United States of America. He shall hold his office during the term of four years, and, together with the Vice President, chosen for the same term, be elected as follows:

2. Each State shall appoint, in such manner as the legislature thereof may direct, a number of electors, equal to the whole number of senators and representatives to which the State may be entitled in the Congress: but no senator or representative, or person holding an office of trust or profit under the United States, shall be appointed an elector.

The electors shall meet in their respective States, and vote by ballot for two persons, of whom one at least shall not be an inhabitant of the same State with themselves. And they shall make a list of all the persons voted for, and of the number of votes for each; which list they shall sign and certify, and transmit sealed to the seat of the government of the United States, directed to the president of the Senate. The president of the Senate shall, in the presence of the Senate and House of Representatives, open all the certificates, and the votes shall then be counted. The person having the greatest number of votes shall be the President, if such number be a majority of the whole number of electors appointed; and if there be more than one who have such majority, and have an equal number of votes, then the House of Representatives shall immediately choose by ballot one of them for President; and if no person have a majority, then from the five highest on the list the said House shall in like manner choose the President. But in choosing the President, the votes shall be taken by States, the representation from each State having one vote; a quorum for this purpose shall consist of a member or members from two thirds of the States, and a majority of all the States shall be necessary to a choice. In every case, after the choice of the President, the person having the greatest number of votes of the electors shall be the Vice President. But if there should remain two or more who have equal votes, the Senate shall choose from them by ballot the Vice President.[4]

3. The Congress may determine the time of choosing the electors, and the day on which they shall give their votes; which day shall be the same throughout the United States.

4. No person except a natural born citizen, or a citizen of the United States, at the time of the adoption of this Constitution, shall be eligible to the office of President; neither shall any person be eligible to that office who shall not have attained to the age of thirty-five years, and been fourteen years a resident within the United States.

5. In the case of removal of the President from office, or of his death, resignation, or inability to discharge the powers and duties of the said office, the same shall devolve on the Vice President, and the Congress may by law provide for the case of removal, death, resignation, or inability, both of the President and Vice President, declaring what officer shall then act as President, and such officer shall act accordingly, until the disability be removed, or a President shall be elected.

6. The President shall, at stated times, receive for his services a compensation, which shall neither be

[4] Superseded by the 12th Amendment.

increased nor diminished during the period for which he shall have been elected, and he shall not receive within that period any other emolument from the United States, or any of them.

7. Before he enter on the execution of his office, he shall take the following oath or affirmation:—"I do solemnly swear (or affirm) that I will faithfully execute the office of President of the United States, and will to the best of my ability, preserve, protect and defend the Constitution of the United States."

SECTION 2

1. The President shall be commander in chief of the army and navy of the United States, and of the militia of the several States, when called into the actual service of the United States; he may require the opinion, in writing, of the principal officer in each of the executive departments, upon any subject relating to the duties of their respective office, and he shall have power to grant reprieves and pardons for offenses against the United States, except in cases of impeachment.

2. He shall have power, by and with the advice and consent of the Senate, to make treaties, provided two thirds of the senators present concur; and he shall nominate, and by and with the advice and consent of the Senate, shall appoint ambassadors, other public ministers and consuls, judges of the Supreme Court, and all other officers of the United States, whose appointments are not herein otherwise provided for, and which shall be established by law: but the Congress may by law vest the appointment of such inferior officers, as they think proper, in the President alone, in the courts of law, or in the heads of departments.

3. The President shall have power to fill up all vacancies that may happen during the recess of the Senate, by granting commissions which shall expire at the end of their next session.

SECTION 3

He shall from time to time give to the Congress information of the state of the Union, and recommend to their consideration such measures as he shall judge necessary and expedient; he may, on extraordinary occasions, convene both Houses, or either of them, and in case of disagreement between them with respect to the time of adjournment, he may adjourn them to such time as he shall think proper; he shall receive ambassadors and other public ministers; he shall take care that the laws be faithfully executed, and shall commission all the officers of the United States.

SECTION 4

The President, Vice President, and all civil officers of the United States, shall be removed from office on impeachment for, and conviction of, treason, bribery, or other high crimes and misdemeanors.

Article III

SECTION 1

The judicial power of the United States shall be vested in one Supreme Court, and in such inferior courts as the Congress may from time to time ordain and establish. The judges, both of the Supreme and inferior courts, shall hold their offices during good behavior, and shall, at stated times, receive for their services, a compensation, which shall not be diminished during their continuance in office.

SECTION 2

1. The judicial power shall extend to all cases, in law and equity, arising under this Constitution, the laws of the United States, and treaties made, or which shall be made, under their authority;—to all cases affecting ambassadors, other public ministers and consuls;—to all cases of admiralty and maritime jurisdiction;—to controversies to which the United States shall be a party;—to controversies between two or more States; between a State and citizens of another State;[5]—between citizens of different States;—between citizens of the same State claiming lands under grants of different States, and between a State, or the citizens thereof, and foreign States, citizens or subjects.

2. In all cases affecting ambassadors, other public ministers and consuls, and those in which a State shall be party, the Supreme Court shall have original jurisdiction. In all the other cases before mentioned, the Supreme Court shall have appellate jurisdiction, both as to law and to fact, with such exceptions, and under such regulations as the Congress shall make.

3. The trial of all crimes, except in cases of impeachment, shall be by jury; and such trial shall be held in the State where the said crimes shall have been committed; but when not committed within any State, the trial shall be at such place or places as the Congress may by law have directed.

[5] See the 11th Amendment.

SECTION 3

1. Treason against the United States shall consist only in levying war against them, or in adhering to their enemies, giving them aid and comfort. No person shall be convicted of treason unless on the testimony of two witnesses to the same overt act, or on confession in open court.

2. The Congress shall have power to declare the punishment of treason, but no attainder of treason shall work corruption of blood, or forfeiture except during the life of the person attainted.

Article IV

SECTION 1

Full faith and credit shall be given in each State to the public acts, records, and judicial proceedings of every other State. And the Congress may by general laws prescribe the manner in which such acts, records and proceedings shall be proved, and the effect thereof.

SECTION 2

1. The citizens of each State shall be entitled to all privileges and immunities of citizens in the several States.[6]

2. A person charged in any State with treason, felony, or other crime, who shall flee from justice, and be found in another State, shall on demand of the executive authority of the State from which he fled, be delivered up to be removed to the State having jurisdiction of the crime.

3. No person held to service or labor in one State under the laws thereof, escaping into another, shall in consequence of any law or regulation therein, be discharged from such service or labor, but shall be delivered up on claim of the party to whom such service or labor may be due.[7]

SECTION 3

1. New States may be admitted by the Congress into this Union; but no new State shall be formed or erected within the jurisdiction of any other State, nor any State be formed by the junction of two or more States, or parts of States, without the consent of the legislatures of the States concerned as well as of the Congress.

2. The Congress shall have power to dispose of and make all needful rules and regulations respecting the territory or other property belonging to the United States; and nothing in this Constitution shall be so construed as to prejudice any claims of the United States, or of any particular State.

SECTION 4

The United States shall guarantee to every State in this Union a republican form of government, and shall protect each of them against invasion; and on application of the legislature, or of the executive (when the legislature cannot be convened) against domestic violence.

Article V

The Congress, whenever two thirds of both Houses shall deem it necessary, shall propose amendments to this Constitution, or, on the application of the legislature of two thirds of the several States, shall call a convention for proposing amendments, which in either case, shall be valid to all intents and purposes, as part of this Constitution when ratified by the legislatures of three fourths of the several States, or by conventions in three fourths thereof, as the one or the other mode of ratification may be proposed by the Congress; provided that no amendment which may be made prior to the year one thousand eight hundred and eight shall in any manner affect the first and fourth clauses in the ninth section of the first article; and that no State, without its consent, shall be deprived of its equal suffrage in the Senate.

Article VI

1. All debts contracted and engagements entered into, before the adoption of this Constitution, shall be as valid against the United States under this Constitution, as under the Confederation.[8]

2. This Constitution, and the laws of the United States which shall be made in pursuance thereof; and all treaties made, or which shall be made, under the authority of the United States, shall be the supreme law of the land; and the judges in every State shall be bound thereby, anything in the Constitution or laws of any State to the contrary notwithstanding.

3. The senators and representatives before mentioned, and the members of the several State legislatures, and all executive and judicial officers, both of the United States and of the several States, shall be bound by oath or affirmation to support this Constitution; but no

---

[6] See the 14th Amendment, Sec. 1.
[7] See the 13th Amendment.

[8] See the 14th Amendment, Sec. 4.

religious test shall ever be required as a qualification to any office or public trust under the United States.

Article VII

The ratification of the conventions of nine States shall be sufficient for the establishment of this Constitution between the States so ratifying the same.

Done in Convention by the unanimous consent of the States present the seventeenth day of September in the year of our Lord one thousand seven hundred and eighty-seven, and of the independence of the United States of America the twelfth. In witness whereof we have hereunto subscribed our names.

Amendments

First Ten Amendments passed by Congress Sept. 25, 1789.

Ratified by three-fourths of the States December 15, 1791.

Amendment I

Congress shall make no law respecting an establishment of religion, or prohibiting the free exercise thereof; or abridging the freedom of speech, or of the press; or the right of the people peaceably to assemble, and to petition the government for a redress of grievances.

Amendment II

A well regulated militia, being necessary to the security of a free State, the right of the people to keep and bear arms, shall not be infringed.

Amendment III

No soldier shall, in time of peace be quartered in any house, without the consent of the owner, nor in time of war, but in a manner to be prescribed by law.

Amendment IV

The right of the people to be secure in their persons, houses, papers, and effects, against unreasonable searches and seizures, shall not be violated, and no warrants shall issue, but upon probable cause, supported by oath or affirmation, and particularly describing the place to be searched, and the person or things to be seized.

Amendment V

No person shall be held to answer for a capital, or otherwise infamous crime, unless on a presentment or indictment of a grand jury, except in cases arising in the land or naval forces, or in the militia, when in actual service in time of war or public danger; nor shall any person be subject for the same offense to be twice put in jeopardy of life or limb; nor shall be compelled in any criminal case to be a witness against himself, nor be deprived of life, liberty, or property, without due process of law; nor shall private property be taken for public use without just compensation.

Amendment VI

In all criminal prosecutions, the accused shall enjoy the right to a speedy and public trial, by an impartial jury of the State and district wherein the crime shall have been committed, which district shall have been previously ascertained by law, and to be informed of the nature and cause of the accusation; to be confronted with the witnesses against him; to have compulsory process for obtaining witnesses in his favor, and to have the assistance of counsel for his defense.

Amendment VII

In suits at common law, where the value in controversy shall exceed twenty dollars, the right of trial by jury shall be preserved, and no fact tried by a jury shall be otherwise reexamined in any court of the United States, then according to the rules of the common law.

Amendment VIII

Excessive bail shall not be required, nor excessive fines imposed, nor cruel and unusual punishments inflicted.

Amendment IX

The enumeration in the Constitution of certain rights shall not be construed to deny or disparage others retained by the people.

Amendment X

The powers not delegated to the United States by the Constitution, nor prohibited by it to the States, are reserved to the States respectively, or to the people.

Amendment XI

Passed by Congress March 5, 1794. Ratified January 8, 1798.

The judicial power of the United States shall not be construed to extend to any suit in law or equity, commenced or prosecuted against one of the United States by citizens of another State, or by citizens or subjects of any foreign State.

Amendment XII

Passed by Congress December 12, 1803. Ratified September 25, 1804.

The electors shall meet in their respective States, and vote by ballot for President and Vice President, one of whom, at least, shall not be an inhabitant of the same State with themselves; they shall name in their ballots the person voted for as President, and in distinct ballots, the person voted for as Vice President, and they shall make distinct lists of all persons voted for as President and of all persons voted for as Vice President, and of the number of votes for each, which lists they shall sign and certify, and transmit sealed to the seat of the government of the United States, directed to the President of the Senate;—The President of the Senate shall, in the presence of the Senate and House of Representatives, open all the certificates and the votes shall then be counted;—The person having the greatest number of votes for President, shall be the President, if such number be a majority of the whole number of electors appointed; and if no person have such majority, then from the persons having the highest numbers not exceeding three on the list of those voted for as President, the House of Representatives shall choose immediately, by ballot, the President. But in choosing the President, the votes shall be taken by States, the representation from each State having one vote; a quorum for this purpose shall consist of a member or members from two thirds of the States, and a majority of all the States shall be necessary to a choice. And if the House of Representatives shall not choose a President whenever the right of choice shall devolve upon them, before the fourth day of March next following, then the Vice President shall act as President, as in the case of the death or other constitutional disability of the President. The person having the greatest number of votes as Vice President shall be the Vice President, if such number be a majority of the whole number of electors appointed, and if no person have a majority, then from the two highest numbers on the list, the Senate shall choose the Vice President; a quorum for the purpose shall consist of two thirds of the whole number of Senators, and a majority of the whole number shall be necessary to a choice. But no person constitutionally ineligible to the office of President shall be eligible to that of Vice President of the United States.

Amendment XIII

Passed by Congress February 1, 1865. Ratified December 18, 1865.

SECTION 1

Neither slavery nor involuntary servitude, except as punishment for crime whereof the party shall have been duly convicted, shall exist within the United States, or any place subject to their jurisdiction.

SECTION 2

Congress shall have power to enforce this article by appropriate legislation.

Amendment XIV

Passed by Congress June 16, 1866. Ratified July 23, 1868.

SECTION 1

All persons born or naturalized in the United States, and subject to the jurisdiction thereof, are citizens of the United States and of the State wherein they reside. No State shall make or enforce any law which shall abridge the privileges or immunities of citizens of the United States; nor shall any State deprive any person of life, liberty, or property, without due process of law; nor deny to any person within its jurisdiction the equal protection of the laws.

SECTION 2

Representatives shall be apportioned among the several States according to their respective numbers, counting the whole number of persons in each State, excluding Indians not taxed. But when the right to vote at any election for the choice of electors for President and Vice President of the United States, representatives in Congress, the executive and judicial officers of a State, or the members of the legislature thereof, is denied to any of the male inhabitants of such State, being twenty-one years of age, and citizens of the United States, or in any way abridged, except for participation in rebellion, or other crime, the basis of representation therein shall be reduced in the proportion which the number of such male citizens shall bear to the whole number of male citizens twenty-one years of age in such State.

SECTION 3

No person shall be a senator or representative in Congress, or elector of President and Vice President, or hold any office, civil or military, under the United States, or under any State, who having previously taken an oath, as a member of Congress, or as an officer of the United States, or as a member of any State legislature, or as an executive or judicial officer of any State, to support the Constitution of the United States, shall have engaged in insurrection or rebellion against the same, or given aid or comfort to the enemies thereof. But Congress may by a vote of two thirds of each House, remove such disability.

SECTION 4

The validity of the public debt of the United States, authorized by law, including debts incurred for payment of pensions and bounties for services in suppressing insurrection or rebellion, shall not be questioned. But neither the United States nor any State shall assume or pay any debt or obligation incurred in aid of insurrection or rebellion against the United States, or any claim for the loss or emancipation of any slave; but all such debts, obligations, and claims shall be held illegal and void.

SECTION 5

The Congress shall have power to enforce, by appropriate legislation, the provisions of this article.

Amendment XV

Passed by Congress February 27, 1869. Ratified March 30, 1870.

SECTION 1

The right of citizens of the United States to vote shall not be denied or abridged by the United States or by any State on account of race, color, or previous condition of servitude.

SECTION 2

The Congress shall have power to enforce this article by appropriate legislation.

Amendment XVI

Passed by Congress July 12, 1909. Ratified February 25, 1913.

The Congress shall have power to lay and collect taxes on incomes, from whatever source derived, without apportionment among the several States, and without regard to any census or enumeration.

Amendment XVII

Passed by Congress May 16, 1912. Ratified May 31, 1913.

The Senate of the United States shall be composed of two senators from each State, elected by the people thereof, for six years; and each senator shall have one vote. The electors in each State shall have the qualifications requisite for electors of the most numerous branch of the State legislature.

When vacancies happen in the representation of any State in the Senate, the executive authority of such State shall issue writs of election to fill such vacancies: Provided, That the legislature of any State may empower the executive thereof to make temporary appointments until the people fill the vacancies by election as the legislature may direct.

This amendment shall not be so construed as to affect the election or term of any senator chosen before it becomes valid as part of the Constitution.

Amendment XVIII

Passed by Congress December 17, 1917. Ratified January 29, 1919.

After one year from the ratification of this article, the manufacture, sale, or transportation of intoxicating liquors within, the importation thereof into, or the exportation thereof from the United States and all territory subject to the jurisdiction thereof for beverage purposes is hereby prohibited.

The Congress and the several States shall have concurrent power to enforce this article by appropriate legislation.

This article shall be inoperative unless it shall have been ratified as an amendment to the Constitution by the legislatures of the several States, as provided in the Constitution, within seven years from the date of the submission hereof to the States by Congress.

Amendment XIX

Passed by Congress June 5, 1919. Ratified August 26, 1920.

The right of citizens of the United States to vote shall not be denied or abridged by the United States or by any State on account of sex.

The Congress shall have power by appropriate legislation to enforce the provisions of this article.

Amendment XX

Passed by Congress March 3, 1932. Ratified January 23, 1933.

SECTION 1

The terms of the President and Vice President shall end at noon on the 20th day of January, and the terms of Senators and Representatives at noon on the 3d day of January, of the years in which such terms would have ended if this article had not been ratified; and the terms of their successors shall then begin.

SECTION 2

The Congress shall assemble at least once in every year, and such meeting shall begin at noon on the 3d day of January, unless they shall by law appoint a different day.

SECTION 3

If, at the time fixed for the beginning of the term of the President, the President-elect shall have died, the Vice President-elect shall become President. If a President shall not have been chosen before the time fixed for the beginning of his term, or if the President-elect shall have failed to qualify, then the Vice President-elect shall act as President until a President shall have qualified; and the Congress may by law provide for the case wherein neither a President-elect nor a Vice President-elect shall have qualified, declaring who shall then act as President, or the manner in which one who is to act shall be selected, and such person shall act accordingly until a President or Vice President shall have qualified.

SECTION 4

The Congress may by law provide for the case of the death of any of the persons from whom the House of Representatives may choose a President whenever the right of choice shall have devolved upon them, and for the case of the death of any of the persons from whom the Senate may choose a Vice President whenever the right of choice shall have devolved upon them.

SECTION 5

Sections 1 and 2 shall take effect on the 15th day of October following the ratification of this article.

SECTION 6

This article shall be inoperative unless it shall have been ratified as an amendment to the Constitution by the legislatures of three-fourths of the several States within seven years from the date of its submission.

Amendment XXI

Passed by Congress February 20, 1933. Ratified December 5, 1933.

SECTION 1

The eighteenth article of amendment to the Constitution of the United States is hereby repealed.

SECTION 2

The transportation or importation into any State, Territory, or possession of the United States for delivery or use therein of intoxicating liquors in violation of the laws thereof, is hereby prohibited.

SECTION 3

This article shall be inoperative unless it shall have been ratified as an amendment to the Constitution by conventions in the several States, as provided in the Constitution, within seven years from the date of the submission thereof to the States by the Congress.

Amendment XXII

Passed by Congress March 24, 1947. Ratified February 26, 1951.

SECTION 1

No person shall be elected to the office of the President more than twice, and no person who has held the office of President, or acted as President, for more than two years of a term to which some other person was elected President shall be elected to the office of the President more than once. But this article shall not apply to any person holding the office of President when this article was proposed by the Congress, and shall not prevent any person who may be holding the office of President, or acting as President, during the term within which this article becomes operative from holding the office of President or acting as President during the remainder of such term.

SECTION 2

This article shall be inoperative unless it shall have been ratified as an amendment to the Constitution by the legislatures of three-fourths of the several States within seven years from the date of its submission to the States by the Congress.

Amendment XXIII

Passed by Congress June 16, 1960. Ratified April 3, 1961.

SECTION 1

The District constituting the seat of Government of the United States shall appoint in such manner as the Congress may direct:

A number of electors of President and Vice President equal to the whole number of Senators and

Representatives in Congress to which the District would be entitled if it were a State, but in no event more than the least populous State; they shall be in addition to those appointed by the States, but they shall be considered, for the purposes of the election of President and Vice President, to be electors appointed by a State; and they shall meet in the District and perform such duties as provided by the twelfth article of amendment.

SECTION 2

The Congress shall have power to enforce this article by appropriate legislation.

Amendment XXIV

Passed by Congress August 27, 1962. Ratified February 4, 1964.

SECTION 1

The right of citizens of the United States to vote in any primary or other election for President or Vice President, for electors for President or Vice President, or for Senator or Representative in Congress, shall not be denied or abridged by the United States or any State by reason of failure to pay any poll tax or other tax.

SECTION 2

The Congress shall have power to enforce this article by appropriate legislation.

Amendment XXV

Passed by Congress July 6, 1965. Ratified February 23, 1967.

SECTION 1

In case of the removal of the President from office or of his death or resignation, the Vice President shall become President.

SECTION 2

Whenever there is a vacancy in the office of the Vice President, the President shall nominate a Vice President who shall take office upon confirmation by a majority vote of both Houses of Congress.

SECTION 3

Whenever the President transmits to the President pro tempore of the Senate and the Speaker of the House of Representatives his written declaration that he is unable to discharge the powers and duties of his office, and until he transmits to them a written declaration to the contrary, such powers and duties shall be discharged by the Vice President as Acting President.

SECTION 4

Whenever the Vice President and a majority of either the principal officers of the executive departments or of such other body as Congress may by law provide, transmit to the President pro tempore of the Senate and the Speaker of the House of Representatives their written declaration that the President is unable to discharge the powers and duties of his office, the Vice President shall immediately assume the powers and duties of the office as Acting President.

Thereafter, when the President transmits to the President pro tempore of the Senate and the Speaker of the House of Representatives his written declaration that no inability exists, he shall resume the powers and duties of his office unless the Vice President and a majority of either the principal officers of the executive department or of such other body as Congress may by law provide, transmit within four days to the President pro tempore of the Senate and the Speaker of the House of Representatives their written declaration that the President is unable to discharge the powers and duties of his office. Thereupon Congress shall decide the issue, assembling within forty-eight hours for that purpose if not in session. If the Congress, within twenty-one days after receipt of the latter written declaration, or, if Congress is not in session, within twenty-one days after Congress is required to assemble, determines by two-thirds vote of both Houses that the President is unable to discharge the powers and duties of his office, the Vice President shall continue to discharge the same as Acting President; otherwise, the President shall resume the powers and duties of his office.

Amendment XXVI

Passed by Congress March 23, 1971. Ratified July 5, 1971.

SECTION 1

The right of citizens of the United States, who are eighteen years of age or older, to vote shall not be denied or abridged by the United States or by any State on account of age.

Amendment XXVII

Passed by Congress September 25, 1789. Ratified May 18, 1992.

No law, varying the compensation for the services of the Senators and Representatives, shall take effect, until an election of Representatives shall have intervened.

Glossary

A

abate—put a stop to a nuisance; reduce or cancel a legacy because the estate of the decedent is insufficient to make payment in full.

absolute guaranty—agreement that creates the same obligation for the guarantor as a suretyship does for the surety; a guaranty of payment creates an absolute guaranty.

absolute privilege—complete defense against the tort of defamation, as in the speeches of members of Congress on the floor and witnesses in a trial.

abstract of title—history of the transfers of title to a given piece of land, briefly stating the parties to and the effect of all deeds, wills, and judicial proceedings relating to the land.

acceptance—unqualified assent to the act or proposal of another, such as the acceptance of an offer to make a contract; the acceptance of a draft (bill of exchange); the acceptance of goods delivered by a seller, or a gift of a deed.

acceptor—drawee who has accepted the liability of paying the amount of money specified in a draft.

accommodation party—person who signs an instrument to lend credit to another party to the paper.

accord and satisfaction—agreement to substitute for an existing debt some alternative form of discharging that debt, coupled with the actual discharge of the debt by the substituted performance.

acknowledgment—admission or confirmation, generally of an instrument and usually made before a person authorized to administer oaths, such as a notary public.

acquired distinctiveness—through advertising, use and association, over time, an ordinary descriptive word or phrase has taken on a new source-identifying meaning and functions as a mark in the eyes of the public.

act-of-state doctrine—doctrine whereby every sovereign state is bound to respect the independence of every other sovereign state, and the courts of one country will not sit in judgment of another government's acts done within its own territory.

adeemed—canceled; as in a specifically bequeathed property being sold or given away by the testator prior to death, thus canceling the bequest.

adjustable rate mortgage (ARM)—mortgage with variable financing charges over the life of the loan.

administrative agency—government body charged with administering and implementing legislation.

administrative law—law governing administrative agencies.

administrative law judge—judicial figure who hears administrative agency actions.

Administrative Procedure Act—federal law that establishes the operating rules for administrative agencies.

administrative regulations—rules made by state and federal administrative agencies.

administrator, administratrix—person (man, woman) appointed to wind up and settle the estate of a person who has died without a will.

admissibility—the quality of the evidence in a case that allows it to be presented to the jury.

adverse possession—hostile possession of real estate, which when actual, visible, notorious, exclusive, and continued for the required time, will vest the title to the land in the person in such adverse possession.

advising bank—bank that tells beneficiary that letter of credit has been issued.

affidavit—statement of facts under oath; executed before a notary public or anyone authorized to administer oaths.

affirm—action taken by an appellate court that approves the decision of the court below.

affirmative action plan (AAP)—plan to have a diverse and representative workforce.

after-acquired goods—goods acquired after a security interest has attached.

agency—the relationship that exists between a person identified as a principal and another by virtue of which the latter may make contracts with third persons on behalf of the principal. (Parties–principal, agent, third person)

agent—person or firm who is authorized by the principal or by operation of law to make contracts with third persons on behalf of the principal.

airbill—document of title issued to a shipper whose goods are being sent via air.

alteration—unauthorized change or completion of a negotiable instrument designed to modify the obligation of a party to the instrument.

alternative payees—those persons to whom a negotiable instrument is made payable, any one of whom may indorse and take delivery of it.

ambiguous—having more than one reasonable interpretation.

answer—what a defendant must file to admit or deny facts asserted by the plaintiff.

anticipatory breach—promisor's repudiation of the contract prior to the time that performance is required when such repudiation is accepted by the promisee as a breach of the contract.

anticipatory repudiation—repudiation made in advance of the time for performance of the contract obligations.

antilapse statutes—statutes providing that the children or heirs of a deceased beneficiary may take the legacy in the place of the deceased beneficiary.

apparent authority—appearance of authority created by the principal's words or conduct.

appeal—taking a case to a reviewing court to determine whether the judgment of the lower court or administrative agency was correct. (Parties–appellant, appellee)

appellate jurisdiction—the power of a court to hear and decide a given class of cases on appeal from another court or administrative agency.

arbitration—the settlement of disputed questions, whether of law or fact, by one or more arbitrators by whose decision the parties agree to be bound.

Article 2—section of the Uniform Commercial Code that governs contracts for the sale of goods.

articles of copartnership—see *partnership agreement.*

articles of incorporation—see *certificate of incorporation.*

articles of partnership—see *partnership agreement.*

assignee—third party to whom contract benefits are transferred.

assignment—transfer of a right. Generally used in connection with personal property rights, as rights under a contract, commercial paper, an insurance policy, a mortgage, or a lease. (Parties—assignor, assignee)

assignor—party who assigns contract rights to a third party.

association tribunal—a court created by a trade association or group for the resolution of disputes among its members.

assumption—mortgage transfers in which the transferee and mortgagor are liable and the property is subject to foreclosure by the mortgagee if payments are not made.

attestation clause—clause that indicates a witness has observed either the execution of the will or the testator's acknowledgment of the writing as the testator's will.

attorney in fact—agent authorized to act for another under a power of attorney.

attorney-client privilege—right of individual to have discussions with his/her attorney kept private and confidential.

attractive nuisance doctrine—a rule imposing liability upon a landowner for injuries sustained by small children playing on the land when the landowner permits a condition to exist or maintains equipment that a reasonable person should realize would attract small children who could not realize the danger. The rule does not apply if an unreasonable burden would be imposed upon the landowner in taking steps to protect the children.

authorities—corporations formed by government that perform public service.

automatic perfection—perfection given by statute without specific filing or possession requirements on the part of the creditor.

automatic stay—order to prevent creditors from taking action such as filing suits or seeking foreclosure against the debtor.

B

bad check laws—laws making it a criminal offense to issue a bad check with intent to defraud.

bailee—person who accepts possession of a property.

bailee's lien—specific, possessory lien of the bailee upon the goods for work done to them. Commonly extended by statute to any bailee's claim for compensation, eliminating the necessity of retention of possession.

bailment—relationship that exists when personal property is delivered into the possession of another under an agreement, express or implied, that the identical property will be returned or will be delivered in accordance with the agreement. (Parties—bailor, bailee)

bailment for mutual benefit—bailment in which the bailor and bailee derive a benefit from the bailment.

bailor—person who turns over the possession of a property.

balance sheet test—comparison of assets to liabilities made to determine solvency.

bankruptcy—procedure by which one unable to pay debts may surrender all assets in excess of any exemption claim to the court for administration and distribution to creditors, and the debtor is given a discharge that releases him from the unpaid balance due on most debts.

bankruptcy courts—court of special jurisdiction to determine bankruptcy issues.

battle of the forms—merchants' exchanges of invoices and purchase orders with differing boilerplate terms.

bearer—person in physical possession of commercial paper payable to bearer, a document of title directing delivery to bearer, or an investment security in bearer form.

bearer paper—instrument with no payee, payable to cash or payable to bearer.

bedrock view—a strict constructionist interpretation of a constitution.

beneficiary—person to whom the proceeds of a life insurance policy are payable, a person for whose benefit property is held in trust, or a person given property by a will; the ultimate recipient of the benefit of a funds transfer.

benefit corporation—for-profit corporation that sets a goal to create a public benefit while still providing economic returns to its investors.

beneficiary's bank—the final bank, which carries out the payment order, in the chain of a transfer of funds.

bequest—gift of personal property by will.

best available treatment—a water treatment that is the most current and best available through research, even though it may not be the treatment used most frequently.

best conventional treatment—a water treatment that is generally used among industries; not always the best treatment available.

bicameral—a two-house form of the legislative branch of government.

bilateral contract—agreement under which one promise is given in exchange for another.

bill of lading—document issued by a carrier acknowledging the receipt of goods and the terms of the contract of transportation.

bill of sale—writing signed by the seller reciting that the personal property therein described has been sold to the buyer.

blackmail—extortion demands made by a nonpublic official.

blank indorsement—an indorsement that does not name the person to whom the paper, document of title, or investment security is negotiated.

blocking laws—laws that prohibit the disclosure, copying, inspection, or removal of documents located in the enacting country in compliance with orders from foreign authorities.

blue sky laws—state statutes designed to protect the public from the sale of worthless stocks and bonds.

bona fide—in good faith; without any fraud or deceit.

bond—a debt investment; a loan to a corporation or government entity usually for a defined period of time at a fixed interest rate.

bond indenture—agreement setting forth the contractual terms of a particular bond issue.

book value—value found by dividing the value of the corporate assets by the number of shares outstanding.

breach—failure to act or perform in the manner called for in a contract.

breach of the peace—violation of the law in the repossession of the collateral.

brownfields—land that is a designated Superfund cleanup site but which lies fallow because no one is willing to risk liability by buying the property, even when the hazardous waste has been removed, or property no one is willing to spend the money to remove the hazardous waste.

bubble concept—method for determining total emissions in one area; all sources are considered in an area.

business ethics—balancing the goal of profits with values of individuals and society.

business judgment rule (BJR)—rule that allows management immunity from liability for corporate acts where there is a reasonable indication that the acts were made in good faith with due care.

bylaws—rules and regulations enacted by a corporation to govern the affairs of the corporation and its shareholders, directors, and officers.

C

cancellation provision—crossing out of a part of an instrument or a destruction of all legal effect of the instrument, whether by act of party, upon breach by the other party, or pursuant to agreement or decree of court.

capital stock—declared money value of the outstanding stock of the corporation.

cargo insurance—insurance that protects a cargo owner against financial loss if goods being shipped are lost or damaged at sea.

carrier—individual or organization undertaking the transportation of goods.

case law—law that includes principles that are expressed for the first time in court decisions.

cash surrender value—sum paid the insured upon the surrender of a policy to the insurer.

cash tender offer—general offer to all shareholders of a target corporation to purchase their shares for cash at a specified price.

cashier's check—draft drawn by a bank on itself.

cause of action—right to damages or other judicial relief when a legally protected right of the plaintiff is violated by an unlawful act of the defendant.

cease-and-desist order—order issued by a court or administrative agency to stop a practice that it decides is improper.

certificate of deposit (CD)—promise-to-pay instrument issued by a bank.

certificate of incorporation—written approval from the state or national government for a corporation to be formed.

certificate of stock—document evidencing a shareholder's ownership of stock issued by a corporation.

certified check—check for which the bank has set aside in a special account sufficient funds to pay it; payment is made when check is presented regardless of amount in drawer's account at that time; discharges all parties except certifying bank when holder requests certification.

cestui que trust—beneficiary of the trust.

CF—cost and freight.

Chapter 7 bankruptcy—liquidation form of bankruptcy under federal law.

Chapter 11 bankruptcy—reorganization form of bankruptcy under federal law.

Chapter 13 bankruptcy—proceeding of consumer debt readjustment plan bankruptcy.

charging order—order by a court, after a business partner's personal assets are exhausted, requiring that the partner's share of the profits be paid to a creditor until the debt is discharged.

charter—grant of authority from a government to exist as a corporation. Generally replaced today by a certificate of incorporation approving the articles of incorporation.

check—order by a depositor on a bank to pay a sum of money to a payee; a bill of exchange drawn on a bank and payable on demand.

choice-of-law clause—clause in an agreement that specifies which law will govern should a dispute arise.

chose in action—intangible personal property in the nature of claims against another, such as a claim for accounts receivable or wages.

CIF—cost, insurance, and freight.

civil disobedience—the term used when natural law proponents violate positive law.

civil laws—the laws that define the rights of one person against another.

claim—creditor's right to payment.

Clayton Act—a federal law that prohibits price discrimination.

Clean Air Act—federal legislation that establishes standards for air pollution levels and prevents further deterioration of air quality.

Clean Water Act—federal legislation that regulates water pollution through a control system.

close corporation—corporation whose shares are held by a single shareholder or a small group of shareholders.

close-connection doctrine—circumstantial evidence, such as an ongoing or a close relationship, that can serve as notice of a problem with an instrument.

COD—cash on delivery.

coinsurance clause—clause requiring the insured to maintain insurance on property up to a stated amount and providing that to the extent that this is not done, the insured is to be deemed a coinsurer with the insurer, so that the latter is liable only for its proportionate share of the amount of insurance required to be carried.

collateral—property pledged by a borrower as security for a debt.

comity—principle of international and national law that the laws of all nations and states deserve the respect legitimately demanded by equal participants.

commerce clause—that section of the U.S. Constitution allocating business regulation between federal and state governments.

commercial impracticability—situation that occurs when costs of performance rise suddenly and performance of a contract will result in a substantial loss.

commercial lease—any nonconsumer lease.

commercial paper—written, transferable, signed promise or order to pay a specified sum of money; a negotiable instrument.

commercial unit—standard of the trade for shipment or packaging of a good.

commission merchant—bailee to whom goods are consigned for sale.

commission or factorage—consignee's compensation.

common carrier—carrier that holds out its facilities to serve the general public for compensation without discrimination.

common law—the body of unwritten principles originally based upon the usages and customs of the community that were recognized and enforced by the courts.

common stock—stock that has no right or priority over any other stock of the corporation as to dividends or distribution of assets upon dissolution.

community property—cotenancy held by husband and wife in property acquired during their marriage under the law of some of the states, principally in the southwestern United States.

comparative negligence—defense to negligence that allows plaintiff to recover reduced damages based on his level of fault.

compensatory damages—sum of money that will compensate an injured plaintiff for actual loss.

complaint—the initial pleading filed by the plaintiff in many actions, which in many states may be served as original process to acquire jurisdiction over the defendant.

composition of creditors—agreement among creditors that each shall accept a part payment as full payment in consideration of the other creditors doing the same.

Comprehensive Environmental Response, Compensation, and Liability Act (CERCLA)—federal law that assigns liability for cleanup of hazardous sites.

computer crimes—wrongs committed using a computer or with knowledge of computers.

concealment—failure to volunteer information not requested.

condition—stipulation or prerequisite in a contract, will, or other instrument.

condition precedent—event that if unsatisfied would mean that no rights would arise under a contract.

condition subsequent—event whose occurrence or lack thereof terminates a contract.

condominium—combination of co-ownership and individual ownership.

confidential relationship—relationship in which, because of the legal status of the parties or their respective physical or mental conditions or knowledge, one party places full confidence and trust in the other.

conflict of interest—conduct that compromises an employee's allegiance to that company.

conglomerate—relationship of a parent corporation to subsidiary corporations engaged in diversified fields of activity unrelated to the field of activity of the parent corporation.

consent decrees—informal settlements of enforcement actions brought by agencies.

consequential damages—damages the buyer experiences as a result of the seller's breach with respect to a third party; also called *special damages.*

consideration—promise or performance that the promisor demands as the price of the promise.

consignee—(1) person to whom goods are shipped; (2) dealer who sells goods for others.

consignment—bailment made for the purpose of sale by the bailee. (Parties—consignor, consignee)

consignor—(1) person who delivers goods to the carrier for shipment; (2) party with title who turns goods over to another for sale.

consolidation (of corporations)—combining of two or more corporations in which the corporate existence of each one ceases and a new corporation is created.

conspiracy—agreement between two or more persons to commit an unlawful act.

constitution—a body of principles that establishes the structure of a government and the relationship of the government to the people who are governed.

constructive bailment—bailment imposed by law as opposed to one created by contract, whereby the bailee must preserve the property and redeliver it to the owner.

constructive delivery—See "*symbolic delivery.*"

constructive eviction—act or omission of the landlord that substantially deprives the tenant of the use and enjoyment of the premises.

consumer—any buyer afforded special protections by statute or regulation.

consumer credit—credit for personal, family, and household use.

Consumer Financial Protection Bureau—consumer protection bureau located within the Federal Reserve that now has jurisdiction over all consumer credit issues and statutes.

consumer goods—goods used or bought primarily for personal, family, or household use.

consumer lease—lease of goods by a natural person for personal, family, or household use.

Consumer Product Safety Improvement Act (CPSIA)—federal law that sets standards for the types of paints used in toys, a response to the lead paint found in toys made in China; requires tracking for international production; increases penalties.

contract—a binding agreement based on the genuine assent of the parties, made for a lawful object, between competent parties, in the form required by law, and generally supported by consideration.

contract carrier—carrier that transports on the basis of individual contracts that it makes with each shipper.

contract interference—tort in which a third party interferes with others' freedom to contract.

contract of adhesion—contract offered by a dominant party to a party with inferior bargaining power on a take-it-or-leave-it basis.

contract under seal—contract executed by affixing a seal or making an impression on the paper or on some adhering substance such as wax attached to the document.

contracting agent—agent with authority to make contracts; person with whom the buyer deals.

Contracts for the International Sale of Goods (CISG)—uniform international contract code contracts for international sale of goods.

contractual capacity—ability to understand that a contract is being made and to understand its general meaning.

contribution—right of a co-obligor who has paid more than a proportionate share to demand that other obligors pay their *pro rata* share.

contributory negligence—negligence of the plaintiff that contributes to injury and at common law bars recovery from the defendant although the defendant may have been more negligent than the plaintiff.

Controlling the Assault of Non-Solicited Pornography and Marketing (CAN-SPAM) Act—allows private companies to bring suit against spammers for their unauthorized use of Internet Service Providers (ISPs).

conversion—act of taking personal property by a person not entitled to it and keeping it from its true owner or prior possessor without consent.

cooperative—group of two or more persons or enterprises that acts through a common agent with respect to a common objective, such as buying or selling.

copyright—exclusive right given by federal statute to the creator of a literary or an artistic work to use, reproduce, and display the work.

corporation—artificial being created by government grant, which for many purposes is treated as a natural person.

corporation by estoppel—corporation that comes about when parties estop themselves from denying that the corporation exists.

corporation de jure—corporation with a legal right to exist by virtue of law.

correspondent bank—will honor the letter of credit from the domestic bank of the buyer.

cost plus—method of determining the purchase price or contract price equal to the seller's or contractor's costs plus a stated percentage as the profit.

co-sureties—sureties for the same debt.

cotenancy—when two or more persons hold concurrent rights and interests in the same property.

Council on Environmental Quality (CEQ)—federal agency that establishes national policies on environmental quality and then recommends legislation to implement these policies.

counterclaim—a claim that the defendant in an action may make against the plaintiff.

counteroffer—proposal by an offeree to the offeror that changes the terms of, and thus rejects, the original offer.

course of dealing—pattern of performance between two parties to a contract.

court—a tribunal established by government to hear and decide matters properly brought to it.

covenant against encumbrances—guarantee that conveyed land is not subject to any right or interest of a third person.

covenant of further assurances—promise that the grantor of an interest in land will execute any additional documents required to perfect the title of the grantee.

covenant of quiet enjoyment—covenant by the grantor of an interest in land to not disturb the grantee's possession of the land.

covenant of right to convey—guarantee that the grantor of an interest in land, if not the owner, has the right or authority to make the conveyance to a new owner.

covenant of seisin—guarantee that the grantor of an interest in land owns the estate conveyed to a new owner.

covenants (or warranties) of title—grantor's covenants of a deed that guarantee such matters as the right to make the conveyance, to ownership of the property, to freedom of the property from encumbrances, or that the grantee will not be disturbed in the quiet enjoyment of the land.

credit transfer—transaction in which a person making payment, such as a buyer, requests payment be made to the beneficiary's bank.

creditor—person (seller or lender) who is owed money; also may be a secured party.

crime—violation of the law that is punished as an offense against the state or government.

criminal laws—the laws that define wrongs against society.

cross-examination—the examination made of a witness by the attorney for the adverse party.

cumulative voting—system of voting for directors in which each shareholder has as many votes as the number of voting shares owned multiplied by the number of directors to be elected, and such votes can be distributed for the various candidates as desired.

customary authority—authority of an agent to do any act that, according to the custom of the community, usually accompanies the transaction for which the agent is authorized to act.

cybersquatters—term for those who register and set up domain names on the Internet for resale to the famous users of the names in question.

D

de facto—existing in fact as distinguished from as of right, as in the case of an officer or a corporation purporting to act as such without being elected to the office or having been properly incorporated.

debenture—unsecured bond of a corporation, with no specific corporate assets pledged as security for payment.

debit transfer—transaction in which a beneficiary entitled to money requests payment from a bank according to a prior agreement.

debtor—buyer on credit (i.e., a borrower).

decedent—person whose estate is being administered.

deed—instrument by which the grantor (owner of land) conveys or transfers the title to a grantee.

defamation—untrue statement by one party about another to a third party.

defendant—party charged with a violation of civil or criminal law in a proceeding.

defined benefit plan—an employer established pension fund obligating the employer to make specified future payments to participants upon retirement.

defined contribution plan—a plan providing individual accounts for each employee participant with benefits defined solely on the amounts contributed by each employee with matching contributions by the employer.

definite time—time of payment computable from the face of the instrument.

delegated powers—powers expressly granted the national government by the Constitution.

delegation—transfer to another of the right and power to do an act.

delegation of duties—transfer of duties by a contracting party to another person who is to perform them.

delivery—constructive or actual possession.

demand draft—draft that is payable upon presentment.

demurrer—a pleading to dismiss the adverse party's pleading for not stating a cause of action or a defense.

deposition—the testimony of a witness taken out of court before a person authorized to administer oaths.

depositor—person, or bailor, who gives property for storage.

derivative (secondary) action—secondary action for damages or breach of contract brought by one or more corporate shareholders against directors, officers, or third persons.

development statement—statement that sets forth significant details of a real estate or property development as required by the federal Land Sales Act.

devise—gift of real estate made by will.

devisee—beneficiary of a devise.

direct damages—losses that are caused by breach of a contract.

direct examination—examination of a witness by his or her attorney.

directed verdict—a direction by the trial judge to the jury to return a verdict in favor of a specified party to the action.

disability—any incapacity resulting from bodily injury or disease to engage in any occupation for remuneration or profit.

discharge in bankruptcy—order of the bankruptcy court relieving the debtor from obligation to pay the unpaid balance of most claims.

disclosed principal—principal whose identity is made known by the agent as well as the fact that the agent is acting on the principal's behalf.

discovery—procedures for ascertaining facts prior to the time of trial in order to eliminate the element of surprise in litigation.

dishonor—status when the primary party refuses to pay the instrument according to its terms.

disinherited—excluded from sharing in the estate of a decedent.

Dispute Settlement Body (DSB)—means provided by the World Trade Organization for member nations to resolve trade disputes rather than engage in unilateral trade sanctions or a trade war.

distinctiveness—capable of serving the source-identifying function of a mark.

distribution *per stirpes*—distribution of an estate made in as many equal parts as there are family lines represented in the nearest generation; also known as *stirpital distribution.*

distributor—entity that takes title to goods and bears the financial and commercial risks for the subsequent sale of the goods.

divestiture order—a court order to dispose of interests that could lead to a monopoly.

divisible contract—agreement consisting of two or more parts, each calling for corresponding performances of each part by the parties.

document of title—document treated as evidence that a person is entitled to receive, hold, and dispose of the document and the goods it covers.

Dodd-Frank Wall Street Reform and Consumer Protection Act—federal legislation passed following the financial markets collapse that includes consumer protections as well as market and mortgage lending reforms.

domestic corporation—corporation that has been incorporated by the state in question as opposed to incorporation by another state.

dominant tenement—land that is benefited by an easement.

donee—recipient of a gift.

donor—person making a gift.

double indemnity—provision for payment of double the amount specified by the insurance contract if death is caused by an accident and occurs under specified circumstances.

draft, or bill of exchange—an unconditional order in writing by one person upon another, signed by the person giving it, and ordering the person to whom it is directed to pay upon demand or at a definite time a sum certain in money to order or to bearer.

drawee—person to whom the draft is addressed and who is ordered to pay the amount of money specified in the draft.

drawer—person who writes out and creates a draft or bill of exchange, including a check.

due diligence—process of checking the environmental history and nature of land prior to purchase.

due process—the constitutional right to be heard, question witnesses, and present evidence.

due process clause—a guarantee of protection against the loss of property or rights without the chance to be heard.

dumping—selling goods in another country at less than fair value.

duress—conduct that deprives the victim of free will and that generally gives the victim the right to set aside any transaction entered into under such circumstances.

duty—obligation of law imposed on a person to perform or refrain from performing a certain act.

E

easement—permanent right that one has in the land of another, as the right to cross another's land or an easement of way.

easement by implication—easement not specifically created by deed that arises from the circumstances of the parties and the land location and access.

economic duress—threat of financial loss.

Economic Espionage Act (EEA)—federal law that makes it a felony to copy, download, transmit, or in any way transfer proprietary files, documents, and information from a computer to an unauthorized person.

economic strikers—union strikers trying to enforce bargaining demands when an impasse has been reached in the negotiation process for a collective bargaining agreement.

effects doctrine—doctrine stating that U.S. courts will assume jurisdiction and will apply antitrust laws to conduct outside of the United States when the activity of business firms has a direct and substantial effect on U.S. commerce; the rule has been modified to require that the effect on U.S. commerce also be direct and foreseeable.

effluent guidelines—EPA standards for maximum ranges of discharge into water.

electronic funds transfer (EFT)—any transfer of funds (other than a transaction originated by a check, draft, or similar paper instrument) that is initiated through an electronic terminal, a telephone, a computer, or a magnetic tape so as to authorize a financial institution to debit or credit an account.

Electronic Funds Transfer Act (EFTA)—federal law that provides consumers with rights and protections in electronic funds transfers.

eleemosynary corporation—corporation organized for a charitable or benevolent purpose.

embezzlement—statutory offense consisting of the unlawful conversion of property entrusted to the wrongdoer.

eminent domain—power of government and certain kinds of corporations to take private property against the objection of the owner, provided the taking is for a public purpose and just compensation is made for it.

emissions offset policy—controls whether new factories can be built in a nonattainment area.

employment-at-will doctrine—doctrine in which the employer has historically been allowed to terminate the employment contract at any time for any reason or for no reason.

en banc—the term used when the full panel of judges on the appellate court hears a case.

encoding warranty—warranty made by any party who encodes electronic information on an instrument; a warranty of accuracy.

Endangered Species Act (ESA)—federal law that identifies and protects species that are endangered from development or other acts that threaten their existence.

endowment insurance—insurance that pays the face amount of the policy if the insured dies within the policy period.

entitlement theory—another name for Nozick's theory that we all have certain rights that must be honored and protected by government.

environmental impact statement (EIS)—formal report prepared under NEPA to document findings on the impact of a federal project on the environment.

equitable title—beneficial interest in a trust.

equity—the body of principles that originally developed because of the inadequacy of the rules then applied by the common law courts of England.

escalation clause—provision for the automatic increase of the rent at periodic intervals.

escheat—transfer to the state of the title to a decedent's property when the owner of the property dies intestate and is not survived by anyone capable of taking the property as heir.

estate in fee—largest estate possible in which the owner has absolute and entire interest in the land.

estoppel—principle by which a person is barred from pursuing a certain course of action or of disputing the truth of certain matters.

ethical egoism—theory of ethics that we should all act in our own self-interest; the Ayn Rand theory that separates guilt from acting in our own self-interest.

ethics—a branch of philosophy dealing with values that relate to the nature of human conduct and values associated with that conduct.

ex post facto **law**—a law making criminal an act that was lawful when done or that increases the penalty when done. Such laws are generally prohibited by constitutional provisions.

exculpatory clause—provision in a contract stating that one of the parties is not liable for damages in case of breach; also called *limitation-of-liability clause*.

executed contract—agreement that has been completely performed.

execution—the carrying out of a judgment of a court, generally directing that property owned by the defendant be sold and the proceeds first be used to pay the execution or judgment creditor.

executive branch—the branch of government (e.g., the president) formed to execute the laws.

executor, executrix—person (man, woman) named in a will to administer the estate of the decedent.

executory contract—agreement by which something remains to be done by one or both parties.

exhaustion of administrative remedies—requirement that an agency make its final decision before the parties can go to court.

existing goods—goods that physically exist and are owned by the seller at the time of a transaction.

exoneration—agreement or provision in an agreement that one party shall not be held liable for loss; the right of the surety to demand that those primarily liable pay the claim for which the surety is secondarily liable.

expert witness—one who has acquired special knowledge in a particular field as through practical experience or study, or both, whose opinion is admissible as an aid to the trier of fact.

export sale—direct sale to customers in a foreign country.

express authority—authority of an agent to perform a certain act.

express authorization—authorization of an agent to perform a certain act.

express contract—agreement of the parties manifested by their words, whether spoken or written.

express warranty—statement by the defendant relating to the goods, which statement is part of the basis of the bargain.

extortion—illegal demand by a public officer acting with apparent authority.

F

factor—bailee to whom goods are consigned for sale.

false imprisonment—intentional detention of a person without that person's consent; called the *shopkeeper's tort* when shoplifters are unlawfully detained.

FAS—free alongside the named vessel.

federal district court—a general trial court of the federal system.

Federal Register—government publication issued five days a week that lists all administrative regulations, all presidential proclamations and executive orders, and other documents and classes of documents that the president or Congress direct to be published.

Federal Register Act—federal law requiring agencies to make public disclosure of proposed rules, passed rules, and activities.

Federal Sentencing Guidelines—federal standards used by judges in determining mandatory sentence terms for those convicted of federal crimes.

federal system—the system of government in which a central government is given power to administer to national concerns while individual states retain the power to administer to local concerns.

fee simple defeasibles—fee simple interest that can be lost if restrictions on its use are violated.

fee simple estate—highest level of land ownership; full interest of unlimited duration.

felony—criminal offense that is punishable by confinement in prison for more than one year or by death, or that is expressly stated by statute to be a felony.

field warehousing—stored goods under the exclusive control of a warehouse but kept on the owner's premises rather than in a warehouse.

Fifth Amendment—constitutional protection against self-incrimination; also guarantees due process.

finance lease—three-party lease agreement in which there is a lessor, a lessee, and a financier.

financing statement—brief statement (record) that gives sufficient information to alert third persons that a particular creditor may have a security interest in the collateral described.

fire insurance policy—a contract that indemnifies the insured for property destruction or damage caused by fire.

firm offer—offer stated to be held open for a specified time, under the UCC, with respect to merchants.

first-in-time provision—creditor whose interest attached first has priority in the collateral when two creditors have a secured interest.

first-to-perfect basis—rule of priorities that holds that first in time in perfecting a security interest, mortgage, judgment, lien, or other property attachment right should have priority.

fixture—personal property attached to or adapted to real estate.

floating lien—claim in a changing or shifting stock of goods of the buyer.

FOB place of destination—shipping contract that requires the seller to deliver goods to the buyer.

FOB place of shipment—contract that requires the seller to arrange for shipment only.

forbearance—refraining from doing an act.

forcible entry and detainer—action by the landlord to have the tenant removed for nonpayment of rent.

foreclosure—procedure for enforcing a mortgage resulting in the public sale of the mortgaged property and, less commonly, in merely barring the right of the mortgagor to redeem the property from the mortgage.

foreign corporation—corporation incorporated under the laws of another state.

Foreign Corrupt Practices Act (FCPA)—federal law that makes it a felony to influence decision makers in other countries for the purpose of obtaining business, such as contracts for sales and services; also imposes financial reporting requirements on certain U.S. corporations.

Foreign Trade Antitrust Improvements Act—the act that requires that the defendant's conduct have a "direct, substantial, and reasonably foreseeable effect" on domestic commerce.

forged or unauthorized indorsement—instrument indorsed by an agent for a principal without authorization or authority.

forgery—fraudulently making or altering an instrument that apparently creates or alters a legal liability of another.

formal contracts—written contracts or agreements whose formality signifies the parties' intention to abide by the terms.

Fourth Amendment—privacy protection in the U.S. Constitution; prohibits unauthorized searches and seizures.

franchise—privilege or authorization, generally exclusive, to engage in a particular activity within a particular geographic area, such as a government franchise to operate a taxi company within a specified city, or a private franchise as the grant by a manufacturer of a right to sell products within a particular territory or for a particular number of years.

franchise agreement—sets forth rights of franchisee to use trademarks, etc., of franchisor.

Franchise Rule—FTC rule requiring detailed disclosures and prohibiting certain practices.

franchisee—person to whom franchise is granted.

franchising—granting of permission to use a trademark, trade name, or copyright under specified conditions; a form of licensing.

franchisor—party granting the franchise.

fraud—intentional making a false statement of fact, with knowledge or reckless indifference that it is false with resulting reliance by another.

fraud in the inducement—fraud that occurs when a person is persuaded or induced to execute an instrument because of fraudulent statements.

fraud-on-the-market—a theory that in an open and developed securities market, the price of a stock is determined by the information on the company available to the public, and misleading statements will defraud purchasers of stock even if they do not directly rely on these statements.

Freedom of Information Act—federal law permitting citizens to request documents and records from administrative agencies.

freight insurance—insures that shipowner will receive payment for transportation charges.

full warranty—obligation of a seller to fix or replace a defective product within a reasonable time without cost to the buyer.

funds transfer—communication of instructions or requests to pay a specific sum of money to the credit of a specified account or person without an actual physical passing of money.

fungible goods—homogeneous goods of which any unit is the equivalent of any other unit.

future goods—goods that exist physically but are not owned by the seller and goods that have not yet been produced.

G

garnishment—the name given in some states to attachment proceedings.

general agent—agent authorized by the principal to transact all affairs in connection with a particular type of business or trade or to transact all business at a certain place.

general corporation code—state's code listing certain requirements for creation of a corporation.

general jurisdiction—the power to hear and decide most controversies involving legal rights and duties.

general legacies—certain sums of money bequeathed to named persons by the testator; to be paid out of the decedent's assets generally without specifying any particular fund or source from which the payment is to be made.

general partner—partnership in which the partners conduct as co-owners a business for profit, and each partner has a right to take part in the management of the business and has unlimited liability; general partners publicly and actively engage in the transaction of firm business.

general partners—managers of a partnership who have personal liability for the partnership debts.

gift—title to an owner's personal property voluntarily transferred by a party not receiving anything in exchange.

gift causa mortis—gift, made by the donor in the belief that death was immediate and impending, that is revoked or is revocable under certain circumstances.

good faith—absence of knowledge of any defects or problems; "pure heart and an empty head."

goods—anything movable at the time it is identified as the subject of a transaction.

grantee—new owner of a land conveyance.

grantor—owner who transfers or conveys an interest in land to a new owner.

gratuitous bailment—bailment in which the bailee does not receive any compensation or advantage.

guarantor—one who undertakes the obligation of guaranty.

guaranty—agreement or promise to answer for a debt; an undertaking to pay the debt of another if the creditor first sues the debtor.

guaranty of collection—form of guaranty in which creditor cannot proceed against guarantor until after proceeding against debtor.

guaranty of payment—absolute promise to pay when a debtor defaults.

guest—transient who contracts for a room or site at a hotel.

H

hearing officer (or examiner)—another name for an administrative law judge.

hearsay evidence—statements made out of court that are offered in court as proof of the information contained in the statements and that, subject to many exceptions, are not admissible in evidence.

holder—someone in possession of an instrument that runs to that person (i.e., is made payable to that person, is indorsed to that person, or is bearer paper).

holder in due course—a holder who has given value, taken in good faith without notice of dishonor, defenses, or that instrument is overdue, and who is afforded special rights or status.

holder through a holder in due course—holder of an instrument who attains holder-in-due-course status because a holder in due course has held it previous to him or her.

holographic will—unwitnessed will written by hand.

homeowners insurance policy—combination of standard fire insurance and comprehensive personal liability insurance.

hotelkeeper—one regularly engaged in the business of offering living accommodations to all transient persons.

hull insurance—insurance that covers physical damage on a freight-moving vessel.

I

identification—point in the transaction when the buyer acquires an interest in the goods subject to the contract.

identified—term applied to particular goods selected by either the buyer or the seller as the goods called for by the sales contract.

illusory promise—promise that in fact does not impose any obligation on the promisor.

impeach—using prior inconsistent evidence to challenge the credibility of a witness.

implied contract—contract expressed by conduct or implied or deduced from the facts.

implied warranty—warranty that was not made but is implied by law.

implied warranty of the merchantability—group of promises made by the seller, the most important of which is that the goods are fit for the ordinary purposes for which they are sold.

impostor rule—an exception to the rules on liability for forgery that covers situations such as the embezzling payroll clerk.

in pari delicto—equally guilty; used in reference to a transaction as to which relief will not be granted to either party because both are equally guilty of wrongdoing.

incidental authority—authority of an agent that is reasonably necessary to execute express authority.

incidental damages—incurred by the nonbreaching party as part of the process of trying to cover (buy substitute goods) or sell (selling subject matter of contract to another); includes storage fees, commissions, and the like.

income—money earned by the principal, or property in trust, and distributed by the trustee.

incontestability clause—provision that after the lapse of a specified time the insurer cannot dispute the policy on the ground of misrepresentation or fraud of the insured or similar wrongful conduct.

incorporation by reference—contract consisting of both the original or skeleton document and the detailed statement that is incorporated in it.

incorporator—one or more natural persons or corporations who sign and file appropriate incorporation forms with a designated government official.

indemnity—right of a person secondarily liable to require that a person primarily liable pay for loss sustained when the secondary party discharges the obligation that the primary party should have discharged; an undertaking to pay another a sum of money to indemnify when loss is incurred.

indemnity contract—agreement by one person, for consideration, to pay another person a sum of money in the event that the other person sustains a specified loss.

indenture trustee—usually a commercial banking institution, to represent the interests of the bondholders and ensure that the terms and covenants of the bond issue are met by the corporation.

independent contractor—contractor who undertakes to perform a specified task according to the terms of a contract but over whom the other contracting party has no control except as provided for by the contract.

indorsee—party to whom special indorsement is made.

indorsement—signature of the payee on an instrument.

indorser—secondary party (or obligor) on a note.

informal contract—simple oral or written contract.

informal settlements—negotiated disposition of a matter before an administrative agency, generally without public sanctions.

injunction—order of a court of equity to refrain from doing (negative injunction) or to do (affirmative or mandatory injunction) a specified act.

inland marine—insurance that covers domestic shipments of goods over land and inland waterways.

insider—full-time corporate employee or a director or their relatives.

insider information—privileged information on company business known only to employees.

insolvency—excess of debts and liabilities over assets, or inability to pay debts as they mature.

instruction—summary of the law given to jurors by the judge before deliberation begins.

insurable interest—the right to hold a valid insurance policy on a person or property.

insurance—a plan of security against risks by charging the loss against a fund created by the payments made by policyholders.

insurance agent—agent of an insurance company.

insurance broker—independent contractor who is not employed by any one insurance company.

insured—person to whom the promise in an insurance contract is made.

insurer—promisor in an insurance contract.

integrity—the adherence to one's values and principles despite the costs and consequences.

intentional infliction of emotional distress—tort that produces mental anguish caused by conduct that exceeds all bounds of decency.

intentional tort—civil wrong that results from intentional conduct.

inter vivos gift—any transaction that takes place between living persons and creates rights prior to the death of any of them.

interest in the authority—form of agency in which an agent has been given or paid for the right to exercise authority.

interest in the subject matter—form of agency in which an agent is given an interest in the property with which that agent is dealing.

interlineation—writing between the lines or adding to the provisions of a document, the effect thereof depending upon the nature of the document.

intermediary bank—bank between the originator and the beneficiary bank in the transfer of funds.

interrogatories—written questions used as a discovery tool that must be answered under oath.

intervenors—in administrative actions, third parties who have an interest in the issues being determined by an ALJ.

intestate—condition of dying without a will as to any property.

intestate succession—distribution, made as directed by statute, of a decedent's property not effectively disposed of by will.

invasion of privacy—tort of intentional intrusion into the private affairs of another.

invitee—person who enters another's land by invitation.

involuntary bankruptcy—proceeding in which a creditor or creditors file the petition for relief with the bankruptcy court.

issuer—party who issues a document such as a letter of credit or a document of title such as a warehouse receipt or bill of lading.

J

joint and several liability—disproportionate satisfaction of partnership debt rendering each partner liable for the entire debt with the right to contribution from other partners.

joint liability—apportions partners' responsibility for partnership debt equally.

joint tenancy—estate held jointly by two or more with the right of survivorship as between them unless modified by statute.

joint venture—relationship in which two or more persons or firms combine their labor or property for a single undertaking and share profits and losses equally unless otherwise agreed.

judge—primary officer of the court.

judgment lien—lien obtained through the courts.

judgment n.o.v. (or *non obstante veredicto*, "notwithstanding the verdict")—a judgment entered after verdict upon the motion of the losing party on the ground that the verdict is so wrong that a judgment should be entered the opposite of the verdict.

judicial branch—the branch of government (e.g., the courts) formed to interpret the laws.

jurisdiction—the power of a court to hear and determine a given class of cases; the power to act over a particular defendant.

jurisdictional rule of reason—rule that balances the vital interests, including laws and policies, of the United States with those of a foreign country.

jury—a body of citizens sworn by a court to determine by verdict the issues of fact submitted to them.

K

Kant's categorical imperative—a standard of ethics that requires that we avoid one-sided benefit for us as a result of the conduct or decision.

L

land—earth, including all things embedded in or attached thereto, whether naturally or by the act of humans.

landlord—one who leases real property to another.

law—the order or pattern of rules that society establishes to govern the conduct of individuals and the relationships among them.

lease—agreement between the owner of property and a tenant by which the former agrees to give possession of the property to the latter for payment of rent. (Parties—landlord or lessor, tenant or lessee)

leasehold estate—interest of a tenant in rented land.

legacy—gift of money made by will.

legal title—title held by the trustee in a trust situation.

legatee—beneficiary who receives a gift of personal property by will.

legislative branch—the branch of government (e.g., Congress) formed to make the laws.

lessee—one who has a possessory interest in real or personal property under a lease; a tenant.

lessor—one who conveys real or personal property by a lease; a landlord.

letter of credit—commercial device used to guarantee payment to a seller, primarily in an international business transaction.

letters of administration—written authorization given to an administrator of an estate as evidence of appointment and authority.

letters testamentary—written authorization given to an executor of an estate as evidence of appointment and authority.

liability insurance—covers the ship-owner's liability if the ship causes damage to another ship or its cargo.

libel—written or visual defamation without legal justification.

license—personal privilege to do some act or series of acts upon the land of another, as the placing of a sign thereon, not amounting to an easement or a right of possession.

licensee—someone on another's premises with the permission of the occupier, whose duty is to warn the licensee of nonobvious dangers.

licensing—transfer of technology rights to a product so that it may be produced by a different business organization in a foreign country in exchange for royalties and other payments as agreed.

lien—claim or right, against through judgment or levy.

life estate—an estate for the duration of a life.

limitation-of-liability clause—provision in a contract stating that one of the parties is not liable for damages in case of breach; also called *exculpatory clause*.

limited covenant—any covenant that does not provide the complete protection of a full covenant.

limited defenses—defenses available to secondary parties if the presenting party is a holder in due course.

limited liability company (LLC)—a partnership for federal tax treatment and the limited liability feature of the corporate form of business organization.

limited liability partnership (LLP)—partnership in which at least one partner has a liability limited to the loss of the capital contribution made to the partnership.

limited partner—partner who neither takes part in the management of the partnership nor appears to the public to be a general partner.

limited partnership—partnership that can be formed by "one or more general partners and one or more limited partners."

limited (special) jurisdiction—the authority to hear only particular kinds of cases.

limited warranty—any warranty that does not provide the complete protection of a full warranty.

lineals—relationship that exists when one person is a direct descendant of the other; also called *lineal descendants*.

liquidated damages—provision stipulating the amount of damages to be paid in the event of default or breach of contract.

liquidated damages clause—specification of exact compensation in case of a breach of contract.

liquidation—process of converting property into money whether of particular items of property or of all the assets of a business or an estate.

living trust—trust created to take effect within the lifetime of the settlor; also called *inter vivos* trust.

living will—document by which individuals may indicate that if they become unable to express their wishes and are in an irreversible, incurable condition, they do not want life-sustaining medical treatments.

living-document view—the term used when a constitution is interpreted according to changes in conditions.

lottery—any plan by which a consideration is given for a chance to win a prize; it consists of three elements: (1) there must be a payment of money or something of value for an opportunity to win, (2) a prize must be available, and (3) the prize must be offered by lot or chance.

M

mailbox rule—timing for acceptance tied to proper acceptance.

maker—party who writes or creates a promissory note.

malpractice—when services are not properly rendered in accordance with commonly accepted standards; negligence by a professional in performing his or her skill.

marine insurance—policies that cover perils relating to the transportation of goods.

market power—the ability to control price and exclude competitors.

market value—price at which a share of stock can be voluntarily bought or sold in the open market.

mask work—specific form of expression embodied in a chip design, including the stencils used in manufacturing semiconductor chip products.

mass picketing—illegal tactic of employees massing together in great numbers to effectively shut down entrances of the employer's facility.

maturity date—date that a corporation is required to repay a loan to a bondholder.

means test—new standard under the Reform Act that requires the court to find that the debtor does not have the means to repay creditors; goes beyond the past requirement of petitions being granted on the simple assertion of the debtor saying, "I have debts."

mechanic's lien—claim by laborers or materials suppliers for property improvements.

mediation—the settlement of a dispute through the use of a messenger who carries to each side of the dispute the issues and offers in the case.

merchant—seller who deals in specific goods classified by the UCC.

merger (of corporations)—combining of corporations by which one absorbs the other and continues to exist, preserving its original charter and identity while the other corporation ceases to exist.

minitrial—a trial held on portions of the case or certain issues in the case.

Miranda warnings—warnings required to prevent self-incrimination in a criminal matter.

mirror image rule—common law contract rule on acceptance that requires language to be absolutely the same as the offer, unequivocal and unconditional.

misdemeanor—criminal offense with a sentence of less than one year that is neither treason nor a felony.

misrepresentation—false statement of fact made innocently without any intent to deceive.

mistrial—a court's declaration that terminates a trial and postpones it to a later date; commonly entered when evidence has been of a highly prejudicial character or when a juror has been guilty of misconduct.

money—medium of exchange.

money order—draft issued by a bank or a nonbank.

moral relativists—those who make decisions based on circumstances and not on the basis of any predefined standards.

mortgage—interest in land given by the owner to a creditor as security for the payment of the creditor for a debt, the nature of the interest depending upon the law of the state where the land is located. (Parties— mortgagor, mortgagee)

most-favored-nation—clause in treaties between countries whereby any privilege granted to one member is extended to all members of the treaty.

motion for summary judgment—request that the court decide a case on basis of law only because there are no material issues disputed by the parties.

motion to dismiss—a pleading that may be filed to attack the adverse party's pleading as not stating a cause of action or a defense.

N

National Environmental Policy Act (NEPA)—federal law that mandates study of a project's impact on the environment before it can be undertaken by any federal agency.

National Pollutant Discharge Elimination System (NPDES)—EPA system for regulating point source emissions into water.

national treatment—a WTO requirement in which a country may not discriminate between its own products and foreign products or services.

natural law—a system of principles to guide human conduct independent of, and sometimes contrary to, enacted law and discovered by man's rational intelligence.

necessaries—things indispensable or absolutely necessary for the sustenance of human life.

negligence—failure to exercise due care under the circumstances that results in harm proximately caused to one owed a duty to exercise due care.

negotiability—quality of an instrument that affords special rights and standing.

negotiable bill of lading—document of title that by its terms calls for goods to be delivered "to the bearer" or "to the order of" a named person.

negotiable instrument—drafts, promissory notes, checks, and certificates of deposit that, in proper form, give special rights as "negotiable commercial paper."

negotiable warehouse receipt—receipt that states the covered goods will be delivered "to the bearer" or "to the order of."

negotiation—the transfer of commercial paper by indorsement and delivery by the person to whom it is then payable in the case of order paper and by physical transfer in the case of bearer paper.

Noise Control Act—federal law that controls noise emissions from low-flying aircraft.

nominal damages—nominal sum awarded the plaintiff in order to establish that legal rights have been violated although the plaintiff in fact has not sustained any actual loss or damages.

nonattainment areas—"dirty" areas that do not meet federal standards under the Clean Air Act.

nonconforming use—use of land that conflicts with a zoning ordinance at the time the ordinance goes into effect.

nonconsumer lease—lease that does not satisfy the definition of a consumer lease; also known as a *commercial lease.*

nonnegotiable bill of lading—See *straight bill of lading.*

nonnegotiable instrument—contract, note, or draft that does not meet negotiability requirements of Article 3.

nonnegotiable warehouse receipt—receipt that states the covered goods received will be delivered to a specific person.

notice of dishonor—notice that an instrument has been dishonored; such notice can be oral, written, or electronic but is subject to time limitations.

notice statute—statute under which the last good-faith or bona fide purchaser holds the title.

notice-race statute—statute under which the first bona fide purchaser to record the deed holds the title.

novation—substitution for an old contract with a new one that either replaces an existing obligation with a new obligation or replaces an original party with a new party.

nuisance—conduct that harms or prejudices another in the use of land or that harms or prejudices the public.

O

obligee—promisee who can claim the benefit of the obligation.

obligor—promisor.

ocean marine—policies that cover transportation of goods in vessels in international and coastal trade.

offer—expression of an offeror's willingness to enter into a contractual agreement.

offeree—person to whom an offer is made.

offeror—person who makes an offer.

Oil Pollution Act—federal law that assigns cleanup liability for oil spills in U.S. waters.

open meeting law—law that requires advance notice of agency meeting and public access.

opening statements—statements by opposing attorneys that tell the jury what their cases will prove.

operation of law—attaching of certain consequences to certain facts because of legal principles that operate automatically as contrasted with consequences that arise because of the voluntary action of a party designed to create those consequences.

option contract—contract to hold an offer to make a contract open for a fixed period of time.

order of relief—the order from the bankruptcy judge that starts the protection for the debtor; when the order of relief is entered by the court, the debtor's creditors must stop all proceedings and work through the bankruptcy court to recover debts (if possible). Court finding that creditors have met the standards for bankruptcy petitions.

order paper—instrument payable to the order of a party.

original jurisdiction—the authority to hear a controversy when it is first brought to court.

originator—party who originates the funds transfer.

output contract—contract of a producer to sell its entire production or output to a given buyer.

outstanding—name for shares of a company that have been issued to stockholders.

overdraft—negative balance in a drawer's account.

P

par value—specified monetary amount assigned by an issuing corporation for each share of its stock.

parol evidence rule—rule that prohibits the introduction in evidence of oral or written statements made prior to or contemporaneously with the execution of a complete written contract, deed, or instrument, in the absence of fraud, accident, or mistake.

partially disclosed principal—principal whose existence is made known but whose identity is not.

partner—one of two or more persons who jointly own and carry on a business for profit.

partnership—pooling of capital resources and the business or professional talents of two or more individuals (partners) with the goal of making a profit.

partnership agreement—document prepared to evidence the contract of the parties. (Parties—partners or general partners)

party—person involved in a legal transaction; may be a natural person, an artificial person (e.g., a corporation), or an unincorporated enterprise (e.g., a governmental agency).

past consideration—something that has been performed in the past and which, therefore, cannot be consideration for a promise made in the present.

payable to order—term stating that a negotiable instrument is payable to the order of any person described in it or to a person or order.

payee—party to whom payment is to be made.

payment order—direction given by an originator to his or her bank or by any bank to a subsequent bank to make a specified funds transfer.

Pension Benefit Guaranty Corporation (PBGC)—an insurance plan to protect employees covered by defined benefit plans in case an employer is unable to meet its payment obligations from the employer's pension fund.

per capita—method of distributing estate assets on an equal-per-person basis.

perfected security interest—security interest with priority because of filing, possession, automatic, or temporary priority status.

periodic tenancy—tenancy that continues indefinitely for a specified rental period until terminated; often called a month-to-month tenancy.

personal property—property that is movable or intangible, or rights in such things.

personal representative—administrator or executor who represents decedents under UPC.

per stirpes—method for distribution of an estate that divides property equally down family lines.

physical duress—threat of physical harm to person or property.

plaintiff—party who initiates a lawsuit.

pleadings—the papers filed by the parties in an action in order to set forth the facts and frame the issues to be tried, although, under some systems, the pleadings merely give notice or a general indication of the nature of the issues.

pledge—bailment given as security for the payment of a debt or the performance of an obligation owed to the pledgee. (Parties—pledgor, pledgee)

point sources—direct discharges into bodies of water.

police power—the power to govern; the power to adopt laws for the protection of the public health, welfare, safety, and morals.

policy—paper evidencing the contract of insurance.

positive law—law enacted and codified by governmental authority.

possession—exclusive dominion and control of property.

possibility of reverter—nature of the interest held by the grantor after conveying land outright but subject to a condition or provision that may cause the grantee's interest to become forfeited and the interest to revert to the grantor or heirs.

postdate—to insert or place on an instrument a later date than the actual date on which it was executed.

postdating—inserting or placing on an instrument a later date than the actual date on which it was executed.

potentially responsible parties (PRPs)—those beyond actual polluters who could be responsible for cleanup costs.

power of attorney—written authorization to an agent by the principal.

precedent—a decision of a court that stands as the law for a particular problem in the future.

predatory lending—a practice on the part of the subprime lending market whereby lenders take advantage of less sophisticated consumers or those who are desperate for funds by using the lenders' superior bargaining positions to obtain credit terms that go well beyond compensating them for their risk.

predicate act—qualifying underlying offense for RICO liability.

preemption—the federal government's superior regulatory position over state laws on the same subject area.

preemptive right—shareholder's right upon the increase of a corporation's capital stock to be allowed to subscribe to such a percentage of the new shares as the shareholder's old shares bore to the former total capital stock.

preferences—transfers of property by a debtor to one or more specific creditors to enable these creditors to obtain payment for debts owed.

preferential transfers—certain transfers of money or security interests in the time frame just prior to bankruptcy that can be set aside if voidable.

preferred stock—stock that has a priority or preference as to payment of dividends or upon liquidation, or both.

prescription—acquisition of a right to use the land of another, as an easement, by making hostile, visible, and notorious use of the land, continuing for the period specified by the local law.

presentment—formal request for payment on an instrument.

price discrimination—the charging practice by a seller of different prices to different buyers for commodities of similar grade and quality, resulting in reduced competition or a tendency to create a monopoly.

prima facie—evidence that, if believed, is sufficient by itself to lead to a particular conclusion.

primary offerings—the original distribution of securities by the issuing corporations.

primary party—party to whom the holder or holder in due course must turn first to obtain payment.

primary picketing—legal presentations in front of a business notifying the public of a labor dispute.

primum non nocere—above all, do no harm.

principal—person or firm who employs an agent; the person who, with respect to a surety, is primarily liable to the third person or creditor; property held in trust.

principal debtor—original borrower or debtor.

prior art—a showing that an invention as a whole would have been obvious to a person of ordinary skill in the art when the invention was patented.

private carrier—carrier owned by the shipper, such as a company's own fleet of trucks.

private corporation—corporation organized for charitable and benevolent purposes or for purposes of finance, industry, and commerce.

private law—the rules and regulations parties agree to as part of their contractual relationships.

private nuisance—nuisance that affects only one or a few individuals.

privileges and immunities clause—a clause that entitles a person going into another state to make contracts, own property, and engage in business to the same extent as citizens of that state.

privity—succession or chain of relationship to the same thing or right, such as privity of contract, privity of estate, privity of possession.

privity of contract—relationship between a promisor and the promisee.

privity rule—succession or chain of relationship to the same thing or right, such as privity of contract, privity of estate, privity of possession.

pro rata—proportionately, or divided according to a rate or standard.

probate—procedure for formally establishing or proving that a given writing is the last will and testament of the person who purportedly signed it.

procedural law—the law that must be followed in enforcing rights and liabilities.

process—paperwork served personally on a defendant in a civil case.

product disparagement—false statements made about a product or business.

profit—right to take a part of the soil or produce of another's land, such as timber or water.

promisee—person to whom a promise is made.

promisor—person who makes a promise.

promissory estoppels—doctrine that a promise will be enforced although it is not supported by consideration when the promisor should have reasonably expected that the promise would induce action or forbearance of a definite and substantial character on the part of the promised and injustice can be avoided only by enforcement of the promise.

promissory note—unconditional promise in writing made by one person to another, signed by the maker engaging to pay on demand, or at a definite time, a sum certain in money to order or to bearer. (Parties—maker, payee)

promoters—persons who plan the formation of the corporation and sell or promote the idea to others.

proof of claim—written statement, signed by the creditor or an authorized representative, setting forth any claim made against the debtor and the basis for it.

property report—condensed version of a property development statement filed with the secretary of HUD and given to a prospective customer at least 48 hours before signing a contract to buy or lease property.

prosecutor—party who originates a criminal proceeding.

prospectus—information provided to each potential purchaser of securities setting forth the key information contained in the registration statement.

proxy—written authorization by a shareholder to another person to vote the stock owned by the shareholder; the person who is the holder of such a written authorization.

public corporation—corporation that has been established for governmental purposes and for the administration of public affairs.

public nuisance—nuisance that affects the community or public at large.

public policy—certain objectives relating to health, morals, and integrity of government that the law seeks to advance by declaring invalid any contract that conflicts with those objectives even though there is no statute expressly declaring such a contract illegal.

public warehouses—entities that serve the public generally without discrimination.

punitive damages—damages, in excess of those required to compensate the plaintiff for the wrong done, that are imposed in order to punish the defendant because of the particularly wanton or willful character of wrongdoing; also called *exemplary damages.*

purchase money security interest (PMSI)—the security interest in the goods a seller sells on credit that become the collateral for the creditor/seller.

Q

qualified indorsement—an indorsement that includes words such as "without recourse" that disclaims certain liability of the indorser to a maker or a drawee.

qualified privilege—media privilege to print inaccurate information without liability for defamation, so long as a retraction is printed and there was no malice.

quantum meruit—as much as deserved; an action brought for the value of the services rendered the defendant when there was no express contract as to the purchase price.

quasi contract—court-imposed obligation to prevent unjust enrichment in the absence of a contract.

quasi-judicial proceedings—forms of hearings in which the rules of evidence and procedure are more relaxed but each side still has a chance to be heard.

quasi-public corporation—private corporation furnishing services on which the public is particularly dependent, for example, a gas and electric company.

quitclaim deed—deed by which the grantor purports to give up only whatever right or title the grantor may have in the property without specifying or warranting transfer of any particular interest.

quorum—minimum number of persons, shares represented, or directors who must be present at a meeting in order to lawfully transact business.

R

race statute—statute under which the first party to record the deed holds the title.

race-notice statute—see *notice-race statute.*

Racketeer Influenced and Corrupt Organizations (RICO) Act—federal law, initially targeting organized crime that has expanded in scope and provides penalties and civil recovery for multiple criminal offenses, or a pattern of racketeering.

real property—land and all rights in land.

recognizance—obligation entered into before a court to do some act, such as to appear at a later date for a hearing. Also called a *contract of record.*

recorder—public official in charge of deeds.

recross-examination—an examination by the other side's attorney that follows the redirect examination.

redemption—buying back of one's property, which has been sold because of a default, upon paying the amount that

had been originally due together with interest and costs.

redirect examination—questioning after cross-examination, in which the attorney for the witness testifying may ask the same witness other questions to overcome effects of the cross-examination.

reference to a third person—settlement that allows a nonparty to resolve the dispute.

reformation—remedy by which a written instrument is corrected when it fails to express the actual intent of both parties because of fraud, accident, or mistake.

registered bonds—bonds held by owners whose names and addresses are registered on the books of the corporation to ensure proper payment.

registration requirements—provisions of the Securities Act of 1933 requiring advance disclosure to the public of a new securities issue through filing a statement with the SEC and sending a prospectus to each potential purchaser.

registration statement—document disclosing specific financial information regarding the security, the issuer, and the underwriter.

release—an instrument by which the signing party (releasor) relinquishes claims or potential claims against one or more persons (releasees) who might otherwise be subject to liability to the releasor.

remainder interest—land interest that follows a life estate.

remand—term used when an appellate court sends a case back to trial court for additional hearings or a new trial.

remedy—action or procedure that is followed in order to enforce a right or to obtain damages for injury to a right.

rent-a-judge plan—dispute resolution through private courts with judges paid to be referees for the cases.

representative capacity—action taken by one on behalf of another, as the act of a personal representative on behalf of a decedent's estate, or action taken both on one's behalf and on behalf of others, as a shareholder bringing a representative action.

repudiation—result of a buyer or seller refusing to perform the contract as stated.

request for production of documents—discovery tool for uncovering paper evidence in a case.

requirements contract—contract to buy all requirements of the buyer from the seller.

rescission—action of one party to a contract to set the contract aside when the other party is guilty of a breach of the contract.

reservation of rights—assertion by a party to a contract that even though a tendered performance (e.g., a defective product) is accepted, the right to damages for nonconformity to the contract is reserved.

Resource Conservation and Recovery Act (RCRA)—federal law that regulates the disposal of potentially harmful substances and encourages resource conservation and recovery.

Resource Recovery Act—early federal solid waste disposal legislation that provided funding for states and local governments with recycling programs.

respondeat superior—doctrine that the principal or employer is vicariously liable for the unauthorized torts committed by an agent or employee while acting within the scope of the agency or the course of the employment, respectively.

restrictive covenants—covenants in a deed by which the grantee agrees to refrain from doing specified acts.

restrictive indorsement—an indorsement that restricts further transfer, such as in trust for or to the use of some other person, is conditional, or for collection or deposit.

reverse—the term used when the appellate court sets aside the verdict or judgment of a lower court.

reverse mortgage—mortgage in which the owners get their equity out of their home over a period of time and return the house to the lender upon their deaths.

reversible error—an error or defect in court proceedings of so serious a nature that on appeal the appellate court will set aside the proceedings of the lower court.

revoke—testator's act of taking back his or her will and its provisions.

right—legal capacity to require another person to perform or refrain from an action.

right of escheat—right of the state to take the property of a decedent that has not been distributed.

right of first refusal—right of a party to meet the terms of a proposed contract before it is executed, such as a real estate purchase agreement.

right of privacy—the right to be free from unreasonable intrusion by others.

right to cure—second chance for a seller to make a proper tender of conforming goods.

right-to-work laws—laws restricting unions and employees from negotiating clauses in their collective bargaining agreements that make union membership compulsory.

rights theory—Nozick's theory of ethics that we all have a set of rights that must be honored and protected by government.

risk—peril or contingency against which the insured is protected by the contract of insurance.

risk of loss—in contract performance, the cost of damage or injury to the goods contracted for.

Robinson-Patman Act—a federal statute designed to eliminate price discrimination in interstate commerce.

S

Safe Drinking Water Act—a federal law that establishes national standards for contaminants in drinking water.

sale on approval—term indicating that no sale takes place until the buyer approves or accepts the goods.

sale or return—sale in which the title to the property passes to the buyer at the time of the transaction but the buyer is given the option of returning the property and restoring the title to the seller.

search warrant—judicial authorization for a search of property where there is the expectation of privacy.

seasonable—timely.

secondary meaning—a legal term signifying the words in question have taken on a new meaning with the public, capable of serving a source-identifying function of a mark.

secondary parties—called secondary obligors under Revised Article 3; parties to an instrument to whom holders turn when the primary party, for whatever reason, fails to pay the instrument.

secondary picketing—picketing an employer with which a union has no dispute to persuade the employer to stop doing business with a party to the dispute; generally illegal under the NLRA.

secrecy laws—confidentiality laws applied to home-country banks.

secured party—person owed the money, whether as a seller or a lender, in a secured transaction in personal property.

secured transaction—credit sale of goods or a secured loan that provides special protection for the creditor.

securities—stocks and bonds issued by a corporation. Under some investor protection laws, the term includes any interest in an enterprise that provides unearned income to its owner.

security agreement—agreement of the creditor and the debtor that the creditor will have a security interest.

security interest—property right that enables the creditor to take possession of the property if the debtor does not pay the amount owed.

self-help repossession—creditor's right to repossess the collateral without judicial proceedings.

self-proved wills—wills that eliminate some formalities of proof by being executed according to statutory requirements.

selling on consignment—entrusting a person with possession of property for the purpose of sale.

semiconductor chip product—product placed on a piece of semiconductor material in accordance with a predetermined pattern that is intended to perform electronic circuitry functions.

service mark—mark that identifies a service.

servient tenement—land that is subject to an easement.

settlor—one who settles property in trust or creates a trust.

severalty—ownership of property by one person.

shared powers—powers that are held by both state and national governments.

Sherman Antitrust Act—a federal statute prohibiting combinations and contracts in restraint of interstate trade, now generally inapplicable to labor union activity.

shop right—right of an employer to use in business without charge an invention discovered by an employee during working hours and with the employer's material and equipment.

shopkeeper's privilege—right of a store owner to detain a suspected shoplifter based on reasonable cause and for a reasonable time without resulting liability for false imprisonment.

short-swing profit—profit realized by a corporate insider from selling securities less than six months after purchase.

sinking fund—fixed amount of money set aside each year by the borrowing corporation toward the ultimate payment of bonds.

Sixth Amendment—the U.S. constitutional amendment that guarantees a speedy trial.

slander—defamation of character by spoken words or gestures.

slander of title—malicious making of false statements as to a seller's title.

small claims courts—courts that resolve disputes between parties when those disputes do not exceed a minimal level; no lawyers are permitted; the parties represent themselves.

social contract—the agreement under Locke and Rawls as to what our ethical standards will be.

sole or individual proprietorship—form of business ownership in which one individual owns the business.

soliciting agent—salesperson.

sovereign compliance doctrine—doctrine that allows a defendant to raise as an affirmative defense to an antitrust action the fact that the defendant's actions were compelled by a foreign state.

sovereign immunity doctrine—a doctrine that states that a foreign sovereign generally cannot be sued without its consent.

special agent—agent authorized to transact a specific transaction or to do a specific act.

special indorsement—an indorsement that specifies the person to whom the instrument is indorsed.

specific legacies—identified property bequeathed by a testator; also called *specific devises*.

specific lien—right of a creditor to hold a particular property or assert a lien on the particular property of the debtor because of the creditor's having done work on or having some other association with the property, as distinguished from having a lien generally against the assets of the debtor merely because the debtor is indebted to the lien holder.

specific performance—action brought to compel the adverse party to perform a contract on the theory that merely suing for damages for its breach will not be an adequate remedy.

spendthrift trust—a trust that, prevents creditors of the beneficiary from reaching the principal or income held by the trustee and precludes beneficiary assignments.

spot zoning—allowing individual variation in zoning.

stakeholder analysis—the term used when a decision maker views a problem from different perspectives and measures the impact of a decision on various groups.

stakeholders—those who have a stake, or interest, in the activities of a corporation; stakeholders include employees, members of the community in which the corporation operates, vendors, customers, and any others who are affected by the actions and decisions of the corporation.

stale check—a check whose date is longer than six months ago.

standby letter—letter of credit for a contractor ensuring he will complete the project as contracted.

stare decisis—"let the decision stand"; the principle that the decision of a court should serve as a guide or precedent and control the decision of a similar case in the future.

status quo ante—original positions of the parties.

statute of frauds—statute that, in order to prevent fraud through the use of perjured testimony, requires that certain kinds of transactions be evidenced in writing in order to be binding or enforceable.

statute of limitations—statute that restricts the period of time within which an action may be brought.

statutory law—legislative acts declaring, commanding, or prohibiting something.

stay (or delay) of foreclosure—delay of foreclosure obtained by the mortgagor to prevent undue hardship.

stock subscription—contract or agreement to buy a specific number and kind of shares when they are issued by the corporation.

stop payment order—order by a depositor to the bank to refuse to make payment of a check when presented for payment.

straight (or nonnegotiable) bill of lading—document of title that consigns transported goods to a named person.

strict liability—civil wrong for which there is absolute liability because of the inherent danger in the underlying activity, for example, the use of explosives.

strict tort liability—product liability theory that imposes absolute liability upon the manufacturer, seller, or distributor of goods for harm caused by defective goods.

subject matter jurisdiction—judicial authority to hear a particular type of case.

sublease—a transfer of the premises by the lessee to a third person, the sublessee or subtenant, for a period of less than the term of the original lease.

sublessee—person with lease rights for a period of less than the term of the original lease (also *subtenant*).

subprime lending market—a credit market that makes loans to high-risk consumers (those who have bankruptcies, no credit history, or a poor credit history), often loaning money to pay off other debts the consumer has due.

subrogation—right of a party secondarily liable to stand in the place of the creditor after making payment to the creditor and to enforce the creditor's right against the party primarily liable in order to obtain indemnity from such primary party.

substantial impairment—material defect in a good.

substantial performance—equitable rule that if a good-faith attempt to perform does not precisely meet the terms of the agreement, the agreement will still be considered complete if the essential purpose of the contract is accomplished.

substantive law—the law that defines rights and liabilities.

substitute check—electronic image of a paper check that a bank can create and that has the same legal effect as the original instrument.

substitution—substitution of a new contract between the same parties.

sum certain—amount due under an instrument that can be computed from its face with only reference to interest rates.

summary jury trial—a mock or dry-run trial for parties to get a feel for how their cases will play to a jury.

summation—the attorney address that follows all the evidence presented in court and sums up a case and recommends a particular verdict be returned by the jury.

Superfund Amendment and Reauthorization Act—federal law that expands scope and operation of CERCLA.

Superfund sites—areas designated by the EPA for cleanup.

surety—obligor of a suretyship; primarily liable for the debt or obligation of the principal debtor.

suretyship—undertaking to pay the debt or be liable for the default of another.

symbolic delivery—delivery of goods by delivery of the means of control, such as a key or a relevant document of title, such as a negotiable bill of lading; also called constructive delivery.

T

tariff—(1) domestically—government-approved schedule of charges that may be made by a regulated business, such as a common carrier or warehouser; (2) internationally—tax imposed by a country on goods crossing its borders, without regard to whether the purpose is to raise revenue or to discourage the traffic in the taxed goods.

tax lien—lien on property for nonpayment of taxes.

teller's check—draft drawn by a bank on another bank in which it has an account.

temporary insider—someone retained by a corporation for professional services on an as-needed basis, such as an attorney, accountant, or investment banker.

temporary perfection—perfection given for a limited period of time to creditors.

tenancy at sufferance—lease arrangement in which the tenant occupies the property at the discretion of the landlord.

tenancy at will—holding of land for an indefinite period that may be terminated at any time by the landlord or by the landlord and tenant acting together.

tenancy by entirety or tenancy by the entireties—transfer of property to both husband and wife.

tenancy for years—tenancy for a fixed period of time, even though the time is less than a year.

tenancy in common—relationship that exists when two or more persons own undivided interests in property.

tenancy in partnership—ownership relationship that exists between partners under the Uniform Partnership Act.

tenant—one who holds or possesses real property by any kind of right or title; one who pays rent for the temporary use and occupation of another's real property under a lease.

tender—goods have arrived, are available for pickup, and the buyer is notified.

term insurance—policy written for a specified number of years that terminates at the end of that period.

termination statement—document (record), which may be requested by a paid-up debtor, stating that a security interest is no longer claimed under the specified financing statement.

testamentary capacity—sufficient mental capacity to understand that a writing being executed is a will and what that entails.

testamentary intent—designed to take effect at death, as by disposing of property or appointing a personal representative.

testamentary trust—trust that takes effect upon the settlor's death.

testate—condition of leaving a will upon death.

testate distribution—distribution of an estate in accordance with the will of the decedent.

testator, testatrix—man, woman who makes a will.

theory of justice—the Locke and Rawlsian standard for ethics that requires that we all agree on certain universal principles in advance.

third-party beneficiary—third person whom the parties to a contract intend to benefit by the making of the contract and to confer upon such person the right to sue for breach of contract.

time draft—bill of exchange payable at a stated time after sight or at a definite time.

tippee—individual who receives information about a corporation from an insider or temporary insider.

tort—civil wrong that interferes with one's property or person.

Toxic Substances Control Act (TOSCA)—first federal law to control the manufacture, use, and disposal of toxic substances.

trade dress—product's total image including its overall packaging look.

trade libel—written defamation about a product or service.

trade name—name under which a business is carried on and, if fictitious, must be registered.

trade secret—formula, device, or compilation of information that is used in one's business and is of such a nature that it provides an advantage over competitors who do not have the information.

trademark—mark that identifies a product.

transferee—buyer or vendee.

Transport Rule—the rule promulgated to address downwind pollution from coal and gas-fired power plants.

traveler's check—check that is payable on demand provided it is countersigned by the person whose specimen signature appears on the check.

treasury stock—corporate stock that the corporation has reacquired.

treble damages—three times the damages actually sustained.

trespass—unauthorized action with respect to person or property.

trespasser—person who is on the land of another without permission or authorization.

tripartite—three-part division (of government).

trust—transfer of property by one person to another with the understanding or declaration that such property be held for the benefit of another; the holding of property by the owner in trust for another, upon a declaration of trust, without a transfer to another person. (Parties—settlor, trustee, beneficiary)

trust agreement—instrument creating a trust; also called *deed of trust.*

trust corpus—fund or property that is transferred to the trustee also called *trust fund, trust estate*, and *trust res.*

trustee—party who has legal title to estate and manages it.

trustee in bankruptcy—impartial person elected to administer the debtor's estate.

trustor—donor or settlor who is the owner of property.

tying—the anticompetitive practice of requiring buyers to purchase one product in order to get another.

U

ultra vires—act or contract that the corporation does not have authority to do or make.

unconscionable—unreasonable, not guided or restrained by conscience and often referring to a contract grossly unfair to one party because of the superior bargaining powers of the other party.

underwriter—insurer.

undisclosed principal—principal on whose behalf an agent acts without disclosing to the third person the fact of agency or the identity of the principal.

undue influence—influence that is asserted upon another person by one who dominates that person.

Uniform Probate Code (UPC)—uniform statute on wills and administration of estates.

Uniform Simultaneous Death Act—law providing that when survivorship cannot be established, the property of each person shall be disposed of as though he or she had survived the other.

unilateral contract—contract under which only one party makes a promise.

unincorporated association—combination of two or more persons for the furtherance of a common nonprofit purpose.

universal agent—agent authorized by the principal to do all acts that can lawfully be delegated to a representative.

universal defenses—defenses that are regarded as so basic that the social interest in preserving them outweighs the social interest of giving negotiable instruments the freely transferable qualities of money; accordingly, such defenses are given universal effect and may be raised against all holders.

USA Patriot Act—federal law that, among other things, imposes reporting requirements on banks.

usage of trade—language and customs of an industry.

usury—lending money at an interest rate that is higher than the maximum rate allowed by law.

utilitarians—theory of ethics based on doing the most good for the most people in making decisions.

uttering—crime of issuing or delivering a forged instrument to another person.

V

valid contract—agreement that is binding and enforceable.

value—consideration or antecedent debt or security given in exchange for the transfer of a negotiable instrument or creation of a security interest.

variance—permission of a landowner to use the land in a specified manner that is inconsistent with the zoning ordinance.

vicarious liability—imposing liability for the fault of another.

void agreement—agreement that cannot be enforced.

voidable contract—agreement that is otherwise binding and enforceable but may be rejected at the option of one of the parties as the result of specific circumstances.

voidable title—title of goods that carries with it the contingency of an underlying problem.

voir dire **examination**—the preliminary examination of a juror or a witness to ascertain fitness to act as such.

voluntary bankruptcy—proceeding in which the debtor files the petition for relief.

voting by proxy—authorizing someone else to vote the shares owned by the shareholder.

voting trust—transfer by two or more persons of their shares of stock of a corporation to a trustee who is to vote the shares and act for such shareholders.

W

waiver—release or relinquishment of a known right or objection.

warehouse—entity engaged in the business of storing the goods of others for compensation.

warehouse receipt—receipt issued by the warehouser for stored goods; regulated by the UCC, which clothes the receipt with some degree of negotiability.

warranty—promise, either express or implied, about the nature, quality, or performance of the goods.

warranty against encumbrances—warranty that there are no liens or other encumbrances to goods except those noted by the seller.

warranty deed—deed by which the grantor conveys a specific estate or interest to the grantee and makes one or more of the covenants of title.

warranty of habitability—implied warranty that the leased property is fit for dwelling by tenants.

warranty of title—implied warranty that title to the goods is good and transfer is proper.

wasting assets corporation—corporation designed to exhaust or use up the assets of the corporation, such as by extracting oil, coal, iron, and other ores.

way of necessity—grantee's right to use land retained by the grantor for going to and from the conveyed land.

well-known mark—in international law a mark that both the Paris Convention and TRIPS recognize as deserving protection even if it is not registered in the foreign country; national law determines what "well-known" means but the WIPO offers a list suggesting that the value of the mark, the extent of its use and promotion, and its recognition in the relevant sector of the public are key factors.

White-Collar Crime Penalty Enhancement Act of 2002—federal reforms passed as a result of the collapses of companies such as Enron; provides for longer sentences and higher fines for both executives and companies.

white-collar crimes—crimes that do not use nor threaten to use force or violence or do not cause injury to persons or property.

whole life insurance—ordinary life insurance providing lifetime insurance protection.

will—instrument executed with the formality required by law by which a person makes a disposition of his or her property to take effect upon death.

writ of *certiorari*—the U.S. Supreme Court granting a right of review by the court of a lower court decision.

wrongfully dishonored—error by a bank in refusing to pay a check.

Z

zoning—restrictions imposed by government on the use of designated land to ensure an orderly physical development of the regulated area.

Index